Effective organisational communication

Perspectives, principles and practices

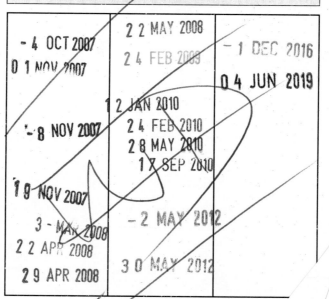

D0784050

We work with leading authors to develop the strongest educational materials in business and management, bringing cutting-edge thinking and best learning practice to a global market.

Under a range of well-known imprints, including Financial Times Prentice Hall, we craft high-quality print and electronic publications which help readers to understand and apply their content, whether studying or at work.

To find out more about the complete range of our publishing, please visit us on the World Wide Web at: www.pearsoned.co.uk

Second edition
Effective organisational communication

Perspectives, principles and practices

Richard Blundel

Prentice Hall
FINANCIAL TIMES

An imprint of **Pearson Education**
Harlow, England • London • New York • Boston • San Francisco • Toronto • Sydney • Singapore • Hong Kong
Tokyo • Seoul • Taipei • New Delhi • Cape Town • Madrid • Mexico City • Amsterdam • Munich • Paris • Milan

Pearson Education Limited
Edinburgh Gate
Harlow
Essex CM20 2JE
England

and Associated Companies throughout the world

Visit us on the World Wide Web at:
www.pearsoned.co.uk

First published in Great Britain as *Effective Business Communication* by Prentice Hall in 1998
Second edition published 2004

Copyright © Prentice Hall Europe 1998
Copyright © Pearson Education Limited 2004

ISBN 0-273-68569-4
ISBN 978-0-273-68569-2

British Library Cataloguing-in-Publication Data
A catalogue record for this book is available from the British Library

Library of Congress Cataloging-in-Publication Data
Blundel, Richard.
    Effective organisational communication: perspectives, principles, and practices/Richard Blundel.
        p.cm.
    Rev. ed. of: Effective business communication. 1998.
    Includes bibliographical references and index.
    ISBN 0-273-68569-4 (pbk.: alk. paper)
        1. Business communication. I. Title: Effective organizational communication. II.
    Blundel, Richard. Effective business communication. III. Title.

HF5718.B584 2004
658.4′5—dc22   2004047204

10 9 8 7 6 5 4 3
09 08 07 06

Typeset by 30 in Stone Serif
Printed by Ashford Colour Press Ltd., Gosport

The publisher's policy is to use paper manufactured from sustainable forests.

Contents

List of figures x
List of tables xii
List of mini-cases xiii
List of case studies xv
Contributors xvi
Preface to the second edition xviii
Acknowledgements xxii

1 Perspectives on communication 1
1.1 Introducing communication 1
1.2 Communicating in organisations: issues and challenges 2
1.3 Stage one: a simple model of the communication process 4
1.4 Feedback, expectations and subjectivity 8
1.5 Organisational communication: key dimensions 9
1.6 Different perspectives on communication 11
Summary 16
Practical exercises 17
Further reading 21
References 21

Part I Principles of communication

2 Breaking barriers: communication in practice 25
2.1 Introduction 25
2.2 Barriers to communication?: identifying underlying causes 26
2.3 Physiological and neurological factors 27
2.4 Social, cultural and ethical barriers 34
2.5 Overcoming the barriers 43
Summary 46
Practical exercises 47
Further reading 51
References 51

3 Using words: verbal communication 53
3.1 Introduction 53
3.2 Clear and concise language: using plain English 54
3.3 The technicalities: spelling, grammar, syntax and punctuation 58
3.4 Beyond plain English? Using language creatively 59

3.5   Spoken English: additional communication issues   64
3.6   Using the language – it is a matter of style   65
3.7   Language and organisation: narrative and discourse analysis   66
Summary   68
Practical exercises   69
Further reading   72
References   73

4   Making pictures: non-verbal communication   75
4.1   Introduction   75
4.2   Using 'pictures' at work   76
4.3   Potential benefits of non-verbal communication   78
4.4   Potential problems with visual media   82
4.5   The use and abuse of graphical data   84
4.6   Visual aspects of corporate identity: an introduction   91
4.7   Human signals: from eye contact to appearance   92
Summary   96
Practical exercises   97
Further reading   100
References   101

5   Developing arguments: persuasive communication   103
5.1   Introduction   103
5.2   Persuasion in organisations   105
5.3   The essential principles: introducing rhetorical argument 106
5.4   The challenge of persuasion: audience, message and context 108
5.5   Persuasive practices: securing attention and arguing well 113
5.6   The ethics of persuasion   116
Summary   118
Practical exercises   119
Further reading   123
References   123

6   Securing feedback: interactive communication   125
6.1   Introduction   125
6.2   Organisational feedback: an initial overview   126
6.3   Securing stakeholder feedback: the case of employees   130
6.4   Practicalities of feedback: designing a form   134
6.5   Feedback, knowledge and organisational learning   136
Summary   138
Practical exercises   139
Further reading   142
References   142

7 Making connections: organisational communication   144

7.1   Introduction   144
7.2   Five 'classic' organisational challenges   145
7.3   Emerging challenges: organisations in the twenty-first century   152
7.4   Organisational communication: reflecting on the challenges   160
Summary   161
Practical exercises   161
Further reading   165
References   165

Part II Communication in practice

8 Letters, e-mail and text messages   171

8.1   Introduction   171
8.2   Business letters: principal uses and channel characteristics   172
8.3   The mysteries of page layout and structure   175
8.4   The style and content of a letter   178
8.5   Business stationery and letterhead design   181
8.6   The decline of the humble 'memo'   183
8.7   E-mail: channel characteristics, formats and applications   184
8.8   Text messaging and beyond: emerging communication issues   189
Summary   190
Practical exercises   190
Further reading   195
References   195

9 Reports, briefing papers and summaries   196

9.1   Introduction   196
9.2   Reports: principal types and purposes   197
9.3   Obtaining a clear specification   198
9.4   Researching and organising the source material   201
9.5   Report writing: drafting stage   201
9.6   Report writing: completion stage   208
9.7   Summarising written material: the vital art   213
9.8   Reflecting on the process of report writing   214
Summary   215
Practical exercises   216
Further reading   219
References   220

10 Advertisements, promotions, news releases and exhibitions   221

10.1 Introduction   221
10.2 Advertising and sales promotion: an overview   223
10.3 Planning an advertising and promotional campaign   224
10.4 Communicating with an advertisement   226
10.5 Public relations – an overview   231
10.6 Successful PR: long-term commitment v short-term fix   232
10.7 Media relations – planning a news release   236
10.8 Exhibitions and events   238
Summary   241
Practical exercises   241
Further reading   246
References   247

11 Interviews, questioning and listening   249

11.1 Introduction   249
11.2 Types of interview   250
11.3 Listening techniques   254
11.4 Questioning techniques and related behaviours   259
11.5 The interviewee's perspective: making the best of it?   264
11.6 Counselling techniques and the manager   266
Summary   267
Practical exercises   268
Further reading   271
References   272

12 Presentations and audio-visual technologies   273

12.1 Introduction   273
12.2 What makes presentations different?   274
12.3 Preparing the presentation materials   275
12.4 The presenter: posture, appearance, voice and memory   276
12.5 Audio-visual equipment and communication practices   283
12.6 On the day itself – final preparations   288
12.7 The presentation: four key elements   290
Summary   295
Practical exercises   296
Further reading   299
References   299

13 Meetings, teams and negotiations   300

13.1 Introduction   300
13.2 Meetings: principal types and purposes   301
13.3 Advantages, disadvantages and channel characteristics   302

13.4 The formal meeting 303
13.5 On being a successful chair 309
13.6 Informal meetings – the benefits of team-working 312
13.7 The rise of the virtual team 317
13.8 Negotiation: applying persuasive communication 319
Summary 326
Practical exercises 326
Further reading 330
References 330

14 Communication in perspective 332

14.1 Introduction 332
14.2 Five questions for organisational communicators 333
Summary 339
Questions for discussion 340
Further reading 344
References 344

Index 347

List of figures

Figure 1.1 A simple linear model of the communication process   5

Figure 1.2 The linear model of communication with feedback   8

Figure 1.3 The multiple dimensions of organisational communication   11

Figure 2.1 Human cognition: four linked mechanisms   28

Figure 2.2 Perception – object recognition   29

Figure 2.3 Three optical illusions   30

Figure 2.4 Human memory processes: a three-stage model   31

Figure 3.1 Selecting a suitable font   57

Figure 4.1 International signs and icons   76

Figure 4.2 Visual images can attract attention   79

Figure 4.3 Striking our target market   84

Figure 4.4 Pie chart with exploded segment   84

Figure 4.5 A component bar chart   85

Figure 4.6 A histogram   86

Figure 4.7 A multiple line graph   87

Figure 4.8 A simple pictogram   87

Figure 4.9 A map illustrating regional data   88

Figure 5.1 A warning poster   112

Figure 6.1 Characterising feedback mechanisms – urgency and complexity 127

Figure 6.2 Example of a form designed to obtain feedback   135

Figure 7.1 Functional and product structures   146

Figure 7.2 Regional offices – a 'Hybrid' structure   147

Figure 7.3 Tall and flat hierarchies: implications for communication 148

Figure 7.4 Stakeholder activism at a manufacturing plant   157

Figure 7.5 Entreprenurial networks: changing connections over time   164

Figure 8.1 A letter in fully blocked layout with 'open' punctuation 175

Figure 8.2 Structure of a business letter   176

Figure 8.3 Example of an ineffective letter   179

Figure 8.4 Typical format for an internal memorandum   183

Figure 8.5 Format of a typical e-mail   184

Figure 9.1 Consistent use of typography: sample hierarchy of headings 207

Figure 9.2 Proof correction symbols   209

Figure 10.1 *Financial Times* advertisement for Chinese new year 2003 224

Figure 10.2 An organisation's dialogue with its stakeholders   232

Figure 10.3 The structure of a typical news release   238

Figure 10.4 Stands at an international trade show   239

Figure 10.5 Elements of a typical display advertisement   242

Figure 10.6 Mapping the customer journey   245

Figure 11.1 Seating layouts for interviews   258

Figure 12.1 Giving a presentation   277

Figure 13.1 A meeting in progress   301

Figure 13.2 Contrasting information flows in a meeting   302

Figure 13.3 A typical committee structure   304

Figure 13.4 Sample agenda and notice of meeting   307

Figure 13.5 Sample narrative minutes   308

List of tables

Table 2.1 Common barriers to communication: probing for 'causes' 26

Table 2.2 A simple activity to 'test' the sensory memory 32

Table 2.3 Hofstede's taxonomic approach to cultural difference 39

Table 2.4 Exploring communication barriers: interpreting the receiver 44

Table 3.1 Grammatical errors, ambiguity and style 59

Table 4.1 Categorising non-verbal communication: some practical examples 77

Table 5.1 Three elements of a rhetorical argument 107

Table 5.2 The basic components of an argument – Toulmin's model 108

Table 5.3 Other forms of persuasive communication 114

Table 6.1 The diversity of organisational feedback: some examples 128

Table 7.1 Five major problems with top management teams 149

Table 8.1 Some examples of widely-used business letters 172

Table 8.2 Listing qualifications and awards: a conventional approach 177

Table 8.3 Statutory disclosure requirements: some practical examples 182

Table 8.4 Direct marketing terminology 193

Table 9.1 Types of report: some practical examples 197

Table 9.2 Getting a report in order: some alternative sequences 203

Table 9.3 Structuring academic dissertations and business reports 204

Table 10.1 Some popular advertising formats 227

Table 10.2 Communication during the 'customer journey' 245

Table 11.1 Main interview types and related communication practices 250

Table 11.2 Sample grid for analysing interview questions 262

Table 13.1 Organisational meetings: overlapping types, purposes and styles 302

Table 13.2 Specialist terminology associated with formal meetings 305

Table 13.3 Indicative communication patterns in the Tuckman model 314

Table 13.4 The concept of team roles: a communication perspective 315

Table 13.5 Alternative negotiation outcomes 320

Table 13.6 Cultural difference in negotiation: an outdated approach? 323

List of mini-cases

1.1 'Shooting Star': communicating in a fast-growing firm   3

1.2 'PromoCo': when temperature became 'noise'   5

1.3 What do we mean by 'effective'?: comparing perspectives   15

2.1 Responding to the challenge of web accessibility   32

2.2 Pearl Harbor 1941: a case of Groupthink?   36

2.3 The missing tourists of Suzhou: de-constructing cultural barriers   42

3.1 The Plain English Campaign   57

3.2 Translating questionnaires in international research   62

3.3 George Orwell on the decline of the English language   65

4.1 The Fairtrade Mark: creating a European identity   80

4.2 Accounts and accountability: communicating financial information   89

4.3 CDP exchanges: a visual approach to cross-cultural interaction   95

5.1 Inform or persuade? The case for speed cameras   104

5.2 'OK Biotec': science and the politics of persuasion   115

5.3 The ethics of persuasion: examples from advertising   117

6.1 When feedback mechanisms fail: explaining 'moral deafness'   129

6.2 Appraisal at 'EnergyCo': 360 degree feedback using questionnaires   132

6.3 Constructing the concept of 'emotional intelligence'   137

7.1 'HeatCo': a clash of organisational sub-cultures   150

7.2 Making connections at Climate Care   155

7.3 Stakeholder dialogue: towards a new perspective?   157

8.1 Letters and paper mail in a digital age   173

8.2 Anarchy in the world of e-mail sign-offs   187

8.3 Texting redundancy: a communication perspective   189

9.1 'Nebulous Phones' and the under-specified reports   200

9.2 Using editing tools in report-writing: a critical assessment   211

9.3 Incorporating reports onto a website: the case of Nokia   214

10.1 Adbusters: challenging corporate advertising?   228

10.2 RSVP*i*™: Managing customer relationships via text   230

10.3 'DozeyToys'– communicating at an international exhibition   240

11.1 Using interviews in an organisational research project   253

11.2 Jean-Jacques and the appraisal interview   256

11.3 Online recruitment: an effective communication channel?   262

12.1 Vocal mechanics: a practical introduction   279

12.2 Presentation technologies: 'death by *PowerPoint*'?   286

12.3 Beating stage fright: 'fight or flight' syndrome   289

13.1 Seating your meeting: the role of design   311

13.2 'Software International': global customer support via virtual teams   318

13.3 The changing face of Chinese negotiation   324

14.1 Leadership, team-working and communication: the 'Global Challenge' 337

List of case studies

A Human contact – more effective than technology?   18

B Translating the Japanese manufacturing model in Thailand   48

C 'Story-telling' – researching organisational narratives   70

D Visual identity, corporate image and strategy – the case of BT   98

E Campaigning against poverty – Oxfam's persuasive communication   120

F Applying 'emotional intelligence' – a tale of two placement students   140

G Entrepreneurial networking – communication as organisation?   162

H 'Infant-plus' baby foods – direct marketing techniques   192

I Getting the message across: annual reports in the internet era   217

J Communicating sustainability in tourism – 'sticking your head above the parapet?'   243

K 'A day in the life of a headhunter': selection interviews   268

L 'LOGOS 05': diary of an international conference delegate   297

M International meetings: a virtual meeting of minds?   328

N Sequencing the human genome – the communication 'race'   340

Contributors

Richard Blundel is a senior lecturer at Oxford Brookes University Business School. He has worked in a number of public and private sector organisations, including periods as a corporate affairs manager in the European office of a large US industrial company and as a marketing research analyst in a specialist consultancy serving the computer industry. His research interests include inter-organisational networks, entrepreneurship, the growth of firms and the relationship between communication and strategic practices.

Naveed Chaudhri has been a member of Oxfam's campaigns staff since 1999, following an earlier career in academic publishing. He has been engaged in grassroots campaigning with the Oxford Oxfam Group for over ten years.

Linda Clark is the founding partner of an executive recruitment and marketing consultancy, specialising in the retail services sector. She has extensive marketing management experience in international retail organisations.

Jackie Clarke is a senior lecturer in marketing and tourism at Oxford Brookes University Business School. She is the co-author of two tourism marketing and management texts. Research interests include tourism sustainability, branding, and consumer behaviour. She has marketing experience in a large aviation and tour operating company, and has conducted research and consultancy in Slovakia, Spain and for a UK-based museum consortium.

Tina Fawcett is a researcher in energy and environmental issues. She has worked for the Environmental Change Institute, University of Oxford, AEA Technology and the Environment Agency. Tina is the co-author, with Mayer Hillman, of *How We Can Save the Planet*, a guide to the implications of climate change, published by Penguin Books.

Richard Foster is an independent consultant with a background as an analyst in the computer services industry. His recent research has involved an assessment of the technical and cultural challenges involved in the planning and implementation of virtual environments.

Daniel Herbert is a senior lecturer in accounting and finance and Oxford Brookes University Business School. He has a background in accounting, both at the UK's National Audit Office and in local government. Dan's recent research activities have included a detailed examination of public sector financial reporting practices and their implications for accountability.

Elspeth Macfarlane is a head of department at Oxford Brookes University Business School. Her teaching and research is in the areas of management skills and human resource management. Elspeth also has extensive commercial experience in human resources management within an international retail chain.

Mark Saunders is head of research at Oxford Brookes University Business School. His research interests include service quality, downsizing, organisational justice and the management of change. He is also co-author of *Research Methods for Business Students* and *Managing Change: a Human Resource Strategy Approach*, which are published by FT Prentice Hall.

Mitchell Sedgwick is a senior research fellow at Oxford Brookes University Business School. He trained as a social anthropologist and has been engaged in ethnographic research on private and public sector organisations over the last two decades. He has held several long-term consultancies at the World Bank and the United Nations, including work on government institutions in Thailand and Laos, and state-owned enterprises in Burkina Faso. His research interests include cross-cultural dynamics at Japanese multinationals and headquarters-subsidiary relations.

Ian Wycherley worked as an accountant in the computer industry before lecturing in management at Oxford Brookes University Business School. He has published research papers on environmental management and also on the management of relationships in industrial networks. Ian has an active interest in the role of storytelling in organisations.

Preface to the second edition

There can be too much communication between people.
Ann Beattie, writer.

Who is this book for?

Effective Organisational Communication has been thoroughly revised and updated in order to meet the changing needs of its readership. The accessible style of the original text has been retained, while academic content, international and inter-cultural perspectives have been greatly enhanced. The revisions have been designed to meet the needs of undergraduate and postgraduate students taking courses such as communication, management skills, international management and organisational behaviour. Whether they are located in the UK, or in other countries, most students will find themselves studying in very diverse multi-national and multi-cultural groups. The new edition places a much stronger emphasis on the implications of such diversity, introducing new theoretical insights and compelling 'real-world' cases studies that highlight the relevant challenges and opportunities. The book's combination of accessibility, up-to-date theory and practical application will also make it a useful resource for students from other disciplines, such as biological science, computing or engin-eering, which often include organisational and managerial themes in their course programmes. It should also be of value to practising managers, who wish to review their own approach to communication, or to coach other employees in this vital and often neglected subject.

What is it trying to achieve?

The purpose of this book is to help you become a more effective communicator. It is concerned with the complex and dynamic mix of written, spoken and visual communication that takes place within and between organisations. We will be looking at people's efforts to communicate in a variety of challenging organis-ational settings, including multinational corporations, international aid agencies, local governments, scientific research teams and start-up ventures. In contrast to many popular texts in this area, *Effective Organisational Communication* is more than simply an instructional manual. Throughout the book, the reader is encouraged to identify connections between the develop-ment of skills in specific communication practices (e.g. drafting more focused and readable reports, communicating more clearly and persuasively in meetings), and a broader set of communication principles. This allows us to consider the likely impact of emerging communication technologies, such as text messaging, alongside more traditional channels. The text also introduces contrasting research perspectives, expanding the scope of the subject and challenging unspoken assumptions about the central theme of 'effectiveness' in communication. By exploring the links between perspectives, principles and practices, you can begin to generalise from your own experiences of communication. It will also help you to develop a more flexible repertoire of skills and stronger critical faculties. As a result, you will be much better placed to deal with new communication challenges.

How is it structured?

Chapter 1 provides a general overview of the book. It introduces the communication process, reviews a number of perspectives and insights and introduces some key themes that are developed throughout the text. It is therefore essential to read this chapter thoroughly, before proceeding. After Chapter 1, the rest of the book is divided into two closely inter-related parts.

Part I – Principles of communication

These six chapters establish a coherent framework for exploring the communication process, drawing on relevant research findings and real-life case studies. Chapter 2 identifies the principal barriers to effective communication and considers how they can be overcome. Subsequent chapters consider the role of words and images in various forms of communication; the communicator's key tasks of developing arguments and the challenge of securing relevant feedback. The final chapter in Part I focuses on the additional issues that arise when you are attempting to communicate within and beyond the boundaries of organisations.

Part II – Communication in practice

The first six chapters provide a comprehensive, practical and critical review of the main communication channels used in today's organisations. Each chapter follows a similar format, introducing the essential elements of the channel, including its strengths and weaknesses, showing how the generic principles of communication can be applied to improve its effectiveness and working through examples of good and bad practices. The final chapter in Part II draws brief conclusions from the preceding chapters and points to some on-going challenges.

The Part I ('principles') chapters build on one another and are therefore best studied in sequence. Part II ('practice') chapters, with the exception of Chapter 14, are entirely self-contained, and can be worked through in any order, depending on your current interests and needs. Chapters 7 and 14 conclude each section, highlighting key themes and emerging issues. This flexible format allows you to explore the links between principles and practice by alternating between the Parts I and II (see the diagram). Each chapter contains several 'mini-cases', practical exercises, an extended case study and detailed suggestions for further reading with full references. These features are designed to confirm your understanding, and to provide practice in applying what has been learnt.

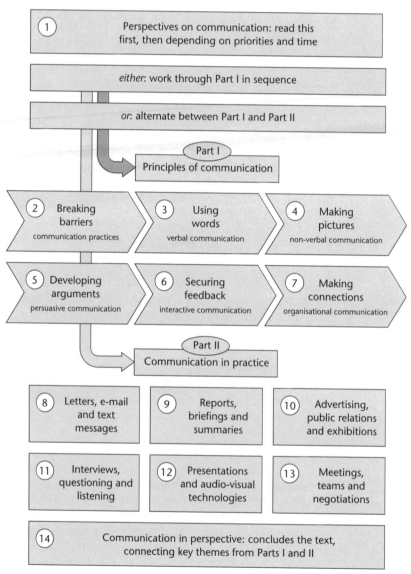

A guide to using this book

How should I approach this subject?

'Effectiveness' in organisational communication is about the skilful application of knowledge. Just as in other fields, such as sports or the performing arts, there is a certain amount of theory and rule learning. However, the only way to improve your personal performance is to practise and the only way to excel is to keep questioning your approach, and to set yourself greater challenges. But there is more to this subject than simply enhancing personal capabilities. Organisations have a profound impact on many aspects of our lives. This is often revealed in controversies over the ways that organisations communicate with key stakeholders, such as employees, customers, suppliers and local communities. In these situations, there is often a pressing need for more *informed* argument. I hope that this book encourages you to take a continuing, *critical* interest in the communication practices of organisations and the people who inhabit them, and that you are able to contribute to these important debates.

Richard Blundel
Oxford
Spring 2004

Companion website and lecturer's supplement

A companion website can be found at **www.booksites.net/blundel**. One of the main themes of this text is that communication is a two-way process. In this spirit, the author and his colleagues welcome comments and any suggestions for new content via the website feedback mechanism.

A lecturer's supplement is available free of charge to tutors adopting the book as a course text. The supplement includes suggested programmes of study, additional exercises, worked solutions and PowerPoint presentation slides. Further details are available on the companion website and all supplements are delivered via the websites.

Acknowledgements

I would like to thank the many colleagues and friends who have contributed to the second edition of this text, including those who have drafted case studies and others who have helped with exercises, illustrations and ideas. I am most grateful to the international panel of reviewers who provided such detailed and perceptive comments on the first edition. Also to all those who have helped by suggesting ideas, supplying materials, responding to questions, or helping with the artwork, including: Clare Allman, Ecover UK; Abigail Ball; Michael Best, University of Massachusetts Lowell; Chris Blackburn; Brian Brown, BT; Ade Brownlow; William Charwood, RSVPi Ltd; Peter Clark, Queen Mary, University of London; Emma Coles; John Colford; Andy Crane, University of Nottingham; Glauco DeVita; Stephen Duhan; Sandy Gordon, National Audit Office; Jonathan Groucutt; Julie Howell, RNIB; Bengt Johannisson, Växjö University; Yan Liu; Phil Morgan; Tom Morton, Climate Care; Edward Mushinga; Abi Murray, Fairtrade Foundation; Fiona Narburgh, Wychavon District Council; Margaret Price; John Prior; Berry O'Donovan; Sonia Rees, Wychavon District Council; Michael Rowlinson, Queen Mary, University of London; Teresa Smallbone; David Smith, Nottingham Business School; Alice Szwelnik; Richard Tallontire, Oxfam GB; Michael Thatcher, Dell Computers; Heather Watters; Clive Wildish. Lastly, I would like to thank those involved in the production process, including my editor Matthew Walker, Camilla Lloyd, Sarah Wild and other colleagues at FT Prentice Hall who supported the project and provided helpful information and guidance.

Publisher's acknowledgements

We are grateful to the following for permission to reproduce copyright material:

Fairtrade logo in mini-case 4.1, p. 81, reproduced by permission; Wychavon District Council sources of income report in mini-case 4.2, p. 90, reproduced by permission; British Telecom logo in Case study D, p. 100, reproduced by permission. BT and the Connected World device are Registered Trademarks of British Telecommunications public limited company; Figure 5.1, reproduced by permission from The Advertising Archive Ltd.; Oxfam logo in Case study E, p. 120, reproduced by permission from Oxfam GB, 274 Banbury Road, Oxford OX2 7DZ. www.oxfam.org.uk; Climate Care logo in mini-case 7.2, p. 155, reproduced by permission; Differentiated network model of stakeholder relationships in mini-case 7.3, p. 158, from *Unfolding stakeholder thinking 2*, Greenleaf Publishing, Andriof *et al.*, 2003; Figure 7.4, reproduced by permission from Oxfam GB, 274 Banbury Road, Oxford OX2 7DZ. www.oxfam.org.uk; RSVPi™ logo in mini-case 10.2, p. 230, reproduced by permission; Figure 10.1 © *Financial Times* 2003; Figure 10.4 PA Photos/EPA, reproduced by permission.

Case study A Human contact – more effective than technology?, © Stephen Overell 2002; Case study M International meetings: a virtual meeting of minds?, © Professor Bhagwati 2001; the author's agent for an extract in mini-case 3.3, p. 65, from 'Politics and the English Language' by George Orwell published in *Shooting an Elephant and Other Essays* © George Orwell 1946, by permission of Bill Hamilton as the literacy executor of the estate of the late Sonia Brownell Orwell and Secker and Warburg Ltd.; Pearson Education Limited for extracts in mini-case 3.2, p. 62 and mini-case 11.1, p. 253 from *Research Methods for Business Students 3/e* by Mark N. K. Saunders, Philip Lewis and Adrian Thornhill published by FT Prentice Hall.

We are grateful to the Financial Times Limited for permission to reprint the following material: Mini-case 8.2 Anarchy in the world of e-mail sign-offs, © *Financial Times*, 23 October 2000; Mini-case 8.3, Texting redundancy: a communication perspective, © *Financial Times*, 31 May 2003; Mini-case 12.2 Presentation technologies: 'death by PowerPoint'?, © *Financial Times*, 9 October 2002; Mini-case 14.1 Leadership, team-working and communication: the 'Global Challenge', © *Financial Times*, 23 November 2001.

For Daniel and Katy

Perspectives on communication

The human mind is like an umbrella, it works best when open.
Walter Gropius, *Bauhaus* architect and designer

Learning outcomes

By the end of this chapter you should be able to:

- appreciate the nature and importance of effective communication within and beyond organisations;
- identify different elements in a simple model of the communication process and give a working definition of the related terminology;
- distinguish the principal dimensions of organisational communication, as used by researchers and practitioners;
- contrast several theoretical perspectives that may provide insights into different aspects of organisational communication;
- explore connections between theory, research evidence and 'real world' communication practices.

1.1 Introducing communication

This book looks at the ways that people communicate in organisations. Its main aim is to help you become a more effective communicator. As the chapter quotation suggests, one of the underlying themes is that effective communication requires an open mind (i.e. a willingness to take on new and unfamiliar ideas). The reason for this is simple. Unless you are open to the needs of your audience, and to the context in which the communication is taking place, your best efforts to communicate are very likely to fail. In today's organisations, you will encounter people from many backgrounds, whose life experiences are entirely different from your own. The context in which you communicate is also likely to be fairly complex and unfamiliar. For example, your employees, customers or suppliers may be located in several different countries, or you may be required to work in a 'virtual team', relying on web-based systems to keep in touch with your colleagues. But having an open mind is not enough. You also need an understanding of the broad principles of communication, a flexible set of practical tools and some experience in applying them in different situations. The book is designed to help you develop your abilities in each of these areas.

This introductory chapter sketches a simple model of the communication process that will be critiqued, elaborated and applied throughout the text. It also provides working definitions of some of the more common terminology used in this subject area, including concepts such as, 'encoding', 'channels' and 'noise'. However, before we move into the theory of communication, it is worth considering two fundamental questions:

● Why is communication such a critical issue for organisations?

● Why is it so difficult to communicate effectively?

1.2 Communicating in organisations: issues and challenges

Human beings are social animals. In a complex technological society, our quality of life, even basic survival, depends on countless successful interactions with other people, mediated through markets, networks and various kinds of organisation. Without these intricate and largely unseen webs of communication, our economic prosperity, social welfare and cultural life would be undermined. Communication can be difficult; history reveals countless occasions when individuals, communities and nations have pursued simpler solutions to their problems, either avoiding the challenge altogether (i.e. 'flight') or using resolving it by force (i.e. 'fight'). Communication can often seem a more demanding and time-consuming option than either 'fight' or 'flight'. This is because, in order for it to be effective, communication requires each party to make some effort to understand the other. However, though it may appear the more difficult option, effective communication does have its rewards. For example, it can help an organisation to achieve:

● satisfied repeat customers, rather than unhappy ex-customers;

● well-motivated employees, rather than an expensive industrial dispute;

● a positive reputation in the wider community, rather than an international boycott of its products;

● innovative and creative strategies, rather than inefficiency, indecision and resistance to change.

Organisations are complex phenomena. As a consequence, effective communicators need to be adept in handling challenges that simply do not arise in ordinary, day-to-day communication (e.g. in your immediate circle of friends). The kind of challenges we need to consider include:

● formal organisation structures, reporting arrangements and procedures;

● cultural diversity, across countries, organisations, departments, employees and other organisational stakeholders;

● intense political, financial and time pressures, competing managerial priorities and demands.

Issues of this kind mean that communicating in organisations is often an uphill struggle. Moreover, the most common challenges are surprisingly similar, whether the organisation is operating in the private, public or voluntary sector. Hence, this book is concerned with communication in human organisations of all kinds. Practical issues are explored through a number of 'mini-cases' and longer case studies set in charitable organisations, government departments, small firms and international companies. Mini-case 1.1 looks at a frequent source of problems, when the communication process fails to keep up with the rapid growth of a new firm.

**Mini-case
1.1**

'Shooting Star': communicating in a fast-growing firm

Communication within an entrepreneurial start-up venture tends to be centralised, informal and face-to-face. The founding owner-managers have direct control over most aspects of the business and are able to keep in direct contact with a small team of employees. Everyone needs to be flexible and there is no need for detailed written procedures; if someone has a problem, they can simply call in and speak to the boss. However, over time, the firm grows in size and complexity. There is an increase in the volume of sales and in the number and variety of customers, more staff are recruited and people begin to specialise in particular tasks. At a certain point, the 'old' approach to communication can become severely stretched.

'Shooting Star' is a biotechnology venture, founded three years ago by two university scientists and a former school friend who worked for an investment company. Following a second round of venture capital financing, the firm has recently moved to a large science park, on the edge of the city. It now employs 15 people. Six of these are research scientists; the others comprise of four laboratory technicians, a finance manager, an office manager, two administrative assistants and a marketing manager. Business is booming, but there are also serious communication problems: the administrators and the scientists are in a constant state of war – every other day the representative of one or other group makes complaints about unreasonable behaviour by the others; the finance manager is worried about an over-spend on the promotional budget; two of the laboratory technicians have just announced that they are leaving for 'better jobs' with another firm on the science park; and yesterday there was a national newspaper report suggesting that the firm's first development project, a new medical treatment for babies, was experiencing problems during its pre-clinical trials.

Shooting Star's three original founders are spending almost all of their time travelling between meetings with investors, medical specialists and pharmaceutical companies. This evening they have at last managed to meet together for a meal. Looking round the table, one of the founders is shocked to see the exhausted faces of her colleagues. She comments, 'You know, I really thought things would get easier once we had got the business going, but now everything seems to be falling apart. What on earth are we doing wrong?'

Questions

1 Review each of the communication problems at 'Shooting Star' and suggest the kinds of communication that appear to be taking place (e.g. do they involve an exchange of emails, a meeting or a telephone conversation?).

2 What do you think is the cause of each of these problems?

3 What changes might the founders make in order to deal with them?

Source: Shooting Star is a fictional organisation.

1.3 Stage one: a simple model of the communication process

Since earliest times, men and women have been speculating on the basic mysteries of human existence: our origins, the purpose of our lives and how we can obtain a better understanding of ourselves and of other people. Over the years, philosophers, theologians and artists have done their best to answer these questions, but it is only in the last few centuries that the process of communication in humans has been the subject of systematic study. Disciplines including, psychology, linguistics, sociology and anthropology have contributed important insights, as have multi-disciplinary and applied specialisms, such as organisation studies, strategic management, human resource management and marketing. This wide-ranging research literature has also created a major challenge for students, teachers and textbook authors.

First, there are well-defended disciplinary and professional boundaries that separate much of the published work. Second, many sub-specialisms have been created, each being concerned with particular types of communication, to the exclusion of others. Third, there has been a great deal of theoretical development, leading to the emergence of several competing perspectives on communication; each of these has its own enthusiastic supporters and dismissive critics, who argue at length about their respective research agendas and methodologies. Later, we will become more familiar with this rich proliferation of ideas, which reflects the real complexity of organisational communication in the new century. However, we begin with a reassuringly simple model of the communication process and introduce some of the basic terminology that is used throughout the text.

The model was developed as part of a now largely-forgotten research project, which investigated the ways that information was communicated in telecommunications systems (Mattelart and Mattelart 1998, Shannon and Weaver 1955). It remains relevant as a source of several key communication terms, and because it has been so widely promoted by communication teachers and practitioners over the last half century. In its simplest version, the model describes a linear (i.e. 'one-way') process that comprises two individuals, a 'sender' and a 'receiver', connected via a conventional telephone landline (see Figure 1.1).

Though this model is simple, it introduces several important concepts. We also need to take note of a number of assumptions on which it is based. The model indicates that the communication process starts when a message is formulated in the **sender's** brain. Having been formulated, the message is then **encoded**. In the case of the telephone call, the process of encoding involves the sender in converting the message into a series of words. The encoded message is then **transmitted** through the microphone and along the telephone line. (Note: In practice, there are two encoding processes here, the second taking place when the microphone converts the words into electrical impulses or – in a digital system – into binary code.) When the encoded message reaches the other end of the line, it has to go through a further process of **decoding**. The signal is converted back into words and the meaning of the words is interpreted by the brain

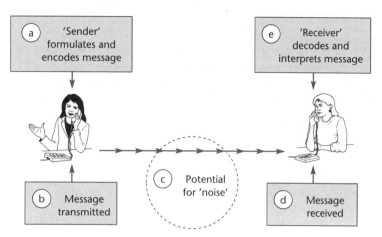

Figure 1.1 A simple linear model of the communication process
Source: Adapted from Shannon and Weaver (1955)

of another person. Once this conversion is complete, the model indicates that the original message has been **received**. This sequence is repeated, with the positions of 'sender' and 'receiver' reversed, creating the basic outline of a telephone conversation. These exchanges can be distorted or interrupted. The original researchers used the word **noise** to refer, literally, to the random electrical crackle that might occasionally interrupt a conversation on an analogue telephone line. The problem continues with today's digital mobile phones, where conversations are sometimes cut short due to a weak or lost signal. In communication theory, the meaning of the term 'noise' is now interpreted much more widely, to include anything that either interrupts or distorts an encoded message, so that it fails to reach the receiver in its original form. For example, if we take this broader view of the communication process, even the temperature in a seminar room can become a source of 'noise' (see Mini-case 1.2).

Mini-case 1.2	**'PromoCo': when temperature became 'noise'**

PromoCo, a Madrid-based sales promotions company, is giving a presentation that is meant to impress some of its most important clients. It is early afternoon in mid-July, and the guests have just enjoyed an excellent four-course lunch, provided by the company. They are directed into a well-furnished seminar room, the lights are dimmed and a digital projector is switched on. The presentation is delivered by a dynamic manager, who speaks clearly and has a well-produced set of slides. However, the air conditioning is not working properly and after a few minutes the room becomes very warm and airless. Members of the audience begin to feel uncomfortable. People shuffle in their seats and whisper to their neighbours. Some remove their jackets, look for windows to open and pass around bottles of sparkling water. One guest, who appears to have enjoyed the complimentary wine at lunchtime, is resting his head on the table and has closed his eyes. The temperature of the room has now become a source of 'noise', distracting the audience from the messages that the presenter, and the company, wishes to convey.

▶

The simple model depicted in Figure 1.1 introduces two further terms, the **message** and the communication **channel**. In the simple model, a message comprises the content that the sender has encoded. Organisational communication is made up of a vast and endless stream of criss-crossing messages. The content of these messages can be broken down into a number of different elements, including raw data, factual information, ideas, opinions, beliefs and emotions. However, these elements are sometimes difficult to distinguish, a point that is well-illustrated by the current debate over climate change and global warming.

Raw data

These may include the results of scientific measurement, such as a series of temperature readings that has not been analysed or put into any meaningful context. Messages containing raw data can be readily transmitted by the sender, but cannot be effectively decoded or interpreted by the receiver, without establishing their context. For example, in the case of the temperature readings, this would include the temperature scale and the dates, times and locations of each reading.

Facts

Facts comprise data that are presented as objective information. That is, they are meaningful and can claim to have some basis in truth or reality. For example, a recent report drew on published scientific research in order to state that the level of carbon dioxide in the atmosphere has risen by a third since the industrial revolution, and that average global temperature has risen by 0.6 degrees centigrade over the same period (IPCC 2001).

Ideas

Ideas are a **more** abstract type of information, presented in the form of concepts, constructs, theories and models, which may have varying degrees of empirical support. For example, the 'enhanced greenhouse effect' is a widely-endorsed scientific theory that connects the burning of fossil fuels (e.g. coal, gas and oil), to an intensification of a natural greenhouse effect of carbon dioxide in the atmosphere, which in turn is leading to global warming (e.g. Fawcett *et al.* 2002: 11–13).

Opinions

Opinions, which may relate to facts or ideas, can be distinguished by their **subjectivity** (i.e. their authority derives from the individual or organisation expressing the opinion, rather than being founded on something that is already proven and more generally acknowledged). For example, in February 2003 the British prime minister expressed his opinion that, 'There will be no lasting peace while there is appalling injustice and poverty. There will be no genuine security if the planet is ravaged by climate change.' (Blair 2003).

Beliefs

Beliefs comprise a strongly-held set of opinions, which is usually linked to an individual's sense of identity and influences daily behaviour. For example, in relation to climate change, some people have made radical lifestyle changes, based on their environmental concerns (e.g. switching from car to cycle journeys, avoiding air travel, offsetting carbon emissions by contributing financially to tree-planting initiatives), while others defend the right to drive fuel-hungry MPVs on the basis of a belief in personal freedom.

Emotion

Emotional energy can be contained in a message, expressing human feelings (e.g. love, anger, joy, bitterness, humour, passion, sentimentality, weariness, hopefulness), in conjunction with other elements, such as facts, or ideas. If this 'affective' element in the message is conveyed to the receiver, it may stimulate similar feelings, often adding to the overall impact. For example, a short television advertisement by the French environmental agency encouraged public support for action against global warming by challenging viewers with the question, 'Do you really want to kill polar bears?' This was followed by a statement to the effect that, by 2060, all of the world's polar bears are going to starve, because the Arctic ice pack will have melted, disrupting their food supplies.

In practice, organisations often exchange messages containing a rich mixture of facts, ideas, opinions and beliefs, often coloured by varying degrees of emotion. In later chapters, we consider how these elements can best be combined in order to deliver the kind of communication we are seeking to achieve. However, whatever is contained in a message, our initial concern is the channel (i.e. the route or technology), that is used to convey it to a receiver. As we saw previously, the original linear model was based on research into a particular channel, the telephone system. Contemporary organisations make use of a number of different communication channels, including: face-to-face meetings and conversations, letters, telephones, e-mails, reports, posters, brochures and video-conferences. Recent technological changes have led to the decline of some channels (e.g. facsimile or 'fax' messaging), and the emergence of others (e.g. SMS or 'text' messaging) in organisational settings. Each of the chapters in Part II deals with specific communication channels. Messages are encoded in different ways, depending on the channel that is used. The form of encoding (e.g. as text, images or sound), is sometimes referred to as the 'medium' of communication. However, it is important to bear in mind that this term is also used to refer to communication channels. For example, when advertising executives talk about different 'media', they are generally referring to television, radio, newspapers, poster sites, etc.

The basic linear approach has introduced some useful terminology, but we need to recognise that it remains a very crude and simplified model of reality, even in the restricted field of the telephone conversation. In the next section, we take a first step in developing a more 'realistic' understanding of the communication process in organisations, by introducing the concepts of feedback, expectations and subjectivity.

1.4 Feedback, expectations and subjectivity

One of the initial modifications of the simple 'one-way' model was to add a **feedback loop** (see Figure 1.2). The term 'feedback' originated in cybernetics, the study of control systems (Boulding 1956, Buckley 1967, Wiener 1948), and introduced an influential 'systems theory' perspective into organisational studies. The thermostat is a very simple feedback mechanism; it regulates the temperature of a building by switching the central heating system on and off when it reaches a pre-set level. In human communication theory, feedback refers to the receiver's response to a message. It is important to note how this differs from the smooth,

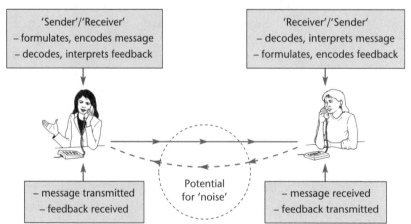

Figure 1.2 **The linear model of communication with feedback**

automatic reaction of a thermostat. Human feedback is much more irregular and unpredictable. Each person might respond to an identical message in a variety of ways, the reaction depending on the way in which a particular message has been perceived. There is a simple thought experiment that demonstrates this point. Imagine yourself walking down a street. Start smiling randomly at the strangers that you pass. How do they react? In all probability, a few people will smile back at you, several may appear hostile or suspicious, others try to ignore you, while quite a few appear completely unaware of either you or your smile (in my own thought experiment, the last group were mostly engaged in mobile phone conversations). A dotted line is used in the revised model, indicating that there is no automatic feedback 'loop' in human communication.

The key lessons from systems theory are that each sub-division of the organisation is affected by activity in other parts. Furthermore, the organisation itself is an 'open system', exposed to a wider environment in which it both experiences competitive threats and finds its collaborative partners (Child 2001). In short, organisations do not operate like thermostats. Rather, their actions are the result of countless human decisions, each of which is based on *subjective* perceptions of the world in which they are operating and their pre-existing values and experiences:

> 'The behaviour of the organization [...] must be interpreted as a result of the image of the executive, directed by his value system. [...] He is a receiver of messages from the receptor of the organization, and his job is to transform those messages into instructions or orders which go out to the effectors. He cannot be regarded, however, as simply a sausage machine grinding out instructions from the messages received. It is more realistic to suppose that between the incoming and outgoing messages lies the great intervening variable of the image. The outgoing messages are the result of the image, not the result of the incoming messages.' (Boulding 1956: 27–28)

The subjective and unpredictable responses of human beings can certainly make life more interesting. For example, they have provided the basis for many humorous cartoons and popular comedy routines. However, because confused feedback gets in the way of mutual understanding, it can have disastrous effects in organisations. For example, it can contribute to industrial accidents, badly-designed products and services, mistreatment of internal and external stakeholders, lack of innovation and poor financial performance. One of our main concerns will be to find ways of overcoming the communication failures that feed these negative outcomes.

1.5 Organisational communication: key dimensions

Organisational communication is a wide-ranging and field of study that spreads across academic disciplines (e.g. psychology, anthropology, organisation studies) and professional specialisms (e.g. marketing, public relations, human resources management). It tackles several different types of communication and makes use of many contrasting theoretical and methodological approaches.

This section introduces something of the variety that is to be found in the communication literature. We begin by examining four of the more common distinctions: verbal and non-verbal, one-way and two-way, inter-personal and mass, internal and external.

Verbal and non-verbal communication

Verbal communication refers to messages coded in the form of words. This may be further sub-divided into spoken (or 'oral') and written forms. Written communication depends on established systems of grammar and punctuation, while spoken communication uses equivalents such as pauses and stress on particular words. Verbal forms of communication raise issues such as using appropriate vocabulary for an audience and translating meanings between different languages. There are also many forms of non-verbal communication. These include 'kinesics' (i.e. human posture, gesture, body language), the use of other visual media (e.g. pictures and signs), and other non-verbal sensory stimuli, such as sounds and smells, all of which can be used to convey a message. In practice, each of these forms can be used simultaneously. For example, text and images are combined in a business report, while presenters make use of words and gestures.

One-way and two-way communication

This distinction refers simply to the direction in which messages are travelling. Some communication channels are inherently 'two-way', such as face-to-face interviews and meetings, with instantaneous feedback. Others may appear to operate in one direction only, including posters and webcasts, but all forms of communication are normally open to some kind of feedback, using techniques such as communication audits or market research. The newer digital communications channels tend to be more 'interactive' than their analogue predecessors. For example, television viewers can now interact with digital broadcasts using their remote control keypads. Similarly, internet technologies, such as 'cookies', can provide organisations with feedback on the way their websites are being accessed.

Inter-personal and mass communication

Until the industrial era, most communication was between individuals, interacting in relatively small groups, primarily through face-to-face channels such as meetings. Mass communication originated with the invention of printing, which allowed people to send the same encoded message to a large number of people. Newspaper and book publishing were the pioneering forms of mass communication in the eighteenth and nineteenth centuries, followed by radio and television in the twentieth century. Today, organisations continue to engage in both inter-personal and mass communication, though the latter tends to be under the control of professional specialists.

Internal and external communication

There has been a long tradition of distinguishing communication that takes place *within* the boundaries of an organisation from that involving the organisation and audiences in the wider world. This distinction is reflected in the different functional areas. For example, human resource managers have tended to focus on employee communication, while public relations, purchasing and marketing managers have dealt with external stakeholders. There has been a similar divide in academic circles, between researchers addressing internal communication processes, and others who are more concerned with corporate communication and media relations. Recently, however, there have been efforts to re-integrate internal and external communication issues, an approach that is also reflected in this text (Cheney and Christensen 2001, Zorn 2002). Researchers point to the increasingly 'blurred' boundaries of today's organisations, and argue that there is an underlying continuity between what have previously been termed 'internal' and 'external' communication processes (see section 7.3).

While these four dimensions of communication do not exhaust the ways that the field might be divided, they at least indicate some of the main areas that we need to address. Each dimension should be seen as overlapping and interconnected. So, rather than slotting them into one of the neat '2 × 2' matrices that are often found in business textbooks, we have used the less tidy but more holistic image of a globe (see Figure 1.3).

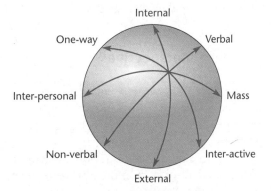

Figure 1.3 The multiple dimensions of organisational communication

1.6 Different perspectives on communication

Our final task in this chapter is to conduct a brief review of some competing views of organisational communication. The aim is to give you a flavour of various perspectives that have informed academic debate in organisation theory and management studies over recent years, and which have also had an impact on everyday communication practices. Writing on the subject of communication ranges from highly instrumental, 'how to' (or 'recipe book') approaches found in most popular management texts, to some extremely abstract academic arguments regarding the nature of human discourse. So why do we need to consider more than one perspective on communication? Communication textbooks tend to emphasise practical techniques, helping students to make better use of particular communication channels (e.g. letters or meetings). In this book, we are aiming to combine the development of relevant skills with an opportunity to reflect on the wider challenges of organisational communication. To achieve this balance, we need to question conventional communication practices, including the assumptions on which they are based. By becoming more aware of the different perspectives used to study communication, we are also better positioned to question the tendency of writers to offer 'pre-packaged' solutions that take insufficient account of local circumstances.

The following overview contrasts four broad academic perspectives on organisational communication: 'modern'; 'interpretive'; 'critical' and 'postmodern' (adapted from Deetz 2001). However, it is important to note the limitations of an exercise of this kind. There is little agreement amongst academics over the precise meaning of concepts such as 'modernism' and 'postmodernism' (Hassard 1999: 193). As a consequence, the category headings, descriptions and boundaries used in this summary remain incomplete and open to revision. However, they should prove a useful reference, illustrating different ways to approach the challenge of communicating in human organisations. You are also likely to encounter a similar range of perspectives elsewhere in organisation theory, management studies and other social science disciplines (e.g. Hatch 1997, Clark 2000, Westwood and Clegg 2001).

'Modern' perspectives

Modernism is associated with the rise of scientific enquiry in the Renaissance and Enlightenment; it remains a dominant way of thinking about the world, but faces challenges from other perspectives, including postmodernism (see below). Modernism's science-based framework emphasises objective measurement, decision-making based on rational calculations (i.e. 'utilitarianism') and progress towards an improved and more general understanding of real world phenomena. Research in this perspective tends to treat organisational communication practices as being readily accessible to researchers, revealing some predictable features that made them open to a degree of managerial intervention and control. Research programmes have often followed the natural science model, seeking law-like generalisations through theory building and empirical testing, frequently making use of quantitative survey data as the basis for detailed statistical analysis of organisations (e.g. Thompson 1967, Pugh and Hickson 1976). Systems theory is another important strand in modernist research. This has tended to treat organisations as rather more complex phenomena that cannot be fully understood using the tools of natural science. For example, greater attention has been paid to the subjective perceptions of people in organisations, leading to more sophisticated explanations of processes such as organisational learning (e.g. Senge 1990, Weick 1979).

'Interpretive' perspectives

Interpretive research in contemporary organisations owes much to the ethnographic tradition in anthropology. In this subject area, it tends to be less concerned with general theory, but aims to reveal the complexity and richness of organisational communication. Ethnographic studies often involve researchers spending long periods 'in the field', using qualitative research methods such as participant observation to record conversations, stories, rituals and other routine events in offices, factories and other organisational settings (Van Maanen 1988). The results are often presented in the form of detailed narratives, accompanied by varying amounts of analysis (Pentland 1999). In contrast to natural science, where researchers can make direct interpretations of objects and processes (e.g. chemical compounds or weather systems), social science researchers are often required to interpret *other people's* interpretations of the world. This fundamental distinction, sometimes referred to as 'the double hermeneutic' (i.e. double interpretation) is an important feature of interpretivist studies. In general, they attempt to conduct research in ways that do not impose the researcher's interpretations of a situation onto the people they are observing.

'Critical' perspectives

The common feature of these perspectives is their broader political agenda, which involves a radical critique of the way power is exercised under industrial capitalism (Alvesson and Willmott 1996). Hence, in the subject area of organisational communication, it has mainly been concerned with ways that communication channels are used to exercise power over employees and other stakeholders. Researchers have used a range of methods, including those associated with modern and interpretive perspectives, but their work can be distinguished by its more sceptical approach to established institutions. One of the central themes in critical organisation and management studies has been the failure of workers and other stakeholders to act in their own interests. Theorists have re-applied earlier concepts such as 'false consciousness' (Gramsci 1971) and distorted communication processes to explain how a particular set of arguments, is transformed into a dominant 'discourse' at the level of the organisation or wider society (Habermas 1984). For example, critical management researchers have investigated 'business process re-engineering' (BPR), an influential managerial fashion/discourse of the 1990s, associated with various practices, including 'delayering' and 'empowerment'. Researchers have studied the strategies of management consultants and other specialists, ranging from their use of the language of 'empowerment' to the ways that they re-invented traditional hierarchical control systems in order to overcome resistance from line managers and other employees (Knights and Willmott 2000).

'Postmodern' perspectives

Postmodernism is often presented as a challenge to the assumptions of modernism, including the way it approaches research. For example, postmodernist theorists have questioned whether it is possible for researchers to take a detached view of their research subjects, and whether there is a possibility of establishing general laws relating to real-world phenomena, such as organisations. The arguments supporting this perspective are complex, but at the core of the postmodernism is the view that there is no neutral access to the world, as modernist researchers assume. Instead, our knowledge is always shaped by language, which is itself a product of society and open to a variety of meanings, depending on the context in which it is used. Consequently, postmodern research has focused on *localised* practices (e.g. Keenoy et al. 1997, Czarinawska 1998). In the field of organisational communication, postmodernists have argued that contemporary trends, such as globalisation and the rise of the internet have left people with 'fragmented identities', in the face of many competing discourses. This means that it is not possible to make any objective, generalisable or unified statements about organisational communication. Instead, research tends to be directed at the deconstruction of particular communication practices (e.g. Livesey's (2002) study, which applies a technique called discourse analysis techniques to study the way that an oil company reported on environmental issues (see section 3.7)).

Each of these perspectives has its supporters and critics. For example, the research aims of modern and interpretive studies are usually presented as apolitical and value-neutral, but critical theorists have argued that both have, to some extent, ignored the political dimension. Postmodernists have criticised interpretivists for representing cultures as unified wholes, rather than reflecting inherent tensions, while modernists have attacked both the interpretive and postmodern perspectives for the absence of coherent theoretical frameworks or sufficiently rigorous research methods. One of the more significant developments in recent years has been the introduction of feminist perspectives on organisational communication. Feminist studies have addressed several issues that had been excluded from much of the earlier work in this area, including, 'the complexities of sex and gender, race and ethnicity, and sexual-social orientation.' (Buzzanell 2000: x). The feminist research agenda can be seen as part of a more general trend towards rethinking the standard approaches to organisational communication (e.g. Wright 2001, Grimes and Richard 2003). Another important feature of this reassessment is the emergence of critics who are pointing to the way that Western cultural assumptions and values have dominated the published work on communication and arguing that greater attention needs to be paid to cultural diversity (Munshi and McKie 2001, De Vita 2001). In other chapters of the book, we consider how diversity is influencing communication practices in a variety of settings.

We have now reviewed four contrasting perspectives on communication, and have developed some provisional ideas about their implications for studying this subject. Mini-case 1.3 revisits these perspectives, highlighting the different ways in which they can shape our understanding of the term, 'effective' when it is applied to organisational communication.

Mini-case 1.3	**What do we mean by 'effective'?: comparing perspectives**

The title of this textbook includes the word 'effective'; similar titles can be found in other subject areas (e.g. 'effective financial management'). But what do we really mean by the word 'effective', firstly in general terms and then when it is applied to organisational communication? The *Concise Oxford English Dictionary* offers the following definition:

> **effective** /ɪˈfɛktɪv/ adj. & n. – *adj.* **1** having a definite or desired effect. **2** powerful in effect; impressive. **3 a** actual; existing in fact rather than officially or theoretically (*took effective control in their absence*). **b** actually usable; realizable; equivalent in its effect (*effective money; effective demand*). **4** coming into operation (*effective as from 1 May*). **5** (of manpower) fit for work or service. – *n.* a soldier available for service. **effectively** *adv.* **effectiveness** *n.* [ME f. L *effectivus* (as EFFECT)].

So, which of these explanations applies to the title of this book? It seems that the first and second definitions are closest to the apparent purpose of the text, which claims that it is 'designed to help you develop your abilities' in various aspects of the communication process. In the first definition, 'effective' communication suggests that you (and other readers) can achieve your intended aims through skilful application of the relevant knowledge and techniques. The second definition goes a little further, so that being effective also means achieving a 'powerful' or 'impressive' result. Both suggest a very 'instrumental' purpose. In other words, that the book is only concerned with helping its readers to achieve what they want to achieve personally, using communication as a tool. So how might the four perspectives on communication broaden our basic understanding of 'effectiveness'?

Modern
In this perspective, we are searching for general rules or principles governing the communication process. By applying these rules in practical situations, we can become more 'effective' in achieving our aims. The underlying assumption is that the process is fairly objective. Communication problems can be defined by the 'sender', who then selects and applies an appropriate solution. For example, Chapter 2 discusses some inherent physiological barriers to communication, such as selective attention and memory loss. Having become aware of this information, the 'sender' is able to design and implement communication channels in ways that seek to overcome the barriers and deliver the message.

Interpretive
In this perspective, we recognise that communication is as much about the meanings constructed by 'receivers' as it is about our performance as a 'sender'. It has been particularly influential in the field of cross-cultural communication, where efforts have been directed at better understanding local customs. In other words, our attention becomes focused on the context in which the interaction is taking place. For example, Chapter 6 considers how organisations secure relevant feedback by becoming more sensitive to the diverse characteristics of their various stakeholders. This perspective can be very revealing, giving us a much better understanding of our own communication practices, including their inherent values and norms. However, it can still be consistent with a rather narrow interpretation of 'effectiveness', based ultimately around our own communication aims.

▶

Critical

In this perspective, we start to raise more radical (i.e. deeper) questions about the communication process. For example, what does effectiveness mean for other actors? What is the impact of choices regarding message content, or between communication channels, on the relative power of different groups within or beyond the organisation? Critical theories challenge (or 'contest') the apparent objectivity of everyday communication practices. For example, in Chapter 7 we consider the changing relationship between organisations and their multiple stakeholders. In this perspective, 'effectiveness' becomes politicised, so we see our own communication aims as being in competition with those of others.

Postmodern

In this perspective, we draw on a combination of interpretivism and critical theory, in an effort to understand what 'effectiveness' might mean in specific organisational settings. As noted in the text, there are many strands of postmodern thinking. However, common themes include the notion that our own communication practices form part of a web of competing narratives, and that these narratives, or 'discourses', are fragmented, socially constructed and have real consequences in the world. By examining, or 'de-constructing', these narratives, we can understand more about the ways in which power is exercised in organisations. For example, in section 3.7, we see how researchers studied a corporate takeover in Singapore by analysing the texts that were produced in and around each organisation. Our understanding of 'effectiveness' has expanded beyond a narrow concern with our own practices. Communication itself has become the raw material for researching the organisation, its activities and their effects.

Questions

1 Outline the main differences between the four perspectives and their approach to studying a subject. Use the word 'organisation' to illustrate your argument.

2 Why might research in the Critical perspective be of interest to someone studying communication in commercial businesses or other types of organisation?

3 What are your own views of the term 'effective' organisational communication? Compare them with those of other students and colleagues and try to prepare an agreed definition that could be applied to organisations of all kinds.

Summary

- Practising effective communication in different organisational settings requires an open mind, which means a willingness to take on new ideas and explore new perspectives.

- While communication in organisations is particularly challenging due to factors such as formal structures, cultural diversity, political, financial and time pressures, efforts to improve communication practices can make a real difference to performance.

- The communication process is often described using a simple linear model, which features senders and receivers. Messages are encoded by senders, transmitted and then decoded by receivers; they are also subject to distortion, or 'noise'.

- Message content, including a mixture of raw data, facts, ideas, opinions, beliefs and emotions, can be conveyed through various channels, such as email, interviews and video-conferences.

- Systems theory has been used to develop more elaborate models of the communication process, which include feedback loops and highlight the importance of subjective perceptions.

- This book takes a holistic view of communication, seeking to integrate conventional dimensions, such as: verbal and non-verbal, one- and two-way, interpersonal and mass, internal and external.

- It also balances an emphasis on practical skills development with deeper reflection on communication practices in today's organisations. This is achieved by drawing on different perspectives – modern, interpretive, critical and postmodern.

Practical exercises

1 'Effective' communicators? Assessing key strengths and weaknesses

Use this exercise to assess your own strengths and weaknesses as you begin this book. Keep the results on file and refer to them again at the end of your studies, noting how far your personal 'strengths' develop and 'weaknesses' are overcome.

(a) At the top of a new page, write down your description: 'An effective communicator is …' Try to sum up the main characteristics in a sentence or two, based on past experience and your reflections on this chapter.

(b) Below this description, divide the page into two columns and use them to list your 'Top Five' communication strengths and weaknesses. What do you do well, and where can you see room for improvement? Use the chapter headings from Part II of this book as a prompt. For example, how effective are you at letter writing, dealing with people on the telephone, giving presentations, being interviewed, 'socialising' informally and so on? Try to be as comprehensive (and honest!) as possible.

(c) Ask a trusted colleague or friend to review your description and comment on your 'Top Five' lists. How does their impression compare with your own?

Seminar option: divide into groups of four or five students and discuss the differences between your descriptions of 'an effective communicator'. Draft a concise statement that incorporates each person's ideas. Finally, add together the ranking scores from each person's 'Top Five' lists and calculate the averages, using these to discover the 'Top Five' strengths and weaknesses for the group as a whole. Use a whiteboard or flipchart to present your results to the rest of the seminar.

2 Jan and Haluk – mis-reading the feedback?

Messages are vulnerable to noise and incorrect de-coding, even when they are delivered 'face-to-face'. Consider the following exchange, which involves a marketing manager, Jan (aged 26) and a sales manager, Haluk (aged 43), in the Copenhagen office of a Japanese electronics company:

Jan   (Walks into the office with a smile, waving several pages of computer print-out at Haluk, who sits at a desk covered with computer print-out paper, books and files, staring at a computer screen) *Well, Haluk, I see that the Regional Sales Report looks a lot better this month!*

Haluk   (Jumps up from the desk and folds arms) *Is that so? 'Looks better', does it? And what exactly do you mean by that?*

Jan   (Shakes head and laughs) *Whoa!, take it easy Haluk, you do not need to be so aggressive!*

Haluk   (Leans back on the desk) *I knew it. You're at it again, Jan, aren't you? Ever since that ...*

Jan   *Look, Haluk, all I am saying is ...* (Gestures with hands)

Haluk   *Alright. Look, just forget it ...Jan. Believe me, I have just about had ...* (a mobile phone on Haluk's desk starts to rings; Haluk turns away from Jan, picks it up and starts speaking) *Hi Gary!* (pause) *No, mate, that's not a problem. So, how was the skiing trip?* (laughs and looks out of the window) *Oh yeah?, I bet she did!* (laughs loudly) *Yeah, yeah...* (pause) *So, what can I do for you, my old friend?*

Jan   *Well that's it!* (Storms out of the office)

(a) Draw up a list identifying what you consider to be the most likely causes of the unsuccessful exchange between Jan and Haluk.

(b) Using your list as a starting point, make suggestions as to how Jan might have avoided this outcome.

(c) Repeat the exercise for Haluk.

(d) Review your responses to the previous questions and try to identify any assumptions you have made about the two people in this exchange.

Seminar option: begin the exercise with two students role-playing the dialogue between Jan and Haluk. Repeat the role-plays, making use of the advice that you have generated in questions (b) and (c).

Case study A   Human contact – more effective than technology?

Contacts mean contracts. Capitalism, associated principally with individualism, has always had its social side. The curious question now being asked is whether it is becoming more sociable as the years go by. In an age when the computer provides limitless opportunities to economise on face-to-face human interaction, networking, flesh-pressing and entrepreneurial schmoozing have never seemed more vital. 'There's no electronic substitute for the occasional exchange of pheromones,' says Ursula Huws, an associate fellow with the Institute of Employment Studies (IES), who has led research into e-working for the European Commission.

   As a commodity, in fact, the business of getting people to eyeball each other – F2F, as it is occasionally known – has been startlingly robust. There is little doubt that international meetings have dipped since September 11 2001 but, domestically, commercial interaction continues to grow. Recent figures from the Meetings Industry Association – which cautiously exclude takings from hotel bars and restaurants – show meetings and conferences account for £7.3bn worth of value to the UK economy. In the year before, it was £6.6bn. Indeed, the necessity of social interaction in business is leading some academics to begin speculating about whether 'F2F business' may be a significant growth area of the economy. Anthony Venables, a professor at the London School of Economics, believes that the clustering of certain activities in cities and locations – the advertising village of Soho, in London, for instance – may be partly explained by 'the efficiency of face-to-face technology'. 'Clustering has become stronger for a number of reasons and one of them may well be that for knowledge-based activities that require brain-storming, trust, body language, context and so on, F2F is simply indispensable.'

Across the European Union, four out of 10 employers now use remote suppliers or back offices supplying services over a telecommunications link. In theory, this could enable a significant relocation of work to cheaper spaces – out of cramped urban hubs such as London, New York and Hong Kong. In addition, new working practices, such as hot-desking, virtual teams and so on, allow clear economies in terms of the amount of physical office space needed per employee. A study by the Royal Institution of Chartered Surveyors (RICS) says companies that use new technology to enable work require an average of 7.7 square metres per employee against a national average of 14.9 square metres. Have such calculations caused the demand for office space in high-density locations to atrophy? No, says RICS. It explains current weak demand in commercial property entirely through the downturn in the economy. The only notice-able impact of technology on the use of business space is the way offices have been reinvented as places for significant social interaction. It is perhaps a sign that work still requires physical presence that many of the changes made to office space involve improving the free flow of communication. Offices are now drop-in points for mobile workers or designed to act as work-oriented 'neighbourhoods'. 'Employers recognise how offices bring people together, forge social capital and strengthen social networks,' says Max Nathan, a researcher with the Work Foundation, a think-tank. 'Employees value the communities and friendships that thrive in office spaces.'

Many of the large number of research projects among universities and institutes into e-work appear to point to apparently paradoxical conclusions. Ms Huws, at the IES, says modern technology has increased the need to meet because the one incontrovert-ible effect of the internet has been to expand the range of communication partners. 'Any business relationship that progresses beyond the most superficial level needs human contact,' she says. 'E-mail breeds misunderstanding.' At the Centre for Research in Innovation Management, at the University of Brighton, researchers have been attempting to isolate which forms of communication can be done successfully online from remote locations. Jonathan Sapsed, who is leading the project involving several high-technology national businesses, says that even with the best groupware and video-conferencing, performance is not as good as when people are together. 'E-mail may be good for group notices and validation but it is less good for knowledge transfer, the resolution of management problems and anything that requires creativity.' Does this suggest the communications revolution has failed to keep its promise of the death of distance? Not exactly. Several experts contend that the effect of the ICT revol-ution is leading to a fragmentation of both economic activity and information. A great deal of information can be swapped electronically – employee payroll and data

▶

management, for instance – and does not require proximity. But, equally, much cannot. Recruitment, deal-making, employee relations and innovation – the more sophisticated end of information sharing – seem to be still dependent on physical presence. Thus the economic dominance of the city as the powerhouse of employment is almost certain to continue, as will the case for 'being there'.

Jane Clarke, co-author of *Wired Working*, a book about the reshaping of work by ICT, says new technology often acts as 'a lubricant' for the older, more important forms of interaction. 'It is certainly no replacement,' she says. 'E-mail can save time and waste time and it takes no sophistication to understand its limits. I often think the information revolution seems to have led to a tendency among employees to manufacture unnecessary meetings.' Even beyond the insidious tentacles of technology, the corporate world seems to furnish endless fresh channels for interaction. Peter Knight, who runs CEO Circle, a networking organisation for global business leaders, says that with the rising pressure to perform and the sense that 'the treadmill is being revved too high' has come a growing feeling of isolation at the top. This has created a need for organisations such as his, which aim to bring together chief executives in solicitous, informal settings. 'No one understands quite so well the unreal expectations they face as other chief executives.' Elsewhere, the pleasures of society translate seamlessly into purely commercial networking. PwC, the accountancy firm, like many others in its sector, runs an alumni network out of its marketing department. There is a dual purpose in bringing together former employees and current ones, says Robert Sandry, business development partner. Partly it is to do with reputation and goodwill – seeing old faces in year groups meeting up once again. But, equally, former employees who have moved on could well turn out to be 'serious buyers of our services'.

Questions

1 Why are human contact and physical presence still considered important to communication in today's organisations?

2 Based on the evidence from this article, and your own personal experience, how do you think the internet has influenced:

(a) communication practices in organisations?

(b) how work activities are organised?

(c) the power of different stakeholders (e.g. employees, customers)?

3 Imagine that you were conducting research on how people use e-mail inside an organisation. Outline a typical research question and the kinds of methods you might use when adopting the four perspectives outlined in the chapter (section 1.7).

Source: Overell (2002). Copyright Stephen Overell. Reproduced with permission.

Further reading

Mattelart and Mattelart (1998) provides a useful historical overview of theories of communication; **Deetz** (2001) gives an alternative view from a broadly 'post-modern' perspective. Two of the most widely discussed approaches to international cultural difference are **Hofstede** (1991) and **Trompenaars** (1994); the text by **Tayeb** (2000) includes some useful commentary and a critique of these theorists. **Hall and Hall** (1990) is a widely-cited text on communication and cultural difference by two of the pioneers in this field. **Alvesson and Willmott** (1996) introduces critical management studies. **Hatch** (1997) is a more general introduction to organisation theory. The edited text by **Buzzanell** (2000) provides a broad overview of recent feminist perspectives on communication. **Jablin and Putnam** (2001) is a wide-ranging academic review of the field, addressing many related specialisms, such as discourse analysis by **Putnam and Fairhurst** (2001) and the relationship between organisational communication and learning **Weick and Ashford** (2001).

References

Alvesson and Willmott (1996) *Making sense of management: a critical introduction*. Sage, London.

Blair, A. (2003) 'Prime Minister's speech on sustainable development', Prime Minister's Office, London. (Available at: www.number-10.gov.uk (accessed 13th August.)

Boulding, K.E. (1956) *The image: knowledge in life and society*. University of Michigan Press, Ann Arbor, Michigan MA.

Buckley, W. (1967) *Sociology and modern systems theory*. Prentice Hall, Englewood Cliffs NJ.

Buzzanell, P.M. (ed.) (2000) *Rethinking organizational and managerial communication from feminist perspectives*. Sage, Thousand Oaks, CA.

Cheney, G. and Christensen, L.T. (2001) 'Organizational identity: linkages between internal and external communication' in Jablin, F.M. and Putnam, L.L. (eds.) *op cit.* (231–69).

Child, J. (2001) 'Trust – the fundamental bond in global collaboration'. *Organizational Dynamics*, 29, 4, 274–88 (Spring).

Clark, P.A. (2000) *Organisations in action: competition between contexts*. Routledge, London.

Czarinawska, B. (1998) *A narrative approach to organisation studies*. Sage, London.

Deetz, S. (2001) 'Conceptual foundations' in Jablin, F.M. and Putnam, L.L. (eds.) *op cit.* (3–45).

De Vita, G. (2001) 'Inclusive approaches to effective communication and active participation in the multicultural classroom: an international business management context'. *Active Learning in Higher Education*, 1, 2: 168–80.

Fawcett, T, Hurst, A. and Boardman, B. (2002) *Carbon UK*. Industrial Sustainable Development Group, Environmental Change Institute, Oxford.

Gramsci, A. (1971) *Selections from prison notebooks*. Lawrence & Wishart, London.

Grimes, D.S. and Richard, O.C. (2003) 'Could communication form impact organizations' experience with diversity?' *The Journal of Business Communication*, 40, 1, 7–27.

Habermas, J (1984) *Reason and the rationalization of society*. Heinemann, London.

Hall, E.T. and Hall, M.R. (1990) *Understanding cultural differences*. Intercultural Press, Yarmouth ME.

Hassard, J. (1999) 'Postmodernism, philosophy and management: concepts and controversies'. *International Journal of Management Research*, 171–95 (June)

Hatch, M.J. (1997) *Organisation theory: modern, symbolic and postmodern perspectives*. Oxford University Press, Oxford.

Hofstede, G. (1991) *Cultures and organisations: software of the mind*. McGraw-Hill, Maidenhead.

IPCC (2001) *Climate change 2001: the scientific basis*. Working Group 1 contribution to the Intergovernmental Panel on Climate Change. (Available at www.ipcc/ch (accessed: 19th August 2003.)

Jablin, F.M. and Putnam, L.L. (eds.) (2001) *The new handbook of organizational communication: advances in theory, research, and methods*. Sage, Thousand Oaks, CA.

Keenoy, T., Oswick, C. and Grant, D. (1997) 'Organisational discourses: text and context'. *Organization*, 4, 147–58.

Knights, D. and Willmott, H. (eds.) (2000) *The reengineering revolution?: critical studies of corporate change*. Sage, London.

Livesey, S.M. (2002) 'Global warming wars: rhetorical and discourse analytic approaches to ExxonMobil's corporate public relations'. *Journal of Business Communication*, 39, 1, 117–48.

Mattelart, A. and Mattelart, M. (1998) *Theories of communication: and introduction*. Sage, London.

Munshi, D. and McKie, D. (2001) 'Towards a new cartography of intercultural communication: mapping bias, business and diversity'. *Business Communication Quarterly*, 64, 3, 9–22.

Overell, S. (2002) 'Wheels of commerce: networking'. *Financial Times*, London edition, 17 (23rd September).

Pentland, B.T. (1999) 'Building process theory with narrative: from description to explanation'. *Academy of Management Review*, 24, 4, 711–24.

Pugh, D.S. and Hickson, D.J. (1976) *The Aston programme, volume 1*. Saxon House, London.

Putnam, L.L. and Fairhurst, G.T. (2001) 'Discourse analysis: issues and concerns'. in Jablin, F.M. and Putnam, L.L. (eds.) *op cit.* (78–136).

Senge, P.M. (1990) *The fifth discipline: the art and practice of the learning organization*. Doubleday, New York.

Shannon, C.E. and Weaver, W.W. (1955) *The mathematical theory of communication*. Illinois University Press, Urbana IL.

Tayeb, M. (2000) International business: theories, principles and practices. FT Prentice Hall, Harlow.

Thompson, J,D. (1967) *Organizations in action*. Wiley, New York.

Trompenaars (1994) *Riding the waves of culture: understanding cultural diversity in business*. Nicholas Brearley, London.

Weick, K.E. (1979) *The social psychology of organizing*. Addison Wesley, Reading MA.

Weick, K.E. and Ashford, S.J. (2001) 'Learning in organizations' in Jablin, F.M. and Putnam, L.L. (eds.) *op cit.* (704–31).

Westwood, R. and Clegg, S (2001) *Point/counterpoint: central debates in organisation theory*. Blackwell, Oxford.

Wiener, N. (1948) *Cybernetics: or control and communication in the animal and the machine*. MIT Press, Cambridge, MA.

Wright, D.K. (2001) 'Editorial: communication research now focuses more on outcomes than outputs'. *Journal of Communication Management*, 6, 3, 206–7.

Van Maanen, J. (1988) *Tales of the field: on writing ethnography*. University of Chicago Press, Chicago.

Zorn, T.E. (2002) Converging within divergence: overcoming the disciplinary fragmentation in business communication, organizational communication and public relations'. *Business Communication Quarterly*, 65, 2, 44–53.

Part I

PRINCIPLES OF COMMUNICATION

CHAPTER 2

Breaking barriers: communication in practice

I talk to the trees, but they don't listen to me, I talk to the birds, but they don't understand.
Clint Eastwood, actor (lyrics from the musical 'Paint your Waggon')

Learning outcomes

By the end of this chapter you should be able to:

- recognise the importance of communication barriers, including the potential cost of unsuccessful communication;

- explore some important psychological, social, ethical and cultural barriers to communication, using relevant research findings;

- evaluate the concept of the communication barrier through practical applications in a variety of channels;

- outline a generic approach to overcoming communication barriers, while also recognising potential constraints and limitations.

2.1 Introduction

Communication is about overcoming barriers, but failure is endemic. All over the world, individuals and organisations are attempting to interact, but the resulting messages are somehow lost or misunderstood. These failures are expensive; the 'cost' of ineffective communication practices is not simply the time and resources wasted in preparing the message. There are also the cumulative effects, including those experienced by the intended receiver, who may have been relying on information contained in the message, and the sender, who assumes it has arrived intact. Consider, for example, the true cost to an organisation of a poorly-executed public relations (PR) campaign. The *initial* cost includes both the PR agency's consultancy fee and the expenses associated with the campaign, but the longer-term damage inflicted on the organisation's image and reputation could be much more costly. As communicators, we are almost always over-optimistic about our messages, assuming they will survive unscathed, all the way from our own brains to those of the receiver. In fact, all messages are vulnerable to the phenomenon of 'noise' (see section 1.3).

This wide-ranging chapter explores a number of different sources of noise, each of which can become a barrier to inter-personal and organisational communication.

We consider how insights from disciplines such as psychology, anthropology and ethics have informed our understanding of human communication processes. Several practical illustrations are used to demonstrate how organisations have succeeded in overcoming sources of noise, facilitating more effective communication. The original conceptualisation of 'noise' referred to technological problems (i.e. electrical interference resulting from the limitations of analogue telephone lines) (see section 1.2). However, as the chapter unfolds it will become clear that communication barriers are primarily the result of human limitations. Consequently, the key to avoiding communication failure is self-awareness on the part of the sender. By reflecting carefully on the needs of the people you are trying to engage with, and on the characteristics of the relevant channels, you will be much better placed to overcome the barriers to communication.

2.2 Barriers to communication?: identifying underlying causes

In order to overcome barriers to communication, it is essential to understand the underlying causes. Isolating the apparent explanations under separate headings is a useful first stage (see Table 2.1). Indeed, the rest of this chapter is structured around a similar set of headings, in order to draw on the relevant areas of research. However, it is essential to recognise that these causal sequences are rather more complicated in practice. For example, consider a situation where an organisation is seeking to communicate more effectively with its deaf employees. It might appear that the basic 'physiological' barrier can be readily overcome through appropriate encoding of messages (e.g. by using a skilled sign language interpreter). However, research into the communication barriers experienced by deaf employees indicates that organisations need to address a much more complex set of social and cultural factors beyond those directly related to hearing loss (Luft 2000).

Table 2.1 **Common barriers to communication: probing for 'causes'**

Apparent 'cause'	Practical example: a more complex explanation?
Physiological	Message in an internal report not received due to blindness; but why was the message not encoded in a suitable format?
Psychological	Message from external stakeholder ignored due to 'groupthink' (Janis 1982); but why has this been allowed to develop in the organisation?
Cultural	Message from organisation misinterpreted by members of a particular cultural group; but why was organisation unaware of cultural diversity?
Political	Message from internal stakeholder not sent because individual is marginalised; but why is the organisation not encouraging a more open climate?
Economic	Message not available to a public sector organisation due to lack of resources; but why is it unable to exert pressure for additional funding?
Technological	Message not delivered due to technical failure; but why was the failure allowed to develop and why are there no back-up systems?

Technological over-optimism and 'blaming the tools'

In a world of mobile phone, video-conferencing and internet technologies, it is easy assume that our communication problems are over. This kind of technological optimism is, of course, actively promoted by those whose job it is to market the latest hardware and software. However, while technology provides ever-faster and more portable communication channels, with increasing carrying capacity (or 'bandwith'), the quality and effectiveness of communication flowing through any channel depends ultimately on the communicative practices adopted by users (Yates and Orlikowski 1992). Just as people tend to make overly-optimistic claims for new technologies, they also have a tendency to distance themselves from poor performance by interpreting the problem in technological terms (i.e. in the words of an old saying, 'the bad craftsman always blames his tools'). When technical failures do occur, the best solution is often to have an alternative technology to act as a fallback (e.g. paper copies of a report to substitute for an electronic version). Other superficially 'technological' problems are generally a cover for human errors, such as selecting an inappropriate channel, or failing to use it effectively.

The following sections review some of the contributory factors, influencing the quality of inter-personal and organisational communication. We begin with human physiology and consider how our capacity to deal with information is affected by interaction between the brain, sensory organs and other parts of the human body. The purpose of these short, non-technical reviews is to draw attention to the complex and multi-layered nature of human communication. Note: Additional commentary on selected references is given in the Further reading section at the end of this chapter.

2.3 Physiological and neurological factors

The sensory and information processing capabilities of human beings exceed those of the most advanced computers. However, because these capabilities are exercised by organic and self-conscious beings, their underlying mechanisms lack the standardisation and predictability of machines. Research suggests that our ability to communicate with one another is profoundly influenced by three inter-related mechanisms:

● **alertness and attention**: affecting what data our senses manage to pick up;

● **perception**: resulting in different interpretations of the same sensory data;

● **memory**: affecting the messages we retain and those we can subsequently recall.

This section explores these four processes – alertness, attention, perception, memory – in a non-technical way, highlighting the implications for communicators (see Figure 2.1). The key lesson is that the capabilities of different people will vary in each of these areas, affecting their ability to communicate. Furthermore, the *same* individual can display wide variations at different points in time.

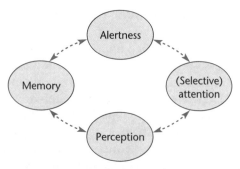

Figure 2.1 **Human cognition: four linked mechanisms**

Variations in level of alertness

Physiological and behavioural functions are influenced by a long-term cycle of alertness, known as the 'cicardian rhythm' (popularly known as the 'body clock'), which traces the daily cycle of light and dark. Disturbances in these patterns can affect the performance of shift workers and air travellers, for example. People not only experience long-term changes in what is termed 'tonic alertness' during the day, but also a number of shorter-term variations in the level of arousal, which are stimulated by events in their immediate environment. The shorter-term change, known as 'phasic alertness', is a common feature of humans and other animals. For example, it can be observed when a cat's ears begin to twitch on hearing a new sound, or when a dozing student is startled into life on hearing his name called out in a seminar. When receivers are repeatedly exposed to the same stimuli, they become 'habituated' to it, the response is no longer activated, and the message blends into the background. This adaptation has important implications for communicators. For example, it is one reason why advertisers are constantly searching for novel and more dramatic ways to deliver their messages, in order that their impact is maintained.

The role of selective attention

Since humans are bombarded by so many different stimuli, the brain has to ration out its processing power. We can only 'pay attention' to a small fraction of this mass of incoming sensory data. People have also learnt to jump from one source to another – a common application of this skill is switching between rival conversations in a noisy bar. However, selective attention can work against communicators. Contemporary audiences have become accustomed to a world of electronically mediated and visually-oriented communication, ranging from 'channel-hopping' through satellite television programmes to absorbing information in the form of ten-second 'sound bites', accompanied by equally short video images. There is evidence that these social and technological developments are influencing public expectations regarding the length and format in which messages are encoded. This represents a major challenge for organisations that need to convey long or complex messages, particularly where they are better suited to extended verbal or text-based argument.

Powers of perception: constructing the world around us

We integrate information that is supplied by each of the senses in order to construct a meaningful interpretation of the world around us (Roth and Bruce 1995). Humans have very advanced powers of perception. In many cases we are able to re-construct a whole picture, or concept, from a tiny scrap of visual information. For example, it is often possible to recognise a friend's face, when it is glimpsed for a moment in the midst of a large crowd of people. We can also identify whole objects from fragmentary evidence (see Figure 2.2). This ability is useful to communicators, suggesting that it is not always necessary to spell out the entire message. Indeed, many of the most effective forms of communication rely for their appeal on this imaginative capability. For example, many of the greatest works of art are noted for the way that they leave the spectator to interpret missing or ambiguous elements.

Figure 2.2 Perception – object recognition

However, it is also important to recognise the inherent limitations of this impressive sensory system. Research using simple optical illusions, such as those reproduced here (see Figure 2.3), has indicated that human perceptions are based on a hypothesis or 'best guess' from the evidence that the senses have managed to collect. If the evidence is ambiguous, people can misinterpret it and even 'see' things that do not exist. These misattributions are not limited to visual signals; inter-personal communication is also profoundly affected by our perceptions of other people. We make these judgements according to various cues, but research indicates that some have a particularly powerful effect. These 'central traits', such as a person's location on the 'warm–cold' continuum, lead people to infer other characteristics. For example, once we have identified someone as 'warm', they are also likely to be perceived as being, 'sociable, popular, happy, good-natured and humorous.' (Hargie 1997: 48). These perceptual limitations provide an important lesson for communicators, particularly in contexts where clarity of communication is the primary objective.

These three examples indicate some unusual features of our capacity to process visual stimuli.

(a) An ambiguous image: which way is the cube facing?

(b) An image that is 'impossible' in three dimensions.

(c) An implied image: we can 'see' a white, upward-pointing triangle, though it is not present on the printed page.

Figure 2.3 Three optical illusions

Remembering

In some folk traditions, witches were accused of 'memory-snatching', a crime that involved stealing the contents of people's minds. Today, we are more likely to explain the limitations of human memory with reference to stressful lifestyles, information overload, old age and the effects of alcohol. In any event, memory loss is clearly a major challenge for the communicator. In many cases, the primary concern is with ensuring that certain messages are retained, but there are also occasions when the purpose of a message is supported by people's ability to forget. Psychologists have identified three distinct processes of memory – registration, storage and retrieval. While there is considerable debate over the intermediate mechanisms, this relatively straightforward three-stage model has provided communication researchers with a useful framework for discussion (e.g. Argyle 1972, Hargie *et al.* 1994). We adopt a simplified model in order to address some of the practical implications of these processes (see Figure 2.4).

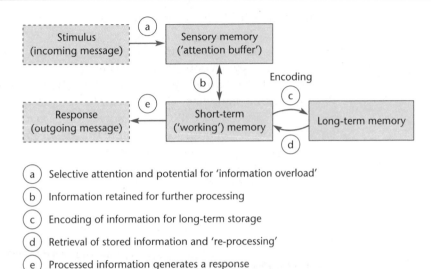

(a) Selective attention and potential for 'information overload'

(b) Information retained for further processing

(c) Encoding of information for long-term storage

(d) Retrieval of stored information and 're-processing'

(e) Processed information generates a response

Figure 2.4 **Human memory processes: a three-stage model**

In some respects, the brain acts like the 'left luggage' office at a railway station. It accepts a message, holds onto it for you, and returns it when you return to request it some time later. Registration of an incoming message is closely related to selective attention, reviewed in the previous paragraph. The key lesson for the communicator is that this process is unlike the kind of storage available on a computer disc, where the encoded message is held indefinitely in an unchanged state. Research suggests that, storage of a message in the human brain can occur at three distinct yet related levels, known as the sensory memory (or 'attention buffer'), the short-term (or 'working') memory, and the long-term memory. Each of these memories appears to have set 'time limits'.

The sensory memory acts as a kind of temporary collection-point for incoming stimuli of all kinds; this limit is often identified as either six or seven separate pieces of information. Once the 'attention buffer' is full, any additional information of the same type causes it to overflow, resulting in the loss of some of the original stored material. Communication specialists have argued that you can stretch this physiological limit by 'chunking' information into larger units (e.g. combining separate letters to form a word or a string of numbers in the form of a date). A proportion of the in-coming messages may then progress to the part of the process, entering the short- and the long-term memory, but there appears to be a great deal of filtering at both intermediate stages. The whole process is also affected by the person's current state of mind. Again, it appears that 'chunking' the information can help with retention, because it imposes some kind of meaning on the information. However, it is important to note that each person processes incoming stimuli in a unique way. This uniqueness is the result of factors such as differences in prior experience, which lead to the recognition of particular patterns connecting new 'information' with that already held in the sensory, working or long-term memory. For this reason, it is difficult to work from someone else's lecture notes, for example; in effect, they have been 'customised' to a particular set of memories and references.

These features of human memory raise a number of practical issues for the communicator. For example, it may be important to consider how long the receiver needs to retain your message. Assuming that it is necessary to retain it for more than a few seconds, how can the you increase the chances that it will pass through the intermediate filters and into the longer-term memory? Table 2.2 summarises a simple activity that can be used to assess your own abilities, and those of friends and colleagues. (Note: Other exercises associated with this chapter provide an opportunity to explore the practicalities of engaging with the sensory, working and long-term memory.)

Table 2.2 A simple activity to 'test' the sensory memory

Introduction
The limits of sensory memory can be demonstrated with a simple activity, which can also be conducted as a 'thought experiment'. Could you, for example, remember two minutes' worth of information long enough to record it on paper? Your level of recall should vary depending on the type of material conveyed. (Note: In a simpler variant of this activity, the first list of 20 random numbers may be re-presented as five 'chunked' dates, in the form: '1945, 2004 …'.)
Meaningless information, out of context
Read out a list of 20 random numbers, between 1 and 100. Speak clearly at normal speed; it should take no more than 15 seconds. Now ask people to write down as much of the message as they can remember. Compare these records with the original.
Meaningful information, in context
Record a weather forecast, as it is printed in a daily newspaper; this should take no more than two minutes. Ask ten prepared factual questions on *specific details* from the forecast. How much of the message is either forgotten or recalled incorrectly?
Information in narrative ('story') form
Read a short narrative, including lots of visual imagery (e.g. *'they crossed a rickety wooden bridge over a cool mountain stream...'*) a children's story would be ideal for this purpose. Again, ensure the story lasts a maximum of two minutes, and follow it with ten prepared factual questions. Is recall any better than in the other examples?

Mini-case 2.1 deals with a current issue that is related to physiological barriers to communication, the challenge of ensuring that web-based materials are designed in a way that makes them accessible to all users.

Mini-case 2.1	**Responding to the challenge of web accessibility**

The web has become an important communication channel, providing people with access to news, information, commercial markets, political debate and educational services. As a consequence, web accessibility has become a major issue for organisations of all kinds. A person's access to the web can be restricted for a number of reasons, including: physical disability, language differences, literacy levels and low bandwith connections. Each of these will create a barrier to communication, unless organisations make an effort to design and implement their web presence appropriately. This case focuses on accessibility issues related to the ability/disability of users.

▶

The World Wide Web Consortium (W3C) is an international not-for-profit organisation, based in North America. As part of its Web Accessibility initiative (WAI), it has developed a detailed set of Web Content Accessibility Guidelines (WCAG 1.0), designed to ensure that websites provide improved access to people with disabilities. The accessibility guidelines are available from the W3C website (www.w3c.org). They deal with design requirements, including the provision of captions with audio content to overcome hearing-related disabilities, and described graphics for those with visual disabilities. Many of the guidelines, such as consistent navigation features, will be beneficial for all users, whatever their ability/disability. The official language of the W3C site is English, but WCAG and related support documents have been translated into many other languages. WAI highlights the fact that at least 10 per cent of the population of most countries has disabilities, and that organisations cannot afford to deliberately miss out on this market. In addition to the ethical and equity-based arguments for constructing more accessible websites, WAI has identified a number of potential benefits for organisations. These include: increased market share and audience reach, more flexible and efficient websites, with lower development and maintenance costs, a public demonstration of corporate social responsibility, which should enhance the organisation's image, and a reduced legal liabilities in countries with strong equal opportunities legislation.

Useability initiatives in the UK: RNIB's campaign for good web design

There are around two million people in the UK with sight problems. The Royal National Institute for the Blind (RNIB) helps anyone with a sight problem with imaginative and practical solutions to everyday challenges. This voluntary sector organisation also campaigns to change society's attitudes, actions and assumptions, so that people with sight problems can enjoy the same rights, freedoms and responsibilities as fully-sighted people. In 1999, RNIB launched a Campaign for Good Web Design, in order to promote the creation of web products and experiences that could be used by everyone, regardless of ability/disability, technology and circumstance (www.rnib.org.uk). This has contributed to a lively debate, with some strong divisions of expert opinion on the question: is it possible to design a web interface that suits the needs of everybody? The following responses were quoted in a public debate, hosted by RNIB in 2002:

- If you research your user requirements well, you should find that everyone doesn't want the same thing. The web experience should be delivered in the way the users want.
- Although we're all different, people pretty much do things the same way. When we start to offer interfaces that work in different ways we start to force different groups of people to learn different ways of doing things. The aim should be to allow site users to do whatever they want while offering a user experience that is as consistent as possible.
- For me, the most successful design is that which allows the user to "socialise" the design for their own needs.

Commenting on this debate, Julie Howell, leader of the RNIB's Good Web Design Campaign concluded that it was essential to involve users in the design process:

'It is becoming clear that adopting the W3C/WAI guidelines is not enough to ensure that visually impaired people will be able to make full use of a website. The inclusion

▶

of users with disabilities at every stage of the design testing cycle would seem to be the ideal way to ensure that any resulting website is both fully accessible to and usable by people with disabilities.'

Regulatory developments are increasing the pressure on organisations with poorly designed and inaccessible websites. In March 2003, the UK's Disability Rights Commission (DRC) announced that is would be investigating one thousand public and private sector websites for their ability to be accessed by Britain's 8.5 million disabled people. Announcing the investigation, the DRC's Chair, Bert Massie said:

'The DRC wants to see a society where all disabled people can participate fully as equal citizens and this formal investigation into web accessibility is an important step towards this goal.'

Questions

1 What is your own experience of website accessibility? Compare your thoughts with those of colleagues and draft a list of the most significant problems you have experienced when attempting to communicate using this channel.

2 Read the relevant guidelines, available from the W3C/WAI and RNIB websites. Sample a selection of public, private and voluntary sector websites, assessing them against these guidelines.

3 Re-read Julie Howell's comment on improving accessibility. Why do you think it is 'not enough' for organisations to follow the W3C/WAI guidelines? What is the wider lesson for organisations seeking to overcome communication barriers?

Sources: RNIB (2002), DRC (2003) WAI (2003). Case prepared by the author with acknowledgement to Julie Howell.

2.4 Social, cultural and ethical barriers

The simple model of communication, outlined in Chapter 1, takes little account of the context in which the message is being sent and received. In practice, both senders and receivers are part of a wider social and cultural setting, which has an impact on the ways in which they communicate. In this section, we review three of the more important barriers to communication within and between social groups. The first relates to the social psychological phenomenon of conformity, a process in which the norms, values and behaviours of an individual begin to follow those of the wider group. The second concerns cultural differences, where individuals in one social group may have different norms, values or behaviour to individuals associated with another grouping. The third barrier is caused by ethical constraints exerted by the organisation itself. Social conformity, ethical dilemmas and cultural difference are necessary features of social life. However, in certain circumstances (e.g. where there is an excessive degree of conformity or, where cultural differences are left un-bridged), they can become both a symptom and a cause of communication failure.

Excessive conformity as a barrier to communication

In the mid-twentieth century, psychological research began to explore the pathological features of excessive conformity. In the shadow of major social evils of the period, including the Holocaust, researchers tried to discover why individuals were willing to take actions as part of a group that they would never contemplate as individuals. In the 1970s, a North American researcher, Janis (1982), introduced the term 'groupthink' to explain an extreme type of conformity occurring within close-knit groups. Janis illustrated the argument with real-world case studies that drew on recent US political and diplomatic crises (i.e. the 'Bay of Pigs' confrontation between the US and USSR in the early 1960s, the gradual escalation of the Vietnam War and the Watergate scandal of the early 1970s). These events were characterised by a number of managerial and communication failures, including: an incomplete survey of alternatives; inadequate reflection on strategic objectives; failure to examine risks of the preferred option; poor information search; selective bias in processing available information; failure to re-appraise alternatives; and failure to work out contingency plans.

Subsequent research has supported the view that groupthink can occur in any highly cohesive group that is insulated from the influence of others, has a single-minded leadership, is under stress and has no clear-cut solution to its problems. Unfortunately, these conditions can be found in many organisational contexts, ranging from defective decision making in senior management meetings to situations such as a hostage-taking incident, where the participants may be exposed to real and imminent danger (Cohan, 2002, Smith 1984). Janis's original research studies identified eight classic symptoms of groupthink:

1 An illusion of invulnerability, contributing to excessive optimism and risk-taking behaviour.

2 Collective rationalisation of the problem, which discounts negative feedback and neutralises problematic information.

3 An unquestioning belief in the inherent morality of the group and its cause, enabling it to ignore moral and ethical considerations.

4 Applying negative stereotyping to outsiders (or 'out-groups') and opponents, and to proposals that would lead to a change.

5 Direct pressure on dissenters to conform and reach consensus, so that any minority views are suppressed.

6 Self-censorship by group members, who suppress any personal objectives, concerns or areas of disagreement.

7 An illusion of unanimity, arising from the other factors, masking any underlying divisions.

8 Emergence of self-appointed 'mind-guards' to protect leaders, filter information, deflect opposition and exert pressure on dissenters.

A brief appraisal of the list indicates that each of these factors in isolation is a potential barrier to communication. The key contribution of Janis (1982) was to highlight the ways in which they can become self-reinforcing in an organisational setting, and connecting that process to observed effects, such as poor decision making.

Harvey (1988) outlines an interesting, and subtly different, case of communication barriers operating between members of a group, which he termed, 'The Abilene Paradox' (or 'AP'). The Abilene Paradox takes its name from an incident in the life of his own family, which provoked him to reflect on the problem of communicating personal feelings to others. The following quotation summarises what took place during a miserable trip to Abilene, Texas:

> 'During a dust storm on a scorching 104-degree West Texas day, four adults piled into an unairconditioned car and drove 35 miles to eat at a cafeteria in Abilene. In the midst of a subsequent family argument during which each family member attempted to blame the others for the disaster, it was discovered that none of the four family members had really wanted to go to Abilene. No-one had vetoed the idea since each had thought, incorrectly, that everyone else had wanted to go.' (Kim 2001: 169–70)

While there are many similarities between the processes identified as 'groupthink' and 'AP', there are also some important differences. For example, under groupthink the cohesiveness of the group is the primary driver, and group members are actively involved in the reinforcement process. By contrast, individuals in the 'AP' scenario appear to take a more passive role, simply 'going along with' a course of action out of a fear of upsetting other members of the group (Kim 2001: 175–6, 180–1).

Mini-case 2.2 presents one of Janis's original cases, which deals with the causes and momentous consequences of groupthink in the US Navy during the Second World War.

Mini-case 2.2	Pearl Harbor 1941: a case of Groupthink?

In his original research, Janis (1982) included a case study of groupthink based on events at Pearl Harbor, Hawaii, in December 1941. The case was used to illustrate how communication failures in the US Navy's high command left its Pacific fleet open to attack by Japanese forces. The following paragraph is a brief summary of the evidence.

It is December 1941, more than two years after the onset of war in Europe. The US remains a neutral power, but Admiral Kummel, Commander-in-Chief of the US Navy's Pacific Fleet, knows that war with Japan is imminent. Though he is clearly under considerable pressure, the Admiral has a detailed strategy in place. Unfortunately, this strategy does not incorporate the possibility that his home naval base, Pearl Harbor on the island of Hawaii, could be the target for an initial attack. During the autumn, military intelligence has been suggesting that such an attack is a distinct possibility. There is also an accumulation of supporting evidence. For example, it is known that Japanese embassy staff on the island of Hawaii have been burning their files. Though incoming intelligence of this kind is under discussion by Admiral Kummel and his staff, they appear consistently to put an incorrect interpretation on it. In particular, officers are filtering out facts that do not fit with their existing interpretation, while emphasising any piece of evidence that reinforces it. Furthermore, this selective attention to the evidence has spread beyond the Admiral's immediate circle, to influence other Naval officers operating from the island. It is now five hours before the attack, on the morning of 7 December 1941. Two US minesweepers identify a submerged submarine just outside Pearl Harbor. However, neither thinks it necessary to report this information to its superiors at the Naval base.

The subsequent three hour-long attack on Pearl Harbor becomes the worst disaster in US naval history; some 2,340 people are killed and 19 vessels are destroyed. Admiral Kummel and his US Army counterpart, Lt-General Short, are relieved of their posts and held responsible for their lack of preparedness, prior to the Japanese attack.

Questions

1 Compare the summary of this case to the list detailing the symptoms of groupthink. Identify plausible examples of these symptoms and note how each may have affected the communication process.

2 Review recent news stories, looking for the symptoms of groupthink in a public, private or voluntary sector organisation. How were the organisation and its stakeholders affected by this phenomenon?

3 More recent information, unavailable when the original case study was prepared, suggests that the US received warnings of a Japanese attack, from British intelligence and other sources, but that this was witheld from the local commanders, on the orders of President Roosevelt. The suggestion is that the President needed to influence US public opinion, which had been strongly opposed to war. Does this undermine the concept of groupthink? What are the wider implications for our understanding of barriers to communication?

Source: Janis (1982, adapted).

Moral silences? Barriers to ethical behaviour

Bird (2002) discusses three communication-related barriers to ethical behaviour in business organisations. These barriers can be summarised briefly in the following terms: 'moral silence', which means failing to speak up about issues that are known to be wrong; 'moral deafness', meaning a failure to hear or attend to moral concerns raised by others; and 'moral blindness', or the failure to recognise the moral implications of actions.

The author summarises his thesis:

> 'Many people in business fail to speak up about their moral convictions. They fail to do so in a number of different ways. As a result, many of the ethical issues and concerns facing business are not addressed as fully, as clearly, and as well as they would be if people voiced their concerns. Moral silence is occasioned and reinforced by the correlative phenomena of moral blindness and moral deafness as well as the quite contrary practice of giving voice to moralistic concerns.' (Bird 2002: 4)

There are strong parallels between the communication barriers identified in this study and the effects of excessive conformity, identified in the concepts of 'groupthink' and the 'Abilene Paradox' (Sims 1992). In both cases, organisations undertake actions that would not have been contemplated by the individuals operating independently. The interesting question from our perspective is the extent to which individual and organisational communication practices might overcome these barriers, so that opposition is voiced and concerns are attended to. We revisit this theme in our discussion of feedback mechanisms (see section 6.2 and Mini-case 6.3).

Cultural difference as a barrier to communication

Cultures shape the way we think and behave. They can be seen as both shaping and being shaped by our established patterns of communication. However, people are often unaware of the profound impact of cultural forces. It is when we experience contrasting cultures at close hand that these forces become more apparent. Nations, occupations, organisations, teams and other social groupings all share a tendency to develop distinctive cultures. The influence of the classic definition by the anthropologists Kroeber and Kluckholm (1952) can be seen in the work of many later organisational researchers (e.g. Brown and Starkey 1994). It is rather convoluted, but remains of interest for its comprehensiveness and the emphasis placed on communication:

> 'Culture consists of patterns, explicit and implicit, of and for behaviour [It is] acquired and transmitted by symbols, constituting the distinctive achievements of human groups, including their embodiments in artefacts; the essential core of culture consists of traditional (that is historically derived and selected) ideas and especially their attached values; culture systems may, on the one hand, be considered as products of action, on the other as conditioned elements of further action.' (Kroeber and Kluckholm 1952: 181)

Cultural diversity is clearly a valuable feature of human societies. However, when people from dissimilar cultures get together, they can encounter powerful barriers, limiting their capacity to communicate. We all have our own anecdotal examples of what is sometimes termed, 'culture clash'. In some cases, the consequences can be simply amusing, or at worst, mildly embarrassing. However, a failure to deal appropriately with cultural difference can also lead to disastrous outcomes for individuals and organisations. This section begins with one of the classic studies of cultural difference in modern organisations, which follows Kroeber and Kluckholm's (1952) approach to cultural systems as shared sets of ideas, transmitted across time through symbols and learned practices, shaping the perceptions and behaviour of individuals and social groups. Having outlined its key themes, and noted some important limitations, we consider a newer and more interactive perspective on the role of culture in international organisations.

The Dutch researcher, Geert Hofstede, drew on the work of earlier cultural researchers in order to test the 'convergence thesis', the view that the world's population is becoming more alike, with national cultural difference squeezed out by the process of globalisation, symbolised by universally-available consumer products such as Coca-Cola and MTV. Hofstede's original study, which was conducted in the late 1960s, involved a large questionnaire-based survey of employees of the international computer company IBM. The findings were published in 1980, with a second edition in 2001 (Hofstede 2001). The survey respondents included several different occupational groups, located in the company's various national subsidiaries. Using a statistical clustering technique, Hofstede was able to distinguish four key dimensions that appeared to characterise particular cultures. A fifth dimension, relating to time orientation, was added in subsequent extensions of the research (Hofstede 2001: 351–72). Table 2.3 offers a brief commentary on the original dimensions.

Table 2.3 **Hofstede's taxonomic approach to cultural difference**

Dimension	Comment
Individualism/collectivism	This dimension is reflected in the ways that managers communicate. In collectivist cultures, there is a stronger emphasis on reaching consensus but may be less room for individual initiative. Individualist cultures appear more argumentative but, arguably, may be more likely to generate creative solutions.
Power distance	This dimension relates to inequalities between senior managers and subordinates. Power, distance and status affects the way that information flows up and down the hierarchy, and the levels at which decisions are made.
Uncertainty avoidance	This dimension reveals differences in how willing managers are to tolerate unstructured, unclear situations. Managers from 'high' uncertainty avoidance cultures tend to plan activities in more detail, which can be associated with rigid, inflexible procedures. Those from 'low' uncertainty avoidance cultures tend to 'muddle through'.
'Achievement'/'relational'	This dimension affects the core values of and practices of organisations rooted in a particular national culture. For example, 'achievement' cultures (referred to as 'masculine' in Hofstede's original study and retained in the 2001 edition) emphasise material gain and aggressive competition, while 'relational' (or 'feminine') cultures are higher on creativity and mutual support.

Hofstede's famous definition of culture highlights the differences that are measured across these dimensions. He treats culture as 'the collective programming of the mind that distinguishes the members of one group or category of people from another' (Hoftede 2001: 9). His work, along with that of other researchers, including Trompenaars (1994), is grounded in the perspective of culture as an enduring source of difference. As such, it has contributed strongly to the convergence debate (e.g. Hickson 1997, Tayeb 2000: 441). It is certainly the case that 'culture clash' remains an important barrier to communication, but there are increasing doubts about the continuing relevance of this perspective in the multi-cultural settings of many contemporary organisations (Holden 2002).

Towards a deeper understanding of cultural difference?

Before moving on to consider an alternative perspective, it may be useful to analyse a typical 'culture clash' scenario, described by the British writer Handy (1996); similar examples can be found throughout the international management literature. The case describes problems experienced when two teams of engineers were drawing up the contract for a collaborative project involving a French and a British company. Members of the French team wanted each part of the contract signed before moving on to the next one. The British team interpreted this as a lack of trust on the part of the French and resisted their request. However, the French team saw reluctance to sign the documentation as displaying a lack of commitment on the part of the British. Fortunately, someone eventually spotted the cultural obstacle and defused the situation. Otherwise, the negotiation could have broken up, resulting in a costly delay.

This kind of mutual incomprehension across national cultures is a potential barrier to communication. Consequently, the 'lesson' of the story, i.e. the need to improve inter-cultural awareness, remains an important one. However, there are some problems with this kind of analysis. Above all, there is the danger of relying on shorthand, stereotypical accounts of culture that ignore local- and individual-level factors. Much popular writing on inter-cultural communication falls into this trap, reducing the complex and subtle issues of cultural difference into over-simplistic anecdotes or comparative tables.

Reliance on these crude characterisations as a basis for doing business across cultural boundaries can be compared to the use of a foreign language phrase-book when travelling abroad. The phrasebook might help you to undertake basic tasks (e.g. booking a hotel, ordering a meal), but would be of no help whatsoever in more demanding tasks, such as reading a novel or listening to an opera. This argument is developed by the authors of a text highlighting the complexities of inter-cultural communication from a 'Chinese' perspective:

> 'Many paradoxical statements are made [by Westerners] about Chinese society. This is partly because authors are not being clear about just which Chinese society they are talking about. It is common, unfortunately, to mix up quotations from ancient classics, observations made about overseas Chinese immigrants in the UK or North America, and observations made in Taiwan and in Mainland China. This makes as much sense as trying to describe what the "English" are like by quoting Chaucer and mixing observations made in London, Capetown, and Peoria, Illinois.' (Pan *et al.* 2002: 118)

For this reason, the authors note that their own research was conducted in the southern Chinese city of Guangzhou (Canton). They see it as providing well-researched statements that cover this narrower geographic scope. They avoid making claims about China as a whole, on the reasonable basis that, 'it would be very difficult to generalise meaningfully about what is approximately one fourth of the world's population' (*ibid*: 118).

There are many problems with the way that culture is interpreted, both in popular discussion and in the research literature. Difficulties that often arise include: a failure to explore underlying assumptions; a tendency for perceptions of 'the other' to become distorted; and an under-emphasis on the ambiguities associated with multiple cultural identities:

● **Hidden assumptions**: Many research studies are themselves 'culture-bound', containing implicit assumptions regarding key issues such as gender and disability. A notable example of this lack of awareness was once displayed by a researcher presenting the results of a study on transport and mobility. The statistics were challenged by a member of the audience, but the researcher could not understand the reason for the anomaly, '[T]hen suddenly the light dawned. "Oh", he exclaimed to general guffaws from the audience, "you're including *children*."' (Ashe 2001: 12)

● **Subjective perceptions**: The ways that we interpret other cultures is subject to distortion, in the sense that people tend to focus attention on those areas that most differ from, or most resemble, their own experience. This phenomenon is exemplified by the Victorian explorer's command, 'Take me to your leader!', which superimposes domestic assumptions about a hierarchical social organisation onto another, unknown culture. Interpretivists have argued that, because perceptions are bound to differ, according to the nature of the observer, cultural difference must be re-interpreted as a subjective construct. Hence, it is misleading to represent cultural systems in an 'essentialist' framework, such as a typology, which implies that categories are stable, homogenous and can be measured objectively (Holden 2002: 27–9).

- **Multiple-dimensions**: Many of the existing characterisations of cultural difference give a misleading impression of universality. This ignores the many sources of ambiguity, including multiple cultural identities (e.g. where people may regard themselves simultaneously as French, black, Catholic, female and European), and the ways that these are negotiated over time. The preoccupation with 'culture clash' gives a misleading impression of the real experience of today's international organisations, because it emphasises confrontations between two unitary cultures. The reality is that most international organisations are *multi*-cultural, made up of people from many different national, social and economic backgrounds, reflecting the kinds of multiple-identities referred to above. As Tayeb (2000: 323) has noted, 'confining behaviour to a handful of dimensions presents a simplistic and unidimensional picture of reality.' We need to consider many other situational factors in order to explain how people behave differently under different conditions.

What are the implications of these developments for our approach to culture and communication? It would be unrealistic to claim that we can engage in a truly 'cross-cultural' approach to organisational communication, within the confines of a concise textbook, which has an unavoidably 'Western' orientation. However, we can begin to take a more critical approach to the established forms, or 'genres', of communication that are found in 'Western', and primarily Northern European, settings, and to the principles that underpin them (Yates and Orlikowski 1992, Holden 2002, Pan et al. 2002). In order to achieve this aim, we will intersperse a critical survey of communication principles and practices with a number of case-based illustrations drawn from these newer 'cross-cultural' contexts. A useful starting point for this process is to reconsider the story of the blind men and the elephant, which is often used to highlight the challenge of understanding a multi-faceted problem.

The blind men and the elephant: a helpful analogy?

This classical Indian story is frequently used as an analogy for the task of understanding complex and multifaceted phenomena, such as human organisations and cultures. It concerns a group of blind men who encounter an elephant for the first time. One man grabs its tail and says, 'so an elephant is thin, like a rope'. Another man touches its hide and says, 'You are wrong, an elephant is rough and flat like a wall.' A third feels for its leg and says, 'Not at all, it is tall and round like a tree ...', and so on. The men are unable to agree on the true nature of the elephant. Since each man is aware of only one part of the animal, they are left with different perceptions of the whole. The analogy goes some way to explaining the obstacles faced by those researching human organisations and their communication practices. However, if we reflect on the story for a moment, it is clear that one important perspective is missing. Mini-case 2.3 recounts another typical story of mutual misunderstanding arising from 'culture clash'. This time our task is to de-construct the barriers from *both* sides, in order to get a deeper understanding of the resulting interactions.

Mini-case 2.3	**The missing tourists of Suzhou: de-constructing cultural barriers**

Two English women were visiting Shanghai and decided to sign up for a guided tour around Suzhou, a neighbouring city famous for its gardens and canals. The tour was organised by a local travel agency that catered primarily for Chinese speakers. The travel agent did not speak English, but one of the English women had a basic grasp of spoken Mandarin. After an extended conversation, involving a lot of repetition, double-checking and occasional miming, the trip to Suzhou was confirmed. The travel agent was unfamiliar with catering for foreigners, but he was confident that the arrangements would work out well. The women were given train tickets from Shanghai to Suzhou and badges that included the name of the travel company. The travel agent told them that they were to be met by a guide. She would identify herself by holding up a board that listed members of the tour party. The two women carefully wrote down their full names for the travel agent, in what was (to him) an unfamiliar western alphabet. The plan was that he would fax the names to the guide in preparation for the tour.

The following day the two women arrived at Shanghai railway station. The women were not sure whether the guide was to going meet them at Shanghai or Suzhou, but since there was nobody at Shanghai who looked like a tour guide, they got on the train. On arriving at Suzhou an hour later, badges prominently displayed, they could not see anyone holding a board displaying their names. Being the only foreigners getting off the train, the two women were immediately surrounded by a crowd of local traders trying to sell maps and taxi rides. After several fruitless minutes wandering around Suzhou station forecourt, local traders in tow, they noticed a woman holding a board with some Chinese characters written on it. They approached the woman, hoping she might be able to help them. It was quickly established that she was the guide they had been looking for. The guide was rather irritated with the English women, as they were holding up the rest of the party, who had already assembled near the tour minibus.

In their defence, the English women pointed out that their names were not displayed on the board she was holding. In addition, none of the other members of the party appeared to be wearing the tour company badges, which they had assumed were some kind of back-up system. The tour guide was amazed at these comments. She pointed to her board. It contained several lines of Chinese characters, one of which included the phrase:

两个英国女士

LIANG GE YING GUO NU SHI

In translation, the phrase means, 'two English women'. As the tour guide gathered everyone into the bus, the two women shook their heads and reflected on the experience. After all, who could have possibly failed to spot something as obvious as that?

Questions

1 This story exemplifies several common communication barriers, some of which have multiple causes. Prepare a list of these barriers and the associated causes.

2 Suggest how each of the participants might have helped to overcome the barriers you have identified. Why do you think they failed to take the relevant actions?

3 Cross-cultural communication issues are often presented from a predominantly 'Western' viewpoint. Why is it important to address cultural difference from multiple perspectives? How might this case be re-drafted to give equal emphasis to non-Western perspectives?

Source: Co-authored with Tina Fawcett.

2.5 Overcoming the barriers

Having reviewed some of the main barriers to communication, it is time to develop some constructive proposals for overcoming them. In doing so, we necessarily move into a more practical and instrumental way of thinking. Throughout the book, the emphasis is on active questioning, rather than learning pre-packaged solutions. However, it is possible to outline our approach in very broad terms. This can be summarised as three connected activities: taking the receiver more seriously; thinking more clearly about the message; and delivering the message skilfully. The following paragraphs introduce these activities at a generic level. They will be elaborated in later chapters, when we take a more detailed look at different aspects of communication, and their application in specific channels.

Taking the receiver more seriously

There are a number of things that the sender can do to minimise the risk of communication failure. Firstly, the communicator can take responsibility for ensuring that messages are delivered, rather than losing interest at the point at which they are 'sent'. As this chapter has indicated, the outcome of any communication is ultimately dependent on the receiver. Therefore, when framing any message, it is important to consider the receiver's pre-existing attitude, expectation and degree of involvement. In some cases, this could involve some background research. For example, it may be necessary to discover what the receiver already knows about the content of a message, how they feel about the topic (e.g. is it likely to interest, frighten, annoy or bore them?), and their perceptions of the sender (i.e. does the organisation, or its representatives, have sufficient credibility to convey or to reinforce the message?). Table 2.4 illustrates the challenge of understanding a receiver's needs. Read through the remarks made and try to suggest the likely reason for communication failure and how it might have been avoided, bearing in mind that the reasons for non-communication are often more complex than they might at first appear.

Table 2.4 **Exploring communication barriers: interpreting the receiver**

Receiver	Surface evidence (a sample statement)
Information services manager, US-owned software company	'Believe me, Jack, that young woman from the Hamburg office just has no idea. I've been in the computer software industry 25 years and I've never heard such garbage ...'
Foreign aid agency worker in a post-conflict country	'You know, I'm sure he said first right and then take the second turning on the left after the road junction, then left at the third round-about... but we seem to have ended up on a construction site!'
Investment analyst at an after-lunch company presentation	'Did she say sales were up by 25% in the last 12 months? I thought it said 20% on the projection slide. I could really do with a break; this presentation has gone on so long I've almost lost the will to live!'

Thinking more clearly about the message

Young children have a refreshingly honest tendency to express the first thing that comes into their minds. For example, a child travelling on a bus has few inhibitions when confronted by something unfamiliar, prompting questions such as, 'Mummy, why is that man wearing a funny hat?' Adults tend to take more care over their communication. For example, they may anticipate a negative reaction and adjust their message in order to avoid this outcome. A great deal of inter-personal communication, including casual everyday conversation, is spontaneous. In other words, it is not prepared in advance. This is not the case for a large part of the communication that takes place in organisations, where many messages need to be thought out carefully before being delivered. This preparation is necessary for a variety of reasons. Perhaps most commonly, it is because the message content is either complex or contentious, or because the audience is widespread and diverse. There are various useful techniques for generating and organising ideas, before attempting to communicate them. One of the simplest is to make use of diagramming techniques (e.g. Buzan 1995). The guiding assumption is that it is often easier to express, share and structure ideas if they have been presented in a visual format (see section 3.2). For example, by using large sheets of paper or a whiteboard, a whole group of people can become involved, working through the problem together. Diagrams can also be used to work out a logical order in which to present the material to an audience, an important factor in many communication channels, including written reports and verbal presentations (see Box 2.1).

Delivering messages skilfully

There are three general rules for effective delivery of any message, whatever media and channels are used. The first, focusing your attention on the receiver, rather than on yourself as the sender, is particularly relevant to inter-personal communication, but also has implications for other channels. The second is concerned with the way messages are coded, while the third returns us to the receiver, and the key issue of securing appropriate feedback:

Box 2.1

Simple sketch (or 'spider') diagrams can help in various communication tasks, from note-taking to the analysis and presentation of a complex problem. Our minds appear to work by association, and the diagram provides a visual link between different words and ideas. Firstly, to generate ideas: instead of simply listing points down a page, write your main subject word in the centre of a blank sheet of paper. Begin to draw a series of lines from it, labelled with linked ideas. The following simple example is based on the topic, 'Holidays':

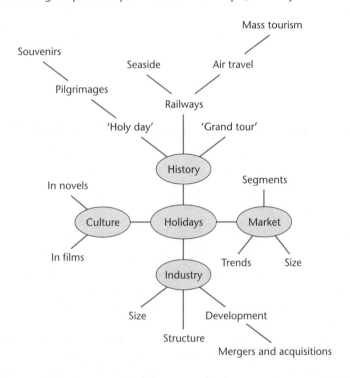

Now, to structure those ideas into a report or presentation, consider the logical links between them. The material can be organised in various ways, including: importance, urgency, simple to complex, and chronological order. This is always a matter of judgement, based on the material you need to communicate and the needs of your audience. As a practice exercise, imagine that you have been asked to give a talk, with five minutes' notice, on a topic about which you know virtually nothing. Experiment with diagramming to generate related ideas on the topic, and use a second diagram to order these ideas. If possible, deliver a talk based on what you have prepared. Did the diagrams help in this task? Were you surprised at how much was stored away in your mind?

- **Focusing on the receiver**: Self-consciousness is a common barrier to inter-personal communication. For example, a very nervous presenter will find it difficult to convey credibility, or to deliver a message that is both coherent and engaging. Failing to focus attention on the receiver can also contribute to the mis-interpretation of any feedback that is received (e.g. a hostile response at a press conference may be interpreted as a personal attack, and the underlying source of the hostility may be left unexplored).

- **Using multiple channels and encoding**: If the receiver is likely to find a message difficult to absorb, the likely solution involves using more one than communication channel (e.g. sending an e-mail and making a follow-up telephone call), and on encoding messages in several ways (e.g. including both text and graphics in a report). The use of multiple channels and encoding can have the effect of reinforcing a message, which is particularly important when the task involves a degree of persuasive communication (see section 5.1). This also increases the likelihood that the messages will be in an appropriate format, when an organisation is engaging with diverse audiences. However, in multiplying these variables, there is also an increased scope for inconsistency between the different channels and forms of encoding (e.g. where a spokesperson's words are contradicted by a written statement). Organisations often exert tight operational controls on their communication channels in an effort to minimise this kind of problem. However, there are difficult trade-offs between the degree of control exercised and the organisation's ability to engage more flexibly with its multiple stakeholders (see section 7.3).

- **Securing appropriate feedback**: Given the open system characteristics of human communication, it is essential to check for any responses from receivers. Feedback allows the sender to make adjustments to the content and format of messages. As noted above, it is important to assess 'negative feedback' in as objective a manner as possible. However, it is generally difficult for individuals and organisations to avoid taking criticism personally.

Even with thorough preparation, there are bound to be some communication failures. However, it is possible to learn from the experience and seek to avoid making a similar mistake in future. Poor communication practices are difficult to rectify, whether they occur at the individual or the organisational level. The most effective communication practitioners, like those in other fields, are never satisfied with their most recent effort. Rather, they strive for *kai-zen*, or continuous improvement. Given a reasonable level of self-confidence, self-awareness and determination, it is possible to make use of constructive criticism and 'un-learn' past practices.

Summary

- Communication failures are endemic, often resulting in significant costs and harm to the organisation and its stakeholders.
- It is important to understand the underlying causes of communication failures, which may involve a range of factors, physiological, psychological, cultural, political, economic and technological.
- Communicators need a basic understanding of physiological processes including differences in alertness, selective attention, powers of perception and memory, and their potential impact on communication.
- It is also important to consider social and cultural barriers, including a tendency towards excessive conformity in social groups ('groupthink'), moral silence and the complex issues arising from cultural diversity.

- While it is dangerous to rely on pre-packaged 'solutions', there are a number of simple techniques, such as diagramming, that can help people to overcome particular communication barriers.

- In more general terms, barriers can be overcome by taking the receiver more seriously, and by thinking more clearly about the content, format and delivery of messages, including the use of multiple channels and forms of encoding.

Practical exercises

1 The art of listening

Writing in the *Harvard Business Review* back in 1952, the American management writer, F.J. Roethlisberger identified listening as a key factor in effective inter-personal communication:

> 'The biggest block to personal communication is man's inability to listen **intelligently, understandingly** and **skilfully** to another person.' (emphasis added)

(a) Do you agree with Roethlisberger's assessment? Give examples to support your argument.

(b) Roethlisberger refers to 'skilful' listening. What do you consider to be the main skills of a good 'listener'? Draw up a list and compare yours with those prepared by colleagues.

(c) How is the 'art' of listening affected by factors such as cultural difference and technological innovation? Give examples to illustrate these influences.

(d) Assess your own capabilities as a listener, by reflecting on recent occasions when you have been in this role. Compare your own assessment to that of a friend or close colleague. How well do they match?

2 Avoiding the question: deliberate communication barriers

In some situations, receivers may construct their own, deliberate barriers to communication. For example, in a broadcast interview, the tactic of pretending not to hear or to misunderstand the sender is often used as a defensive shield against unwelcome questions. Professional politicians and corporate spokespersons may make more or less 'artful' attempts at avoiding the questions that are being posed. Sophisticated media training, often provided by former journalists, helps them to replace a meaningful answer to the interviewer's question with their own pre-prepared statement, an essentially meaningless remark, or a carefully-worded 'sound bite', designed to catch the attention of other media organisations. These 'pseudo-answers' can sound very convincing. For this reason, both interviewers and audiences need to be alert if they are to identify examples of deliberate non-communication. The exercise is designed to improve your skills in detecting these behaviours.

(a) Make a recording of an interview on radio and/or television. Replay it several times, so that you are familiar with the exchanges. (Note: If possible, obtain a written transcript of the programme; these are sometimes available from the broadcaster's website.)

(b) Try to identify examples where the interviewee's response ignores the question, answers a different question, or fails to give a meaningful reply.

(c) What tactics does the interviewer use in order to obtain answers to the original questions posed? How successful are these tactics?

(d) Can you think of any other situations where people put up deliberate barriers to communication? How are these barriers challenged?

Case study B	**Translating the Japanese manufacturing model in Thailand**

This case study is based on a larger research project, which investigated the ways that multinational companies attempt to transfer their domestic working practices to foreign subsidiaries (Sedgwick 1999, 2000). The extract focuses on Japanese automobile and consumer electronics manufacturing plants in Thailand and assesses their efforts to introduce concepts such as quality circles, job rotation and on the job training.

The Japanese manufacturing model
Organisational style in Japanese manufacturing stresses task flexibility and dependency between organisational segments of the manufacturing process. The system is based on strong information flows throughout the organisational hierarchy generated by a work-force capable of communicating efficiently and accurately. Ideally the system devolves authority – over a limited sphere of activities – down to lower levels than would be the case in a traditional 'Fordist' model associated with Western manufacturing systems. Thus workers, who are generally highly trained both at school and at the company itself, appear to have a high degree of autonomy over their specific tasks while at the same time pushing a great deal of information about those tasks into the system.

The Japanese manufacturing model draws on many years of hands-on experience and long-term knowledge building. In addition, many of its practices have been adopted by manufacturers across the world. The broad acknowledgement of the strengths of the Japanese model has reinforced the confidence of Japanese managers, especially at firms with strong manufacturing traditions, such as those reported in this case. This process has also been encouraged by the Japanese media, where a vast array of publications target an avid audience of business managers and engineers. As a con-sequence, Japanese managers carry a fairly stable model of management to their assignments overseas. They also have an understandable expectation that this home-grown, and internationally-praised, model should be perpetuated in their companies' foreign subsidiaries. So, how successful are Japanese multinationals in transferring this model to Japanese subsidiaries in Thailand?

Life on the shop floor
Industrial managers do not spend any significant amount of time pondering either the contents or boundaries of models; they are relevant to the extent that they provide guidelines for action. Let us have a look then at some specific activities associated with Japanese management. The most convenient place to find readily observable action is on the shop floor itself. In industrial production 'quality control' (QC) has a wide breadth of potential meanings, but the activity most closely tied with quality control in Japan is **QC circles**. These are small group activities in which, typically, assembly line workers share ideas about how to solve minor problems on their lines. Ideas are tested

by gathering data from the line that can be analysed using simple statistical measures. 'Circles' are based on the intuitive logic that a worker who is thinking, while he is doing, can make valuable suggestions regarding how work can be conducted more productively. As such, QC circles constitute perhaps the best known application of non-Fordist manufacturing concepts. In the process of participating in circles, workers are assumed to become more interested in their jobs, more engaged with their colleagues, and more highly committed to the company.

While there are of course variations in Japan, QC circles tend to meet regularly once or twice a week near the shop floor, after work, for 30–40 minutes. Workers are not paid for their participation. By contrast, in Thai plants, QC circles were conducted under overtime pay conditions. In many plants they were dropped altogether, or were never present, because of heavy production deadlines. In all plants with active QC circles comparatively rudimentary analytical tools were utilised to identify the sources of production difficulties. Through **job rotation**, a typical worker at a large firm, who is likely to spend an entire working career in that firm, will change tasks and learn new skills. Over the course of a career this broad, hands-on knowledge of the factory should generate more competent managers, as workers rise through the ranks. Job rotation and **on the job training** (OJT) combine to form a system in which workers in Japan are given early responsibility for learning new tasks on a functioning line – where mistakes immediately affect output – with guidance from more experienced co-workers. Awareness of the effect on all line members of a worker's failure to quickly learn new tasks is deliberately used to motivate new line members. By contrast, in Thailand, the researcher observed very few cases of job rotation among workers in the factories studied. Thai workers were reluctant to change tasks. They interpreted such changes as an indication that they were judged incompetent in their current jobs. In addition, they did not want to separate themselves from the social relationships they had established with their co-workers.

Japanese managers were satisfied with this arrangement as it generated stability on the production line and did not require that they retrain workers for new tasks. Meanwhile, the calculation by Japanese managers on how intensively to rotate Thai engineers was based essentially on whether it was best to spread out limited engineering manpower by frequent rotation or keep good engineers focused on tasks they could manage consistently. The latter option was viewed as safer, and overwhelmingly prevailed. On the job training predominated in Thai factories. However, this was explained in interviews with Japanese managers as a response to high demand for output, as opposed to the 'best choice' for training as it would likely be articulated in Japan. The managers also took more time in moving new workers onto production lines, so that mistakes could be more tightly controlled. They felt that Thai workers had plenty of potential but were inexperienced and poorly trained when they were first employed. On the job training was therefore supplemented by limited classroom work, covering assembly methods.

In the automobile plant, classes were conducted by Japanese foremen flown in from Japan with a Thai manager translating; the written materials in the classroom were in Japanese or English and the whole experience appeared frustrating for all involved. In the consumer electronics plant, manuals had been translated into Thai, and most of the training was conducted by Thai engineers. However, observations of the training sessions suggested that the tutors were insecure in their knowledge of Japanese methods.

Muda-dori (time and resource management) is highly valued among Japanese manufacturers as a general paradigm under which waste, defined both in physical terms and in terms of time, is cut out of the production process. It includes **just-in-time** (JIT) delivery of parts by both external and in-house suppliers. In Thailand, plant lay-out reflected the JIT scheme. For example, every tool, machine, and supply bin was positioned in a designated spot so it could be used most efficiently in the production process. However, more complex measures, such as making additional calculations to identify waste on production lines – a common QC circle activity in Japan – was avoided. Instead, waste reduction on the lines in Thailand was the responsibility of production engineers, as in traditional Western systems. The notion of earlier segments of the production line creating products 'just-in-time' for their 'customers' further along in the production process was poorly developed. Just-in-time delivery by outside suppliers, even Japanese-owned suppliers, was not attempted. Indeed, Japanese managers joked among themselves that they knew of one Japanese automobile assembler which had a year's worth of supplies stockpiled on its huge lot.

Translating working practices – just a matter of time?
The research suggests that Japanese managers in Thailand either chose, or were forced, to limit the use of Japanese shop floor practices. This may, in part, be due to the fact that the plants were start-ups, in operation for around five years, with a largely inexperienced labour force. Many of the Japanese managers in these plants said that they fully expected shop floor and production systems to match those in place at 'sister plants' in Japan within 10 to 15 years. This was not the case, however, in another Japanese subsidiary, which had manufactured motor vehicles in Thailand for over 30 years. Whereas the average age of workers in the start-ups was 24 years, most workers in the older plant had 'grown up with the company'. They had joined young and stayed – the average age was now 37 years. The president of this company told the researcher that, try as he had, he simply could not get these production systems in place in Thailand to any degree that approached their use in Japan.

Since no product may be released from the factory at below standard quality, intense production pressures, combined with human and physical resources on the ground, have produced a set of manufacturing methods in Thai subsidiaries very much at odds with the Japanese ideal. Production systems in Thailand are managed from above, with decisions controlled tightly by a centralised cadre of managers and engineers oriented to a top-down flow of information. From the evidence of this study, it appears that large-scale Japanese manufacturing multinationals in Thailand have reproduced those traditional 'Western' practices that they learned to avoid at home.

Note: gender difference in the case study firms

The case study does not address gender issues specifically. However, over 98% of the Japanese, Western, and Thai engineers in these companies, were male, as were assembly line workers in motor vehicle plants. By contrast, in the consumer electronic plants, women accounted for around 45% of assembly line workers. An interesting distinction, between Japanese plants in Japan and the subsidiaries in Thailand was the relatively high proportion of Thai women among non-engineering, 'white collar' staff, typically in jobs involving accounting and data management. Japanese managers often commented that compared with their male counterparts, female Thai staff were highly 'reliable.'

Questions

1 Review the case and identify the main 'messages' that describe the Japanese manufacturing system.

2 List what you see as the main barriers to communicating these messages in the Japanese subsidiary plants in Thailand. Try to support your points with examples from the case material.

3 Compare your list to the types of barriers identified in the chapter, commenting on any patterns that emerge.

4 Prepare a briefing document for managers at one of the plants, outlining a programme to overcome the barriers you have identified.

Source: Written by Mitchell Sedgwick

Further reading

Gross (1996) includes several chapters that offer an accessible introduction to the cognitive and social psychological aspects of communication. **Cooper and Locke** (2000) is an edited text that illustrates how psychological research is applied in particular aspects or organisational life. **Janis** (1982) is the classic work on 'groupthink' and **Bird** (2002) is an interesting analysis of 'moral silence'; **Sims** (1992) brings these two aspects together. There are many studies on cross-cultural barriers to communication and related issues. **Hofstede** (1991) and **Trompenaars** (1994) reflect the dominant approach, while **Tayeb** (1994), **Kirton and Green** (2000) and **Holden** (2002) are examples of more critical interpretations. **English** (2001) reports another approach to breaking down barriers in an international context. **Sedgwick** (1999, 2000) develops themes introduced in Case B.

References

Argyle, M. (1972) *The psychology of interpersonal behaviour* (2nd edn). Penguin, Harmondsworth.

Ashe, A. (2001) 'From Anne Ashe' in *Ahead of time: birthday letters to Mayer Hillman*. Policy Studies Institute, London (11–20).

Bird, F.B. (2002) *The muted conscience: moral silence and the practice of ethics in business*. Quorum, Westport CT.

Brown, A. and Starkey, K. (1994) 'The effect of organisational culture on communication and information'. *Journal of Management Studies*, 31, 807–28.

Buzan, T. (1995) *Use your head*. BBC Books, London.

Cohan, J.A. (2002) '"I didn't know" and "I was only doing my job": has corporate governance careened out of control? A case study of Enron's information myopia'. *Journal of Business Ethics*, 40, 3, 275–99.

Cooper, C. and Locke, E.A. (2000) *Industrial and organizational psychology: linking theory with practice*. Blackwell, Oxford.

DRC (2003) 'Press release: First DRC formal investigation to focus on Web access'. Disability Rights Commission, London (28th March).

English, T. (2001) 'Tension analysis in international organizations: a tool for breaking down communication barriers'. *The International Journal of Organizational Analysis*, 9, 1, 58–83.

Gross, R.D. (1996) *Psychology, the science of mind and behaviour*. Hodder & Stoughton, London.

Handy, C.B. (1996) *Understanding organisations*. Penguin Books, London.

Hargie, O.D.W. (ed.) (1997) *Handbook of communication skills* (2nd edn.). Routledge, London.

Hargie, O., Saunders, C. and Dickson, D. (1994) *Social skills in interpersonal communication* (3rd edn.) Routledge, London.

Harvey, J.B. (1988) 'The Abilene Paradox: the management of agreement'. *Organizational Dynamics*, 17, 16–34 (Summer).

Hickson, D.J. (1997) *Exploring management across the world*. Penguin, London.

Hofstede, G. (2001) *Culture's consequences: comparing values, behaviours, institutions and organizations across nations* (2nd edn.). Sage Publications, London.

Hofstede, G. (1991) *Cultures and organisations: software of the mind*. McGraw-Hill, Maidenhead.

Holden, N. (2002) *Cross-cultural management: a knowledge management perspective*. FT Prentice Hall, Harlow.

Janis, I.L. (1982) *Groupthink*. Houghton Mifflin, Boston MA.

Kim, Y. (2001) 'A comparative study of the "Abilene Paradox" and "Groupthink"'. *Public Administration Quarterly*, 25, 2, 168–89.

Kirton, G. and Greene, A-M. (2000) *Dynamics of managing diversity: a critical approach*. Butterworth-Heinemann, Oxford.

Kroeber, A.L. and Kluckholm, C. (1952) *Culture: a critical review of concepts and definitions*. Harvard University Press, Cambridge MA.

Luft, P. (2000) 'Communication barriers for deaf employees: needs assessment and problem-solving strategies'. *Work*, 14, 51–9.

Pan, Y., Scollon, S. and Scollon, R. (2002) *Professional communication in international settings*. Blackwell, Oxford.

RNIB (2002) 'Press release: RNIB debate sees web usability experts divide over "one size fits all"'. RNIB, London (8th July).

Roth, I. and Bruce, V. (1995) *Perception and representation: current issues* (2nd edn.). Open University Press, Milton Keynes.

Sedgwick, M.W. (1999) 'Do Japanese business practices travel well?: managerial technology transfer to Thailand'. in Encarnation, D.J. (ed.) *Japanese Multinationals in Asia: Regional Operations in Comparative Perspective*. Oxford University Press, New York.

Sedgwick, M.W. (2000) 'The Globalizations of Japanese managers' in Befu, H., Eades, J.S. and Gill, T. (eds.) *Globalization and social change in contemporary Japan*. TransPacific Press, Melbourne.

Sims, R.R. (1992) 'Linking groupthink to unethical behaviour in organizations'. *Journal of Business Ethics*, 11, 9, 651–64.

Smith, S. (1984) 'Groupthink and the hostage rescue mission'. *British Journal of Political Science*, 15, 117–23.

Tayeb, M. (2000) *International business: theories, policies and practices*. FT Prentice Hall, Harlow.

Trompenaars (1994) *Riding the waves of culture: understanding cultural diversity in business*. Nicholas Brearley, London.

WAI (2003) 'Auxiliary benefits of accessible Web design.' W3C Web Accessibility Initiative. (Accessed at: www.w3c.org/WAI/bcase/benefits.html (19th August).)

Yates, J. and Orlikowski, W.J. (1992) 'Genres of organizational communication: a structural approach to studying communications and media'. *Academy of Management Review*, 17, 299–326.

CHAPTER 3

Using words: verbal communication

Prose is words in their best order; poetry is the best words in the best order.
Samuel Taylor Coleridge, poet.

Learning outcomes

By the end of this chapter you should be able to:

- appreciate the importance of written and spoken words in organisational communication;
- apply principles of plain English, in order to produce clear and concise language;
- identify the most common sources of misunderstanding in the use of language, and how they may be avoided;
- explore the ways that the interpretation of spoken language is influenced by paralinguistics;
- develop a more self-aware and flexible use of words, adapting styles to meet the needs of different business situations.

3.1 Introduction

This chapter looks at the ways that words are used, and frequently abused, in organisational communication. It shows how communicators can use fewer words to greater effect. This requires attention to the principles of plain English, but also an imaginative use of the language, ensuring that those words that are used remain both strong and meaningful. The task of constructing text-based messages, whether they are written or spoken, is often very demanding. This is particularly true for people who are attempting to make use of less familiar languages. Getting more of the right words in the right order is not sufficient to transform prose into poetry. However, it should increase the chances that important messages will be conveyed effectively. The chapter covers written and spoken English. It begins by outlining the principles of plain English, and comments on the vexed issues of spelling, grammar and punctuation.

There is a discussion of the difficult balance between clarity, conciseness and the desire to make language compelling and meaningful. We also consider the issue of translation between languages, noting some implications for international organisations, where English is often the adopted language. There is also a review of issues specific to spoken English and a reflection on the use of language as a matter of style. The final section addresses a related topic, the ways that language is used to construct organisational 'stories', and how they influence the communication process.

3.2 Clear and concise language: using plain English

Plain English is a fundamental requirement for most of the written and spoken communication that takes place in organisations. It is often tempting to elaborate or extend the text, in order to provide additional information. For example, a researcher who is drafting a report, based on the findings or a survey may have access to an enormous amount of raw data, providing the basis for many different arguments and reflections. However, the researcher's intended audience, perhaps a marketing director or small sub-committee, is more likely to want a summary document taking up no more than one page of text. The reality is that most senior managers simply do not have time to read large amounts of written material, or even to listen to extended verbal reports. Consequently, the communicator is always required to focus attention on the most important points, and to cut back any superfluous language. Applying plain English principles is also good for the writer or speaker. It forces you to think more clearly about the content of the message, including the central arguments that are being developed (see Chapter 5). (Note: there is even an environmental benefit; imagine the paper and ink cartridges that would be saved if all of the world's written reports were 5 per cent shorter!)

The plea for plain English is something that you are sure to hear from over-burdened managers around the world. It can be reduced to three basic rules:

- using shorter words;
- using fewer words; and
- replacing words with pictures, an under-valued technique that can provide more concise messages, without sacrificing content.

In isolation, these rules may seem obvious, but applying them across a wide range of communication channels requires practice and commitment. At first, time taken to re-draft and refine text might seem wasted. However, the streamlined results are likely to repay that effort many times over.

Using shorter words

English is a particularly rich language. Its older words, with Anglo-Saxon and Nordic roots, have more elaborate counterparts from the 'Romance' languages, derived from Latin, including Norman French. In general, the older words are shorter and more direct. For example, note the difference in length, and also the contrasting tone, in the following sentences:

- Romance: 'The introductory oration was protracted, pedestrian and vacuous.'
- Anglo/Nordic: 'The first speech was long, dull and empty.'

If the shorter word lacks a subtle meaning that you need to convey, it will be necessary to use a longer alternative. However, to make a point clearly and concisely, shorter words must be the general rule.

Using fewer words

It is easy for an unnecessary word to slip into a sentence. Like any intruder, it will do its best to hide, so writers need to be vigilant. How can text be condensed without losing the essential messages? Writers often find it difficult to believe that their text is open to further editing. Consider the following extract, from an imaginary company based in the Netherlands, which demonstrates the process of achieving plainer English. While the language has been exaggerated for effect, similar cases have been reported in many 'real world' organisations (Mini-case 3.1).

Chief Executive's annual address to shareholders: first draft

Of course, it is indeed extremely heartening and reassuring to be in a position where our current shareholders' attention can be drawn to the absence of any seriously negative repercussions affecting active corporate-wide operations. This outcome is one that has arisen as a direct consequence of a not inconsiderable diminution in the principal influential macro-economic indicators over the preceding annual financial reporting period. Moreover, during the course of the period in question, a significant enhancement in the company's overall sales turnover performance and financial profitability measures in the markets of southern continental Europe has been achieved, with a particularly significant and notable improvement in the various countries of the Iberian peninsular region, where it operates. A relatively optimistic trend extrapolation can be forecasted at this stage, suggesting a full realisation or modest improvement on prior-year forecast projections for the indigenous market in those non-alcoholic beverages destined for domestic consumption. A significant and pro-active commitment to the development of our corporate human resources is seen as a necessary and vital prerequisite for the continued upward increase in the company's future fortunes.

The above boxed paragraph contains 180 words. The best way to develop your editing skills is through practical exercises. See how far you can shorten this word count without losing the essence. A shortened version is included below, but make your own attempt at sub-editing before reading on.

There are three main techniques for shortening an existing draft. First, writers can remove non-essential words. For example, sentence openers, such as, 'Of course...' or 'Clearly...' are pure padding. They can be omitted without affecting the message. Some adjectives and adverbs, such as, 'quite', 'fairly' and 'comparatively' are meaningless without a reference point. What, for instance, is meant by, 'a relatively optimistic trend...'? Editors should also delete cosmetic and redundant words, such as, '*pro-active* commitment ...' and 'an upward increase ...'. Second, the writer needs to replace any long-winded (or 'verbose') phrases.

These are often a sign of insecurity on the part of the writer or speaker. People try to compensate for their lack of confidence in the message content by expressing it in grandiose terms. For example, the Chief Executive's reference to '... a not inconsiderable diminution in the principal influential economic indicators over the preceding annual financial reporting period ...' means simply, 'the recession last year'. The third technique is to switch from passive to active voice. The original address is written in the 'passive' voice. This means that it takes the form 'object-verb-subject', rather than the active form, 'subject-verb-object'. Some organisations make extensive use of the passive form. For example, it is the conventional language of most scientific reports. One of the advantages of the passive voice is its ability to suggest objectivity, by removing the author. However, it also requires additional words and is usually less interesting to read.

Here is one way of condensing the Chief Executive's statement, using the simple techniques described above. The text is reduced by more than 50 per cent to just 80 words, with no loss of meaning and with some useful details added. As a bonus, the text has a livelier and more direct tone, which is more appropriate for its intended audience.

Chief Executive's annual address to shareholders: edited version

I am pleased to report that the company is thriving, despite the recession last year. Sales in southern Europe are up 20 million euros from 2004, with margins improving to 15 per cent. Spain and Portugal are stronger, with turnover increasing by 60 million euros and margins of over 17 per cent. We forecast even higher 2005 sales, including 140 million euros in the Dutch retail market. We believe that investing in people will help us to improve our performance.

Using 'pictures' if possible

There is a popular saying, that 'a picture paints a thousand words'. This is true of many organisational messages, where it is more effective to substitute images for spoken or written words. The term 'picture' can be interpreted very loosely for this purpose. For example, in a market research report, you might replace a long and difficult section of text, summarising the results of a survey (i.e. a typical extract would read, 'We found that 16.5 per cent of respondents "agreed strongly", with the proposition, compared to 17.6 per cent who expressed this opinion the previous year, a reduction of 1.1 percentage points. In addition, 28.4 per cent of respondents "agreed", with the proposition, in contrast to a figure of 32.6 per cent the previous year, a reduction of 4.2 percentage points. The figure for the respondents who were "undecided" was 32.8 per cent, representing an increase of 3.6 percentage points from the previous year ...'), with two simple pie charts. Similarly, a long written description of how to get to a particular location can be replaced by a well-drawn route map and section headings can be clarified by selecting appropriate fonts (see Figure 3.1). Chapter 4 considers how various types of manufactured image, and other non-verbal codes, can be used alongside written communication in order to make our messages clearer and more effective.

Times New Roman 18pt

Tahoma 18pt

Book Antiqua bold 18pt

Helvetica bold 18pt

Monotype corsiva 18pt

Arial Narrow 18pt

Continuous text is often printed using fonts like Times New Roman that have *serifs* (i.e. small projections or curls) at the end of each stroke; *sans serif* fonts, such as Tahoma, are more commonly used for titles and headings.

Figure 3.1 Selecting a suitable font

Mini-case 3.1 reviews the activities of an organisation called the Plain English Campaign, which has achieved some notable victories in its efforts to promote principles of the kind outlined in this section.

| Mini-case 3.1 | The Plain English Campaign |

The Plain English Campaign

'We are an independent organisation fighting for crystal-clear language and against jargon, gobbledygook and other confusing language.'

The Plain English Campaign (PEC) is a self-funding organisation, which promotes the principles of plain English from its offices at New Mills in the English Peak District. It was founded in 1979 by a social rights campaigner called Chrissie Maher. Her campaigning activities were first prompted by the deaths of two elderly women, who had been unable to understand the text of an application form that would have provided them with housing benefit. Today, PEC has over 3,000 registered supporters in 70 countries, who can access its services by e-mail, telephone and via it website (www.plainenglish.co.uk). PEC defines plain English on the basis of its effectiveness in communication:

> 'Plain English is something that the intended audience can read, understand and act upon the first time they read it. Plain English takes into account design and layout as well as language.'

Activities and resources

PEC is financed through its commercial services, which include training courses, editorial work, books, magazines and corporate memberships. It also provides a number of free guides, including 'How to write in Plain English', which can be obtained via the website. PEC is probably best known for its annual 'Golden Bull' award for particularly bad examples of written English. The awards achieve a good deal of media coverage, and the offending organisations are usually required to explain the reasons for their poor writing practice.

The 'Crystal Mark'

In 1990, PEC introduced the Crystal Mark as a seal of approval for organisations that would encourage more clear communication with the public. The Crystal Mark has become well established in the UK and is also used in some other English-speaking countries, including the US, Australia and South Africa. Among PEC's criteria for securing the Crystal Mark are: an average sentence length of about 15 to 20 words; 'active' rather than 'passive' verbs; everyday English; use of 'we' and 'you' rather than 'the insured' or 'the applicant'; conciseness; clear, helpful and consistent headings; appropriate type size; and a clear typeface. Documents that meet the required standards can be identified with

▶

the Crystal Mark symbol, subject to verification by PEC. The organisation has also launched an Internet Crystal Mark, which applies similar principles to website design.

Public, private and voluntary sector organisations are becoming increasingly aware of the importance of plain English, both for the purposes of more effective communication and as a defence against legal action. For example, the UK's Unfair Terms in Consumer Contracts Regulations 1999 state that all consumer contracts must be drafted, 'in plain and intelligible language'. Unclear or ambiguous contract terms can be challenged in court, prompting warnings from the Office of Fair Trading. Similar legislation operates in other European Union countries.

Questions

1 Why do you think organisations continue to generate poorly-worded documents, despite the efforts of campaigners such as PEC?

2 Review the PEC website, including the examples of bad practice, and the 'translations' into plain English. Try to find three additional examples, from corporate websites, and produce your own translations, using the guidance provided.

3 What do you see as the additional challenges, if any, when drafting plain English text for use:

(a) in html (i.e. web) format (e.g. a corporate intranet)?
(b) in cross-cultural settings (e.g. the Olympic games)?
(c) in promoting an artistic event (e.g. a theatre or gallery)?
(d) in an oral presentation (e.g. a politician's conference speech)?

Source: Plain English Campaign (2003). Case written by the author, with acknowledgements.

3.3 The technicalities: spelling, grammar, syntax and punctuation

Some people argue that it is not important to correct the spelling, grammar, syntax and punctuation of written communication, particularly when it is for internal use. Short e-mail messages are routinely written in very poor English, with keying errors (or 'typos') and little punctuation. The long-term effects of mobile phone text messaging have yet to unfold, but some commentators argue that it will lead to deterioration in the quality of written and spoken language. The counter-argument is that efforts at achieving correct English are time-consuming and unnecessary. The implication is that errors do not matter, so long as the essential message is clear. It is true that some errors have a very limited effect on communication. For example, a few years ago there was a vociferous campaign to change the wording used on signs above the 'express' checkouts in British supermarkets. The wording was changed from, '10 items or less' to, '10 items or fewer'. The protesters had argued, correctly, that the adjective 'less' referred to a single item (e.g. 'I have less mashed potato than you'), while 'fewer' referred to several separate items (e.g. 'I have fewer chips than you'). Hence, for the checkout signs, 'fewer' was the correct word to use. But was this protest worthwhile? In this instance, the meaning remained clear despite the technical error.

However, errors in spelling, punctuation and grammar often result in misunderstanding, which can lead to costly and unnecessary problems in organisations. Table 3.1 presents a few examples of text, where grammatical errors can make the content ambiguous or difficult to read. Readers who are confident in this area can demonstrate their abilities by correcting these examples; additional guidance is provided in the Further reading section at the end of this chapter, and on the companion website.

Table 3.1 **Grammatical errors, ambiguity and style**

Error	Example
A confused dependent clause	Welsh Rugby Union chiefs gave their full backing to a judge after he jailed a violent player who stamped on an opponent's head for six months.
Too many conjunctions and the absence of punctuation	We sell a range of products to the wholesale market because it is profitable to do so and also since there is the prospect of growth with signs of improvement in the Northern area and some opportunities in the West though we only have one sales representative located there at present whilst the warehousing issue is being resolved and we are rushed off our feet therefore I really do hope that you will be able to bear with us in the meantime because for some reason or other we seem to barely have time to take a breath.
Faulty grammar and punctuation	Our company were very pleased, to have done the presentation for your office, yesterday. As you would have clearly seen the best feature, of our services are, above all their very top qualified technicians. Each one of them have been awarded, full industry certification, and commitment to the job with also an extensive two years training programmes. I hope we can therefore be looking forward, to have heard from you in due course.

3.4 Beyond plain English? Using language creatively

Languages are living phenomena, and the English language is particularly vibrant, as it is in such widespread use across the globe (McCrum et al. 1992; Crystal 2003b). New words and expressions are created all the time, while others are becoming redundant, losing their original meaning and fading away. For example, the last two decades have seen the arrival of terms such as, 'collateral damage', 'global warming', 'snow boarding', 'road rage', 'spin doctors', 'spamming', 'text messaging' and 'virtual business'. In many cases the terms are associated with technologies; consequently, they tend to fall into disuse and their original meanings are forgotten once the technology is superseded. The sheer richness and variety of expression can be of great value to the communicator. However, it also poses major problems. As we have already noted, the essential requirement in effective communication is to generate shared meanings between 'sender' and 'receiver' (see section 1.3). The following aspects of language lend it additional richness, but can also be a source of confusion.

Metaphor, idiom and figurative expression

Words are not always used literally. Metaphor may be used to give a message greater impact, but it is a potential source of confusion. Native English speakers may have experience of different figurative expressions, depending on the particular part of the world in which they acquired their language. The same applies to those who have studied English as a foreign language in a particular setting (e.g. South Africa, Hong Kong or Scotland). Hence, the meaning of a phrase such as 'their comments were met by a stony silence' will be self-evident to some English speakers, but may be unfamiliar to others. Consider, for example, possible meanings of the Ugandan English expression, 'I am another one.' It is used by a person who has done something interesting or unusual; the implication is that there is another part of this person that was previously unknown to others (Mushinga 2003). Indian English has produced many richly visual expressions, which may be also be unfamiliar to users of English in other parts of the world:

> 'Another characteristic of Indian English is the literal translation of idiom, echoing the earlier medieval tradition of translation from French into English of phrases like "a marriage of convenience" and "it goes without saying". Today, there are several such Indian English translations that have become part of a shared vocabulary: "may the fire ovens consume you", "a crocodile in a loin cloth", and comparisons like "as good as kitchen ashes", "as helpless as a calf", and "as lean as an areca-nut tree". Abuse in Indian English is a particularly rich source of idiomatic translation. From masters to servants: "you donkey's husband". From parents to children: "why did I rear a serpent with the milk of my breast?"'
> (McCrum *et al.* 1992: 362)

However, some of this idiomatic language has gained a more universal status, primarily as a result of its use in international contexts, including business organisations. For example, the imagery of gold has long been used metaphorically to describe how people are paid. This has given rise to several common expressions in international business: encouraging people to join a company ('golden handshakes'); allowing them to leave a troubled company painlessly ('golden parachutes'); or using financial inducements to ensure that they conform and remain with the organisation ('golden handcuffs', 'golden collars' and 'gilded cages'). Metaphors are also used to make abstract ideas more concrete. In a speech given in 1947, the British statesman, Winston Churchill, described the post-1945 division of Europe as 'an iron curtain' descending across Europe, 'from Stettin in the Baltic to Trieste in the Adriatic'; this expression passed into history with the symbolic demolition of the Berlin Wall in 1989. Churchill suffered from occasional bouts of depression and created another evocative image, 'black dog', to describe the real physical threat posed by his otherwise intangible illness (Jenkins 2001: 466, 810, 819).

Metaphors are often found in the language of organisations. For example, the 'glass ceiling' is a vivid metaphor that originated in North America, where most of the large corporations are housed in 20 or 30 storey skyscrapers. The top floors of these buildings are commonly reserved for the spacious offices of the chief executive and other senior staff. Hence, 'the glass ceiling' captures the idea that women, in particular, face an unyielding but invisible barrier, blocking their promotion from middle management positions. However, it is important to balance the use of these expressions against the needs of the audience. For example, imagine the challenge if you had to explain the concept of the glass ceiling to an audience that had no prior experience of skyscrapers. Can you suggest any alternative metaphors would convey a similar meaning in a world of single-storey buildings?

Lastly, we should note that communicators can sometimes achieve powerful and persuasive effects by adapting or embellishing an existing figurative expression. For example, the British politician, Dennis Healey was famous for his effective use of language in order to attack his opponents in parliament; he once compared another politician's skills in political debate to being, 'savaged by a dead sheep'. Of course, if such language is to be effective, the reference must be meaningful to the intended audience. For example the idiomatic phrase, 'Pigs will fly' is used by the British to refer to something that is not likely to happen, or to be practical. Another politician, Kenneth Clarke, once elaborated this phrase in a speech attacking the policies of the opposition party. He suggested that, 'It is not just a matter of pigs flying. It is a whole farmyard on a mission deep into space.' This remark was very effective when delivered to a British parliamentary audience, and when reported in the domestic media. However, the same words could be a source of great confusion for anyone who was unfamiliar with the original idiom.

Clichéd and empty language

Some words and expressions become so over-used that they lose their original meaning. The business community is particularly prone to the adoption of fashionable terminology, which is slipped into a sentence for cosmetic effect. For example, 'empowering ...' and 'sustainable ...' became popular terms in the 1990s, but they have become ill-defined and vacuous due to over-use. One of the symptoms of empty and clichéd language is that unrelated expressions are sometimes combined to create bizarre 'mixed' metaphors. For example, a politician once attempted to highlight the greed of company directors with two idiomatic phrases (i.e. 'having a snout in the trough' and 'riding on the gravy train'). However, he inadvertently combined them, creating the entirely *meaningless* phrase, 'having their snouts in the gravy train'.

Euphemism – the deliberate disguise of meaning

A euphemism is an innocuous word or phrase that is used to disguise or reduce the impact of an unpleasant reality. Hence, instead of saying that people have died, we may refer to them as having, 'left us' or, 'passed away'. Similarly, when governments drop bombs on cities, resulting in the death of civilians, official statements contain euphemistic phrases such as, 'forces engaged in a number of surgical strikes against enemy targets', acknowledging the killing of non-combatants and of their own forces with military terminology, such as 'collateral damage' and 'friendly fire'. Euphemisms are a common feature in all forms of persuasive communication (see Chapter 5). However, if the primary objective is clear expression, they are best avoided.

Specialist terminology and technical jargon

Specialist groups, including train-spotters, salsa dancers, economists and brain surgeons, tend to develop their own distinctive vocabulary. Jargon words act as a useful shorthand for terms the group uses regularly. However, they can become a serious obstacle to communication with a non-specialist audience. Because the words are either unintelligible, unfamiliar, or difficult, people tend to lose interest in the written or spoken message. This distancing can also lead to some hostility between groups. For example, the former British Prime Minister, Margaret Thatcher's opinion of the economics profession was once revealed in the passing comment that, 'You and I come by road or rail, but economists travel on *infrastructure*' (Howard 1988: 9 – emphasis added). Even if audiences remain engaged, their attention will be distracted as they attempt to unscramble the meaning of the jargon. The lesson for communicators is to assess their audience before making use of jargon. If they are likely to be unfamiliar with the words, provide a clear explanation (e.g. by including a glossary in a report), or use language that non-specialists can understand.

Each of these elements of the living language, from figurative expressions to technical jargon, becomes more problematic when communication involves non-Native speakers. This is due to the added complication of translating meanings between languages. Mini-case 3.2 deals with this practical challenge: how can we retain the original meaning of a message when it is translated into a number of different languages?

Mini-case 3.2	Translating questionnaires in international research

Translating questions and associated instructions into another language requires care if your translated or target questionnaire is to be decoded and answered by respondents in the way you intended. For international research this is extremely important if the questionnaires are to have the same meaning to all respondents. For this reason, Usnier (1998) suggests that when translating the source questionnaire attention should be paid to:

● **Lexical meaning:** The precise meaning of individual words (e.g. the French word *chaud* can be translated into two concepts in English and German, meaning 'warm' and 'hot');

● **Idiomatic meaning:** The meanings of a group of words that are natural to a native speaker and not deducible from the individual words (e.g. the English expression for informal communication, 'grapevine', has a similar idiomatic meaning as the French expression téléphone arabe, which translates literally as 'arabic telephone');

● **Grammar and syntax:** The correct use of language, including the ordering of words and phrases to create well-formed sentences (e.g. in Japanese the ordering is quite different from English or Dutch, as verbs are at the end of sentences);

● **Experiential meaning:** The equivalence of meanings of words and sentences for people in their everyday experiences (e.g. terms that are familiar in the source questionnaire's context, such as 'dual career household', may be unfamiliar in the target questionnaire's context).

Usnier (1998) outlines a number of techniques for translating the source questionnaire. These, along with their advantages and disadvantages, are summarised in the table below. In this table, the *source questionnaire* is the questionnaire that is to be translated, and the *target questionnaire* is the translated questionnaire. When writing your final project report, remember to include a copy of both the source and the target questionnaire as appendices. This will allow readers familiar with both languages to check that the equivalent questions in both questionnaires have the same meaning.

Translation techniques for questionnaires

	Direct translation	Back-translation	Parallel translation	Mixed techniques
Approach	Source questionnaire to target questionnaire.	Source questionnaire to target questionnaire to source questionnaire; comparison of two new source questionnaires; creation of final version.	Source questionnaire to target questionnaire by two or more independent translators; comparison of two target questionnaires; creation of final version.	Back-translation by two or more independent translators; comparison of two new source questionnaires; creation of final version.
Advantages	Easy to implement, relatively inexpensive.	Likely to discover most problems.	Leads to good wording of target questionnaire.	Ensures best match between source and target questionnaires.
Disadvantages	Can lead to many discrepancies, including those relating to meaning, between source and target questionnaire.	Requires two translators, one a native speaker of the source language, the other a native speaker of the target language.	Cannot ensure that lexical, idiomatic and experiential meanings are kept in target questionnaire.	Costly, requires two or more independent translators. Implies that the source questionnaire can also be changed.

Source: Developed from Usnier (1998).

Questions

1 The case identifies four key aspects of language that need to be addressed when translating documents such as questionnaires. Identify or draft examples of text to illustrate each of these issues.

2 The case highlights a number of practical problems faced by an organisation that operates in multiple languages. Which problems do you consider the most difficult to manage?

3 Can you identify any additional challenges for the multi-lingual organisation? How might they be resolved?

Source: This case is based on an extract from Saunders *et al.* (2003: 300–1). Reproduced with permission.

3.5 Spoken English: additional communication issues

Most of the language issues discussed in previous sections can be applied equally to written and spoken English. This section introduces two additional issues that are particularly relevant when English is spoken, the importance of emphasis and its connection with paralinguistics, the non-verbal behaviours that are associated with the process of speaking.

The importance of emphasis

The meaning of a sentence can be altered radically by 'inflection', changing the pitch of the voice to place emphasis on particular words. Authors may achieve a similar effect in written language by altering the typeface (e.g. using *italicised*, **bold**, UPPER CASE or <u>underlined</u> text). However, the adjustments used in spoken English may be less apparent. Receivers familiar with the spoken language will be able to detect very subtle variations. However, non-native speakers may miss some of these signals. The differences in meaning can be dramatic. For example, consider the simple sentence, 'We don't want your money.' How would different inflections change the message when it is spoken aloud?

(a)   *We* don't want your money ...

(b)   We *don't* want your money ...

(c)   We don't *want* your money ...

(d)   We don't want *your* money ...

(e)   We don't want your *money* ...

In each case, the meaning of the statement is 'qualified' by the emphasis given to a particular word. The inflection signals that listener is to expect a pause, followed by a clause beginning, 'but ...'. Thus, example (d) might continue, 'but we do want *hers*', while example (e) suggests, 'but we do want your *support*. Watch out for this type of mis-interpretation of your intended message in presentations and 'one-to-one' conversations.

Paralinguistics: the role of non-verbal signals

Paralanguage refers to the range of sounds (e.g. 'mmm', 'huh'), intakes of breath and silences that surround the spoken language. These have an important function in conversation. For example, they can be used to indicate that a person is listening, to encourage the speaker to continue or to signal agreement. Paralanguage is one of several forms of non-verbal signalling, including eye contact, facial expression and gesture, that are used to reinforce words, and to introduce subtle differences into their meaning. These signals are also subject to cultural variations, which can on occasion lead to the mis-interpretation of oral messages. The role of non-verbal signals is discussed in more detail in the next chapter (see section 4.7).

3.6 Using the language – it is a matter of style

Written and spoken style can be seen as a combination of all the areas discussed so far. In written channels it relates to issues such as the choice of vocabulary, sentence structure and to the rules of grammar and punctuation. In spoken channels, issues such as punctuation are replaced by those related to paralanguage, intonation and delivery. The styles most commonly used in business writing are sometimes described as 'plain English' (see section 3.2), or 'international English' (McCrum *et al.* 1992; Crystal 2003b). In both cases, the main emphasis is on applying the principles of clarity and simplicity. However, there is no one 'right' way to communicate with words. It is important to develop flexibility, adapting your language style to the requirements of specific messages and readers. Mini-case 3.3 makes an explicit connection between the quality of language and the resulting exchange of ideas. It remains a powerful argument, with many resonances in today's world, where the English language is used so widely:

Mini-case 3.3

George Orwell on the decline of the English language

The writer and journalist, George Orwell was born in 1903 in India. His work includes a documentary account of fighting in the Spanish Civil War, *Homage to Catalonia*, and the well-known novels *Animal Farm* and *Nineteen Eighty-Four*. The following extract is from a short essay in which Orwell comments on the current state of the English language and its impact on the way that people think:

'Most people who bother with the matter at all would admit that the English language is in a bad way, but it is generally assumed that we cannot by conscious action do anything about it. Our civilisation is decadent and our language – so the argument runs – must inevitably share in the general collapse. It follows that any struggle against the abuse of language is a sentimental archaism, like preferring candles to electric light or hansom cabs to aeroplanes. Underneath this lies the half-conscious belief that language is a natural growth and not an instrument which we shape for our own purposes. Now, it is clear that the decline of a language must ultimately have political and economic causes: it is not due simply to the bad influence of this or that individual writer. But an effect can become a cause, reinforcing the original cause and producing the same effect in an intensified form, and so on indefinitely. A man may take to drink because he feels himself a failure, and then fail all the more because he drinks. It is rather the same thing that is happening to the English language. It becomes ugly and inaccurate because our thoughts are foolish, but the slovenliness of our language makes it easier for us to have foolish thoughts. The point is that the process is reversible. Modern English, especially written English, is full of bad habits which spread by imitation and which can be avoided if one is willing to take the necessary trouble. If one gets rid of these habits one can think more clearly, and to think more clearly is a necessary first step towards political regeneration.'

Source: Extracted from 'Politics and the English language' in *Shooting and Elephant and other Essays* (1950). Copyright © George Orwell 1946, by permission of Bill Hamilton as the literary executor of the estate of the late Sonia Brownell Orwell and Secker and Warburg Ltd.

Questions

1 Summarise Orwell's main arguments in 'bullet point' format.

2 Do you agree with Orwell's proposition that there is a link between the state of the language and the quality of decisions made by politicians or other key figures? Give practical examples to support your argument.

3 What do you see as the main opportunities and challenges arising from the wider use of the English language in international organisations, and in global channels such as the internet?

3.7 Language and organisation: narrative and discourse analysis

The final section of this chapter moves from a concern with the form of the language to the 'stories' that it can convey. The interest in organisational stories, and the broader role of narrative in research is shared by the interpretive and postmodern perspectives, as discussed in the opening chapter (see section 1.7). The late 20th century saw an increased interest in the way that language influenced organisations. Researchers in these traditions treated language as more than just a tool for achieving managerial objectives; it became a subject of study in its own right, with research focusing on the ways that language was used to create and shape the organisation, its underlying meanings, identities and practices.

> 'The significance of narrative data lies not just in their richness and near universal availability, but in the fact that they are the same kind of data that organizational members use to plan, enact, interpret, and evaluate their own actions and those of others.' (Pentland 1999: 716)

Empirical studies of organisational narratives have made use of a variety of theoretical frameworks and qualitative research techniques (Livesey 2002a). In contrast to functional approaches to communication, which focus on abstracting general principles, this kind of research tends to concentrate the complexity and richness that is found when language is used in particular settings. However, it can also provide insights into the ways that 'stories' are shaped and deployed in order to achieve strategic purposes (Boje *et al.* 1999: 354). Two recent examples from the management and business communication literature illustrate the kinds of insight that can be obtained by studying communication in this perspective. The theme of story-telling in organisations is discussed further in the case study and Further reading section at the end of this chapter:

Battle in the boardroom (Ng and de Cock 2002)

The researchers study the hostile takeover of one of Singapore's best-known companies ('Cleo') by another long-established business ('Antony'). They use multiple sources, including internal company documentation, such as board minutes and draft minutes, in order to 'craft' their own account of these events. The resulting narrative reveals how a key protagonist, the chairman of the acquired company, 'Cleo', made use of language to secure overall control of the strategic agenda. For example, it shows how he exploited language to present a convincing set of causal connections (i.e. establishing a sequence of causes and effects, that board members and other stakeholders began to accept as the most likely explanation). The 'Cleo' chairman's performance was also strengthened by his ability to draw on selected Chinese cultural themes, such as personal loyalty and filial (i.e. brotherly) piety, in order to play the traditional role of the wise patriarch (*ibid:* 41). This resonated with the board members of both companies, who shared these conventions. By contrast, the chairman of 'Antony', an Indonesian, was seen as less effective in presenting his ideas. He also appeared to suffer from a preconceived view of Indonesians as 'short-term traders' (*ibid*: 33). The authors warn that the narrative, 'should not lead us to see storytelling as automatically dissolving facts' (*ibid:* 42). 'Cleo's' chairman did not rely on words alone, he also surrounded himself with loyal managers and took control of information flows. However, it does indicate how this exercise of power was only possible because he had established 'discursive legitimacy' through his storytelling performances (*ibid:* 42).

Global warming wars (Livesey 2002b)

This paper analyses texts published by the US oil company ExxonMobil, as part of its response to debate on climate change, following the negotiation of the Kyoto Protocol in 1997. In contrast to European oil multinationals, notably BP and Royal Dutch/Shell Group, which modified their strategies in response to evidence from the climate scientists, ExxonMobil maintained an isolationist stance, shared by the US government, which downplayed the threats of global warming and maintained the primacy of fossil fuels (*ibid:* 125–6). The researcher analysed a series of advertorials (i.e. sponsored articles) published in *The New York Times* newspaper during March and April 2000. The research was conducted using two methodological approaches: rhetorical analysis, which explores how texts frame meanings, create understanding and make connections with audiences; and discourse analysis, which is concerned with the broader relationship between the texts and the sociological context in which they are employed (see section 5.3). The following extract illustrates how rhetorical analysis was used in this study:

> '**The texts achieve their effect by altering linguistic meanings and relationships in ways that reshape ExxonMobil's own and other actors' identities. 'Prudence' and 'responsibility' (and their implied opposites) are moral terms used in the ads rhetorically to characterize/construct the agents (scientists, economists, environmentalists, government regulators, energy suppliers and consumers), acts (government regulation, production of energy-efficient fuels), and agencies (science and technology, climate science, economics, public policy) variously interposed in the dramatic scene.**'

For example, an advertorial entitled 'Do no harm', published on 16 March 2000, begins by seeking to undermine scientific evidence on the potential 'harm' associated with climate change. This is achieved by comparing 'different views of the climate change debate' with weather forecasts that are constantly being changed. It argues that there is no proven link between the activities of the company and harm to the environment, then switches to economics, in order to argue that any proposed change in business practices would impose costs and therefore threaten to 'harm' the 'health' of the economy. 'ExxonMobil's argument here produces the conclusion that the problem is not global warming, but the wrong-headed, if not arrogant, views of the climate scientists (and the misguided government representatives and public that trust them), who "believe they can predict changes in climate decades from now"' (*ibid*: 128). 'Precaution,' a word that is usually associated with conservative and measured approaches, and in the climate change debate characterised by environmentalists as necessary to safeguard the 'health' of the planet, is re-interpreted as hasty, if not hysterical action, and an instrument of 'harm.' Rather than precaution, the company calls for a prudent approach, saying: 'a prudent approach to the climate issue must recognize that there is not enough information to justify harming economies and forcing the world's population to endure unwarranted lifestyle changes by dramatically reducing the use of energy now.' (*ibid*: 128–9).

Both of the above studies take a critical approach to the ways that individuals and organisations exploit language, in order to pursue their sectional interests. Narrative studies can provide valuable insights into these processes. In particular, they can help us to grasp the complex challenges that confront organisational stakeholders, as they seek to convey their own messages in the face of the competing 'stories' of other actors. We return to this theme in Chapter 5, which tackles aspects of persuasive communication, including the use of verbal and non-verbal codes.

Summary

- In general, organisational communication is improved through the consistent use of plain and unambiguous language.
- The basic principles of plain English are: use fewer words, use shorter words and use pictures in place of words, where appropriate.
- Editing and summarising text is a key management skill. It involves the removal of redundant words, replacing of long-winded expressions and writing in the 'active' form.
- Plain English means avoiding words and phrases that have lost their meaning, euphemisms that deliberately disguise meaning, and technical terminology, or 'jargon' that is not readily understood by the relevant audience.

- Correct use of grammar, spelling and punctuation is also an important discipline that can reduce the scope for misunderstanding and increase the speed of communication.

- The widespread use of the English language has created a great deal of colour and variety. However, it is important to use local idiomatic expressions with a combination of sensitivity and imagination, ensuring that they are appropriate to the audience.

- In spoken English, communicators also need to be aware of the ways that emphasis on particular words and 'paralinguistics' (e.g. the use of eye contact and facial expression) can influence the interpretation of verbal messages.

- Language is both a medium of communication and a framework for understanding human experience; techniques such as discourse analysis can be used to deconstruct narratives, revealing their constitutive role (i.e. in establishing shared meanings).

Practical exercises

1 Drafting simple instructions

(a) Prepare a draft set of written instructions for someone carrying out one of the following tasks for the *first* time:

- prepare, cook and serve a cheese and mushroom omelette;

- withdraw £50 from a 'cash-point' machine;

- deal with a punctured cycle or car tyre.

(b) Ask someone to test your instructions, and to point out any faults or ambiguities.

(c) Re-draft the instructions to make them clearer and more concise. Use a red pen to mark the changes on the old draft, then write out your revised version on a separate sheet. Compare your final draft with the original.

2 Jargon-busting

(a) Prepare a list of the 'Top Ten' worst examples of jargon in one of the following fields, or in your own specialist area, presenting them in a poster format: Accountancy, Business, Medicine, Computing, Economics, Engineering, Finance, Law, Marketing, Personnel, Purchasing, Sales.

(b) For each jargon word or expression, suggest a sensible alternative that can be understood by a non-specialist. Did you find any jargon words that do not have any 'layperson's' equivalent?

(c) Consider how the problem of jargon and other specialist terminology may be complicated by factors such as translation and cultural difference. How might you overcome these difficulties in an international organisation?

Case-study C

'Story-telling' – researching organisational narratives

The nature of stories

Oral histories, captured in the form of myths and legends, have long been used to store the collective knowledge of tribes and nations. They allowed knowledge to be passed down between generations, before reading and writing became a widespread channel of communication. A story is often a simple tale of how a character desires something – a promotion, for example – meets a difficulty, and struggles to overcome it, using internal resources, such as persistence, luck, or outside help. Human interest arises from the ensuing struggle between a desired outcome and reality (McKee 2003). The management writer, Boje (1991: 111) has defined a story as, 'an oral or written performance involving two or more people interpreting past or anticipated experience.' This definition highlights the active role of the receiver, who reads or listens to the story. Good story-tellers employ various techniques to interact with the receiver, increasing their motivation and enjoyment. For this reason, it is generally more effective for stories to be told face-to-face, rather than through indirect channels, such as e-mail. A 'good' story is an accessible and immersive experience that can exclude other thoughts in the mind of the receiver (Denning 2000). Stories are more vivid, engaging and entertaining than most types of organisational communication, such as formal policy documents, memos or statistical reports (Swap *et al.* 2001). For this reason, they can be used to communicate more memorable and persuasive messages (Morgan and Dennehy 1997). An often-overlooked characteristic of stories is that the 'truth' lies in the meaning that they convey to the receiver, rather than in the accuracy of the events that are portrayed (Gabriel 2000).

How stories are used in organisations

In some fields, like journalism, education and sales, stories have an especially significant role. However, stories are told and passed on in organisations of all kinds. People are natural story-tellers, and the stories they tell help employees to give meaning to their work. Management educators and writers also use stories, adapting old myths for inspiration or drafting case studies to communicate practical examples (Greco 1996). Most of the stories found in business settings are relatively short, taking less than five minutes to tell (Boje 1991, Swap *et al.* 2001), yet these short stories can still be effective. For example, they can be the turning point in a long meeting, where people have been considering large amounts of factual data and statistical charts. If someone says, 'I think that's similar to what Sally did when...', the quality of attention changes, as other members of the meeting engage with this narrative. In these situations, even if other people disagree with the point of the initial story, they are likely to respond with a story of their own (Cohen and Prusak 2001, Collinson and Mackenzie 1999, Greco 1996).

Stories from respected executives have become a preferred approach in teaching leadership effectiveness in many of today's companies (Ready 2002). They can be useful in explaining how the political process works in an organisation, and to pass on tacit knowledge. Stories are used in training courses in organisations to improve the recall of the message (Snowden 2001), and as a more relaxing alternative to traditional exercises such as ice-breakers and role-plays (Parkin 1998). They can also be used to establish social norms and values in an organisation, as the following example illustrates:

Bill Hewlett used to work for General Electric (GE) and observed that the company had lots of security systems to protect their materials and equipment. Many employees felt that this showed that GE did not trust them. Some people wanted to teach GE a lesson, so they stole from the company, despite the security systems. Later, after starting his own company, Bill Hewlett once discovered a locked store cupboard at one of his own factories. He broke it open using a bolt-cutter, and left a note saying, 'don't ever lock this door again'. As the story was repeated around the company, it had the effect of reinforcing more general levels of trust between managers and employees (cited in Dennehy 1999).

The next story also conveys organisational values, but with more threatening or negative connotations:

Ryan was a senior manager who had two fishbowls in his office. In one were goldfish, in the other, a piranha. Ryan asked each of his staff to pick a goldfish that was most like themselves (spotted, dark, etc.). Then, when Ryan was displeased with someone, he would ask the person to take his or her goldfish and feed it to the piranha (cited in Frost 2003).

Most current stories are negative or neutral about the organisation, while positive ones tend to refer to the past (Gabriel 2000). Some researchers have argued that 'good' stories, whether positive or negative, are more believable than bad ones (Taylor et al. 2002). The implication of this idea, that a skilled story-teller can manage the meaning of events in an organisation, is exploited in various forms of persuasive communication, from sales to public relations. However, it also suggests that less powerful actors in an organisation – as well as external stakeholders, such as community groups – can gain additional power by telling of a good story well. Consider the following examples of positive and negative stories, their sources and their effects on various audiences:

UPS is an international parcels delivery company, based in the US. There are many stories circulating within the company concerning drivers who have delivered parcels no matter what the weather. Similar messages were also presented in the company's public advertising campaigns. The stories had a strong human element. For example, in one case an eight-month pregnant manager was said to have covered for another employee in order to ensure that the deliveries were made on time (cited in Cohen and Prusak 2001).

The Union Pacific railroad company is also based in the US. During the 1990s, various stories circulated amongst employees and customers relating to the company being unreliable. Employees had started to call it the 'Utterly Pathetic' railroad. Some stories had a dark humour, which added to their effectiveness. For example, it was said that a locomotive engineer got so fed up with the railroad's incompetence that he decided to commit suicide. He went outside, lay on the tracks – and starved to death (cited in Coutu 2003).

The implication is that, given their power and potential consequences, managers should take an interest in the kinds of stories that are being told in their organisation. They might also consider how best to influence these stories, though it is likely that heavy-handed intervention will prove counter-productive, encouraging a further outbreak of 'anti-stories'. The final story in this case was presented in a paper by the organisational researcher, Karl Weick (1996). It is based on real events, concerning a 'Wildlands' (i.e. forest) fire-fighters. Read this re-interpretation of the story then answer the questions below:

> Bob was a strong, experienced fire-fighter, working in the Wildlands. He had fought many different types of fire in ten years, and felt he had seen it all. One hot summer's day, he was fighting a fire with a new recruit called Jim. The two men worked hard, sweat streaming down their faces, their vision obscured by the smoke, and their mouths dry with the heat. Despite their efforts, the fire grew more intense. Jim lost his nerve, dropped his spade and backpack, and ran for safety. Bob called after him that the fire was nearly under control. A nearby tree exploded with a crash, and the wind blew flames towards Bob, nearly cutting him off. Bob turned and ran, still carrying his gear. Strong as he was, the equipment slowed him down in the dense undergrowth, and the fire caught up with him. He was trapped, and died of his injuries. (Note: Adapted from Weick 1996.)

Questions

1 Reflect on your reactions to the story (e.g. What pictures came into your head as your read it?; Could you hear the characters talking?; What feelings did you experience?) and consider what aspects of the story prompted these reactions.

2 What do you think is the basic message of the story?

3 How else could the message have been conveyed?

4 In what circumstances do you think that telling the story would be more suitable or effective than the other methods?

5 Do you think that managers should be trained to tell stories? Give your reasons.

6 Try to identify five examples of how stories could be used effectively in an organisation.

Source: Written by Ian Wychertey.

Further reading

Crystal (2003b), McCrum *et al.* (1992) and Bryson (1991) are informative and often entertaining tours of the English language, its history and development around the world. Crystal (2003a) is a comprehensive reference; there are also many helpful guides to writing style, such as: Economist (2001), Urdang (1991) and Inman (1994). Lodge (1988) is a comic novel, written by a professor of English literature, which explores the communication problems between an academic and a factory manager, due to the different language that each employs. Boje (2001) and Gabriel (2000) are academic overviews of current approaches to studying narratives and storytelling in organisations; Tietze *et al.* (2003) is an accessible introduction. Denning (2000), Swap *et al.* (2001), McKee (2003) and Snowden (2001) discuss practical applications of storytelling in knowledge creation and other areas of communication.

References

Boje, D.M. (1991). 'The storytelling organization: a study of story performance in an office supply firm'. *Administrative Science Quarterly*, 36, 106–26.

Boje, D.M. (2001) *Narrative methods for organizational and communication research*. Sage, London.

Boje, D.M., Luhman, J.T. and Baack, D.E. (1999) 'Hegemonic stories and encounters between storytelling organizations'. *Journal of Management Inquiry*, 8, 340–60.

Bryson, B. (1991) *Mother tongue*. Penguin, London.

Cohen, D. and Prusak, L. (2001) *In good company: how social capital makes organizations work*. Harvard Business School Press, Harvard MA.

Collinson, C. and Mackenzie, A. (1999). 'The power of story in organisations'. *Journal of Workplace Learning*, 11, 1, 38–40.

Coutu, D.L. (2003). 'Sense and reliability: a conversation with celebrated psychologist Karl E. Weick'. *Harvard Business Review*, 81, 84–9 (April).

Crystal, D. (2003a) *The Cambridge encyclopedia of the English language* (2nd edn.). Cambridge University Press, Cambridge.

Crystal, D. (2003b) *English as a global language* (2nd edn.). Cambridge University Press, Cambridge.

Dennehy, R.F. (1999) 'The executive as storyteller'. *Management Review*, 40–3 (March).

Denning, S. (2000) *The springboard : how storytelling ignites action in knowledge-era organizations*. Butterworth-Heinemann, Oxford.

Economist, The (2001) *The Economist style guide*. Profile Books, London.

Frost, P.J. (2003) *Toxic emotions at work*. Harvard Business School Press, Boston MA.

Gabriel, Y. (2000) *Storytelling in organisations: facts, fictions and fantasies*. Oxford University Press, Oxford.

Greco, J. (1996) 'Stories for executive development: An isotonic solution'. *Journal of Organisational Change Management*, 9, 5, 43–74.

Howard, P. (1988) *Winged words*. Hamish Hamilton, London.

Inman, C. (1994) *The Financial Times style guide*. FT Pitman, London.

Jenkins, R. (2001) *Churchill*. Macmillan, London.

Livesey, S.M. (2002a) 'Interpretive acts: new vistas in qualitative research in business communication. A guest editorial'. *Journal of Business Communication*, 39, 1, 6–11.

Livesey, S.M. (2002b) 'Global warming wars: rhetorical and discourse analytic approaches to ExxonMobil's corporate public relations'. *Journal of Business Communication*, 39, 1, 117–48.

Lodge, D. (1988) *Nice work*. Penguin Books, London.

McCrum, R., Cran, W. and MacNeil, R. (1992) *The story of English* (new and revised edn.). Faber and Faber, London.

McKee, R. (2003) 'Storytelling that moves people'. *Harvard Business Review*, 81, 51–5 (June).

Morgan, S. and Dennehy, R.F. (1997) 'The power of organizational storytelling: a management development perspective'. *Journal of Management Development*, 16, 7, 494–501.

Mushinga, E. (2003) Personal correspondence.

Ng, W. and De Cock, C. (2002) 'Battle in the boardroom: a discursive perspective'. *Journal of Management Studies*, 39, 1, 23–49.

Orwell, G. (1950) *Shooting an Elephant and Other Essays*. Secker and Warburg, London.

Parkin, M. (1998) *Tales for trainers*. Kogan Page, London.

Pentland, B.T. (1999) 'Building process theory with narrative: from description to explanation'. *Academy of Management Review*, 24, 4, 711–24.

Plain English Campaign (2003) 'About the Campaign'. Plain English Campaign, New Mills [available at www.plainenglish.co.uk (accessed 16th July)].

Ready, D.A. (2002). 'How storytelling builds next-generation leaders'. *MIT Sloan Management Review*, 63–9 (Summer).

Saunders, M.N.K., Lewis, P. and Thornhill, A. (2003) *Research methods for business students* (3rd edn.). FT Prentice Hall, Harlow.

Snowden, D.J. (2001) 'Story telling as a strategic communication tool'. *Strategic Communication Management*, 28–31 (April/May).

Swap, W., Leonard, D., Shields, M. and Abrams, L. (2001). 'Using mentoring and storytelling to transfer knowledge in the workplace'. *Journal of Management Information Systems*, 18, 1, 95–114.

Taylor, S.S., Fisher, D. and Dufresne, R.L. (2002). 'The aesthetics of management storytelling'. *Management Learning*, 33, 3, 313–30.

Tietze. S., Cohen, L. and Musson, G. (2003) *Understanding organizations through language*. Sage, London.

Urdang, L. (1991) *The Oxford thesaurus: an A-Z dictionary of synonyms*. Oxford University Press, Oxford.

Usnier, J-C. (1998) *International and cross-cultural management research*. Sage, London.

Weick, K.E. (1996) 'Drop your tools: an allegory for organizational studies'. *Administrative Science Quarterly*, 41, 2, 301–13.

CHAPTER 4

Making pictures: non-verbal communication

'What is the use of a book', thought Alice, *'without pictures or conversations?'*
Lewis Carroll, *Alice in Wonderland* (Chapter 1)

4.1 Introduction

Organisations make use of a wide variety of non-verbal forms of communication. Most, though not all, involve encoding a message in some kind of visual image, hence the title of this chapter. However, the 'pictures' that are reviewed in the following section are not limited to those embedded in material artefacts, such as charts in a business report or photographs on a website. We are also concerned with the visual signals that people exchange, often unconsciously, as part of their everyday inter-personal communication: for example, the gestures and body language that reinforce our words, or simply express our state of mind, in meetings and presentations. Non-verbal signals can have a powerful effect. For example, a well-designed reception area and smiling, smartly-dressed staff are likely to have a positive influence on a prospective customer, reinforcing verbal statements about 'professionalism' and 'customer service', that have been made in the company's promotional literature. By contrast, a recruitment interview panel may be unable to avoid a negative assessment of an interviewee, due to factors such as physical appearance and eye contact, irrespective of the verbal communication that is taking place in the interview room. Our purpose, in drawing this wide variety of images together, is to provide the basis for a general discussion regarding the role and importance of non-verbal communication in organisations, and the ways that non-verbal coding interacts with written and spoken forms. We explore the potential advantages and the most common problem areas, highlighting some of the ways that these difficulties can be avoided or overcome. Several of the themes are elaborated in later chapters, including a short section on the special problems of creating and maintaining a visual identity for your organisation, which is expanded in Chapter 10.

4.2 Using 'pictures' at work

In some situations, visual images can replace written or spoken words entirely. Their role in these cases is often to overcome context-specific barriers to communication, and the substitute images have been developed to meet the needs of the environment in which they are used. For example, traders on traditional commodities exchanges and bookmakers at racetracks overcome the twin problems of noise and distance with elaborate hand signals that instantly communicate information relating to market prices. International organisations have also overcome barriers in the use of written language by replacing text with pictures. For example, in airport terminals, signs indicating facilities such as restaurants and exits are universally recognised, conveying simple messages without words. Standardised signs, or 'icons', have also been adopted in computer software programs, allowing them to be used worldwide (see Figure 4.1).

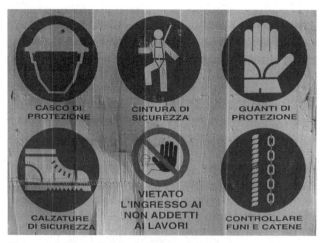

Figure 4.1 **International signs and icons**

The other main function of visual images, in organisations as in other areas of life, is to reinforce written or spoken words. This reinforcement occurs in many different ways, for example:

- A skilled conference speaker uses an outstretched arms gesture to make the audience feel more directly involved in the presentation.
- A finance director giving a presentation to City analysts uses bar graphs and pie charts to display the raw data from a complex profit forecast in a clearer and more attractive way.
- A brochure-designer searches photographic libraries to find a suitable image to support the central messages that appear in the text of an organisation's annual report.

Table 4.1 indicates something of the variety of forms in which people communicate without the direct use of written or spoken words. Specialist researchers in this field have introduced various terms to describe these activities. For example, the word 'kinesics' is sometimes used to refer to various forms of body language, including eye contact, facial expression, posture and gesture, while 'proxemics' refers to the role that personal distance and physical space plays in communication (see section 4.7). In addition, the field of 'paralinguistics', introduced in the previous chapter, refers to the different ways that spoken language is modified by the actions that surround it, including the pace of delivery, tone of voice and use of silence (see section 3.5). However, it is important to note that any categorisation into different 'types' is necessarily artificial, since it does not reflect the 'holistic' reality of organisational communication (see section 1.6). In practice, messages are often communicated through a rich, flexible and simultaneous combination of verbal and non-verbal forms. Consider the kinds of messages that are being sent, consciously or unconsciously, in each of the following examples. Is the meaning clear and unambiguous in each case? To what extent are the messages under the control of the sender? What other factors might intervene to influence the receiver's interpretation of these non-verbal signals?

Table 4.1 Categorising non-verbal communication: some practical examples

Human (primarily visual	Practical examples
Eye contact	Interviewee does not look at interviewer while speaking.
Facial expression	Negotiator smiles at representative of other party.
Gesture	Chief executive folds arms during press briefing.
Posture	Members of a team lean forward during discussions around a table.
Personal distance and touch	Manager puts arm around employees' shoulders.
Personal appearance	Web design consultant arrives at company offices in casual clothes.
Manufactured (primarily visual)	**Practical examples**
Signs and symbols	Corporate logo is redesigned following acquisition.
Representational images	Photographs of all employees placed on corporate intranet.
Physical appearance and space	Offices re-painted in bright colours, with open-plan layout.
Use of other senses	**Practical examples**
Hearing	World music played by retail call centre as customers wait for service.
Smell	Hospital uses essential oils to counter smell of disinfectant.
Touch	Company selects thick embossed card covers for promotional brochure.

4.3 Potential benefits of non-verbal communication

The potential benefits of non-verbal forms of communication are most obvious on those occasions when people are forced to rely too heavily on bare words. For example, there are times when e-mail exchanges are inadequate, and it becomes essential for sender and receiver to meet face-to-face, or at least to gain some additional paralinguistic richness through a telephone conversation. 'Pictures' can be quickly assimilated. They can also help to simplify an otherwise complex message, attract the attention of an audience, motivate them to act, and help them to retain a message, once the original stimulus has gone.

Rapid communication of messages

People are all very adept at 'speed reading' visual messages. If you ask someone a question, for example, their facial expressions (e.g. a smile, raised eyebrows or a grimace), can communicate the answer instantaneously, and long before the spoken reply. The more subtle human signs can only be detected in face-to-face settings, but some can be employed in technologically-mediated forms of communication, such as video conferencing, with the prospect of further applications as the quality of visual imaging is enhanced. Manufactured signs, such as those used on roads and motorways, also have the capacity to convey essential information quickly and easily.

Simplification of complex messages

There is a general requirement in organisations to simplify messages, so that they can be readily understood by non-specialists, and by people who do not have sufficient time to absorb a detailed verbal explanation. For example, the key findings of a research study may be displayed as bar charts, pie charts, cluster plots, etc., enabling an audience to *visualise* the information (see section 4.5). Flow diagrams can be used to summarise a manufacturing process, or to explain how a piece of furniture is assembled, without the use of extended verbal descriptions. For example, the dynamic Swedish furniture retailer IKEA has many years' experience in designing multi-language instruction leaflets for its 'flat pack', home-assembly products. IKEA leaflets are based on simple line drawings in a numbered sequence. The easily understood instructions, combined with good basic product design and manufacture, ensure that the same instructions can be readily understood by the company's customers, whether they are French, Czech, Italian or British. Graphics can also be used to explain relationships and actions that would be difficult to convey in text or spoken words, due to their linear and sequential form (Sayer 2000: 149). For example, an organisational structure chart is used to describe a configuration, rather than a sequence of events; it would be very tedious and confusing to present this kind of information verbally.

Securing audience attention

A striking image can make us stop and look, exploiting 'phasic alertness' (see section 2.3). For example, Figure 4.2 is likely to have been one of the first things you noticed on turning this page. Dramatic or unexpected images can be used in many situations, including newspapers, advertisements, brochures, presentations and exhibition stands. Consider, for example, how an advertising agency might convey the following unpalatable message to an audience of young adults:

> **'Though you are young now, you will need financial support in your old age. It is therefore time to start thinking about a pension.'**

In this case, the message was conveyed as part of a television advertising campaign for a pensions provider. The agency created a storyline involving an elderly man who attempted to dress and act like a teenager. It became evident that the man was engaged in a very belated attempt to enrol himself on a pension plan. The imagery was powerful, combining visual 'humour' with a sobering reminder to its intended audience that they too must start to face the realities of financing their retirement. However, in a world that is increasingly saturated with strong visual images, organisations have to work ever harder to secure the attention of their audience. This often involves differing judgements. For example, in 2003, the children's charity Barnardos, launched a fund-raising and awareness campaign that included photos of a baby with a cockroach and syringe in its mouth. These powerful and provocative photos prompted complaints by the public and were withdrawn.

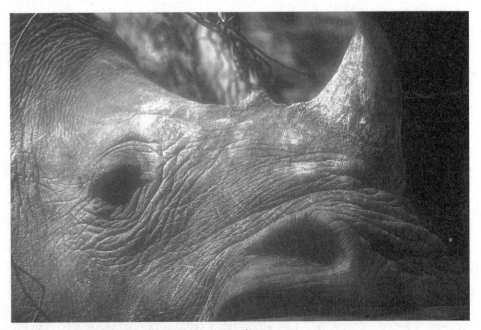

Figure 4.2 **Visual images can attract attention**

Persuading and motivating

As we have already noted, non-verbal signals can reinforce a verbal message, adding to its persuasive power. For instance, the small business manager at a bank is likely to give your financing request a more sympathetic hearing if you arrive smartly-dressed, rather than in a scruffy jumper and torn jeans. In the same way, an attractively packaged product or service can encourage repeat purchases, especially if its appearance is consistent with the prospective buyer's own values and self-image. Of course, negative images, such as a pile of rubbish outside an expensive restaurant, will have the opposite effect – particularly if the visual stimulus is accompanied by an unpleasant smell. (Note: The role of images as persuaders is considered in more detail in Chapter 5.)

Making messages memorable

Lastly, non-verbal signals can help to get your message into a receiver's short- or long-term memory (see section 2.3). Some of these 'pictures' remain potent over many years. For example, in the late twentieth century, the computer company IBM was using the image of the pioneering cinema comedian, Charlie Chaplin, in its advertising campaigns. Other visual symbols, such as those associated with the major world religions, are even more enduring. Corporate and product advertising makes extensive use of visual 'hooks' to establish and build brand awareness and longer-term reputation. Repeated exposure to a strong image will increase the likelihood that the target audience will retain the connected messages. For this reason, organisations need to pay particular attention to aspects of their visual identity, ranging from trade marks and corporate logos to the face of a key spokesperson (see section 4.6).

Mini-case 4.1 reviews the recent evolution of a visual identity and the messages that it seeks to convey. It concerns a certification mark, which is being used to endorse fairly-traded products across Europe.

Mini-case 4.1	The Fairtrade Mark: Creating a European identity

Consumers in the North rely on many products, such as tea, coffee and chocolate, that are sourced from other parts of the world. These products have been exposed to large fluctuations in world commodities markets, and the producers – often including small farmers – have been unable to secure their livelihoods. Development agencies identified the role that consumers might play, if they were able to purchase products on a fairly traded basis. Inspection and audit ensures that producers meet agreed Fairtrade standards, which includes issues such as local participation and the reinvestment of Fairtrade premiums to improve social conditions or economic infrastructure.

In 1989, the Netherlands introduced the first Fairtrade label, 'Max Havelaar', which acted as a seal of approval for products bought from registered suppliers according to Fairtrade criteria. The first Fairtrade product in the UK was launched in 1994. At present, there are labelling initiatives in 17 countries, covering an expanding product range. The UK's original Mark consisted of two interlocked 'F's in upper case letters (i.e. facing one another, the right hand letter being inverted). A re-designed Mark, illustrated below, was introduced in 2002 as part of a harmonisation initiative across Europe. In May 2003, a MORI survey reported that 25 per cent of the UK population recognised the Fairtrade Mark. Understanding of this image had also increased, as measured by the number of respondents correctly associating the symbol with the strap-line, 'Guarantees a better deal for Third World Producers.' Brands carrying the Fairtrade Mark now account for 14 per cent of the UK's roast and ground coffee market.

In the UK, the Mark is certified by the Fairtrade Foundation, which issues detailed guidance on the certification process and the correct use of the Fairtrade Mark by users and licensees. For example, it specifies four ways in which the symbol and the qualifying statement (or 'strapline') can be presented, plus minimum sizes, accept-able colours and positioning on product packaging. In addition to the visual aspects, there are guidelines for copywriters, including the requirement that the expression 'Fairtrade' always be presented as a single word, with an upper case 'F' and lower-case 't'. The Foundation is part of an umbrella body, Fairtrade Labelling Organisations (FLO) International, which has the aim of establishing a single inter-national Fairtrade label. Additional details on the Fairtrade Foundation can be obtained at: www.fairtrade.org.uk. The Fairtrade Mark is illustrated below, in one of the four available variations:

Questions

1 Were you aware of the Fairtrade Mark, in supermarkets, other food retail outlets, or high-street coffee chains such as Costa Coffee or Starbucks?

2 How would you assess the effectiveness of the Mark, based on the potential benefits outlined in the previous section?

3 The inverted 'F' mark was a simple but effective visual device. What do you think were the arguments for replacing it with the present symbol?

4 Can you identify any potential challenges for the Fairtrade Mark, as it is extended into new product areas (e.g. clothing) and geographic markets?

Source: Fairtrade Foundation (2003) and the author.

4.4 Potential problems with visual media

In Chapter 3, we saw how inappropriate use of language is a source of problems for individuals and organisations. This section considers how non-verbal signals can also generate unintended and problematic results. There are three potential sources of difficulty. First, a particular 'picture' may not be consistent with other aspects of the message that is being sent. Second, it may not be suitable for the receiver that the sender is trying to reach. Third, its meaning may be altered according to the context in which it is being received. People often spend excessive amounts of time on the words and numbers that are encoded in their messages, but ignore or under-emphasise the non-verbal element. As a result, receivers' negative interpretations of the associated 'pictures' may undermine the effectiveness of the delivered message. Technological improvements in digital imaging, graphics software and colour printing have made it easier to integrate relatively sophisticated images into estab-lished communication channels, such as reports and presentations. However, these tools have created their own problems, as the task of design has transferred from technical specialists, such as graphic designers, to untrained and often inexperi-enced people. The following points cover some of the more common pitfalls, when we make use of 'pictures' in both their human and manufactured forms.

Inconsistency

Non-verbal communication can be a source of two types of inconsistency, which can reduce the effectiveness of the central message by confusing, and probably alienating, receivers. First, the non-verbal signals may not correspond to other forms of encoding, such as spoken or written words: for example, if a welcome message from an unsmiling hotel receptionist will be interpreted, perhaps cor-rectly, as superficial and insincere. Similarly a human resource department report or presentation, promoting health and safety issues will be undermined if the authors inadvertently include old photographs showing scrap materials blocking a factory gangway or workers not wearing protective clothing. In both cases, the inconsistencies may not be apparent to the sender. However, they can have a powerful effect on those receiving the combined message.

The second inconsistency is between the visual signal and the 'reality' that it is supposed to represent. Hence, even if the receptionist is smiling when wel-coming the hotel guest, the facial expression may not be effective without substantiation, such as previous evidence of good customer service at this hotel. In the case of manufactured images, media researchers have pointed to the greater 'visual literacy' or sophistication of contemporary audiences. The idea is that, because people are routinely exposed to so many highly-processed images, they have become sceptical about their value (Klein 2000: 279–310). For example, in the late twentieth century, holiday brochures became notorious for their use of misleading photography, which gave a false impression of hotels and resorts; consumers became wary of these 'glossy' images, so that their use became counter-productive. Charts, maps and diagrams can also misrepresent their source data in various ways (see section 4.5).

Inherent unsuitability

Some 'pictures' are simply unsuitable for their intended purpose. For example, it is difficult to imagine how a dishevelled physical appearance would enhance a message within an organisation, except perhaps where the sender is trying to demonstrate that they have been working all night to complete a piece of work. One of the most common failings in representational images, such as photography and video, is the use of over-familiar or clichéd material. For example, almost every university prospectus includes pictures of tutors pointing earnestly at computer screens and of newly-graduated students throwing their hats in the air. Because they are so over-used, these images are less likely to attract attention. They can also send unintended messages to their audience. For example, an annual report that is full of 'stock' pictures of factory sites and smiling workers might convey an impression of the organisation as old-fashioned and uncreative. Stereotypical images, including many popular representations of women, children, people with disabilities and people from less-developed countries have also been subject to criticism. Organisations, including charities and campaign groups, need to pay attention to the implied messages that these images convey.

Context-related meaning

The meaning of 'pictures' can vary between contexts and over time, in much the same way as it does with words (see section 3.4). However, in the case of non-verbal communication, there is arguably an even greater potential for differences in interpretation, particularly in relation to human signals, such as gesture and eye contact. Consider, for example, the different implications of physical proximity between passengers standing in a crowded train, a group of friends celebrating at a party and two strangers involved in an verbal argument. These differences are further complicated by cultural factors. We are aware, from research and anecdotal observation, that regional and national cultures have generated contrasting approaches to common human signals, including the role of eye contact, the conventional meaning of particular gestures and the appropriateness of touching other people during a meeting or conversation (see section 4.7). These differences extend to the interpretation of manufactured images, including photographs, drawings and even physical artefacts like ceramics (Moeran 1997).

Consider the following situation. You are sitting in a presentation on the subject of marketing strategy in an international consulting firm. The presenter decides to 'liven up' one of the slides by adding the image of a military jet firing air-to-surface missiles. The accompanying text reads, 'Striking our target market' (see Figure 4.3). An illustration of this kind will have varying effects, depending on the background and nature of each member of the audience. For example, people with an interest in aircraft may simply try to identify the plane, those involved in recent anti-war campaigns will find the imagery offensive, while anyone unfortunate enough to have experienced a real bombing raid will be drawn into unpleasant recollections of past events. The implication is that communicators need to take care in their use of manufactured images, always considering how receivers might interpret them.

Striking our target market!

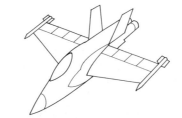

• How do we increase the IMPACT of our
multimedia promotional campaign?

Figure 4.3 **Striking our target market**

4.5 The use and abuse of graphical data

Graphs and charts can be very effective ways to encode numerical information. However, it is easy to confuse an audience by selecting the wrong type of graphical image to represent your data, or by constructing an image incorrectly (Tufte 1990). Furthermore, research suggests that incorrectly designed graphics can influence the receiver's decision making, raising a number of broader policy issues (Tufte 1997; Arunachalam *et al.* 2002). This section reviews a few of the more popular types of graphs and charts, noting some of the ways that they can be used and abused.

Pie charts

Pie charts are used to show the relative size of different items making up a total. For example, the breakdown of quarterly sales by region, or audience figures by age group. Conventionally, the largest segment is placed at the 'top' of the pie, with other segments following in a clockwise direction. Each segment should be labelled, normally with figures indicating the value and percentage share.

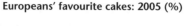

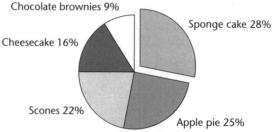

Figure 4.4 **Pie chart with exploded segment**

The overall total should also be stated. This usually takes the form of a separate label inserted below the graphic. If there is a requirement to emphasise a particular segment, it may be 'exploded' (see Figure 4.4). Problems may arise when there are too many segments, making the graphic unclear. In these situations, it may be possible to aggregate some of the data into larger segments, so simplifying the graphical presentation. Component bar charts offer an alternative method of displaying this kind of data.

Bar charts

Bar charts are also used to compare the values of different items. They can be presented in either vertical or horizontal formats. The major advantage of bar charts over pie charts is that individual values can be easily read off against a scale, which should always be inserted on the appropriate axis. Bar charts are normally drawn with separated bars of equal width. Because each bar represents discrete data, it should not be linked to other bars using a line. More complex data can be presented using either multiple or component bar charts (see Figure 4.5). In all cases, it is important to avoid distorting the data by introducing a 'false zero' in the vertical axis. The scale should run from zero, but in some cases (e.g. in order to highlight particular changes), the scale is broken. If this is done, it becomes essential to indicate the break clearly, to ensure that the reader interprets the data correctly. The convention is to mark the break with two 'zig-zag' lines through the axis.

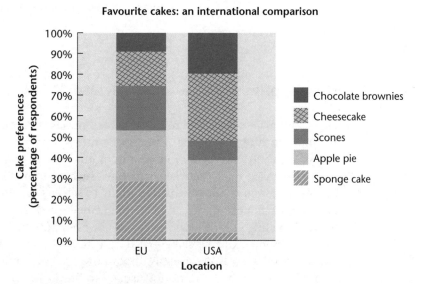

Figure 4.5 **A component bar chart**

Histograms

Histograms are sometimes confused with bar charts, but they can be differentiated according to the types of data they represent. Histograms are used for *continuous* data sets, such as a frequency distribution showing mortality rates by age of population. Bar charts are for *discrete* or *non-continuous* data, such as a comparison of mortality rates in five different countries. Histograms should be drawn with the bars touching, reflecting the continuous nature of their source data (see Figure 4.6). If there are large intervals in the data with low values, these can be combined to create some bars that are wider than others. In a histogram, the overall trend is sometimes shown by linking the tops of each bar with a curved line, or by superimposing a moving average.

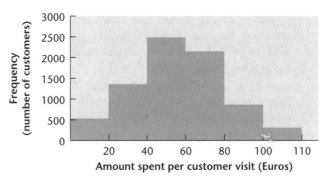

Figure 4.6 **A histogram**

Line graphs

Line graphs are often used to present continuous data, including various kinds of time series (e.g. tracking inflation or unemployment rates over the last 30 years). Typically, two or more lines are plotted on the same graph, so that comparisons can be made between variables, such as trends in personal disposable income and house prices. It is important to select suitable scales, line types and labelling so that each line can be distinguished (see Figure 4.7). It is also possible to combine line graphs with histograms or even bar charts; different data values can be presented on the same graph by using two scales on the left- and right-hand vertical axes. However, it is important to avoid overloading the graph with information. The better option is usually to break the data down into a number of simpler graphs, with suitable explanatory text.

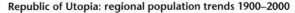
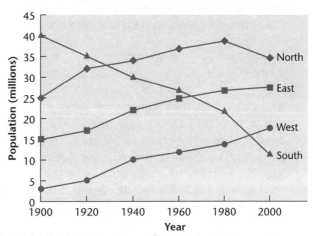

Figure 4.7 **A multiple line graph**

Pictograms

Pictograms are based on the idea that data may be more appealing and informative if it is turned into a representative image. For example, a breakdown of the number of employees in different parts of an organisation may be illustrated using a picture made up of 'matchstick' people, each of which represents 100 employees. The most common pitfall associated with pictograms is the misrepresentation of quantities. The main source of distortion is a lack of clarity over the scale, which may be one dimensional, like the linear scales used in graphs and bar chart, but can also take a two-dimensional form. For example, imagine that the finance director of a housing association wants to show that the average market price of houses has doubled between 1995 and 2005. The person preparing her presentation draws two houses, one twice the height of the other. The finance director rejects this pictogram, arguing that it distorts the argument. Why? Because it implies that house prices have quadrupled, since the *area* taken

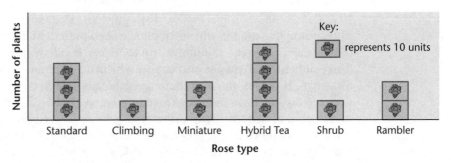

Figure 4.8 **A simple pictogram**

up by the 2005 house is four times that representing prices in 1995. At their simplest, pictograms may be little more than an elaborate version of more conventional graphics, such as a bar chart (see Figure 4.8).

Maps

Maps can be used to represent all kinds of data that have a spatial or geographic dimension. For example, regional differences in sales revenues, average household income, crime rates or number of business start-ups are often indicated by colouring or shading the relevant national or administrative boundaries (see Figure 4.9). However, maps can also be misleading. This is because the relative *size* of the areas shaded is usually unrelated to the data that is being displayed. For example, parliamentary constituencies vary in size according to population density (i.e. rural constituencies are much larger than those in urban centres). A map that is coloured according to the political party holding each constituency would therefore tend to exaggerate the representation of those parties that were strongest in rural areas, while understating those associated with towns and cities.

Our sales in Europe: 2005

Figure 4.9 **A map illustrating regional data**

The illustrations used in this section have been presented in a straightforward two-dimensional format. Computer packages now offer a range of supposedly 'three-dimensional' graphs and charts, which may appear to make data look more attractive. However, most of these are generally 'blocked-out' versions of the traditional two-dimensional formats (e.g. a conventional line graph is transformed into a series of ribbons). The cosmetic benefits of blocked-out graphs and charts are usually outweighed by the problems of interpretation. The most obvious obstacle is that the lines and bars in 'three-dimensional' graphics cannot be lined up against the relevant scale. This makes it difficult to determine the relevant data values.

Mini-case 4.2 shows how graphics have been used in an effort to better inform people about local government spending. This is a particularly demanding communication challenge, given the range of abilities in the use of numbers and the level of public interest in the details of public sector financial statements.

| Mini-case 4.2 | Accounts and accountability: communicating financial information |

Local councils in the UK spend more than £78 billion (€117bn) per annum on a wide range of local services. As part of a wider effort to increase local accountability, and to encourage local communities to become more involved in civic activity, central government encouraged councils to make a greater effort to communicate their spending plans and past financial performance. The traditional communication channel used for this purpose is the highly formalised cycle of drafting and publishing financial statements, a process that is broadly comparable to that undertaken by public and private limited companies. Councils are under a strict legal obligation to prepare and publish a set of financial accounts each year. The accounts are intended to explain to local ratepayers, and any other interested individuals or groups, how the council has raised, spent and managed its financial resources over the previous 12 months.

In an effort to regulate these reports, the government and the professional accounting bodies have produced a set of guidelines that councils have to adhere to. This guidance specifies the information that must be included in the accounts and the methods to be used in calculating the relevant figures. Each set of accounts must contain the following items: an explanatory foreword; a statement that explains the accounting policies that have been used to prepare the accounts; the actual accounting information, presented in a standardised format; and notes that explain in more detail how the figures in the accounts have been arrived at. The detailed guidance is made available in a document, called the 'Code of practice on local authority accounting in the United Kingdom: a statement of recommended practice', which is published by a professional body, the Chartered Institute of Public Finance and Accountancy (CIPFA 2003). The CIPFA guidance seeks to ensure that all councils produce reports that present information in the same format and in the same individual statements. It also ensures that the published accounts of councils are comparable. This means that it should be possible for users to compare the level of spending of different councils in key areas (e.g. transportation, education or social services), because the relevant figures are disclosed in both sets of accounts, and are also calculated on the same basis.

Meeting the communication challenge
Although the CIPFA guidance serves a useful purpose, it does leave local councils facing some difficult communication issues. For example, the guidance does not indicate how councils should actually display the information that is included in their reports. Councils have to find their own ways to convey what is often quite complex financial information, to a number of different audiences with a wide range of needs and interests. Research indicates a wide variation in the performance of councils in producing clear and well-designed reports. In the worst examples, the accounts are simply presented as large tables of financial data, with very limited explanation and interpretation. By contrast, some of the best reports reflect a conscious effort to present these figures in a clear and understandable way, taking full account of the requirements of different stakeholder groups.

▶

Wychavon District Council provides services for approximately 47,000 households in the English county of Worcestershire. The extract reproduced below is from the Council's annual statement of accounts for 2002–2003. The table and bar chart show the council's main sources of income from taxes (on households and businesses), grants, fees and charges made for services and interest earned on money they have invested. Alongside the table and chart, the authors have included a brief narrative explanation of the figures and some related comments. The Wychavon report illustrates how one local council has made significant efforts to present accounting information in a clearer and more understandable way.

Where the money came from

The following table and chart provides an analysis of our main sources of income for the year and compares the position to the previous financial year.

Sources of income	2001/2002 £000's	2002/2003 £000's
1 Council Tax-Payers	4,020	4,125
2 Business Rates	4,218	4,768
3 Government Grants	16,807	18,032
4 Fees & Charges & Other	3,331	3,982
5 Interest	3,172	2,725
6 Collection Fund Surplus	41	0
	31,589	33,632

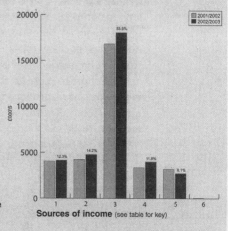

The government provides our main source of income in the form of specific and general grants. The government also determines the amount of business rates we receive. Our council tax income grew by only 2.5% in the year in line with our financial strategy. Overall, our income from fees and charges showed an increase of 20% due to an increased demand for chargeable services.

Source: Wychavon DC. Reproduced with permission.

Questions

1 What types of stakeholder do you think might be interested in the accounts of a local council? What problems might there be in communicating accounting information to each of these audiences?

2 Review the sample materials. Discuss the advantages and disadvantages of the council's chosen format, with its combination of graphs, tables and narrative.

3 Can you think of other ways to present the information shown in this example? How would your approach be affected if the information were being presented on a website, rather than as a printed document?

4 Companies also have to prepare accounts for a number of different stakeholder groups. Compare and contrast the challenges faced by companies and councils in communicating financial information.

Source: CIPFA (2003), Office of the Deputy Prime Minister (2003), Wychavon DC (2003). Case prepared by Dan Herbert, with acknowledgements to Fiona Narburgh and Sonia Rees.

4.6 Visual aspects of corporate identity: an introduction

The image of a 'start-up' or one-person business is closely associated with the individual who runs it. However, larger organisations inevitably become more impersonal. As a result, there have been concerted efforts to manage the corporate 'image', that is, the way that human organisations, ranging from businesses to entire countries, are perceived by their various audiences or 'publics' (Olins 2000). This is reflected in a corporate visual communication industry that is currently valued in excess of £2.1 billion in the UK alone (Donaldson and Eyre 2000). As organisations make changes in strategic direction, they find it necessary to review aspects of their visual identities. The most obvious visual elements open to managerial control are corporate symbols and logos. Some of these have very long associations (e.g. the simple red triangle, associated with UK-based brewing company, Bass, since the 18th century).

Shell, an Anglo-Dutch petrochemicals company, also has a long established visual identity. Shell's distinctive symbol, also represented in the company name, was the choice of its founder, Marcus Samuel. It is a reference to his father's previous business activities, which included trading seashells in mid-nineteenth century London. Organisations can also become associated with particular colours as a result of their historical development. For example, Shell's use of red in its colour scheme dates back to a tactical decision in the 1890s, when the company needed to differentiate its oil containers from the blue tins used by its international rival, Standard Oil (Yergin 1991: 63–70).

Many large corporations have undergone repeated changes of identity, reflecting shifts in strategic direction or a desire to escape previous associations. In the 1990s, several of the more celebrated corporate 'makeovers' have attracted criticism, due to the high costs involved and to the perception that some of the changes were superficial, making little difference to the organisation's current performance or future potential. It appears that the more excessive spending programmes have been curtailed, reflecting the difficult trading conditions of recent years. There have also been examples of organisations redeploying their visual communication budgets in a more emergent or 'bottom-up' manner, opening up new channels of communication with employees. For example, Donaldson and Eyre (2000) report on a culture change initiative at the UK's second largest electrical retailer, Comet, which made extensive use of video interviews with members of staff and customers across the country. This simple example demonstrates how visual communication can be used in radically different ways, in order to address strategic issues regarding corporate identity and the more fundamental question of corporate image; how organisations are perceived by their key stakeholders.

The theme of visual identity and its complex relationship with corporate strategy and image is developed in the case study at the end of this chapter. The implications for practice are explored as part of a broader discussion of corporate advertising (see sections 10.3 and 10.4) and public relations (see sections 10.5 and 10.6). In the next section, we return to the personal level and consider how individuals deploy visual signals, ranging from eye contact to physical appearance, to convey messages without necessarily making use of words.

4.7 Human signals: from eye contact to appearance

This section considers how human beings generate non-verbal signals, and the kinds of messages they convey. These 'human' signals are particularly evident in direct inter-personal communication, but many of them can also be conveyed through mediated communication channels, such as video recordings, photographs and even paintings. The received messages are often complicated by the fact that they are derived from a *combination* of intentional and unconscious non-verbal signs. Researchers have studied the ways that these signs are produced through: eye contact and behaviour ('oculesics'); facial expression, gesture and posture ('kinesics'); personal distance, use of space and touch ('proxemics'); and through the impression made by a person's physical appearance. In practice, senders are often unaware of how these combined non-verbal messages are being interpreted. Consequently, they may not recognise inconsistencies between these signs, their spoken words and any associated 'paralanguage' (see section 3.6). The potential for communication problems is further increased by the many different cultural conventions attached to the use of these non-verbal signals. The following categorisation illustrates the resulting challenges with some practical examples; you can probably add others from your own experience.

Eye contact and behaviour

Use of the human eye can have a powerful influence on inter-personal communication. For example, in most contemporary Western cultures, there is an automatic expectation that people engaged in a conversation will maintain a fairly constant degree of eye contact. While staring fixedly into the eyes of another person might be regarded as aggressive, looking away from their face during a conversation, even for a brief period, will generally be interpreted negatively. It signals either a lack of interest in the conversation that is taking place, or that the person averting their gaze is untrustworthy. This practice is in stark contrast to some cultural traditions, where withholding eye contact signals respect for the status of the person speaking. (Note: It seems likely that similarly deferential practices once existed in Western societies, reflecting more hierarchical forms of social organisation.) The influence of these conventions is highlighted in the way that we interpret video images of an interview. If the interviewee is unfamiliar with television, she may continue to look at the person asking questions off-camera, rather than looking into the lens. For viewers accustomed to the Western practices, the *apparent* lack of eye contact will stimulate negative connotations in much the same way as a 'face-to-face' interaction. Like the other non-verbal signals discussed in this section, national cultural differences attracted considerable interest from researchers, and result in 'self-help' literature to guide unwary travellers and international managers (e.g. Hall (1959), Hall and Hall (1990), Harris and Moran (1996)). The eye is also used in very subtle ways, often in conjunction with facial expressions, to convey various states of mind. These can also be conveyed in manufactured representations of the human face, including video images and photography.

Facial expression

Humans are capable of a great variety of facial expressions. As with other signalling systems, including human language, we learn these expressions from others and their inherent meanings are shared within cultural groups. There is mixed research evidence on the ability of those outside a culture to make a correct interpretation of its facial codes. Facial expressions are sometimes difficult to interpret, even within the bounds of a culture. Consider, for example, Leonardo da Vinci's celebrated portrait, *Mona Lisa* (circa 1502). Popular fascination with the mysterious 'smile' of this Florentine woman has been explained as resulting from the artist's deliberate efforts to leave the corners of her mouth and eyes indistinct, and therefore her mood open to interpretation (Gombrich 1978: 227–9). Some facial expressions are highly culture-specific. For example, raising an eyebrow has a sexual connotation in China, while smiling sometimes signals regret or embarrassment; the meanings of both signals contrast with those ascribed in other cultures, including those of the West (Dou and Clark 2002: 60). However, psychological studies have indicated a near-universal ability in recognising seven basic human emotions; anger, disgust, fear, happiness, sadness and contempt (Eckman 1992). There is also strong anecdotal evidence for this phenomenon in the countless images of faces from around the world that we see in newspapers, television programmes and other mass media. Furthermore, it seems likely that with repeated exposure to other cultures, through working in international organisations or viewing global mass media images, people do learn to make these interpretations.

Gesture and posture

Similar issues arise with respect to human gesture and other aspects of what is sometimes termed, 'body language', including the way people sit and stand in relation to one another. Gestures can act as useful 'shorthand', conveying a simple message rapidly and overcoming other obstacles, including language differences. For example, the 'thumbs up' and 'thumbs down' hand gesture may be used by workers on a noisy construction site or by tourists seeking confirmation that their hotel room is booked, or that they are taking the correct route. Problems can arise when culture-specific gestures are mis-interpreted; travellers' tales are full of examples where seemingly 'innocent' gestures convey a different, and sometimes offensive, message in another culture. Gesture and posture, like facial expression, can also have different meanings *within* a cultural group. For example, putting an arm around the shoulders of another person can indicate personal affection or solidarity. However, in some organisational contexts it suggests a power relationship (e.g. a senior manager may be permitted to make this gesture to a subordinate, but it would be considered 'inappropriate' if it was carried out the other way around). There are also close connections between the use of these signals and the ways that people position themselves in physical space.

Personal distance and touch

Cultural groups have different assumptions regarding the use of space between people and the appropriateness of physical contact during face-to-face communication (Hall and Hall 1990). Again, we can see that these norms are largely unconscious and highly context-dependent. For example, British people tend to retain a greater personal distance and engage in much less direct physical contact than their Italian or Spanish counterparts. However, these general conventions are superceded in certain situations, such as taking the elevator in an office building or travelling on the London Underground in the rush hour. In both situations, conventional rules on proximity are modified and close contact is tolerated, with the strict proviso that people avoid any form of eye contact. Again, if a person experiences what appears to be an unnecessary attempt to break with their established norms for proximity and touch, the resulting signals are largely negative. For example, if other people get 'too close' or become too tactile (e.g. repeatedly touching the receiver's arm while talking), they will be perceived as over-familiar, 'pushy' (i.e. using excessive persuasion), or aggressive. Similarly, people who are 'not close enough' or insufficiently tactile, according to the receiver's normal expectations, will be perceived as cold, untrustworthy or hostile. International communicators can also 'learn' and adapt to these differences, though some of the subtleties may be more difficult to overcome. For example, where one group has prior expectations of another, it may be disconcerting to find that behaviour has been adapted to local norms.

Physical appearance

Receivers may be influenced by various aspects of another person's appearance, from the state of their hair to the style of their shoes. We signal various messages by our (largely inherited) physical features, and more deliberate, 'manufactured' aspects of our appearance, such as clothing, jewellery and other accessories. In an organisational context, these elements may be combined to signal valued attributes, such as personal status (e.g. displaying an ostentatiously expensive suit or wristwatch), professionalism (e.g. the white coat of a clinical specialist or research scientist), or other capabilities (e.g. the self-consciously non-conformist appearance of 'creative' staff in an advertising agency or a performing arts organisation). In some cases, these signals are standardised, through the use of organisational dress codes or uniforms, both of which are designed to send out a consistent message about the organisation and its values.

As in the other areas discussed, the most common communication problems related to physical appearance arise from differing expectations and conflicting norms. For example, some large corporations have experimented with a relaxation of their formal dress codes (i.e. the so-called, 'dress-down Friday'). In some instances, these initiatives have proved problematic, with employees struggling to maintain their normal standards of professionalism and more formally-dressed visitors feeling isolated and uncomfortable. In certain contexts, clothing can still be a source of contention, often arising from differences in religious or ethical position. For example, women wearing the burkha have experienced resistance in some Western organisations. However, like other non-verbal signals discussed in this section, dress codes and related signals have been subject to change as international organisations begin to develop shared meanings and, in some cases, to acknowledge a greater diversity of practices (Holden 2002).

Mini-case 4.3 outlines a novel approach to modifying cross-cultural communication practices, which has been applied successfully in various international organisations. It makes use of visual cues, ranging from product brochures to meeting agendas, in order to prompt interaction between groups of people from different cultural backgrounds.

| Mini-case 4.3 | CDP exchanges: a visual approach to cross-cultural interaction |

Traditional approaches to dealing with cross-cultural interactions are modelled on the experiences of a traveller, arriving in a foreign country for the first time. They focus on resolving the errors and confusion that arise from a lack of familiarity with local communication practices (e.g. Hall and Hall 1990). As we noted in earlier chapters, confrontations of this kind – between two distinct cultures – are still relevant to communicators. However, many international organisations are facing a different challenge, as they seek to negotiate *new* patterns of behaviour that are suited to multi-cultural settings. Pan *et al.* (2002) outline an approach, described as the Communication Portfolio Display (CDP) exchange, that responds to this challenge. The authors argue that professional communication in international settings cannot be standardised around the practices of a single social or cultural group. Their method encourages people to learn directly from those with whom they need to interact. This is based on the thesis that, 'successful communication in the international workplace requires a *self-reflective* understanding of the processes of communication' (*ibid:* 5 – emphasis added). The core activity involves an exchange of 'best case' examples of professional communications materials, providing the basis for reflective discussion and feedback:

> 'To give an example, we could imagine that we have a small team of buyers based in Frankfurt who have established contact with producers of supplies in Guangzhou, China. The buyers will be going to China and the Chinese team will be visiting Frankfurt, as the relationship is expected to last over a period of at least several years. A traditional approach to the intercultural aspects of this program would be to provide training to the German team in Chinese communicative and cultural practices and also, if at all possible, to provide training to the Chinese team in German practices.' (*ibid:* 5)

The authors note that this approach is unlikely to be achieved, given the shortage of suitable training materials and consultants, particularly those whose technical expertise can be combined with language skills in Cantonese, rather than Mandarin Chinese. The alternative approach involves some or all of the team members compiling a professional CDP. The portfolio would include readily-available items, such as product brochures, business cards, letters, e-mails and CVs (or 'resumés'). Participants would also try to find materials that indicated how other communication channels, including formal meetings and presentations, were conducted. The portfolios would then be used to stimulate discussion within and between the teams:

▶

'These CDPs would then be exchanged between the two teams. Each team would then conduct a "focus group" discussion of the materials from the point of view of their communicative effectiveness. That is, they would say what seemed confusing to them, what was missing, what seemed excessive or unnecessary, or whatever adjustments might be needed to improve their ability to understand. These comments and reflections would then be returned to the other team for them to consider and digest.' (*ibid: 5–6*)

The authors emphasise that the primary purpose of the exchange is not to isolate cultural, national or personal differences, but rather to encourage participants to reflect on the effectiveness of these practices, and to encourage a process of mutual learning. The desired outcome is that the people concerned are able to adjust their own practices to some extent, in order to achieve a better way of communicating within that particular setting.

Questions

1 How does the CDP approach differ from traditional work on cross-cultural difference? For each one, what do you consider to be its main advantages and disadvantages in a multi-cultural setting?

2 The portfolio of material provides a visual stimulus for discussion. How might it be extended to illustrate other, less tangible communication channels, such as interviews or team discussions?

3 Experiment with creating your own CDP, which could include a recently-produced report, set of presentation slides and CV. Compare your portfolio to that produced by other students or colleagues, reflecting on the changes that may be necessary in order to meet everyone's communication needs.

Source: Hall and Hall (1990), Pan *et al.* (2002). Case prepared by the author.

Summary

- Organisations make use of a wide range of non-verbal signals, including visual images, or 'pictures', both human and manufactured.

- There are many potential advantages of non-verbal encoding: messages are quickly assimilated, complex content can be simplified, the attention of an audience can be caught, and messages can be more memorable. In addition, images are often powerful persuaders and motivators.

- The most common problems arise when 'pictures' of all kinds are used carelessly (i.e. images are either inconsistent, inherently unsuitable or inappropriate in a particular context).

- Graphs and charts can be used to present data in more informative and appealing ways. However, it is important to use the most appropriate type and format, ensuring that you communicate a clear and undistorted impression of the underlying figures.

- The visual identity of an organisation needs to be well thought-out and linked to its real values and activities. Managing the identity of a large business involves a complex mixture of strategic and practical issues,

- Communicators also need to be aware of how 'human' signals, such as eye contact and gesture, influence the communication process. This is particularly important in multi-cultural contexts where there is a need to acknowledge diversity in the use of these codes.

Practical exercises

1 Designing icons, symbols and diagrams

The meaning behind the images reproduced in Figure 4.1 can be absorbed 'at a glance', avoiding the need for a verbal explanation. The images are also designed to be understood instantly by people from a wide variety of cultures and language groups. With these requirements in mind, design your own images for the following purposes:

(a) a computer icon for instant access to a home shopping service

(b) a directional sign indicating the police station at an international airport

(c) 'no overtaking' and 'cycle workshop ahead' signs for use on a cross-border cycle route

Based on the discussion and illustrations in the chapter (see section 4.3), sketch a suitable visual image to meet the following requirements:

(d) a diagram, which explains exactly how to carry out one of the following tasks without the use of words:

- prepare, cook and serve a mushroom omelette;

- withdraw money from a 'cash-point' machine;

- repair a punctured bicycle tyre.

(e) A visual identity for a new range of 'green' (i.e. environmentally-friendly) consumer products, either household detergents, paints or clothes. The manufacturer needs to build a distinctive and memorable image in the domestic retail market.

What aspect did you find most difficult in preparing each image? How should your rough drafts be improved, when redrawn by a professional artist, to make them more effective?

2 Unacceptable images? The ethical dimension

Manufactured images can be powerful communicators. At one extreme, horrific war photography has forced national governments and the United Nations to change their policies, whilst at the other, beautiful landscapes have been used to promote everything from tourism to shampoo. Like any powerful communication technique, the application of these non-verbal signals is open to abuse. For example, in a notorious Nazi propaganda film of the 1930s, the anti-Semitic verbal commentary was reinforced through the use of close-up images of rats scurrying through the contents of an abandoned house. What kinds of ethical constraints should be placed on the way that images are used in organisational communication? Imagine that your objective was one of the following:

(a) to warn drivers of the serious dangers of speeding

(b) to persuade young people not to start smoking

(c) to persuade smokers to continue purchasing your brand

(d) to inform schoolchildren about drugs or contraception.

Identify examples of the kinds of images you would consider both useful and acceptable to reinforce a verbal message in one of these cases. What kinds of images, if any, do you see as unacceptable for the stated purpose. Give a reasoned explanation for your choice. Supporting materials can be found in texts on business ethics, such as Bowie (2002).

Seminar option: This exercise requires all group members to pay particular respect to the views of others. Share your conclusions with the rest of the group. Discuss the issues arising, including any significant differences of opinion between individuals. Was there any consensus on the kinds of images that would be unacceptable in these circumstances? Were decisions based mainly on ethical judgements, or more practical concerns?

Case-study D

Visual identity, corporate image and strategy – the case of BT

The nature and dynamics of corporate visual identity are exemplified in the history of one of Europe's leading providers of telecommunications services, British Telecommunications plc (BT). A combination of technological innovation, market liberalisation and a changing socio-economic context have prompted changes in BT's corporate and business strategies, which have also been reflected in the organisation's evolving visual identity and its image in the minds of key stakeholders, including industry regulators, investors, customers and suppliers.

From private enterprise to state monopoly
As in other countries, most of the UK's telephone network was once under the control of the state. BT's origins date back to the 1840s, when the first generation of telecommunications companies began to introduce electric telegraph services. Many new companies competed in the early burst of innovation. By the late 1860s this was already a thriving international business, with submarine cables connecting Europe with North America. The UK's inland telegraph system, including some related manufacturing businesses, was transferred to the state in 1870, a decade before Alexander Graham Bell's initial experiments with the telephone. The newly-emerging generation of telephone companies competed with the state-run 'General Post Office' (GPO). However, from 1912 until its privatisation in 1984, the state was the monopoly supplier of telephone services for domestic and business use, other than in a few municipalities.

Creating a new identity: privatisation and beyond
During its existence as part of the GPO, the precursor of BT had no separate identity. During the 1970s, telecommunications activities were separated from other parts of the Post Office and, in 1981, they came under the control of a separate public corporation, which operated under the name *British Telecom*. At this time, promotional

materials used in display and television advertising featured a cartoon bird, named *Buzby*, whose voice was provided by a well-known British comedian. The company's partial privatisation in November 1984, when over 50 per cent of the company's share capital was sold to the public, was the first in a series of privatisations of state-owned utilities that continued into the 1990s. The privatised company, which adopted the legal title, 'British Telecommunications plc', was now actively traded on the London Stock Exchange, and in other international exchanges. With its new commercial freedom, the company was positioned to respond to new competition in the UK, and to expand its operations globally. However, it was still popularly identified by the shortened trading name, 'British Telecom', combined with a simple logo based on the initial 'T' in upper case, outlined by a circle.

By the early 1990s, the company needed a more radical redesign to reflect its new strategic ambitions. The name and logo were still functioning effectively in its domestic markets, but problems arose when using this identity internationally. The main problem was the logo, which was almost identical to that of several other national telecommunications organisations, including the Spanish company, *Telefonica*. This restricted its potential as a registered trade mark, and made it unsuitable as a distinctive, international 'brand'. The adopted name, *British Telecom* was also perceived in some markets as 'conservative and unexciting, reliable but not forward-looking'. Above all, it suggested that the company was national, rather than international in scope. Design consultants were asked to review the overall corporate identity. The subsequent re-design was more than simply 'cosmetic'. It followed a six-month research study, geared to the company's vision of becoming the most successful worldwide telecommunications group. It was also explicitly linked to changes in company structure, culture and operations. The new logo featured a 'piper', comprising a 'listener' (reproduced in red in the full colour versions), and a 'teller' (reproduced in blue). This was meant to symbolise two-way communication, enabling customers to talk to one another, a central element in BT's business mission. The symbol was also seen as universal, conveying a similar message across different cultures. The use of a human figure was designed to highlight the personal element in the company's activities. On the practical side, the logo had to be suitable for a wide range of applications, from payphone kiosks to stationery. It had to be reproducible in monochrome and in a four-colour format, and it had to look equally effective displayed on a computer screen or moulded into a plastic product. Other aspects of the re-design included improved typefaces and documentation. The new visual identity was accompanied by a change of name. The company adopted its initial letters 'BT' as a replacement trading name, while retaining the full corporate name for formal documents, such as contracts and share certificates.

'Connecting your world': BT in the 21st century

The 1990s saw further developments in BT's activities, including the expansion of internet-related businesses, and the company entered the new century with four main lines of business: BT Retail, BT Wholesale, BT Global Services and BT Openworld. Its new strategic priorities include: putting broadband services 'at the heart of BT'; creating a 'media enabled network'; and providing 'solutions and other value-added services for multi-site corporate customers in Europe'. This has contributed to a further reassessment of BT's brand identity. In 2003, the company's 'piper' symbol was replaced by a multi-coloured globe, a design that had previously been adopted for 'BT Openworld'.

As with its predecessor, the logo is made available in full-colour and monochrome versions, in order to meet different applications (see below). The new design was associated with a new brand vision, that was summarised in the corporate slogan, 'Connecting your world'. The new identity makes bolder use of colour, intended to demonstrate characteristics such as 'dynamism' and 'freshness'. The designers have also selected photographic images that support the brand vision, for use in both consumer and business markets. Lastly, while the 'BT' lettering is unchanged, the company has introduced new typography, to be used in all communication channels (e.g. brochures, advertisements, websites). The new typography is also designed to reinforce the identity in a consistent way.

Questions

1 Review the decisions made by BT in relation to its visual identity. How important do you think it was for the organisation to make these changes? What would the implications have been, if it had made a different choice at each stage?

2 Compare the names and logos of three international telecommunications companies (or similar organisations operating in anther sector), based on published materials (e.g. annual reports, websites). How effective do you consider these elements, in conveying a distinctive and appropriate identity for the organisation?

3 Draft a short report (maximum 800 words), outlining a proposed visual identity for BT, or a similar organisation. Ensure that your proposal covers the relevant practical issues (e.g. use of colour) when reproducing the identity in various formats. Justify your choices, with reference to the strategic aims of the organisation.

Source: BT (2003a, 2003b). BT logo reproduced with permission.

Further reading

This chapter has covered various forms of non-verbal communication. Beginning with business graphics, **Tufte** (1990) and (1997) has written beautifully-produced and inspiring source-books on this subject; other texts such as **Morris** (1999), **Richey** (1994) and **Saunders** *et al.* (2003) include more straightforward practical advice on presenting statistical data graphically. **Arunachalam** *et al.* (2002) is an example of empirical research into the impact of graphical information on decision making. **Olins** (1989, 2000, 2003) is a key source on elements of visual identity and its relationship to corporate image, from a leading practitioner. There are many research studies on aspects of non-verbal communication in inter-personal settings, mostly with a national cultural emphasis. **Hall** (1959) was a pioneering anthropological study, with more recent sources including **Hall and Hall** (1990), and contributions to edited texts such as **Jackson** (1995) and **Joynt and Warner** (1996).

References

Arunachalam, V., Pei, B.K. and Steinbart, P.J. (2002) 'Impression management with graphs: effects on choices'. *Journal of Information Systems*, 16, 2, 183–202.

Bowie, N.E. (ed.) (2002) *The Blackwell guide to business ethics*. Blackwell, Oxford.

BT (2003a) 'The company: BT group archives'. Available at www.btplc.com (accessed 6th August).

BT (2003b) 'Basic elements'. Branding guidelines document, supplied by BT brand helpdesk. British Telecommunications plc, London.

CIPFA (2003) *Code of practice on local authority accounting in the United Kingdom: a statement of recommended practice.* The Chartered Institute of Public Finance and Accounting, London.

Donaldson, A. and Eyre, K. (2000) 'Using visual communication to drive change'. *Strategic Communication Management*, 32–5 (December).

Dou, W-L. and Clark, W.C. (2002) 'Appreciating diversity in multicultural communication styles'. *Business Forum*, 24, 3–4, 54–61.

Eckman, P. (1992) 'An argument for basic emotions'. *Cognition and Emotion*, 6, 169–200.

Fairtrade Foundation, The (2003) 'Recognition of the Fairtrade mark soars [press release]'. Fairtrade Foundation, London (May).

Gombrich, E.H. (1978) *The story of art* (13th edn.). Phaidon Press, London.

Hall, E.T. (1959) *The silent language*. Doubleday, New York.

Hall, E.T. and Hall, M.R. (1990) *Understanding cultural differences*. Intercultural Press, Yarmouth ME.

Harris, P.R. and Moran, R.T. (1996) *Managing cultural differences: leadership strategies for a new world of business*. Gulf Publishing, Houston TX.

Holden, N. (2002) *Cross-cultural management: a knowledge management perspective*. FT Prentice Hall, Harlow.

Jackson, T. (1995) *Cross-cultural management*. Butterworth-Heinemann, London.

Joynt, P. and Warner, M. (1996) *Managing across cultures: issues and perspectives*. International Thomson, London.

Klein, N. (2000) *No logo*. Flamingo, London.

Moeran, B. (1997) *Folk art potters of Japan: beyond an anthropology of aesthetics*. Curzon Press, Richmond.

Morris, C. (1999) *Quantitative approaches in business studies* (5th edn). FT Prentice Hall, Harlow,

Office of the Deputy Prime Minister (2003) *Statistical release: July 2003.* HMSO, London.

Olins, W. (1989) *Corporate identity: making business strategy visible through design*. Thames & Hudson, London.

Olins, W. (2000) *Trading identities: why countries and companies are taking on each others roles*. Foreign Policy Centre, London.

Olins, W. (2003) *On brand*. Thames & Hudson, London.

Pan, Y., Scollon, S. and Scollon, R. (2002) *Professional communication in international settings*. Blackwell, Oxford.

Richey, T. (1994) *The marketer's visual tool kit: using charts, graphs and models for strategic planning and problem solving*. American Marketing Association / AMACOM, New York.

Saunders, M.N.K., Lewis, P. and Thornhill, A. (2003) *Research methods for business students* (3rd edn.). FT Prentice Hall, Harlow.

Sayer, A. (2000) *Realism and social science.* Sage, London.

Tufte, E.R. (1990) *Envisioning information*. Graphics Press, London.

Tufte, E.R. (1997) *Visual Explanations: Images and Quantities, Evidence and Narrative.* Graphics Press, London.

Wychavon DC (2003) *Statement of accounts 2002–2003*, Wychavon District Council, Pershore.

Yergin, D. (1991) *The prize: the epic quest for oil, money and power.* Simon and Schuster, London.

CHAPTER 5

Developing arguments: persuasive communication

Only free men can negotiate. Prisoners cannot enter into contracts ...
Public statement by Nelson Mandela, February 1985 (Mandela 1991: 511)

Learning outcomes

By the end of this chapter you should be able to:

- appreciate the role of persuasive communication in various organisational contexts;
- identify the principal factors leading to successful and unsuccessful outcomes;
- review established theoretical perspectives regarding motivation and decision making;
- apply verbal and non-verbal forms of communication in order to secure attention, develop arguments and secure agreement;
- address ethical aspects of persuasive communication.

5.1 Introduction

Everyone is involved in persuasion. Sometimes we are seeking to persuade others. For example, a manager needs a volunteer to work over the weekend in order to complete a project, or a trades union negotiator calls for improvements in working conditions. However, for much of the time we are on the receiving end of another person's efforts to affect, convert, convince, exhort, induce, influence, prompt, sway, urge or otherwise win us over. Many of these persuasive messages are highly sophisticated, the product of technical specialists, associated with advertising agencies, public relations consultancies and the emerging breed of political 'spin doctor' (Hollingsworth 1997, Michie 1998, Miller and Dinan 2000). These professionals are sometimes accused of exerting undue influence, or even 'brain-washing', their audiences. In reality, the starting point for persuasive communication is that the receiver must have some freedom in responding to persuasive messages, and an underlying ability to choose between alternative courses of action. As the opening quotation suggests, without freedom, there is no scope for negotiation and therefore no need to persuade. In a relatively free and democratic society, audiences have some scope for accepting or rejecting the messages they are sent. As a result, even the 'professional' communicators cannot guarantee the outcome of their efforts at persuasion.

This chapter focuses on the roles that persuasive communication can play within and between organisations. It reviews various types of persuasion that you are likely to encounter at work, plus some that everyone experiences as citizens and consumers. We also reflect on the key elements that people use to construct an argument, and apply the principles of rhetorical argument in a number of practical cases. Many messages contain degrees of persuasion, though they may be quite subtle and easy to overlook. For example, when an eager job applicant selects particular clothing for an interview, it is not purely a personal preference; it is a conscious choice, designed to influence the decision of the interview panel through non-verbal signals (see section 4.7). Similarly, as Mini-case 5.1 demonstrates, the purpose of a road traffic sign identifying a speed camera is not simply to provide information; it is a calculated attempt to change the behaviour of drivers.

Mini-case 5.1	Inform or persuade? The case for speed cameras

Inform or persuade? The case for speed cameras

Driving at excessive speeds is a well-known source of accident and injury on the world's roads. There have been many initiatives from governments, transport departments and the police, designed to persuade drivers to comply with local speed limits, the most common being to penalise offenders with fines and endorsements on their driving licences. However, the traditional method, of using police vehicles to stop offenders, is costly and can create potentially hazardous distractions on multi-lane roads with heavy traffic flows; other drivers travelling in both directions tend to slow down for a short period, creating a 'ripple' effect in the traffic (Oesch 2002: 1). Speed cameras have been introduced in many countries since the 1990s, to record on film the registration numbers of vehicles travelling at more than the approved speed. Research has demonstrated the effectiveness of this method of speed control. For example, researchers in the Canadian state, British Columbia, reported a 7 per cent decline in crashes and up to 20 per cent fewer deaths in the year following introduction of cameras (Chen *et al.* 1998). A subsequent review of eight pilot schemes in the UK reported significant reductions in the number of fatal and serious injuries (Department for Transport 2003). Drivers are usually advised of the possible presence of speed cameras by warning signs, of the kind illustrated below.

However, there are many more signs than cameras. Consequently, one of the most contentious issues arising from the use of cameras has concerned their identification (Department for Transport 2003). Some have argued that it is more effective to publicise the location of each camera, using channels such as websites. There was a change of policy in the UK, so that cameras are currently painted in bright yellow, rather than the dull grey that was used previously. The effect is to highlight their presence to passing motorists, at least during daylight hours. Some people have questioned the logic of this approach, though it has the support of agencies such as the UK's Department for Transport. There has also been considerable debate regarding the emerging market in electronic devices to detect the presence of speed cameras, with some commentators seeing it as improving road safety, while others argue that it helps speeding motorists to avoid facing proper legal penalties. Most reports seem to suggest widespread public support for the installation of cameras. For example, there is an active campaign in the city of New York for the provision of additional speed cameras, plus 'red light' cameras at traffic intersections. It is also supported by groups such as Transport 2000, who promote the interests of pedestrians and cyclists as part of their wider campaigning activities. However, there is also vocal opposition from some organisations representing the interests of drivers, which has also been reflected in driving magazines. Several independent websites have been set up to campaign against the use of speed cameras and some motorists have taken direct action to undermine the process (e.g. people setting fire to speed cameras, or using imitation licence plates in order to avoid detection). While the overall number of cameras continues to increase, one of the original schemes, which operated in British Columbia, has since been terminated.

Further information on speed cameras is available at the following websites: www.dft.gov.uk, www.highwaysafety.org and www.transport2000.org.uk. Details of other government sources and campaigning websites can be obtained via search engines.

Questions

1 Review the case and identify the persuasive elements in the 'messages' that are being sent by the speed cameras and the associated warning signs.

2 Assess both sides of the argument regarding the identification and colouring of speed cameras. Which approach do you see as more persuasive?

3 Suggest other types of persuasive message, which might replace or complement those represented by speed cameras and warning signs.

Source: Chen *et al.* 1998, Oesch 2002, Department for Transport 2003. Written by the author.

5.2 Persuasion in organisations

Though persuasive communication is used in all areas of organisational life, some functions are particularly 'persuasion-rich'. The basic dynamics of persuasion are evident in various types of inter-personal communication, such as the interactions taking place in meetings and interviews. However, in some of these, such as advertisements and press releases, the persuasive element is very explicit throughout. In other channels, including reports, letters and e-mails, persuasion may play a more subtle and intermittent role, forming part of the overall message. Consider the different ways that persuasive communication operates in the following practical examples:

- **Advertising**: Persuasive techniques are used to secure the attention of a target audience and to increase its subsequent recall of the message. Contrary to popular opinion, many adverts are concerned with ideas, such as building brand 'identity' and 'values', rather than action, in the form of an immediate purchase decision (Chapter 10).

- **Public relations (PR) and lobbying**: Public relations practitioners are often ridiculed as 'hooray Henries' swilling gin and tonic, or cynical manipulators oiling the wheels of power. Neither stereotype is entirely accurate. Public relations is mainly concerned with managing the links between an organisation and the people outside, including customers, local communities and journalists. Lobbying means presenting an organisation's case to the key decision makers. Today, this is mostly done using briefing documents, lunchtime meetings and other PR tools; though the traditional meetings in the lobbies (i.e. corridors) of parliaments do still occur. These specialised forms of persuasion are used by all types of organisation, including companies, trades unions, single issue campaigners and charities (see Chapter 10).

- **Interviews**: Job interviews can often involve efforts at persuasion from both sides. Candidates are seeking to convince the panel that they are the right person for the job, while the organisation is trying to attract the strong candidates to accept job offers. Employers also want unsuccessful candidates to leave with a positive impression of their organisation, because this is essential to their longer-term efforts at recruitment. Persuasion can also be a factor in other types of interview, such as an employee performance appraisal (see Chapter 11).

- **Business meetings and negotiations**: In committee meetings and project team briefings, people often have to work hard, persuading others to accept their novel or controversial ideas and proposals. There are also those occasions when one party wants to deliver an effective counter-argument against another individual or group (see Chapter 13).

The next section introduces the underlying principles of persuasion, which draw on the concepts of rhetoric and argument. These principles are then applied to a series of practical challenges, indicating some of the ways in which organisational communication can be made more persuasive.

5.3 The essential principles: introducing rhetorical argument

The essential principles of persuasive communication have been understood for many centuries. They can best be summarised by returning to one of the sources of contemporary approaches to language, and the ways that it can be used in order to develop arguments. The term 'rhetoric' is used quite loosely today.

However, its role in argument derives from the Ancient Greek term for an orator or speaker, where *têchnê rhêtorikê* referred to the skills required to construct an eloquent speech. When the Greek philosopher Aristotle (384–322 BC) explored the structure of arguments, he managed to isolate three fundamental elements: *ethos*, or the credibility of the person presenting the argument; *logos*, the internal logic of the argument; and *pathos*, which equates with the emotional dimension. He defined rhetoric as, 'an ability, in each particular case, to see the available means of persuasion'. (Aristotle 1991: 36, Skerlep 2001: 180). These elements remain a useful framework for analysing persuasive messages. For example, if we reconsider the challenge of persuading people to refrain from drug abuse, it is clear that each of these elements has been exploited at various times (e.g. endorsement of anti-drugs messages by sports or music celebrities, publication of statistical reports detailing the consequences of abuse and personal appeals by parents and survivors). In addition, we might also anticipate that communicating a message in a channel that combines these elements (e.g. a face-to-face presentation to school children, given by a former addict, who can present a clear and passionate case against drugs), has the potential to be more persuasive than messages that contain these elements in isolation (see Table 5.1).

Table 5.1 **Three elements of a rhetorical argument**

Element/type of argumentation	Practical example
Ethos: credibility of the person or organisation presenting the argument.	An organisation with a poor reputation appoints a new senior executive who is well-regarded by key stakeholders.
Logos: internal logic of the argument presented.	A government department issues a detailed research study that makes the case for its policy proposals.
Pathos: appeals to emotion in support of the other elements	A police force asks the parents of a victim of crime to join in a televised public appeal for information.

Analysing arguments: applying Toulmin's (1957) model

There are several approaches to the study of rhetorical argument, reflecting the broad social scientific distinctions outlined in section 1.7. This section focuses on work conducted within the 'normative/modern' perspective, which is primarily concerned with the ways in which speakers influence their audiences, 'through the *intentional* use of speech' (Ovarec and Salvador 1993: 183 – emphasis added). Toulmin (1957) is one of the most influential figures in this tradition. His model of argumentation has been used to analyse the different components of an argument and their logical connections, both for research purposes and to help people improve their skills in presenting arguments. It begins from the idea that any argument consists of someone making an assertion or 'claim' with the aim of gaining general acceptance among a group of people. For example, the research director of an engineering company may be seeking board approval to invest in a research project involving a novel technology, which is currently at a development stage (see Table 5.2).

Table 5.2 **The basic components of an argument – Toulmin's model**

Component	Description	Example
Claim	The assertion that is put forward for acceptance.	Research manager claims that the new product merits further capital investment.
Grounds	Relevant data forming basis for the argument.	Research report highlights product's performance and market potential.
Warrant	Rules or principles for linking a 'claim' to its 'grounds'.	What is generally regarded as relevant and strong research evidence.
Backings	Evidence supporting the 'warrant' in this particular case.	Details of the people who conducted the research, experience, methods used, etc.
Qualifiers	Phrases that place conditions or limits on the strength of the 'claim'.	Report states that, 'Product performance has been rated "excellent" in all applications tested *so far*' (emphasis added).
Rebuttals	Exceptional conditions, beyond the scope of the 'claim', that would otherwise undermine the argument.	Project will fail if a rival firm is successful in developing a product based on the next generation technology.

Source: Toulmin (1957), Von Werder (1999: 674–8), Skerlep (2001: 185)

The potential value of Toulmin's model is in helping communicators to reconstruct and learn from previous arguments. It can also be used to encourage a more analytical approach to the managerial tasks of decision making and presenting the outcomes to stakeholders (Skerlep 2001: 185). In the next section, we continue in this modernist perspective by considering the practical challenge of managing the process of persuasion in an organisational setting.

5.4 The challenge of persuasion: audience, message and context

In this section, we proceed with the simplifying assumption that persuasion is primarily a process of argument and counter-argument. Consequently, the main focus of the communicator's effort is on constructing a 'winning' argument. However, even in this narrow view of persuasive communication, we need to consider several broader questions. The answers to these questions are important, because they will inform the content of any persuasive message, its structure and the channels through which it is directed. The main issues to be addressed are: the nature of the audience; the nature of the message that is being conveyed; and the context in which the persuasive communication is taking place.

Assessing the nature of the audience

One of the most challenging tasks is to make a satisfactory assessment of your audience. The following list of questions indicates some of the more common issues that may require clarification or further research:

- What previous experience do they have, either of you as an individual, or the organisation that you represent?
- What do they already know, and how do they feel, about the subject matter of your message?
- What do you know about their personality and their current state of mind?
- Are you trying to persuade one individual or a large number of people?
- Are they able to act independently, or are they playing the role of representatives or agents of another organisation?
- What other factors that might be persuading them in the opposite direction?

Researchers have explored the background to these questions at various levels of analysis. For example, a recent survey-based study distinguished five broad decision-making styles among senior executives. The authors suggested that these styles were relatively permanent characteristics of the individuals concerned and argued that persuasive communications would be more likely to succeed if they were tailored to the appropriate style:

> **'Executives make it to the senior level largely because they are effective decision makers. Learning mostly from experience, they build a set of criteria that guides them. Each decision is influenced by both reason and emotion, but the weight given to each of these elements during the decision-making process can vary widely depending on the person.' (Williams and Miller 2002: 66)**

It is certainly useful to gain a better understanding of individuals that you are seeking to persuade directly (e.g. the line manager with whom you are negotiating). Theories of human motivation may be of relevance here, though there is considerable debate over the relevance of classical 'content' theories, such as Maslow's (1943, 1987) 'hierarchy of needs', Alderfer's (1972) modified needs hierarchy and McClelland's (1988) categorisation of four key 'motives', often associated with its application in entrepreneurship research. Similarly, 'process' theories of motivation, many of which are based around concepts of 'expectancy' can be suggestive (e.g. Lawler 1973). However, subsequent research by psychologists has highlighted conceptual and methodological limitations when they are applied to organisational settings (e.g. Van Eeerde and Thierry 1996). Organisational theorists and strategy researchers, concerned with complex processes of persuasive communication and strategic decision making, have also pointed out that these processes operate across many different levels of analysis, including the actions of individual managers, interaction between powerful sub-groups within the organisation, and wider economic, social and cultural influences (e.g. Barnett and Burgelman 1996, Lewin and Koza 2001).

Assessing the message: content and purpose

We now turn to some questions concerning the message that you are trying to convey. One set of questions relates to the content of the message. For example, does it comprise facts, ideas, opinions or a mixture of all three? Is it relatively simple or complex? Is the content likely to be surprising, or unwelcome or threatening to your audience, or to those they represent? In making this assessment, it is important to pay particular attention to the emotional (or 'affective') aspects of the message, since these can have a decisive effect on the outcome (see section 6.5). Organisational communicators often make the mistake of over-emphasising the cognitive aspects of their arguments, assessing them as logical and well-substantiated. This ignores the fact that audiences are human. In some cases, their powerful and sometimes unpredictable emotional responses will be fully capable of overwhelming the most impeccable logic and the carefully-collected evidence that supports it. Non-rational aspects can become decisive when those you are attempting to persuade feel that their personal values, interests, security, or sense of identity is under threat. For example, during the international outbreak of SARS (Sudden Acute Respiratory Syndrome) in 2003, many public agencies, including local authorities in the Canadian city of Toronto, struggled to convince local populations that the threat had been contained. Popular fear of this previously unfamiliar disease proved more powerful than the dry statistics of reported incidents, and organisations that sought to persuade on the basis of their established reputation, found their credibility being challenged.

There is a related set of questions concerning the underlying purpose of the message. Some persuasive messages have relatively modest objectives, but others are more demanding, requiring a corresponding increase in effort on your part. The following simple classification of objectives distinguishes between efforts to change what the receiver knows, what they believe, and how they currently behave.

Changing facts and ideas

If the relevant facts are clear and non-contentious, this simple form of persuasion is relatively easy, as the following dialogue makes clear. If senders have access to relevant supporting evidence (i.e. 'grounds', as identified in Toulmin's model), which they are capable of presenting in a straightforward manner, receivers will be persuaded to change their minds. If you want to practise your skills in deconstructing arguments, analyse the following dialogue using the model outlined in Table 5.2:

Emily: So, Ifor, are you coming to the team briefing?

Ifor: You're crazy! It's only nine o'clock.

Emily: Sure, but didn't you know? Jay re-scheduled it yesterday.

Ifor: You can't be serious, it's always at 11. Anyway, I'm sure someone would have told me.

Emily: Yes, it's definite. I have checked with his PA, and there's an e-mail to confirm it – take a look if you don't believe me.

Ifor: OK, you win. Well, let's get a move on then, or we'll be late!

However, in some circumstances it can be far more difficult to persuade people to accept novel, complex or controversial facts and ideas. The pioneering scientist, Galileo Galilei (1564–1642), encountered violent opposition when he presented evidence that supported the 'heliocentric' theory of Nicholas Copernicus (i.e. the strange notion that the Earth revolved around the Sun, rather than the other way around). The new theory was seen as undermining the prevailing 'world view', which also legitimated the religious and political power structures of the time. First, Galileo's book was banned by religious authorities. He was subsequently forced to deny his 'revolutionary' ideas and spent the rest of his life under house arrest. Many examples from more recent history indicate that many people today remain unwilling to tolerate evidence suggesting that their world has changed.

Changing beliefs and values

Though they contain facts and ideas, a person's beliefs and values are bolstered by other powerful factors, such as self-image, cultural background and pressure exerted by a peer group (e.g. fellow scientists, or other members of a team, department or professional association). Therefore, if you are seeking to influence a receiver's beliefs and values, it is essential to consider more than the basic information content of the message. For example, imagine that you are working for an international retail organisation, which is re-positioning itself on the basis of enhanced customer service, after many years pursuing a low-price, 'pile it high and sell it cheap' strategy. Many of the managers running local stores have been working for the company since graduation; their average age is 52 years. How can the regional operations director begin to persuade local area managers to implement the new strategy? Successful persuasion, in the face of such entrenched beliefs, may take some time. The pattern of communication is also likely to include a strong inter-personal and emotional dimension. In a dramatic example of this phenomenon, recorded as part of a television documentary, a member of a white supremacist group 'switched sides' and joined forces with an anti-racist campaign. For this individual, the catalyst for change was a close friendship with a work colleague who happened to be black. It required emotive pressure of a personal relationship, rather than the force of logical argument, to provide the energy needed to drive such a radical change.

Changing actions and behaviour

Influencing another person's actions can be very straightforward. For example, asking a colleague to send you a copy of her report or asking someone to speak at a meeting does not normally require much persuasive effort. Full-scale persuasion only arises where the receiver has an in-built resistance towards the proposed action or change in behaviour. These fundamental behavioural changes also require more than simply polite and rational discussion. For example, in countless public health campaigns, efforts have been directed at discouraging people from activities such as smoking, drug abuse and 'unsafe' sex. These campaigns have made use of posters, leaflets and other communication channels, containing messages that present frank and unambiguous information on the related risks (see Figure 5.1). Can this type of communication compete effectively against peer group pressure and slick commercialisation? In some cases, direct contact with people who have experienced the consequences has proved more persuasive.

Figure 5.1 A warning poster

Source: The Advertising Archive Ltd. Reproduced with permission.

Assessing the context of persuasion

As in other forms of communication, ineffective outcomes may result from the sender's failure to fully grasp the context in which the persuasive message is being received. For example, is it happening *within* an organisation (e.g. encouraging employees to improve service quality, seeking to overcome a conflict between rival departments), or in the *outside* world (e.g. attracting new customers to purchase a product, lobbying the government to increase spending on sports or the arts?). The approach to persuasion may also be affected by timescale and by the activities of other parties. Different strategies are required if you are under pressure to achieve a quick result, or where other actors are actively competing for the 'hearts and minds' of your audience.

The process of questioning should encourage the communicator towards creative solutions, designed to overcome the barriers that have been identified. For example, if the persuasive message involves a novel concept (e.g. a new technology, or unfamiliar work practice), the task of persuasion is likely to be much more difficult. Having identified this potential barrier, the communicator can take it into account when designing a message. In this case, the 'solution' may be to convey the novel content of the message using language and concepts that the audience already understands, and where there is already some common ground. The most persuasive communicators display a combination of awareness and flexibility, recognising and exploiting the fundamental self-interest of their audience:

> 'When what you have to say clearly intersects with what the other person wants or needs or cares about, you have given [them] a primary, compelling reason for listening. You're not actually demanding that he/she give up self-involvement. You're just piggy-backing on some part of the listener's own momentum ... you're defining your message as another facet of his or her ongoing life concerns.' (Hamlyn 1989: 38)

5.5 Persuasive practices: securing attention and arguing well

The communication practices most commonly associated with persuasion are efforts to secure attention (e.g. the salesperson's 'cold calling' technique or the advertiser's eye-catching design), and engaging in argument. In both cases, the result depends on the skill with which communication channels are selected and exploited. There are a number of generic 'recipes' for securing the attention of receivers, the secondary aim being to ensure the optimum pre-conditions for 'delivering' the message. While the appropriateness of particular techniques may vary, depending on local circumstances, one or more of the following stimuli may generate a positive response:

- **Addressing people by name**: The use of personal names exploits the capacity for selective perception; it increases phasic alertness and can make people feel involved. Referring to a specific group in an audience, such as 'the team from our Zurich office', has a similar effect. Non-verbal cues, such as direct eye contact and gestures, are also used to attract attention in face-to-face settings, such as meetings and seminars.

- **Posing questions**: As problem-solving animals, humans find it difficult to resist a challenging question. For example, at the start of a presentation, the speaker might simply turn the opening statement into a question (e.g. 'Thank you for coming along this afternoon. Tell me, why do you think our main competitor has doubled its sales figures in the last six months?'). Visual puzzles are another form of question that can attract attention in various communication channels, including display posters and television advertisements.

- **Being provocative**: Persuasive communication often makes use of provocation, in order to stimulate initial awareness. This may be combined with other techniques, such as asking a question. For example, a British marketing consultancy once used a banner headline comprising the phrase, 'Are you bloody brilliant?', as the opening line of a job advertisement; it attracted attention and conveyed something about the distinctive culture of the firm. Non-verbal cues, including gestures and manufactured images, can also be provocative. For example, in the 1990s, Italian fashion company Benneton achieved high levels of awareness with a controversial poster and magazine campaign that included photographic images of an AIDS patient, a new-born baby and the bloodstained uniform of a dead soldier.

- **Using different channels and encoding**: We have considered how text-based argument and imagery may be used to construct and convey a persuasive message. These types of encoding lend themselves to conventional channels, such as presentations and promotional literature. However, organisations have access to other persuasive techniques, relying on different channels and forms of encoding. For example, imaginative communicators may be able to exploit other human senses. Sound, music, smell and taste can have a particularly strong persuasive impact, by-passing cognitive processes (i.e. the receiver's intellect), and making a direct impact at the level of the emotions and instincts. In some situations, they may also engage forms of 'direct action' in order to get their message across (see Table 5.3):

Table 5.3 Other forms of persuasive communication

Encoding/potential channels	Comments
Music and other sounds (e.g. soundtracks to advertisements, 'muzak' in retail outlets, 'on hold' music for call centres, hazard warning signals)	Music is sometimes described as 'organised sound'. Throughout history, sounds of all kinds have been used in persuasive communication. Songs have always been used to attract prospective lovers, whilst drums were beaten in order to terrify the enemy and lead reluctant soldiers into war. Because it is based on regular patterns, melody is readily absorbed and remembered. As a result, music provides a kind of mental 'hook' onto which other messages can be tagged. Advertising is often reinforced in this way. Ceremonial music at public events, such as the Olympic Games, plays a similar motivational role.
Taste and smell (e.g. food outlets, perfume retailers, creating 'mood' in buildings and public spaces, warning of gas escape)	Though the sense of smell in humans is less developed than that of other animals, it remains an influential stimulant. As the smell of cooking emerges from a restaurant, passers-by begin to feel hungry and may decide to stop for a meal. The multi-million pound perfume industry prospers on the belief that its well-packaged aromas have a persuasive effect on users and those they want to attract. Smells can seduce, stimulate, warn and repel (e.g. bitter tastes are added to household chemicals to deter young children). The related sense of taste shares many of these attributes. However, there are obvious practical limitations on the use of these stimuli in organisational settings.
Direct action	People are often persuaded by actions rather than rational arguments. Direct action is usually associated with political protest movements, but it can also be effective in a business environment. A research scientist wanted to convince the materials company '3M' that his invention had real market potential. Instead of using the conventional persuasion methods of formal presentations and feasibility studies, he produced a trial batch of his *entirely new* stationery product, distributing it to the secretaries of 3M's senior executives. The product proved very popular and supplies soon ran out. The secretaries, who were unable to obtain more stock, told their bosses just how useful the product was. Thanks to this direct action, the development project was approved and the '*Post-it note*' became a highly successful product worldwide.

The other side of the argument? Persuasion as interaction

As the earlier discussion indicated, the heart of persuasion involves communicators in constructing a coherent argument, supported by credible evidence and addressing both cognitive and affective aspects. However, the simplified model that we have adopted up to this point has one major limitation. While it has taken some account of the audience, as part of the process of designing an argument, our approach remains locked into the linear (or 'one-way') model of communication (see section 1.3). This ignores the fact that persuasion is an *interactive* process, involving all parties in a negotiation of meanings. The classic error, repeated by many organisations, is in attempting to sustain an argument that is grounded in their own initial position rather than engaging in a *genuine* interaction with those they are seeking to persuade. Mini-case 5.2 highlights the need to take the other party's perspective more seriously.

Mini-case 5.2	'OK Biotec': science and the politics of persuasion

The environmental campaigning organisation, *Green Earth* have alleged that an international biotechnology firm, OK Biotec is polluting a waterway and harming wildlife, including the 'Bay Gull', an endangered sea bird.

The senior management of OK Biotec are mostly former scientists. They are justifiably proud of their technical innovation record. The company is internationally recognised as a centre of excellence in all of the technical issues relating to the supposed pollutant. It has also obtained independent scientific reports, stating that:

- the company's outflows have no measurable effect on local concentrations of the chemical concerned;
- the birds are indeed being harmed, but the culprit is a *different* pollutant, which is being released by a number of other companies in the area.

The Chief Executive Officer of OK Biotec is Professor Katia Kleen, an experienced scientist who founded the company as a 'spin-out' from her former university, which is the world-leading research centre in this field. Professor Kleen decides to take a direct approach. She issues a strongly-worded press release, dismissing the campaigners' evidence as 'amateurish' and 'subversive'. Attached to the press release is a 15-page technical survey of the laboratories, incorporating all of the evidence from the independent researchers. Confident that the company is in the clear, Professor Kleen and her family leave town and enjoy a relaxing weekend at a country house hotel. And the result? Later in that same weekend, the *Sunday Inquisitor* publishes a front-page colour photograph of people in biological warfare suits, taking samples of a bright orange liquid pouring from an outfall pipe. Their headline blazes: '*Kleen says it's OK to poison the Bay*'. The article continues on page two, illustrated with another large colour photograph of dead and dying Bay Gull chicks in a nest.

Television news teams from surrounding countries catch up with Professor Kleen in the early hours of Sunday morning. She is filmed in the luxurious surroundings of the country house hotel, surrounded by the aftermath of a champagne celebration. On Monday, the newspapers are filled with outraged comments from politicians and members of the public. Their perception, based on edited highlights from the television interviews, is that Professor Kleen and her company are acting in a complacent, incompetent, secretive and uncaring manner. The independent technical reports are completely forgotten. OK Biotec's share price collapses and trading is temporarily suspended. Two days later, a trespassing tabloid journalist is pursued by an OK Biotec security guard. In the ensuing confusion, he is accidentally savaged to death by an over-enthusiastic guard dog. The entire Board of OK Biotec is forced to resign.

Three years later, the pollution continues unabated, the Bay Gull has become extinct and OK Biotec continues to get the blame. Professor Kleen has just secured a deal with a magazine publisher, in which she intends to tell her side of the story. In retrospect, it seems that the company's senior management team could have been more persuasive in this situation, to the benefit of the Bay Gull, and everyone concerned.

Questions

1 Identify what you consider to be OK Biotec's key communication errors.

2 Which messages had the greatest persuasive power for: (a) the OK Biotec management team; (b) the media; (c) the general public?

3 With the benefit of hindsight, devise an alternative communication strategy for OK Biotec. In doing so, suggest how the company should have responded at each stage, noting the likely media reactions.

Source: Written by the author, based on real events. 'OK Biotec' is a fictional organisation.

5.6 The ethics of persuasion

The circus promoter P.T. Barnum was known for the cynical maxim, '*There's a sucker born every minute*'. This suggests that persuasion is a relatively straightforward task, and that its purpose is to win a 'one-off' victory against a gullible opponent. Hopefully, this chapter has demonstrated that 'effectiveness' in persuasive communication cannot be judged by our ability to mislead or deceive an audience. In organisational settings, this kind of 'win–lose' approach to persuasion is generally counter-productive, because the long-term reputation of the organisation will be damaged by repeated efforts to 'sucker' its various stakeholders. This lesson has become even more relevant in the era of the internet, which provides an instantaneous channel for discontented stakeholders to communicate their dissatisfaction around the world. Consequently, the techniques of persuasive communication that have been outlined in this chapter will only be effective if receivers are taken seriously throughout the process. Of course, there are other reasons for behaving honestly, beyond this pragmatic concern with 'bad publicity'. Since the 1990s, many organisations have begun to take a more serious interest in business ethics and corporate governance. Under pressure from consumers, shareholders, journalists and governmental regulators, organisations of all kinds (i.e. including corporations, charities and public agencies) have begun to develop codes of conduct to regulate their activities. Persuasive communication raises a number of ethical issues. The most obvious of these is the use of lies and deception in areas such as advertising and selling (Carson 2002). Other areas include employee, supplier and shareholder relationships. In many cases, unethical persuasive practices are also likely to be either illegal or contrary to industry standards. Ethical issues relating specifically to persuasive communication can be divided into three broad categories, relating to the purpose, content and delivery of messages. Mini-case 5.3 considers some of the more contentious issues, using examples from the advertising industry.

Mini-case 5.3	The ethics of persuasion: examples from advertising

The advertising industry has long been the subject of criticism in ethical debates (e.g. Packard 1957). However, persuasive communication can also be regarded as unethical in many other contexts, ranging from job interviewing to the conduct of shareholder meetings. Consequently, examples from advertising are used here to illustrate issues that can be applied more widely:

- **Unacceptable purposes?** The intended purpose of certain messages may be considered unacceptable, but the picture is complicated by significant geographic and cultural variations in the ways that ethical standards are applied. For example, in the UK, television advertising targeted at children is closely regulated, but in some countries *all* advertising to children is banned. Similarly, it is illegal to advertise political parties and religious groups on UK television, though this practice is permitted in some countries, including the US. There have been increasingly stringent controls on the advertising of cigarette brands, again with some variation between countries.
- **Unacceptable content?** The previous section referred to Italian fashion retailer Benneton's advertising campaign, which featured graphic images of contemporary issues, including the bloodstained uniform of a soldier and a deathbed scene in a hospital ward. The campaign was criticised on the grounds that it exploited its sources in order to promote an unrelated and relatively superficial consumer product. Other frequent arguments have concerned nudity in advertisements, the portrayal of women and children, and comic stereotyping of other nationalities. These concerns also tend to be culture-specific, a factor that is normally taken into account by advertisers, on grounds of self-interest as much as ethics.
- **Unacceptable channels and encoding:** Some of the techniques developed to persuade audiences have subsequently been dismissed as unethical. For example, 'subliminal' techniques that fool the senses by projecting text or images for very short periods so that they are not readily apparent to the conscious mind. These forms of advertising have been outlawed for many years. However, technologies such as video text messaging are likely to present new challenges to the limits of acceptability. More traditional techniques, such as the 'hard sales' pitches perfected by unscrupulous dealers in double-glazing, time-share property and religion, are a continuing source of irritation and ethical debate. There is a degree of regulation of direct sales activities; the UK's 'Telephone Preference Service', for example, allows telephone subscribers to request their removal from the 'cold call' lists of direct sales firms. However, cases of undue pressure and mis-representation seem to be all too common.

Advertising and marketing professionals are often keenly aware of these ethical issues (e.g. Kotler *et al.* 2001). However, these efforts are not always communicated to external stakeholders. Reporting his research on marketing ethics, one North American academic noted with surprise that nearly half of the ethical codes in the organisations he studied were treated as *internal* documents. He concluded that ethical issues should be debated openly, across the boundaries of the firm:

▶

'Since marketing is at the forefront of a firm's external communication, discussion of ethical issues should not be a foreign concept. Going forward, the necessity for clear and candid communication to surmount ethical problems seems mandatory... Further examination of what factors lead to candour/openness/transparency in marketing is needed.' (Murphy 2002: 175–6)

Questions

1 Find recent examples of advertising materials, of any kind, that might be regarded as 'unethical' under each of the three categories. Discuss your assessments with other students or colleagues, noting any differences of viewpoint and the basis of these arguments.

2 Why do you think that so many organisations appear to be treating their marketing-related ethical codes as internal documents? How would you suggest that an organisation communicated with stakeholders, regarding these ethical codes?

3 Using the advertising examples as a guide, try to identify equivalent ethical issues that apply to other forms of persuasive communication (e.g. negotiations). Should these practices also be subject to ethical codes? If so, how might they be worded?

Source: Kotler *et al.* (2001), Carson (2002), Murphy (2002). Written by the author.

Summary

- Persuasion is an essential element in organisational communication, conveyed in all types of channel and present in many messages, which attempt to influence the ideas, beliefs or behaviours of receivers.

- While some organisational functions, such as marketing and public relations, are particularly 'persuasion-rich', persuasive communication plays an intermittent role in all areas of the organisation.

- The basic structure and content of persuasive messages, including the three fundamental elements of *ethos*, *logos* and *pathos*, can be related to established principles of argument (or 'rhetoric').

- The scale of the persuasive task depends on the nature of the sender, the receiver, the message and the context in which it is being communicated;

- Deliberate efforts at persuasion involve securing attention and developing a strong, coherent argument, which addresses the receiver's perceptions and feelings.

- Non-verbal signals, including images, music, smell and direct action, can act as powerful persuaders. Words alone may be insufficient; persuasive communication is often based on a creative use of multiple communication channels and forms of encoding.

- Persuasive communication raises important ethical issues for organisations, relating to the purpose and content of persuasive messages, and to the ways that they are conveyed.

Practical exercises

1 Are you convinced?

We have all experienced being persuaded to do something, to change an opinion or alter our behaviour. Much of this persuasion relates to fairly trivial issues, but occasionally we are persuaded to make a more significant change. Spend a few minutes thinking back on an occasion when you were persuaded to change your mind:

(a) What type of change was involved? Was it concerned with facts, concepts, beliefs, behaviour – or a mixture of these?

(b) What persuasive techniques were used on you?

(c) How did you respond to this persuasive effort?

(d) Ultimately, what do you think was *decisive* in making the change?

Seminar option: If you are working in a group, compare your answers with others. Does the type of persuasion appear to vary, depending on the subject matter? Can you reach any conclusions about the most effective persuaders?

2 The ultimate persuasion challenge?

(a) Divide into groups and spend 15 minutes devising the most difficult persuasive communication task you can imagine. It can involve a commercial business, a voluntary organisation or a public sector body. Write out the task on a large sheet of paper, specifying the message to be communicated, the sender, the receiver(s) and the general context. Use the following sample task as a model for structuring the information. (Note: This example can also be used as an alternative group task, or by those studying independently.)

A persuasive communication challenge: sample task

Sender	The city council
Receivers	Local personal and business tax payers
Message	Seeking agreement to increase local personal taxes by 45 per cent and business taxes by 24 per cent in the next financial year; the funds are needed for essential public services and economic development work.
Context	There is high regional unemployment, particularly among the 'under 25' and 'over 50' age groups. Local hospitals and schools are laying off staff due to budget cuts. It is also essential to encourage inward investment.

(b) Exchange your task with another group, and spend 30 minutes developing a communication proposal, designed to overcome the problem that you have been set. Try to be as creative and convincing as possible, whilst basing all your arguments on the perceptions of the *receivers*. If time allows, present your solutions and discuss how effectively you have made use of all available media and techniques.

Campaigning against poverty – Oxfam's persuasive communication

This case study is based on the reflections of a member of Oxfam's full-time campaign staff, based in Oxford. The author, Naveed Chaudhri, writes in a personal capacity and views expressed in the case study are not necessarily those of Oxfam GB.

Background

Oxfam GB, a development organisation dedicated to finding lasting solutions to poverty and suffering, is one of the UK's biggest charities. Founded in 1942, Oxfam today works in more than 80 countries around the world. There is now a family of 12 Oxfams, which together form Oxfam International. The aim of Oxfam International is to maximise impact on poverty by co-ordinating work of these individual members.

With wide public recognition, Oxfam GB undertakes a range of activities: it is a charity retailer, a responder to disasters, a funder of development projects, and a campaigner for change. Oxfam's mission statement gives a broad mandate for this wide range of activities, providing a clear moral message and a basis for all its public communications.

Oxfam is explicitly a campaigning organisation. It states: 'To overcome poverty and suffering involves changing unjust policies and practices, nationally and internationally, as well as working closely with people in poverty.' Recent Oxfam campaigns include seeking tighter UK arms-control legislation, pushing for funding for basic education for all, and arguing for the need to reform the world trade system. With limited resources, development charities can only help a tiny fraction of those in need, whereas improving policies and practices on these issues could potentially have a far wider effect on poverty.

Trust: the basis of Oxfam's legitimacy

It is important to put Oxfam's campaigning into perspective. Its core work is to put the funds of generous donors to good use in practical ways, to improve the lives of particular classes of beneficiaries. Without a continuing record of effective poverty relief, Oxfam would have no moral grounding for the opinions it expresses. This record is the basis both of enormous public trust, and, crucially for campaigning success, of widespread respect from politicians of all parties. Under UK charity law, Oxfam must ensure that its public statements are based on sound knowledge, and are necessary to achieve its defined charitable objectives. This is vital for any development charity seeking to campaign for change.

Inevitably, campaigners enter the political arena. The desire to speak out may conflict with the need to remain impartial, and with the need to retain broad-based public support. Campaigners must be able to communicate their concerns in a way which balances these competing pressures, in an often complex and rapidly-changing environment.

Ethical dilemmas: Iraq and Afghanistan

In early 2003, Oxfam recommended that there should not be US and British military intervention in Iraq. Although concerned not to be seen to be aligned with the anti-war movement (for the sorts of reasons outlined above), Oxfam's experience warned of the likely humanitarian situation following military action, a concern which was subsequently shown to be justified. A year or so earlier, however, Oxfam's call for a pause in the US bombing in northern Afghanistan to allow in food supplies before the onset of winter was unheeded, yet the feared widespread famine did not occur. Underlying these different concerns, justified or otherwise, was a single issue for Oxfam's credibility: whether entering publicly into the political arena would cause more harm or good. If the effect Oxfam could have on those particular situations was likely to be positive, would speaking out nevertheless have repercussions for its ability to work effectively in other parts of the world? Would the public's trust in the organisation be damaged?

Marshalling the arguments – and the support

Of course, it does matter very much that Oxfam gets the arguments right, and its 60 years' experience of working with poor people all around the world is perhaps its greatest asset. But campaigning is about far more than just lobbying at a policy level, and the knowledge Oxfam can bring to a discussion is just the starting point. Politicians need to be convinced that Oxfam's arguments are right; they also need to be given a reason to act. Thus the potential for bringing about the implementation of policy recommendations should be the measure of success when planning a campaign. This will rely on the different channels of influence which can be utilised, and, usually, on the level of popular support (or perceived popular support) for a campaign. Being right is of little use without some prospect, albeit sometimes over the long term, that one can change the political agenda for the better.

More than just 'marketing an idea'

Campaigning is seen by some as ultimately about marketing an idea, and campaigning organisations certainly have much to learn from the corporate sector about marketing tools and strategies. However, campaigning is much more than this. Far more than with any commercial product, people's loyalty to an idea is vital, and so the moral purpose underlying the campaign is paramount. Not only this, but the way in which one campaigns – the way in which one deals with people – is as important as the message itself. No matter how compelling the analogy with marketing, an organisation such as Oxfam, renowned for its humanitarian concern, would ignore this at its peril. And perhaps this is a lesson Oxfam can give to commercial companies: that a tangible concern for people should be at the heart of successful brands.

Complex problems, simple messages? Understanding Oxfam's audiences

The problems with which Oxfam deals are complex, the factors affecting people living in poverty many and varied. Oxfam's recent *Make Trade Fair* campaign is a good example, dealing with the labyrinthine details of the global trade system, yet needing to win the support of thousands, if not millions, of ordinary people in order to influence decision makers, in the face of very powerful vested interests.

Communicating these concerns requires a different approach for different audiences, with varying levels of detail required, depending on their levels of interest and knowledge.

The largest number of potential supporters, perhaps motivated by a desire for the 'system' to be fair, but with a limited desire or opportunity to take action, needs convincing by very clear communications, setting out the moral arguments briefly and compellingly. This level of mass communication must be underpinned by the trust referred to above. It is also where the skills of mass marketing, including the increasing use of new technology (i.e. what is now termed 'e-campaigning') come into their own. Other audiences include campaigns activists, politicians, trades unions, local, regional and national media, companies, and other non-governmental organisations. Each audience needs its own communications strategy, depending on the issues involved, and the importance of that audience in the matrix of potential influences on the relevant decision makers.

Not only do levels of engagement vary, but the motivations of these different audiences can be radically different. For example, an activist may be motivated to promote fairly-traded products by detailed explanations of the mechanisms by which the benefits to poor producers are guaranteed; yet average consumers will need to be convinced primarily of the quality of the product, coupled with a general belief that by buying it, they are making a positive contribution to the cause.

There are many other communications challenges for campaigners to face, including the need to address cultural sensitivities; to work alongside others living in very different circumstances; to work increasingly on a global scale for increased impact; and to use new technologies as campaigning tools. Nevertheless, the basic principles of campaigning remain the same, and to be successful, Oxfam needs to win the battle of both hearts and minds.

Questions

1 Re-read the case and identify examples of the ways in which Oxfam constructs and delivers persuasive messages, making use of relevant material from the chapter (e.g. Aristotle's fundamental distinction between the three elements of rhetoric: *ethos*, *logos*, and *pathos*).

2 What do you consider to be the main differences between persuasive communication in a campaigning organisation, such as Oxfam, and that taking place in a commercial organisation, such as a food retailer?

3 What are the main barriers to communication with Oxfam's various audiences? How are they being overcome?

4 Oxfam has developed a number of web-based resources, including the 'e-campaigning' activities referred to in the case. Review these resources (www.oxfam.org.uk) and prepare a short presentation (i.e. four bullet pointed slides, plus notes) evaluating each resource in terms of its persuasive potential.

Source: Written by Naveed Chaudhri

Further reading

Much of the research on persuasive communication has been conducted within specialist disciplines, such as buyer behaviour, advertising, sales and public relations; additional references are included in Chapter 10. **Skerlep** (2001) includes a reasonably accessible introduction to the theories of rhetorical argument, tracing it back to the classic study by **Toulmin** (1957). **Von Werder** (1999) also makes use of Toulmin's framework in a complex empirical study, exploring how Daimler-Benz reached an important strategic decision through argument. **Williams and Miller** (2002) report a much simpler study, arguing persuasion techniques should be adapted to the decision-making styles of business leaders. **Cooper and Locke** (2000) and **Warr** (1996) address some related psychological issues in work contexts. **Livesey** (2002) is an interesting case study, analysing the persuasive communication of a large corporation using rhetorical and discourse analysis techniques. **Bowie** (2002) is a useful edited 'reader' covering various aspects of business ethics, including those related to marketing, addressed by **Murphy** (2002) selling and advertising, by **Carson** (2002).

References

Alderfer, C.P. (1972) *Existence, relatedness and growth*. Macmillan, London.

Aristotle (1991) *The Art of Rhetoric* (Lawson-Tancred, H (ed.)). Penguin, London.

Barnett, W.P. and Burgleman, R.A. (1996) 'Evolutionary perspectives on strategy'. *Strategic Management Journal*, 17, 5–19.

Bowie, N.E. (ed.) (2002) *The Blackwell guide to business ethics*. Blackwell, Oxford.

Carson, T.L. (2002) 'Ethical issues in selling and advertising'. in Bowie, N.E. (ed.) *op cit.* (186–205).

Chen, G., Wilson, J., Mehle, W. and Cooper, P. (1998) *Interim evaluation report: photo radar program one year after introduction of the violation ticket phase*. Insurance Corporation of British Columbia, Victoria.

Cooper, C.L. and Locke, E.A. (2000) *Industrial and organizational psychology: linking theory with practice*. Blackwell, Oxford.

Department for Transport (2003) 'Speed cameras'. Department for Transport, London. (Available at: www.dft.gov.uk/roadsafety (accessed 12th August).

Hamlyn, S. (1989) *How to talk so people listen*. HarperCollins, London.

Hollingsworth, M. (1997) *The ultimate spin doctor: the life and fast times of Tim Bell*. Hodder and Stoughton, London,

Kotler, P., Armstrong, G., Saunders, J. and Wong, J. (2001) *Principles of marketing: the European edition* (3rd edn.). FT Prentice Hall, Harlow.

Lawler, E.E. (1973) *Motivation in work organizations*. Brooks/Cole, Monterey CA.

Lewin, A.Y. and Koza, M.P. (2001) 'Empirical research in co-evolutionary processes of strategic adaptation and change: the promise and the challenge'. *Organization Studies*, 22, 6, v–xii (Special Issue on: Multi-level Analysis and Co-evolution).

Livesey, S.M. (2002) 'Global warming wars: rhetorical and discourse analytical approaches to ExxonMobil's corporate public discourse'. *Journal of Business Communication*, 39, 1, 117–48.

McClelland, D.C. (1988) *Human motivation*. Cambridge University Press, Cambridge.

Mandela, N.R. (1994) *Long walk to freedom: the autobiography of Nelson Mandela*. Little, Brown and Company, London.

Maslow, A.H. (1943) 'A theory of human motivation'. *Psychology Review*, 50, 307–96 (July).

Maslow, A.H. (1987) *Motivation and personality* (3rd edn.). Harper and Row, New York.

Michie, D. (1998) *The invisible persuaders: how Britain's spin doctors manipulate the media*. Bantam, London.

Miller, D. and Dinan, W. (2000) 'The rise of the PR industry in Britain, 1979–98.' *European Journal of Communication*, 15, 1, 5–35.

Murphy, P.E. (2002) 'Marketing ethics at the Millennium: review, reflections and recommendations'. in Bowie, N.E. (ed.) *The Blackwell guide to business ethics*. Blackwell, Oxford (165–85).

Oesch, S.L. (2002) *Statement before the Maryland House of Delegates, Commerce and Government Matters Committee: automated speed enforcement* (5th February). Insurance Institute for Highway Safety, Arlington VA.

Ovarec. C. and Salvador, M. (1993) 'The duality of rhetoric: theory as discursive practice.' in Poulakos, T. (ed.) *Rethinking the history of rhetoric: multidisciplinary essays on the rhetorical tradition*. Westview Press, Boulder CO (173–92).

Packard, V. ([1957] 1997) *The hidden persuaders: the classic study of the American advertising machine*. Penguin, London.

Skerlep, A. (2001) 'Re-evaluating the role of rhetoric in public relations theory and in strategies of corporate discourse'. *Journal of Communication Management*, 6, 2, 176–87.

Toulmin, S. (1957) *The uses of argument*. Cambridge University Press, Cambridge.

Van Eeerde, W. and Thierry, H. (1996) 'Vroom's expectancy models and work-related criteria: a meta-analysis'. *Journal of Applied Psychology*, 81, 5, 575–86 (October).

Von Werder, A. (1999) 'Argumentation rationality of management decisions'. *Organization Science*, 10, 5, 672–90.

Warr, P. (1996) *Psychology at work*. Penguin Books, London.

Williams, G. and Miller, R.B. (2002) 'Change the way you persuade'. *Harvard Business Review*, 80, 65–73 (May).

CHAPTER 6

Securing feedback: interactive communication

Half of the money I spend on advertising is wasted; the trouble is, I don't know which half.
William Hesketh Lever, consumer product manufacturer

Learning outcomes

By the end of this chapter you should be able to:

- recognise the wide variety of responses stimulated by organisational activity and the importance of securing feedback effectively;
- identify the different characteristics of organisational feedback and the mechanisms that are used to collect and process this information;
- critically assess specific feedback mechanisms employed in relation to the organisation's employees and its customers;
- make connections between feedback mechanisms and other organisational and managerial issues, such as knowledge management, organisational learning and emotional intelligence.

6.1 Introduction

As William Hesketh Lever recognised, the challenge in securing feedback is not simply to obtain information but to secure feedback that is both relevant and of high quality. Lever's problem was echoed more recently by the chief executive officer of Hewlett Packard, who commented, 'If HP knew what HP knows we would be three times as profitable.' This chapter is concerned with the ways that organisations secure feedback from their internal and external stakeholders, and from the wider environment in which they operate. By 'feedback' we are referring to the diverse range of responses elicited by messages that are sent out by organisations. Feedback is essential to any open system, facilitating interaction and enabling it to adapt and meet the changing demands of its environment (see section 1.5). In reviewing feedback mechanisms, we concentrate on the implications for communication, but also engage with a much wider debate concerning the ways that organisations manage knowledge and learn from their collective experience. An organisation requires feedback from all of its stakeholder groups if it is to continue to function effectively. The quality of this feedback depends, in turn, on the effective use of particular communication channels. For example, marketing departments have to maintain a close watch on qualitative and quantitative changes in demand (e.g. the emergence of a new fashion trend, a collapse in consumer spending), in order that their company's products remain competitive. They do so using a number of channels, including survey questionnaires, focus group interviews and the analysis of weekly sales reports. Organisational managers of all kinds need to obtain feedback from their colleagues and business partners. Failure to secure this feedback can lead to serious dysfunctional effects, such as under-achievement and internal conflict.

The sheer diversity of organisational feedback, and the many channels through which it is conveyed, make it difficult to generalise about the techniques for securing effective feedback. However, it is possible to identify some general principles. The chapter begins with an overview of the main kinds of feedback, including their inherent characteristics and the form in which messages are received. It is followed by a closer examination of the feedback mechanisms that enable organisations to obtain information from one of their major stakeholder groups – their employees. We then consider the practicalities of form design, illustrating the challenges of constructing an apparently simple communication channel for the purposes of feedback. The chapter concludes with a brief discussion that highlights connections between the main themes of this chapter and related research, in the areas of knowledge management, organisational learning and emotional intelligence.

6.2 Organisational feedback: an initial overview

There is an astonishing diversity of organisational feedback mechanisms, but they are rarely subjected to systematic analysis. This section presents an initial critical review of the types of feedback that are secured in different parts of the organisation, highlighting their inherent characteristics and the communication channels through which they are typically conveyed. We have already noted that communication channels vary in the extent to which they facilitate feedback (see section 1.5). In the case of feedback, we can identify two distinct dimensions relating to the quality of the messages conveyed: their degree of urgency and their inherent complexity. Both dimensions need to be taken into account when designing and assessing feedback mechanisms:

- **Degree of urgency**: In some situations, the prime requirement is to secure *immediate* feedback on a particular organisational activity. For example, the engineers at a hospital need to know at once if there is a technical fault in a piece of medical equipment. The message is urgent because any delay is likely to affect service delivery, which could endanger the lives of patients. In other parts of the hospital (e.g. in the human resources department, where an employee's annual appraisal interview is processed), there is less urgency regarding the timing of the process.

- **Inherent complexity**: For some forms of feedback, the prime requirement is to convey very *complex* messages relating to the organisation. For example, at the headquarters of a restaurant chain, a dissatisfied customer's verbal complaint may be a mixture of factual information, subjective perceptions and strong human emotions. Complex messages of this kind can also contain a degree of ambiguity, requiring the organisation to interpret the meaning of the message (i.e. it may be difficult to identify the underlying cause of the complaint from the initial message). By contrast, much of the feedback collected by the restaurant chain will comprise relatively straightforward data (e.g. standardised accounting reports sent to the finance department by each restaurant on a regular basis).

When these two dimensions are represented graphically, we are given some indication of the variety of feedback mechanisms employed in organisations (see Figure 6.1). Figure 6.1 suggests the relative strengths of several common feedback mechanisms in terms of their information richness and immediacy of response. Many other examples could be added, and their position may be open to debate, depending on the particular circumstances in which they are being employed. Note that the categorisation 'low' degree of urgency in Figure 6.1 does not imply lack of importance, but only that the message contained in this feedback is not highly time-sensitive.

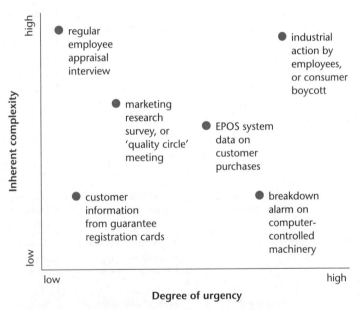

Figure 6.1 **Characterising feedback mechanisms – urgency and complexity**

Examining the diversity of feedback mechanisms

Organisational feedback is encoded in many different forms, ranging from numerical data on the management accountant's paper printouts to the spoken words and gestures of a protestor during the annual shareholder's meeting. As these two examples illustrate, feedback can also be collected in many different locations, within and beyond the physical boundaries of the organisation. However, one of the challenges for communicators is to ensure that this collection actually takes place. We have seen how any message can be obstructed or distorted by powerful barriers, operating at the level of individuals, groups, the organisation and the wider environment. Consequently, the quality of the feedback obtained will depend a great deal on the context in which it is sent and the degree to which it is under organisational control. For example, statistical process control data collected inside a company's production plant may be highly reliable. By contrast, most organisations find it extremely difficult to gauge public reactions to their proposed or enacted strategies. In contrast to feedback from the production line, the latter involves less reliable types of data collection. Moreover, messages from the public are likely to be more complex and their responses are open to a variety of interpretations.

Table 6.1 The diversity of organisational feedback: some examples

Area of activity or stakeholder group	Typical feedback mechanisms	Comment
Suppliers	Bids from suppliers Informal contacts	Quantitative and qualitative data, collected via formal and informal processes in a purchasing department.
Production	Quality audits Production statistics	Quantitative and qualitative data, primarily collected via formal processes in a production department.
Employees	Appraisal process Job satisfaction surveys Staff turnover rates Response to job adverts 'The grapevine'	Mainly qualitative data, collected via formal and informal processes at a number of locations.
Customers	Sales data Market research Customer complaints	Quantitative and qualitative data, collected via formal processes in sales, marketing and customer service departments.
Local community/ general public	Stakeholder consultations Media coverage	Primarily qualitative data, may be collected formally by corporate affairs and informally by other members of staff.
Financial community	Accounting statements Analysts reports Informal contact	Quantitative data (from accounts) and qualitative data, collected more informally by accountants, treasury managers and senior executives.
Management accounting	Accounting statements Variance reports	Primarily quantitative data, collected formally by cost accountants.

In the case of organisational feedback, one of the biggest challenges is to ensure that messages are conveyed beyond the point of collection, in order that other parts of the organisation are aware of any incipient problems. Like other messages, feedback may need translating across functional or departmental borders. Consider, for example, a Chinese manufacturer of hi-fi equipment, who is exporting to international markets. Feedback received by the European sales team may indicate that there is resistance to some cosmetic features of the product design. However, unless this information is conveyed – in an appropriate format – to the company's research and development department in Shanghai, there may be a costly delay in remodelling the product. For senior executives, the main concern is to ensure their exposure to relevant streams of feedback from *all parts* of the organisation. Clearly, those at the centre of the organisation are not in a position to absorb all of the incoming information in detail. However, subject to appropriate filtering, their exposure to a diversity of feedback can enable senior executives to make important connections, informing their strategic decision making (e.g. Grant 1996, Kay 2000, Spender 1996). For example, by synthesising feedback obtained from multiple stakeholders, the organisation will be better positioned to embark on a major acquisition, diversification or divestment. This is not a trivial task, and organisations often struggle to maintain an effective flow of information. Mini-case 6.1 considers how organisational feedback mechanisms can fail in respect of ethical issues, a form of 'moral deafness' that can have disastrous results for all concerned.

Mini-case 6.1	When feedback mechanisms fail: explaining 'moral deafness'

In his book, *The muted conscience*, Frederick Bruce Bird explores an interesting and important question for all organisational communicators, which was first introduced in section 2.4. Given that all individuals have moral concerns, why do they so often fail to voice these concerns in the organisations where they work? Bird suggests that 'moral silence' is reinforced by various forms of 'moral deafness' and 'moral blindness'. In other words, people manage to ignore emerging ethical issues. Those who do speak out, the so-called 'whistle-blowers', often face a great deal of hostility in their organisation. They can find their careers undermined and may even face threats of physical violence. The fear of experiencing these problems can act as a powerful disincentive on individuals. Also, at the organisational level, it seems that there are institutional obstacles to feedback of this kind. (Note: Although the author does not make this connection, these concepts can be linked to Janis's (1982) concept of 'groupthink' and the 'Abilene paradox' (see section 2.4), which suggest how social psychological factors might contribute to the process).

Nestlé and infant formula: a case of 'moral deafness'?
In Bird's definition, 'People are morally deaf to the degree that they do not hear and do not respond to moral issues that have been raised by others' (Bird 2002: 55). He identifies five types of moral deafness:

- as inattentiveness
- as not being ready to hear bad news
- as not seeking out bad news
- as not comprehending
- as not taking into consideration the accounts of others

One of the cases cited as an example of moral deafness concerns Nestlé, one of the world's largest branded foods manufacturers. Nestlé has been engaged in more than two decades of argument with campaigning organisations over its strategy for marketing infant powdered milk formula in developing countries. In the early 1980s, the company was criticised publicly for promoting formula in situations where its use was bound to increase infant mortality, due to the poor quality of local water supplies and the risk that the product would be used incorrectly. Campaigners argued that advertising and sales

▶

promotion techniques were being used to persuade mothers to abandon breast-feeding in favour of the infant formula. The initial response from Nestlé's board of directors, which was captured in a televised international press conference, was widely-regarded as both arrogant and defensive. Protests were organised in response to perceived inaction on the part of the company. Nestlé found its products boycotted by student unions, religious groups and other organisations involved with development issues.

Over subsequent years, Nestlé has made significant changes to its marketing and promotional practices. It has also engaged in a long and expensive public relations campaign, which has sought to engage in a dialogue with campaigners. The company has a separate section on its website (www.babymilk.nestle.com) addressing issues such as the company's compliance with international codes of practice. For example, it states that:

> 'Nestlé leaves the recommendation of appropriate breast-milk substitutes to health professionals and for almost 20 years has stopped all promotion of infant formula to the public. This commitment to a ban on promotional materials means: no advertising, no store promotions, no price incentives, no "milk nurses" and no to educational materials mentioning infant formula.' (Nestlé 2003)

However, campaign groups such as Baby-milk Action continue to exert pressure on the company, using its website (www.babymilkaction.org) to present a case against the company and to encourage people to boycott its products. This long-running debate has been given a new urgency in the context of the AIDS epidemic, which has created additional demand for infant formula and dietary supplements.

Questions

1 What factors do you think may have contributed to the apparent 'moral deafness' of Nestlé in the early 1980s?

2 What kinds of communication channel have operated to change the company's position since the initial protests? Can the current situation still be regarded as 'moral deafness' in Bird's definition?

3 Describe a recent example of an organisation displaying moral deafness, blindness or silence. How might the development of technologies, such as e-mail and the internet, have affected these phenomena?

Sources: Baby Milk Action (2003), Bird (2002), Nestlé (2003). Written by the author.

6.3 Securing stakeholder feedback: the case of employees

This section considers some of the main feedback mechanisms used in relation to the key internal stakeholder group for all organisations – its employees. Similar exercises could be conducted for each of the main external stakeholder groups, including customers, suppliers and local communities. In selecting this stakeholder group, our aim is to examine the patterns of *communication* that underpin these feedback mechanisms, rather than to address them from a specifically human resources management (HRM) perspective.

There are many ways for organisations to obtain feedback from employees, relating to issues such as their performance in work tasks, their degree of satisfaction with the job, managers, colleagues and the work environment, and internal perceptions of the organisation. Feedback may be collected by line managers and human resources specialists, but it is doubtful whether these different sources are always integrated. In this section we consider four typical communication channels in brief, before focusing our attention on an increasingly popular channel, the '360-degree appraisal'.

● **Job satisfaction surveys**: Many organisations use questionnaire survey techniques to obtain feedback from employees. The questionnaires are sometimes presented in another guise (e.g. a 'communication audit'), and are often conducted by external research consultancies in order to overcome employees' concerns regarding anonymity. This channel is likely to generate a mixture of qualitative and quantitative data, relating both to specific issues (e.g. identifying problems with the catering facilities) and to employee attitudes (e.g. degree of support for a proposed organisational restructuring). Data are analysed and summarised in order to provide feedback to senior managers and human resources departments, normally in the form of a written report or verbal presentation. Surveys can provide a broad yet concise overview, highlighting key differences between departments and types of staff, for example. However, there is a danger that important messages will be lost during the intermediate stages of the process.

● **Staff turnover rates**: This deceptively simple measure may be of more relevance in larger organisations, where there are enough employees to allow for the identification of trends. Increased staff turnover may indicate a number of things, including dissatisfaction with the job or the organisation, fears over its future, or a highly competitive job market. Similarly, reduced turnover may be interpreted positively (i.e. staff enjoy working for the organisation), or negatively (i.e. they are only staying on in the hope of large redundancy payments). To interpret the data correctly, it is necessary to complement statistical analysis of turnover rates (e.g. between different time periods, or across departments and geographic locations) with qualitative data. This may range from informal feedback from managers to a more elaborate system of 'exit interviews' with departing members of staff.

● **Response to job advertising**: Organisations need to be aware of the state of the employment market, particularly when they are seeking large numbers of new staff, or have a shortage of people in a particular specialism. A decline in the level of interest in job advertisements may be measured in terms of number of initial enquiries, number of applications received or quality of applicants. Each of these measures may indicate various possibilities. For example, the market may have become more competitive, the organisation may no longer be perceived as an attractive employer, or the pay and conditions for a specific post are not sufficient to attract good candidates.

● **'The grapevine'**: This informal and unofficial channel can provide some of the richest feedback from employees. However, because messages pass primarily by word of mouth, in corridors, canteens and bars, senior managers find them elusive and difficult to assess. Even where they have access to these messages, the information may be transient, inconsistent and unreliable. Grapevines are a common source of mis-information, particularly when an organisation is facing threats or uncertainties. Rumours may flare up for a short period of time, and information received from one part of the organisation may be contradicted by that from another source.

Each of these channels provides feedback on employees, though the quality and format of the information varies significantly according to which channel is selected. The 360-degree appraisal has become a widely-adopted feedback mechanism, which tackles several limitations identified in earlier forms of appraisal. It integrates information from several different sources in order to provide a more reliable basis for appraising employees.

360-degree appraisal

The 360-degree performance review has grown in popularity as a result of the problems encountered with other forms of appraisal. The term '360-degree' refers to the idea that employees' assessments should be based on feedback from several sources, including their peers, subordinates, supervisors and sometimes external stakeholders such as customers (Marchington and Wilkinson 2002: 329). From a communication perspective, the primary advantage of this approach is that multiple-rater assessments provide information that has greater validity, and that has the potential to be more persuasive when it is presented to the employee. The practice of giving and receiving 360-degree feedback should also generate valuable information at an organisational level, better informing strategic decision making. It can also foster a climate of more open communication in the organisations where it is adopted, something that is particularly appropriate for new organisational forms (see section 7.3). Mini-case 6.2 illustrates how 360-degree feedback was implemented in one large organisation.

| Mini-case 6.2 | Appraisal at 'EnergyCo': 360-degree feedback using questionnaires |

EnergyCo extracts, refines and distributes crude oil products to a worldwide market. As part of its policy of continuous improvement, the company involves all of its middle managers in a process of 360-degree feedback. Initial data for the feedback are collected using a questionnaire that is distributed via the organisation's intranet to each manager's line manager, their peer group and those who report directly to them. The manager also completes the questionnaire. Although completion of these questionnaires is not compulsory, over 95% of employees fill in and return them. The questionnaire focuses on those aspects of a manager's performance that EnergyCo considers are essential to its survival in the global energy market and, in effect, describes the standards that are expected of its employees. These are known in EnergyCo as, 'essential managerial skills and behaviours' and are grouped under the sub-headings of: 'leadership', 'people management', 'commitment', 'customer focus', 'communication', 'teamwork', 'adaptability', 'planning' and 'innovation'. The person completing the questionnaire rates the performance of the manager across 45 indicator statements grouped under these nine sub-headings. For each of these statements the person completing the questionnaire is also asked to indicate the importance of the behaviour or skill to that manager's role. This is illustrated by the following extract from the questionnaire, which covers the 'communication' sub-heading:

Skills or behaviours	Actual performance						Importance					
	Never	Rarely	Sometimes	Usually	Mostly	Always	None	Very little	Little	Reasonable	Considerable	Critical
Communication												
15. Open in dealings with others	1	2	3	4	5	6	1	2	3	4	5	6
16. Offers clear, concise, timely feedback	1	2	3	4	5	6	1	2	3	4	5	6
17. Builds networks with others	1	2	3	4	5	6	1	2	3	4	5	6
18. Trusts employees	1	2	3	4	5	6	1	2	3	4	5	6

Answers to the questions are treated as strictly confidential. Individual replies are not disclosed to the manager who only sees their results aggregated into tables. The tables show their peers' view, the view of those who report directly to them, as well as their own view and that of their line manager. A local university produces these tables independently, acting as external consultants to EnergyCo. If there are any additional comments on the questionnaire, the consultants ensure that these are anonymised before being included in an individual manager's feedback report.

Making use of the feedback
Initially, each feedback report is used as the basis for the annual Staff Development Review between the manager, their line manager and a member of the human resources department. Differences in responses are considered and possible reasons explored. As part of this process, any areas where the manager's performance needs improvement are considered, and an action plan is agreed jointly. Although it is not EnergyCo's policy to make feedback reports available generally to other employees within the company, a number of middle managers at EnergyCo have agreed to discuss their results with their peers and those who report directly. This has enabled them to obtain more detailed feedback.

Questions

1 Why do you think the feedback questionnaire is completed by the manager receiving feedback in addition to their line manager, peer group and those who report directly to them?

2 Why do you think the data from the feedback questionnaire for peers and those reporting directly to the manager are aggregated into tables rather than the completed questionnaires being given to each manager?

3 How might data collected from 360-degree feedback questionnaires, such as that used by EnergyCo, be used by a human resources department to inform an organisation-wide training and development strategy?

Source: This case was prepared by Mark N. K. Saunders, drawing on experience of implementing 360-degree feedback programmes. 'EnergyCo' is a fictional organisation.

6.4 Practicalities of feedback: designing a form

The preceding discussion has been concerned with the broad principles of communicating feedback. This section looks at one practical application of these principles, the task of designing a form. These humble documents can be an important communication channel, enabling the organisation to collect pre-specified information in a structured way (see Figure 6.2).

The form designer needs to address the following questions:

- **What do I really need to know?** There is a fine balance between asking too little and too much. It is a waste of resources to collect and analyse unnecessary information. In addition, an over-long form may alienate the person who has to complete it. On the other hand, missing out a key question can have disastrous results. For example, when a customer enquiry form fails to ask for a contact telephone number or e-mail, essential for any follow-up calls.

- **Are the questions clear, concise and acceptable?** Questions and instructions must be unambiguous and readily understood by anyone who might need to complete the form. The Plain English Campaign has fought a long battle with government agencies and businesses for clear language in forms and other documents (see Mini-case 3.1). It is also important to avoid questions that might upset the respondent, leading to a non-response, or even a complaint. For example, 'ethnic monitoring' questions that are now included in most job applications need to be worded carefully, accompanied by a written assurance that they play no part in the selection process.

- **Is the structure logical?** Again, it is important to focus on the needs of the person completing the form. If the layout is unclear, or the sequence of questions is unusual, it will lead to confusion and irritation. The result will be that the responses are either incomplete or, more seriously, may include errors and mis-representation.

- **Does the form encourage a positive response?** Taking care over the previous three points should help to increase the response rate and ensure that useful information is obtained. It is also possible to motivate the person who is *investing their time* in completing the document with an attractive form design and incentives for completion. It is relatively easy to produce a professional-looking document using standard wordprocessing software, particularly with the help of the templates provided with the more popular programs. Some forms contain intrinsic incentives for completion. For example, a job application form holds out the prospect of employment, while a tax return comes with a threat of a financial penalty if it is not sent back by a certain date. In some cases, it may be necessary to provide additional incentives, such as free product samples, prize draws, competitions and charitable contributions.

'TrainCo' **Customer feedback form**

TrainCo would like to hear your comments on our services. Please take a few minutes to complete this simple online form. All feedback will be reviewed by TrainCo staff and we aim to respond to specific requests within 5 working days.

Which service did you use?   ○ Local/commuter
○ Inter-city
○ International/sleeper

Which station did you travel from?   ALPHAVILLE

Which station did you travel to?   ALPHAVILLE

When did you start your journey?   01 ▲▼ JAN ▲▼ Date
01 ▲▼ AM ▲▼ Time

What type of feedback are you sending?   ○ Suggestion
○ Complaint
○ Request for information
○ Compliment

Please type your suggestion, complaint, request or compliment in the box below

Would you like a response from TrainCo?   ○ Yes   ○ No

If you have requested a response, please insert your contact details

Last name

First name (or initials)

Address

Town or City

Post or zip code

E-mail address

Phone number (day)   please include area codes

Phone number (evening)

How would you like us to contact you?   ○ E-mail   ○ Phone   ○ Letter

Click here to send your feedback to TrainCo   SEND FORM

Click here to clear the form and start again   START AGAIN

TrainCo thanks you for your comments

Figure 6.2 Example of a form designed to obtain feedback

6.5 Feedback, knowledge and organisational learning

At the beginning of the chapter we noted that any discussion of organisational feedback mechanisms is bound to connect with a much broader debate concerning knowledge management and organisational learning. This section highlights three themes from that debate, which have a particular significance for the communication process:

- the distinction between single- and double-loop learning;
- the relationship between tacit and explicit knowledge; and
- the ongoing debate concerning individual- and organisational-level knowledge.

These brief introductions should also provide useful links for those studying related subjects, including organisation theory, strategy and change management. The chapter closes by returning to the individual level and the popular concept of 'emotional intelligence'.

- **Single- and double-loop learning**: This long-established distinction refers to the different levels at which feedback may be absorbed (Argyris and Schön 1978). In single-loop learning, the individual or organisation simply responds to the incoming message, while double-loop learning involves a deeper reflection on the reasons for the message, creating new perspectives and more substantial changes in activity. For example, a single-loop response to a decline in product sales might be to reduce production, whereas a double-loop response would be to re-think the whole marketing strategy.

- **Explicit and tacit knowledge**: Many writers have attempted to distinguish 'tacit' knowledge, which is a product of the direct experience of an individual or group, and 'explicit' knowledge, which has been separated from practice (e.g. in the form of a textbook). From our perspective, the key features of tacit knowledge are that it is difficult to communicate, because it cannot be separated from the processes in which it was created, and where it is being applied (Spender 1996: 67). For example, the practical knowledge of the game possessed by a leading football player (or a leading football team) can be observed in action, but the people concerned would find it difficult to transfer their knowledge to others. By contrast, explicit data, such as the statistics recording number of goals scored by a team over many seasons, can be readily communicated.

- **Individual and organisational knowledge**: A common complaint in the organisation learning literature is the tendency to treat these as functionally equivalent, when there are clear differences in the ways that knowledge is handled at the level of the individual person and the organisation. For example, we know that the way that ideas are generated in a team of people during a 'brainstorming' session cannot be reduced to the activities of its individual members. This has led some researchers to explore the dynamic relationship between tacit/explicit and individual/collective knowledge in organisations (e.g. Penrose 1959, Spender 1996, Nonaka and Takeuchi 1995).

Mini-case 6.3 returns us to the role that people can play in securing feedback, as we review the concept of 'emotional intelligence'. This idea emerged in the mid-

1990s, a product of research into managerial cognition and its relationship with human emotion. It has since become one of the most popular techniques for improving feedback at the level of the individual manager. Its proponents claim that, by paying greater attention to the emotional element in our communication, managers can enhance their own performance and that of their organisation. (Note: This theme is developed in the case study at the end of this chapter, which applies the concept of emotional intelligence to the experience of two placement students in an international firm).

Mini-case 6.3	Constructing the concept of 'emotional intelligence'

Researchers have been taking an increasing interest in the role of emotion in organisations, including its role in communication (e.g. Shuler and Sypher 2000, Kramer and Hess 2002). One of the underlying themes in this work is that a focus on cognition (i.e. processes of rational thinking and expression) is insufficient; organisations need to take greater account of the emotional, or 'affective' dimension (i.e. how people process and express their feelings).

The concept of 'emotional intelligence' was first identified by two US-based researchers, Salovey and Mayer (1990), who were concerned with the way that people gain an understanding of emotion as part of a larger project on the interaction between emotion and cognition. John D. Mayer has subsequently defined emotional intelligence as, 'the ability to perceive, to integrate, to understand and reflectively manage one's own and other people's feelings' (cited in Pickard 1999: 50). He emphasises that this is not the same as simply having good 'social skills', or knowing how to behave in a particular situation:

> 'We are making visible the capacity of these people who think intuitively about emotion. You can have social skills but completely miss the emotional content of what's happening around you.' (Mayer, cited in Pickard 1999: 50)

One of the implications of the term 'intelligence', is that the emotional dimension has a critical part to play in the information processing that takes place in humans. In short, we may be able to improve our thinking by managing this aspect more effectively. The concept of emotional intelligence was popularised by Daniel Goleman, a science writer on the *New York Times* with a background in psychology. Goleman's (1996) book, *Emotional intelligence: why it can matter more than IQ*, summarised the research evidence and provided practical examples, demonstrating its potential. Drawing on Salovey and Mayer's (1990) original 'domains' of emotional intelligence, he has identified four fundamental 'capabilities', each of which is composed of a specific set of competencies. The following listing was presented in an article that linked emotional intelligence to leadership skills (Goleman 2000: 80):

- self-awareness: emotional self-awareness, accurate self-assessment and self-confidence;
- self-management: self-control, trustworthiness, conscientiousness, adaptability, achievement orientation, initiative;
- social awareness: empathy, organisational awareness, service orientation;
- social skill: visionary leadership, influence, developing others, communication, change catalyst, conflict management, building bonds, teamwork and collaboration.

▶

There are now several distinct approaches to emotional intelligence, each of which has its own methodologies. For example, UK-based researchers Dulewicz and Higgs (2000) have developed an emotional intelligence (EQ) measurement scale, which is based on psychometric testing in the form of questionnaire surveys, applied to managers attending training courses. The results were subjected to a principal components (or 'factor') analysis, revealing independent factors. The authors have developed a model, relating 'EQ', 'IQ' (intelligence quotient) and 'MQ' (managerial intelligence) to personal performance. However, while adopting Goleman's EQ and MQ measures, they question whether the terminology is appropriate, given that IQ (or 'intelligence quotient') measures have resulted from a much longer and more thorough period of testing (*ibid*: 366). Meanwhile, Mayer and his colleagues have developed their own research scales, which are based on participants undertaking practical tests. For example, people are asked to identify a range of emotions from images of human faces. Another test comprises a statement such as, 'Susan was angry, then Susan was ashamed.' Participants are asked to suggest what might have happened in-between, based on a range of multiple-choice answers (Pickard 1999: 53).

Questions

1 Why might the concept of 'emotional intelligence' be of value to organisational communicators? What limitations can you identify? Illustrate your answer with five practical applications, from any area of organisational life.

2 Is emotional intelligence an exclusively Western concept? Consider its likely relevance to different national and organisational cultures.

3 Some writers on emotional intelligence suggest that the emotional intelligence of leaders is contagious, so that their 'mood' is quickly disseminated throughout the organisation (Goleman *et al.* 2001). How might you 'test' this idea? If it is valid, what are the practical implications for organisational communication?

Sources: Goleman (2000), Goleman *et al.* (2001), Pickard (1999). Written by the author.

Summary

- Organisations make use of many different kinds of feedback, conveyed through a range of communication channels.
- Feedback can be assessed along two key dimensions, urgency and inherent complexity of the message.
- The major challenges for organisations are to synthesise information from multiple sources, and in a variety of formats, and to ensure openness to feedback, avoiding barriers such as 'moral deafness'.
- Various feedback mechanisms can be used to secure feedback from employees, a key internal stakeholder. These include employee appraisals, job satisfaction surveys, staff turnover rates, responses to job advertisements and organisational 'grapevines'.

- Even simple feedback mechanisms, such as forms, involve many practical questions. These include an assessment of the information needed, and issues related to the structure and content of the channel.

- The capacity to encourage interactive communication through feedback mechanisms is closely related to other organisational and managerial topics in the fields of knowledge management, organisational learning and emotional intelligence.

Practical exercises

1 'Sun, Sea and Sand' – designing an evaluation form

You are the customer services manager at 'Sun, Sea and Sand' international holiday villages, which has several sites in Italy, Spain, Portugal, and Greece. You need to evaluate your customers' experience of the range of watersports, the restaurant-bar and children's daytime activities taking place at your sites. You aim is to obtain this information by using an evaluation form that is distributed to each guest at the end of their holiday.

(a) Prepare an evaluation form, suitable for this purpose. What questions do you need to ask? What factors do you need to consider in designing the layout?

(b) Make a photocopy of your form and ask another person to complete it, taking on the role of a guest at one of your resorts. (Note: Copying your form onto an A3-sized sheet of paper and folding it on the longest side will give you a useful A4-sized brochure format).

(c) Review the completed form. Did *the other person* find it clear and unambiguous? Did *you* get the information you expected and required? Consider any ways in which the form could be improved.

(d) Refer back to the opening sections of the chapter. How would you classify this method of collecting feedback? Would other methods be more appropriate? Give your reasons for this assessment.

2 Analysing organisational feedback mechanisms

(a) Re-read the opening sections of this chapter, which discuss the diversity of feedback mechanisms used in organisations.

(b) Conduct a review of the feedback mechanisms operating in your own university, workplace, or another selected organisation. Apply the frameworks in Figure 6.1 and Table 6.1 to analyse these mechanisms. (Note: You may need to focus on a specific part of a larger organisation, such as one department in a university.)

(c) Comment on your findings. For example: Is there any pattern to the kinds of mechanisms employed? Are there any apparent 'gaps' in the information flows? If so, how might you rectify the situation?

| Case study F | Applying 'emotional intelligence' – a tale of two placement students |

Introduction

This is a fictionalised case, based on the author's research. Students studying for a degree at 'New City University' have the option of taking a business placement during their third year. This provides students with experience of a graduate-like role, and the opportunity to practise and enhance their skills, thus increasing their employability at graduation. Many organisations offer such placements, and in doing so provide themselves with an opportunity to assess prospective graduate applicants 'on the job' in exchange for a fair salary. Prior to leaving the university to embark upon their placement, many students worry about their technical knowledge, organisational ability and time management skills. While these may be important, it is communication skills – including levels of emotional intelligence – that are more likely to result in a successful or unsuccessful year. Consider the case of two students, Theo and James, who are applying for a placement at 'Nova Communications' an international media communications company. Both students have achieved similar marks in their university course so far.

Theo and James begin their placements

Following an application and two interviews, Theo and James are delighted to be offered a year placement with this well-known and widely-respected organisation. The students are both assigned to the marketing division where they are to work within the e-marketing department and report to the same line manger, Josef Kant. Their new manager is 53-years-old and has worked for the organisation for 15 years. Although technically and commercially very gifted, he is very demanding of his team and has a reputation for poor interpersonal skills and an exceptionally bad temper. Josef's outbursts are legendary and he prides himself that he has managed to breed a 'culture of fear' in his department. Colleagues and his line mangers have told him in the past how his negative behaviour affects morale and productivity, but he usually replies that he, 'couldn't care less'. Josef has refused to change and his attitude is summed up in the comment, 'Who cares? I can retire in five years' time.'

James and Theo appear to settle quickly into the department, and begin to produce work of a similar standard. However, it becomes obvious that the two students differ greatly in their ability to handle interpersonal relations. This is particularly clear from the very different ways that they deal with Josef, their 'difficult' boss.

James's story

James is the first to experience Josef's unique 'management style'. Josef calls him in to discuss some work that James has completed, but which does not meet with Josef's approval. Josef interrogates James, shouting and making threats to curtail the placement, 'if you don't get your act together'. James leaves the room upset, demotivated and confused but having no indication of how his performance could be improved. James expects the other team members to be supportive, but unfortunately Josef's culture of fear and bullying means that other team members either ignore what is going on, look after themselves or – worse still – adopt similar bullying techniques to Josef! The result is that James spends much of his time trying to avoid any contact with Josef. He also avoids completing tasks, has frequent days off sick and often 'goes missing' during the day.

Theo's story

Theo has similar encounters with Josef, but handles them very differently. When Josef criticises him, he is able to separate the content from the behaviour, listen to the arguments and understand what is required for improvement and acceptance. He also asks assertive questions until he is sure that he understands. Although Theo feels uncomfortable at Josef's behaviour, he does not allow it to affect his desired outcome, which is to complete the task on time and to the best of his ability. Although, like James, he is fearful of how Josef will react during these meetings, he works hard to develop some rapport with his boss, understanding that he has to succeed in this relationship in order to progress in his role.

The consequences for James and Theo

At first James, clearly wanting to save face, pretends to Theo that he is coping with the situation. However as time goes on, Theo becomes aware of the despair that his colleague is suffering. Gradually, he persuades James to confide in him, so that he can offer some help. Theo tries to encourage James to deal more openly with the situation and confront the issues. However, James seems either unwilling or unable to do so. His performance is beginning to spiral out of control and he no longer has any real belief in himself. James struggles on to the end of the placement year, busying himself with non-threatening routine tasks. His only consolation is that Theo is willing to tackle most of the more demanding tasks, particularly those involving direct contact with Josef. The two students return to university with very different placement experiences. Theo has had a very successful year, enhancing both his technical knowledge and his transferable skills, whereas James is totally demoralised. The feedback that he receives from the company states that he is, 'not a team player, lacks drive and motivation and does not handle criticism well'. Furthermore, James still has no idea how he might overcome the difficulties he has experienced. He looks forward to a return to university life, but is now dreading the prospect of a graduate job.

The sequel

Back at 'Nova Communications', it appears that Josef has finally overstepped the mark. The morale of his department is at an all-time low, trust has evaporated and Josef has lost any ability to motivate or develop his staff. To his delight, and that of his department, the company introduces a voluntary redundancy programme and Josef is pensioned off early.

Source: Written by Elspeth Macfarlane.

Questions

1 Analyse the emotional intelligence of: (a) Josef, (b) James and (c) Theo, using the dimensions outlined in the main part of this chapter (see Mini-case 6.3 in particular).

2 How could Josef have improved his communication with James?

3 Faced with similar circumstances in the future, what could James do to achieve better results?

4 Using the emotional intelligence framework, consider how you would assess yourself under each of the key dimensions. Try to identify at least two areas for further development.

Further reading

Brown and Duguid (2000) is a straightforward account of managerial techniques for handling feedback and other forms of organisational knowledge. **Pedler** *et al.* (1997) and **Senge** (1990) are widely-cited works on the subject of learning organisations, a vast literature that coincides with our discussion of feedback mechanisms. **Lähteemäki** *et al.* (2001) offer a critique of organisational learning. **Baumard** (1999) is a more demanding text for those interested in the way that organisations handle tacit knowledge. Other useful sources include **Nonaka and Takeuchi** (1995), **Grant** (1996) and **Spender** (1996). **Salovey and Mayer** (1990) pioneered the concept of emotional intelligence (EQ). **Goleman** (1996) popularised the concept and proposed techniques to improve emotional awareness and related skills, including (2000, 2001) on leadership. **Dulewicz and Higgs** (2000) identify an approach to measuring EQ. **Duckett and Macfarlane** (2003) apply the EQ concept in an empirical study. There are many texts on research methods, including **Saunders** *et al.* (2003). (See also Further reading in Chapter 9).

References

Argyris, C. and Schön, D.A. (1978) *Organizational learning: a theory of action perspective.* Addison-Wesley, Reading MA.

Baby Milk Action (2003) 'The Nestlé boycott'. (Available at: www.babymilkaction.org (accessed 27th August).)

Bird, F.B. (2002) *The muted conscience: moral silence and the practice of ethics in business.* Quorum, Westport CT.

Baumard, P. (1999) *Tacit knowledge in organizations.* Sage, London.

Brown, J.S. and Duguid, P. (2000) 'How to capture knowledge without killing it'. *Harvard Business Review*, 78, 73–80 (May-June).

Duckett, H. and Macfarlane, E. (2003) 'Emotional intelligence and transformational leadership in retailing.' *The Leadership & Organization Development Journal*, 24, 6, 309–17.

Dulewicz, V. and Higgs, M. (2000) 'Emotional intelligence: a review and evaluation study'. *Journal of Managerial Psychology*, 15, 4, 341–72.

Goleman, D. (1996) *Emotional intelligence: why it can matter more than IQ.* Bloomsbury, London.

Goleman, D. (2000) 'Leadership that gets results'. *Harvard Business Review*, 78, 78–90 (March–April).

Goleman, D., Boyatzis, R. and McKee, A. (2001) 'Primal leadership: the hidden driver of great performance'. *Harvard Business Review*, 79, 43–51 (December).

Grant, R.M. (1996) 'Toward a knowledge-based theory of the firm'. *Strategic Management Journal*, 17, 109–22 (Winter Special Issue).

Janis, I.L. (1982) *Groupthink.* Houghton Mifflin, Boston MA.

Kay, J. (2000) 'Strategy and the delusion of Grand Designs'. in: *Mastering strategy: the complete MBA companion in strategy.* Pearson Education, Harlow (5–10).

Kramer, M.W. and Hess, J.A. (2002) 'Communication rules for the display of emotions in organizational settings'. *Management Communication Quarterly*, 16, 1, 66–80.

Lähteemäki, S., Toivonen, J. and Mattila, M. (2001) 'Critical aspects of organizational learning research and proposals for its measurement'. *British Journal of Management*, 12, 113–29.

Marchington, M. and Wilkinson, A. (2002) *People management and development* (2nd edn.). CIPD, London.

Nestlé (2003) 'Babymilk issue facts'. (Available at: www.babymilk.nestle.com (accessed 27th August).)

Nonaka, I. and Takeuchi, H. (1995) *The knowledge-creating company: how Japanese companies create the dynamics of innovation.* Oxford University Press, Oxford.

Pedler, M., Burgoyne, J. and Boydell, T. (eds.) (1997) *Towards the Learning Company* (2nd edn.). McGraw-Hill, Maidenhead.

Penrose, E.T. ([1959] 1995) *The theory of the growth of the firm* (3rd edn.). Oxford University Press, Oxford.

Pickard, J. (1999) 'Sense and sensitivity'. *People Management*, 48–56 (28th October).

Saunders, M.N.K., Lewis, P. and Thornhill, A. (2003) *Research methods for business students* (3rd edn.). FT Prentice Hall, Harlow.

Salovey, P. and Mayer, J.P. (1990) 'Emotional intelligence'. *Imagination, Cognition and Personality*, 9, 185–211.

Senge, P.M. (1990) *The fifth discipline: the art and practice of the learning organization.* Doubleday, New York.

Shuler, S. and Sypher, B.D. (2000) 'Seeking emotional labour: when managing the heart enhances the work experience'. *Management Communication Quarterly*, 14, 1, 50–89.

Spender, J.C. (1996) 'Organizational knowledge, learning and memory: three concepts in search of a theory'. *Journal of Organizational Change Management*, 9, 1, 63–78.

CHAPTER 7

Making connections: organisational communication

Man is not the enemy of man, but through the medium of a false system of government.

Thomas Paine, political theorist

Learning outcomes

By the end of this chapter you should be able to:

- explore the relationship between organisations, inter-organisational networks and today's communication practices;

- evaluate well-established communication challenges presented by organisations, including the formal structures and managerial hierarchies, top management teams, organisational cultures, sub-cultures and unofficial communication channels;

- consider the impact of emerging challenges, including the inter-related issues of information and communications technology, the blurring of organisational boundaries and dialogue with multiple stakeholders;

- reflect on the contribution of organisational theory and related research programmes, including more recent work on stakeholders and inter-organisational networks.

7.1 Introduction

Individuals and organisations engage in a frequently uneasy mix of collaboration and competition (Lado *et al.* 1997, Child and Faulkner 1998). For example, colleagues within an organisation may be competing for promotion opportunities, yet also collaborating to achieve corporate objectives. Similarly, organisations often find themselves forming strategic alliances to share knowledge, capabilities or other resources, while continuing to compete in other spheres. Success or failure in these endeavours depends to a great extent on the quality of interaction between the relevant individuals and groups. Previous chapters have reviewed some of the broad principles of communication, primarily at the level of *inter-personal* interaction. This chapter concludes Part I by extending the scope to the level of *organisations* and the *inter-organisational networks* in which they operate.

Communication failures are a common feature of organisational life, which can create intense frustration for all those affected. Though they are frequently the product of more complex organisational problems, people have a strong tendency to associate failures with their most obvious symptoms. In practice, responses are likely to take the form of personalised and often emotionally-charged criticism of high-profile individuals and groups. Of course, the capabilities and performance of individual managers can make a great deal of difference. However, it should be possible to distinguish weaknesses in 'management' from those that can be attributed to individual managers (Watson 1994). The value of organisational research is in helping us to probe beneath the surface level and to reveal more about the underlying causes. With a better understanding of the relevant mechanisms, we have the potential to make more substantial improvements in communication practices, and to create healthier and more productive organisations.

This chapter begins with a brief review of the more common challenges faced by managers, focusing on formal structures, hierarchies, top management teams and the endemic issues associated with organisational cultures and sub-cultures. The remaining sections respond to emerging organisational challenges, including the increasing use of information and communication technologies, the blurring of organisational boundaries and the additional complexity posed by recent developments in stakeholder thinking.

7.2 Five 'classic' organisational challenges

This section explores five themes from organisational research and practice that have had a particularly strong and lasting relationship with the way people communicate. The first three – formal structures, hierarchies and top management teams – are, to some degree, under the control of senior managers. The fourth and fifth – organisational culture and the informal 'grapevine' – are rather more elusive yet profoundly important influences on communication.

Organisation structure: always a compromise?

Every type of organisation, beyond the simplest sole practitioner or entrepreneurial start-up, needs a degree of formality in its structure and procedures. Formal structures are necessary for a number of reasons. For example, they help managers to allocate tasks and responsibilities between defined functions (e.g. marketing, finance, production), and they provide the basis for a clear a chain of command. Formal structures are typically presented in the form of an organisational chart, showing the upward, downward and lateral connections between named individuals, job roles or departments. Managers can select from a number of different structures, which have been applied in different organisations in the past. Organisational researchers in the twentieth century identified a number of factors that were associated with the structures selected by organisations, including:

- size of organisation,
- technology used,
- type of activity,
- goals or objectives,
- competitive environment.

The guiding principle, which emerged from these 'contingency' approaches to management, is that an organisation's structure should 'fit' the functions it carries out and the environment in which it operates (Pugh *et al.* 1968, Pugh 1997). At its simplest, this suggests two approaches to structuring a business, the 'functional' structure, which prioritised internal operations and the 'product'-based structure, which was oriented around factors in the external environment, typically the organisation's markets (see Figure 7.1):

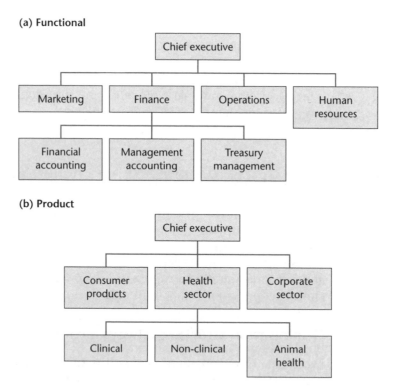

Figure 7.1 **Functional and product structures**

Functional structures have tended to be more efficient ways of organising 'production' but are less flexible in responding to changes in the 'market', whether it is a commercial customer or the users/consumers of a public sector service. By contrast, product-based structures can be more effective in meeting customer needs but are less well co-ordinated internally. In other words, each option represents an unavoidable compromise, which is signalled by the resulting communication flows.

Some organisations have attempted to 'get the best of both worlds', by introducing mixed or 'hybrid' structures. Examples include the typical regional office structure, where each region has its own set of functions, with 'dotted line' links to head office (see Figure 7.2), and the 'matrix' structure, where functional and product reporting lines are combined in a cross-hatched pattern. (Note: The matrix structure is revisited in a practical exercise at the end of this chapter).

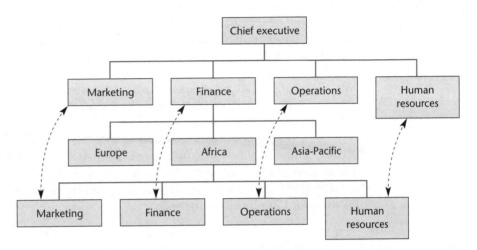

Figure 7.2 **Regional offices – A 'Hybrid' structure**

Since the choice of formal structure contributes to distinctive patterns of internal and external communication, managers need to consider the potential trade-offs arising from their structuring decisions. The paradoxical implications of these decisions are highlighted in other research, which looks more broadly at how organisations are configured. For example, March (1991) contrasts the requirements for successfully 'exploring' (i.e. being innovative and entrepreneurial, creating new knowledge) and 'exploiting' (i.e. being cost-efficient, securing the maximum return from previously-acquired knowledge). In order to 'explore', the organisation needs to be structured in a way that allows for overlapping and fairly loose connections. However, a structure of this kind would be highly inefficient if it was applied to exploitation. Burns and Stalker (1961) also made reference to this fundamental dilemma, and used it to qualify their much-cited discussion of efficiency and innovation under 'organic' and 'mechanistic' management systems. In practice, some organisations have achieved a great deal of flexibility, adapting their mode of organising in order to meet these different demands. For example, a study of factories processing sugar beet revealed that they switched between organic and mechanistic forms of organisation at different times of the year. Furthermore, these changes in the management system followed a regular pattern, reflecting the highly seasonal nature of the organisation's core activities. (Clark 2000: 241–5).

Managerial hierarchies: the case for 'delayering'?

The distances between people in organisations can be vertical, horizontal or geographic. Vertical distance is a measure of the degree of 'hierarchy', the number of levels in an organisational structure. Horizontal (or lateral) distance relates to the number of groupings at a particular level in the hierarchy. Together, these create the overall shape of the organisation. For example, large industrial corporations and government departments have tended to adopt 'tall' hierarchies, with many layers of management and relatively few staff reporting to the managers at each level. By contrast, high technology and consulting firms are typically 'flat' hierarchies, with few managerial levels (see Figure 7.3). Since the 1980s, large organisations of all kinds have been cutting out levels of management (i.e. 'delayering'), with the stated aim of reducing operating costs and improving information flow. In retrospect, many observers have noted that the overly aggressive delayering has created new problems, such as the loss of essential 'tacit' knowledge (i.e. situation-specific, experienced-based knowledge, often built up over many years and difficult to communicate to others) (Nonaka and Takeuchi 1995). It also left certain managers over-burdened with too many lines of communication to subordinates.

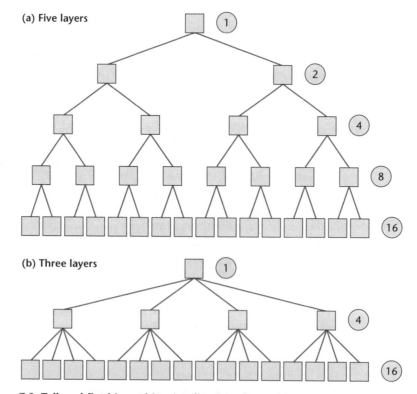

Figure 7.3 **Tall and flat hierarchies: implications for communication**

Top management teams: a block on communication?

The one person who really *should* be in touch with the entire organisation is the chief executive. The person in this role needs to deliver compelling messages to internal and external stakeholders, but also to be open to feedback on strategically important and urgent issues. However, many factors can conspire to block communication from flowing in either direction. Because of the complexity of a large organisation, the chief executive has to depend on others for feedback on performance, guidance on strategic direction and, in some cases, to convey messages from the centre. Incoming information is, of necessity, delivered in a highly summarised form. As a result, there is considerable scope for top management team (TMT) members to pursue internal political ambitions, furthering the interests of their own part of the organisation or attacking the performance of other areas, rather than addressing common strategic concerns. In short, TMTs form a critical link between the chief executive and the rest of the organisation. This has prompted a great deal of research on the composition and dynamics of these teams, focusing on issues such as decision-making capabilities, good governance and accountability. (Note Section 13.5 includes a broader review of communication in teams.) These studies have pointed to serious problems, experienced by many chief executives with respect to their TMTs. For example, Hambrick (1995) reports the results of in-depth interviews with 23 chief executives of major companies headquartered in the US and Europe. His research identifies five clear categories of problem, from the perspective of the chief executive: inadequate capabilities of an individual executive; common team-wide shortcomings; harmful rivalries; groupthink; and fragmentation (see Table 7.1).

Table 7.1 **Five major problems with top management teams**

Problem	Comment
Inadequate capabilities of an individual executive	The most common problem was the executive whose business area was delivering profits but whose short-sighted behaviour endangered its longer-term future.
Common team-wide shortcomings	The most commonly-cited limitation was that the team lacked relevant skills and experience for a radically-changed external environment, often reflecting the historic pattern of job advancement.
Harmful rivalries	These conflicts may seem inevitable, given the aggressive, achievement-oriented nature of many senior executives, and the tendency to build and defend personal 'empires' or 'fiefdoms'.
Groupthink	This pathological feature, which has been associated with overly-cohesive decision-making groups facing external threats, was discussed in section 2.4.
Fragmentation	In stark contrast to groupthink, there is an absence of cohesion in the top management team, with minimal interaction between senior executives, each of whom is operating in relative independence.

The fragmentation problem in TMTs is partly due to the characteristics of organisations and to their strategic direction. For example, in large corporations with highly diversified operating units, based in unrelated industries (i.e. the traditional 'conglomerates'), there may be little need for interaction between members of the TMT.

In contrast, the senior executives of a company engaging in intensive product-market (or internal process) innovation will need to meet regularly, often in face-to-face settings, in order to co-ordinate and make the many mutual adjustments that are required (Hambrick 1995: 117–18). Other factors influencing the degree of integration/fragmentation include factors relating specifically to chief executives, including the time they have been in post, their efforts to bring in new team members and the prospect that they may be about to depart. The key point, from our perspective, is that communication patterns at the top of the organisation may be fundamentally altered over time as a result of the internal dynamics of the TMT.

Organisational culture and sub-culture: managing difference?

Organisations tend to develop distinctive cultures that are both signified and reproduced through communication practices, including initiation rites, myths/stories and symbols. People can quickly begin to identify with an organisational grouping, particularly when they have shared experiences, interests and goals. Equally, they can find it difficult to interact with others whose cultural associations differ. Organisational cultures cross-cut the national differences discussed in previous chapters. For example, it is evident that the organisational culture of IBM is different, in almost every way, from that of other computer manufacturers originating in the US, such as Dell or Compaq. Furthermore, these organisational cultures are to a large extent reflected in the companies' operations around the world. Cultures include self-perpetuating structures, leading like-minded people to be recruited into organisations, while encouraging those unsuited to move on. The picture is further complicated, because various departments and occupational groupings within an organisation are also likely to display their own distinctive norms, values and communication practices; these are usually termed organisational 'sub-cultures'. For communicators, one of the key challenges is how to manage the 'interface' between organisational cultures and sub-cultures in order to facilitate better internal and external communication. Mini-case 7.1 considers the impact that these sub-cultures can have on communication within the organisation.

Mini-case 7.1	'HeatCo': a clash of organisational sub-cultures

'HeatCo': a clash of organisational sub-cultures

It is all-out war at 'HeatCo', a large European company manufacturing specialised heating and ventilation equipment. The accounts clerks are refusing to process invoices, customers are cancelling orders and the Sales Director is engaged in a 24-hour shouting match with the Finance Director in the main corridor. What has led to this crisis? The accountants are responsible for producing accurate and reliable performance figures for all areas of the company. They follow their profession's 'conservatism' principle, always understating profits if the figures are uncertain. The accountants are scrupulous, methodical and insist on following procedures. Financial control is their top priority. They think that HeatCo's salespeople are flashy, disorganised loud-mouths. They spend all their time in the office and have a suspicion that the overseas expense claims are being fiddled. The sales team is responsible for securing orders and achieving ambitious sales targets. Its members are natural optimists and extroverts, able to take the 'knocks' when a big order falls through. They are flexible and energetic, always on the move in the UK and abroad. They hate paperwork. Creating business is their top priority, especially since the MD launched the company's new attack on the European market. The sales team thinks that HeatCo's accountants are sad, boring bureaucratic nit-pickers. Sales figures were down in the previous quarter, and the sales team are under pressure to perform. In the rush to record details of new orders, sales-people are not filling in all the necessary details on the forms. As a result, the accounts department has been sending out incorrect invoices, and is having to handle subsequent customer complaints. Accounts clerks keep calling the sales office in order to check these forms, but the people they need are never around. The Chief Accountant has started sending warning memos to members of the sales team, but these have only exacerbated the problem: 'Who does that [expletive deleted] bean counter think he is?' complained one irate Sales Manager. 'He really should get out more', added a colleague, as they marched briskly into the bar of the Budapest Hilton.

Questions

1 You are a communications consultant, hired by the MD of HeatCo. Discuss the possible short-term actions you could take to deal with the communication breakdown between these departments.

2 Prepare a short report (300 words maximum), outlining your chosen solution and arguing why it would be the most effective in overcoming the organisational problems identified in this case.

3 Organisational communication issues often mask deeper problems. Review recent news stories and identify an example of an organisation where communication problems proved to be the symptom of more serious organisational problems. What role did communication play in the outcome?

Source: Case prepared by the author, based on real events. 'HeatCo' is a fictional organisation.

Mini-case 7.1 describes a typical inter-departmental conflict, involving sales and accounting specialists. Divisions of this kind were once a very common phenomenon in many large organisations. However, there are signs that some of these traditional divisions, both of culture and knowledge, are being eroded. Faced with an intensification of external competitive pressures, companies have restructured their internal operations, removing many of the horizontal and vertical divisions that characterised the organisational hierarchies of the twentieth century. As a result of 'delayering', many employees have taken on additional roles. In the case of sales managers, there is now a general requirement for new recruits to demonstrate high-level accounting and finance skills, in addition to those previously associated with the sales professional. As sales departments become more fluent in the 'language' of accounting, there should be scope for more productive interactions with professional accountants. The more general transition from departmental 'silos' to multi-tasking project teams has the potential to reduce some long-established sources of communication problems in organisations. However, the emergence of more fluid and boundary-less organisational forms raises its own set of issues for the communicator (see section 7.3).

'I heard it on the grapevine': unofficial communication channels

Company grapevines consist of overlapping, informal networks of friends and colleagues who circulate information around an organisation, often during lunch breaks or social events. From an organisational perspective, grapevines can be very effective 'unofficial' communication channels. This is because they are often considerably faster than conventional routes, are more likely to gain the attention of employees, and do not require any investment in communications infrastructure. For these reasons, managers occasionally make use of grapevines to release their official messages, by placing rumours that prepare the ground for a subsequent formal, officially-sanctioned announcement. However, grapevines can also become counter-productive. For example, in a time of uncertainty, such as restructuring or redundancy, harmless gossip is often replaced by misinformation. In these conditions, grapevines tend to distort and exaggerate messages as they are passed around. The best antidote to the exaggeration of unsubstantiated stories is for managers to act quickly and decisively. In some cases, organisations invest considerable resources searching for the source of negative stories (i.e. dealing with the symptoms rather than the cause). The more insightful approach, and that most likely to produce results, is to treat the material circulating on the grapevine as feedback, enabling managers to better interpret and respond to the underlying cause (see section 6.3)

7.3 Emerging challenges: organisations in the twenty-first century

While the 'classic' challenges outlined in the previous section continue to influence communication practices, many new issues are emerging, which are also having profound effects on today's organisations. Here, we review three closely-related developments: the mediating role of digital technologies; blurred organisational boundaries; and the rise of stakeholder thinking in public, private and voluntary sector organisations.

Digital technologies: transforming the pace and place of work

Information and communications technologies (ICTs) have transformed the working lives of many people. Two of the key changes relate to the pace at which people work, and the places in which it is undertaken. For example, the widespread introduction of mobile phones from the mid-1990s introduced a new era of mobile computing, so that employees could remain in contact with corporate intranets, wherever they were located. Instantaneous interaction, via e-mail and other forms of data transfer, has had mixed results. From an employee's perspective, the positive outcomes have included the creation of new and more flexible ways of working, which have suited particular lifestyles. Against this, the new technologies have been seen as increasing managerial control over employees through computer-enabled monitoring of work activities. They have also intensified the pace of work in many situations (e.g. the intrusion of e-mails and text messages, often requiring immediate response, into the home environment). The introduction of remote working provides a useful illustration of these processes. With the expansion of broadband connections, employees can obtain real-time access to corporate intranets in many locations, including their home-based offices. It has also become cost-effective for organisations to provide their staff with the equipment needed to enable remote working; additional costs (i.e. capital equipment and line rental) are more than offset by the substantial reduction in corporate office overheads. In one of the pioneering remote working initiatives, a large computer company equipped all of its office workers to work from home. This enabled the company to manage some 13,000 employees from offices that could accommodate a maximum of 3,000.

The most widely-cited employee benefits relate to lifestyle issues. Home workers are able to spend more time with their families at important times of the day (e.g. before and after school). However, remote working has created a number of communication challenges requiring careful consideration and management. Cultural change is probably the biggest hurdle. The traditional, hierarchical management systems found in many large organisations represent powerful barriers to change. For example, removing employees from a manager's 'line of sight' can lead to a perceived loss of power and status. The remote worker can also find that the initial novelty is replaced by a feeling of being distanced from the organisation, leading to loss of direction and motivation. It is easy for the employee to lose the sense of belonging that was present in the office environment, a perception that may be reinforced by other forms of marginalisation (e.g. in relation to internal politics and career advancement). Informal face-to-face communication and 'networking' (e.g. coffee machine conversations, impromptu meetings, afterwork celebrations), add to the richness of office life and cannot be duplicated in the home office. In short, there is no technologically-mediated substitute for 'face time', a term that is itself a product of the 'virtual' era.

How should organisations address these communication challenges? One of the most important requirements is a programme of training and cultural adjustment, for managers and all those involved in remote working. The courses need to cover every aspect of remote working, including technological and procedural aspects: for example, time management, arrangements for supervision, reporting progress, and obtaining additional support when it is needed. Perhaps the most important element is a code of conduct, an agreement of what is expected by both parties. Its importance reflects the fact that remote working is a relatively new communication genre (Orlikowski and Yates 1994, Yates and Orlikowski 2002), in which the ways of organising are still being resolved. Organisations may adopt different strategies with regard to 'face time', but it appears that regular visits to the office (e.g. at least once a week), may be valuable, providing access to informal channels and helping to reinforce a sense of belonging. Remote working has proved valuable for all parties, where it addresses issues of this kind. However, some tasks are more readily adapted to the remote working mode. The most straightforward tasks are those involving mainly bilateral communication (e.g. the remote worker receives the necessary information on a task from the office intranet, completes the task and sends it back to the point of origin). The communication issues become rather more complex in the case of 'virtual teams', where there is a need for intensive multi-lateral communication, requiring co-ordination of several people in different 'remote' locations (see section 13.6).

Blurred boundaries? Strategic alliances and network forms

The borders of organisations are becoming increasingly blurred. A complex com-bination of factors, ranging from the introduction of 'total quality management' (TQM) concepts to the privatisation of public utilities and the out-sourcing of non-core activities, transformed the industrial landscape. In the second half of the last century, many industries were dominated by large 'multi-divisional' cor-porations, operating as discrete, vertically-integrated and relatively well-defined entities (Chandler 1962, Galbraith 1967). While 'big business' corporations and their public sector counterparts have survived, their resources and capabilities are increasingly based upon strategic alliances, joint ventures and various types of inter-organisational network (Birkinshaw and Hagström 2000, Child and Faulkner 1998, Ebers 1999). Networks are neither a new, nor a newly-discovered, phenomenon. However, they have been recognised as a distinctive way of co-ordinating economic activities that can be distinguished from the internal hierarchy of the firm and the invisible hand of the market:

> 'Network governance involves a select, persistent and structured set of autonomous firms (as well as non-profit agencies) engaged in creating products or services based on implicit and open-ended contracts to adapt to environmental contingencies and to co-ordinate and safeguard exchanges. These contracts are socially – not legally – binding'. (Jones *et al.* 1997: 913)

The tendency to organise activity across administrative boundaries raises some fundamental questions regarding the ways that organisations communicate. For example, researchers have focused on issues related to:

- trust (e.g. how is it established and maintained in networks?);
- intellectual property (e.g. how can information flows be protected from imitators?);
- knowledge creation (e.g. how is the process maintained when activities are outsourced?).

There are, as yet, only tentative answers to many of these questions. However, in broad terms we can conclude that managers need to invest time and effort in actively developing relationships. (Note: This issue is addressed in the case study at the end of this chapter.) They should also consider both the short and longer-term implications of any network connections that they make, including their likely impact on relationships with other stakeholders, and on the potential for organisational learning.

Mini-case 7.2 considers how one company made use of the internet to organise an innovative 'virtual' business, which might be also characterised as an inter-organisational network. The case highlights the challenges and opportunities it faces as the company seeks to connect a number of different stakeholders, and to communicate an unfamiliar message in a clear and convincing way.

Making connections at Climate Care

Climate Care is an innovative company, founded in 1998 by an entre-preneur based in Oxford, England. The company's aim is to 'help individuals and organisations reduce their own impact on global warm-ing' (Climate Care 2003). The primary cause of global warming, and global climate change more generally, is carbon dioxide emissions from the use of fossil fuels, such as coal, oil and gas. In the UK, individuals are directly responsible for one half of national carbon dioxide emissions, from energy use in homes and for personal transport. Climate Care offers to 'offset' the carbon dioxide emissions of their customers. This means that the company invests in practical projects, which either reduce carbon dioxide emissions, by saving energy or using renewable energy, or by planting and maintaining forests, which can absorb carbon dioxide from the atmosphere. This is quite a complex and unfamiliar marketing proposition, which requires careful communication. Because Climate Care is selling a service (i.e. a guarantee of carbon dioxide offsets), rather than a physical product, the web is an ideal channel for delivering supporting information and persuasive messages. What the end-customer needs is reassurance that the proposition is genuine and that the offset projects are worthwhile. In addition, the interactive nature of websites allows people to use a simple tool to calculate their own impact on the climate; they can then begin the process of offsetting those emissions.

The virtual business: connecting Climate Care's partners
Climate Care sells carbon offsets directly to individuals and through a network of part-ner organisations, including the Co-operative Bank, the Environmental Transport Association, Explore Worldwide and Journey Latin America. Partners may offer services with 'built-in' carbon offsets (e.g. mortgages from the Co-operative Bank include an automatic annual offset), or as an optional feature. Many of the partner organisations are travel companies, providing offsets for the carbon dioxide generated by air travel. In most cases, the partner organisations are buying their own offsets from Climate Care, as well as recommending them to potential customers. The company's website (www.climatecare.org) provides hyper-links, highlighted by corporate logos, which connect its customers to partners' websites. Many customers buy their offsets directly from Climate Care through its website, but they also come via Climate Care's partners. The following illustration follows a prospective 'indirect' customer through the process. You are considering a trekking holiday in Peru with Journey Latin America (JLA), but are concerned about the environmental impact of your trip. The 'Responsible Travel' page on JLA's site provides a link that enables you to purchase a carbon dioxide offset through Climate Care. Clicking this link takes you to a jointly branded Climate Care/ JLA webpage titled 'Offset your air travel emissions with Journey Latin America and Climate Care'. It provides basic information about Climate Care as a company, explains the concept of offsets and shows how JLA is offsetting the business air miles of its own employees. This page links to one that allows you to select your flight details by origin and destination. You choose a return flight from Manchester to Lima and this infor-mation is used to calculate the relevant carbon dioxide emissions, and the cost of offsetting them with Climate Care. If you decide to book the holiday, you can then choose to pay Climate Care for this offset.

▶

Questions

1 Re-read the case and sketch a simple organisational diagram, identifying the different connections between Climate Care and other actors, and noting the communication channels that are used.

2 What do you see as the major communication challenges facing Climate Care? Refer back to the discussion in this chapter, and preceding chapters in this part of the book, in order to prepare a list of suggestions as to how the company might respond to these challenges.

3 Identify another example of a virtual business, which connects a number of separate organisations/individuals using web-based technologies. Compare the relevant websites, and any other communication channels used by these businesses, noting any similarities or differences.

Source: Climate Care (2003). Case prepared by Tina Fawcett.

The rise of stakeholder thinking

The concept of stakeholder thinking was popularised by the North American writer, R. Edward Freeman, in a book entitled, *Strategic Management: a Stakeholder Approach*. Freeman's definition of stakeholders emphasises the idea that an organisation's strategy-making engages with many different actors:

'**A stakeholder in an organization is (by definition) any group or individual who can affect or is affected by the achievement of the organization's objective.**' **(Freeman 1984: 25)**

The stakeholder approach to organisational strategy can be seen as complementary to network perspectives, discussed previously (Andriof and Waddock 2002: 39–41). Freeman's central argument was that an exclusive focus on a corporation's 'shareholder value' (i.e. a financial indicator based on the income yield and growth of its share capital) provided an inadequate guide for determining strategic direction.

'**If in the past the focus was on enhancing shareholder value, now it is on *engaging* stakeholders for long-term value creation.**' **(Andriof *et al.* 2002: 9 – emphasis in original)**

This may seem a new, and perhaps rather idealistic concept. However, its roots can be traced to the work of pioneering economists, Adam Smith's [1759] *The Theory of Moral Sentiments* and [1776] *An Inquiry into the Nature and Causes of the Wealth of Nations*, being important early sources. Smith connected economic and ethical issues in a holistic way, anticipating the 'open systems' view of organisations (Boulding 1956). However, this social and moral grounding was largely overlooked in the subsequent application of Smith's ideas (Skinner 1987, Andriof *et al.* 2002). Critics of 'free market' economics have argued that its narrow focus on shareholder value has contributed to negative outcomes for other stakeholders, including employees, consumers, local communities and the natural environment (i.e. poor working conditions, sub-standard products, damage to local economies, atmospheric pollution). Increasing concern over these effects has been reflected in an intellectual debate regarding the appropriate relationship between business and society (e.g. Galbraith 1967, Schumacher 1974). It has also sparked waves of activism by various stakeholder groups, including trades unions, consumers associations and environmental campaigners (see Figure 7.4).

Figure 7.4 Stakeholder activism at a manufacturing plant

Source: Reproduced with permission from Oxfam GB. www.oxfam.org.uk

There are several strands of stakeholder research. Many studies attempt to classify stakeholders into categories, representing their relationship with the organisation. One popular application of these ideas is to 'map' the relative power and interest of different actors, including anticipated changes in these two dimensions, in an effort to guide public relations activities. Mini-case 7.3 reviews a more recent trend in the field of stakeholder thinking, which concentrates on the kind of engagement taking place in stakeholder relationships, highlighting some of the links between organisational communication, corporate responsibility and accountability.

Mini-case 7.3	Stakeholder dialogue: towards a new perspective?

The development of stakeholder thinking over the last two decades has seen greater attention paid to ethical issues and increasing concern with the concept of stakeholder dialogue, mutual engagement and responsibility (Friedman and Miles 2002). These developments have involved both academics and practitioners. For example, the telecommunications company BT has now identified six stakeholder groups that are particularly critical to the success of its business. Reporting on its progress in this area, the company refers to specific communication channels that are used to engage in a dialogue with each group of stakeholders (e.g. customer dialogue occurs through Customer

▶

Liaison Panels, customer surveys and Telecommunications Advisory Committees) (cited in: BT 2003). Descriptions of this kind may give the impression of a well-defined process. However, the implications of maintaining a genuine dialogue with multiple stakeholders are rather more complex. Freeman's original (1984) 'spoke and wheel' model of stakeholder relationships was quite straightforward, with the organisation at the centre and each stakeholder occupying a separate spoke. However, in practice, organisations tend to engage with networks of stakeholders rather than isolated actors (i.e. stakeholders may be connected to one another, or to their own set of stakeholders). Organisations also have to deal with *internal differences* in their stakeholders (e.g. the marketing department in a supplier firm may have different interests to the production department). The resulting 'differentiated network' model of stakeholder relationships highlights the importance of communication across organisational boundaries, in order to constitute, manage and maintain these complex connections (Crane and Livesey 2003: 43).

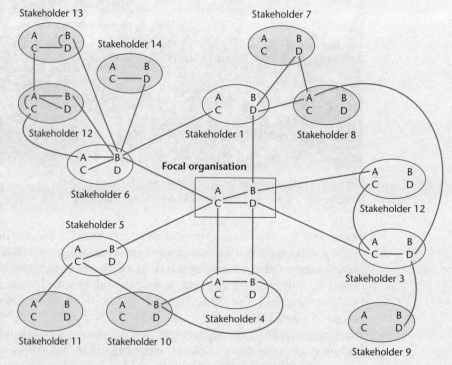

Differentiated network model of stakeholder relationships
Source: Crane and Livesey 2003: 42. Reproduced with permission.

So what are the implications for communicators? Conventional approaches to corporate communications suggest that corporations need to adopt coherent and uniform message strategies, reflected in practices such as the use of detailed manuals for corporate identity (e.g. the use of company logos and slogans), clearance procedures for news releases and standardisation of website designs. The objective here is to communicate a core set of values and coherent arguments, or 'stories' (e.g. Kitchen and Schultz 2001) . There are often good reasons for opting for this integrated approach, including the need to avoid accusations of hypocrisy and inconsistency, and to show a clear and unambiguous change in strategic direction or focus:

'Communicating a uniform message to stakeholders may be particularly important when an organisation is attempting to orchestrate change and/or protect a firm's image. Thus, when Shell revised its general business principles to reflect its growing commitment to the natural environment and human rights, the overarching message of its communication campaign was that profits and principles (responsible behaviour) had to go hand in hand.' (Crane and Livesey 2003: 44–5)

Yet there is a real contradiction between the aims of integrated corporate communication and the demands of engaging in a genuine dialogue with stakeholders. If an organisation is to engage in a *genuine* (i.e. two-way) dialogue across its differentiated network of stakeholder relationships, it needs to be open to processes such as, 'mutual education, joint problem-solving and relationship-building' (*ibid:* 47). These dispersed and unpredictable interactions are likely to work against the centralised, integrated and managed communication of corporate messages.

'The acceptance – even embracing – of uncontrollability and inconsistency poses a significant challenge for the dialoguing organisation. Dialogue by its nature (when it is genuine at least), takes time, is not efficient, cuts against hierarchical control, and does not assume a predetermined fixed understanding of how things (the world) are or what should be done. In contrast, modern organisations are typically dominated by decision-making models that prioritise consistency and control. Dialogue may therefore, on the one hand, have paralysing effects on organisations and their stakeholders, preventing them from reaching consensus and action; or, on the other hand, may result in them splitting and falling apart.' (*ibid:* 51)

In practice, organisations fall short of engaging in genuine dialogue. Instead, they adopt more superficial forms of interaction with stakeholders, which may amount to little more than providing an opportunity for stakeholders to express their views (e.g. an 'interactive' web forum on a corporate website, which posts comments from corporate critics, with counter-arguments from the organisation or third party sources). This limited engagement has been termed 'monologic dialogue', because one-way communication (i.e. a monologue) masquerades as real interaction. It can also become counter-productive (from the perspective of the organisation), where stakeholders perceive it as an attempt at manipulating or controlling dissent.

Questions

1 Why do you think that many organisations are paying more attention to their stakeholders, as evidenced by research and by corporate stakeholder reporting of the kind undertaken by BT?

2 Search the web, or other sources, for examples of 'genuine' and 'monologic' dialogue between organisations and their stakeholders. Discuss your reasons for selecting these examples and comment on their effectiveness from the perspective of the organisation.

3 Prepare a short report (maximum 1000 words) suggesting how a named organisation (select an example from the public, private or voluntary sector) might begin to engage in genuine dialogue with its key stakeholders.

Sources: Andriof *et al.* (2002), Friedman and Miles (2002), BT (2003), Crane and Livesey (2003). Case prepared by the author, with acknowledgements to Andy Crane and Samantha Miles.

7.4 Organisational communication: reflecting on the challenges

Difficulties in communication can be both a symptom of an underlying problem in the organisation, and a contributory factor, perpetuating and even worsening the original problem. Unless the root cause of the problem is tackled, any communication-based 'solution' will be correctly perceived as purely cosmetic, and hence discredited. Senior managers often make the mistake of assuming that short-term solutions (or 'fixes'), particularly those relying solely on technology, are sufficient to deal with deep-seated structural problems (e.g. those arising from underlying economic, political or cultural factors). For example, they may organise a meeting or web presentation in the belief that all that is needed is to 'get the message across' more effectively. Part I of this book, and Chapter 6 in particular, has emphasised the importance of two-way communication. However, it is also important to recognise that even the most sincere efforts at dialogue may have limited impact on more fundamental organisational problems. Indeed, increased contact between the parties may even exacerbate the conflict, due to 'noise', incorrect de-coding and distorted feedback (Newell *et al.* 2002). For this reason, managers also need to reflect on the broader pressures acting on their organisations, and to incorporate this understanding into their communication strategies and practices. Human organisations have always represented a compromise between differing requirements and objectives. As a result, a certain amount of tension is inevitable. In fact, organisations actually *need* a degree of tension in order to work effectively. If completely freed of stress, they are likely collapse into a kind of directionless inertia. However, when stress levels become *excessive*, everyone connected with the organisation begins to suffer and to under-perform.

This chapter has reviewed some 'classic' organisational issues, including decisions regarding structure, hierarchy, culture and sub-culture and has explored their close relationship with communication practices. We have also considered the impact of emerging trends, including the proliferation of ICTs, increasing reliance on inter-organisational networks and a greater concern with stakeholder dialogue. Changes of this kind require us to reconsider established approaches to organisational communication, including the frameworks that we use to understand these phenomena. For example, Chapter 1 indicated one of the standard distinctions in the literature, between 'internal' and 'external' communication. In today's organisation, managers need to think in much broader terms, addressing the blurred boundaries of the organisation and the complex relationships in which it is engaged. Any meaningful communication strategy must take full account of an organisation's connections with multiple stakeholders, including suppliers, collaborative partners, consultants, contracted-out personnel and customers.

Summary

- Communication failures can be both a symptom of, and a contributor to, organisational problems. It is essential to get to the root cause, rather than relying on cosmetic solutions or technical fixes.

- Decisions regarding formal structures are always a compromise between factors such as efficiency and effectiveness, reflecting internal and external pressures. Like other structural changes, such as de-layering, they can have a significant impact on communication.

- Top management teams, which connect chief executives to the rest of the organisation, are vulnerable to communication failures, including 'group-think' and fragmentation.

- Communication is often particularly difficult at the boundaries of organisational cultures and sub-cultures, due in part to their distinctive norms, values and practices. Such problems can be reduced using multi-tasking project teams.

- Digital information and communications technologies, blurred organisational boundaries and stakeholder thinking have posed new challenges, the common feature being a need for more flexible and interactive approaches to communication.

Practical exercises

1 Mergers and acquisitions: 'marriages made in heaven'?

Find a recent corporate merger or acquisition story from the *Financial Times* or other source. Based on the information that you have obtained about the companies involved, prepare a short report (maximum 1,000 words), outlining the communication strategy that you would adopt to ensure that the 'marriage' is a successful one. The kind of background issues you investigate will depend on the needs of the case, but might include some of the following:

- The history of each company – how did it grow?
- The cultural origins of each company – still tied to 'home' country?
- Technologies used by each company – degree of automation?
- Types of employee – professional, manual, craft skills?
- The nature of the products and services – innovative or traditional?
- Markets and customers – types and locations?
- Other key stakeholder issues – any significant sources of opposition?

2 Communicating across a matrix?

Matrix structures are an attempt to combine the benefits of product-based and functional structures by operating both *simultaneously* and with equal weight being given to each 'arm' of the matrix. Some universities, for example, have experimented with this type of structure; the 'products' are the courses and the 'functions' are the academic departments and other services. A typical matrix structure chart for a university is shown below:

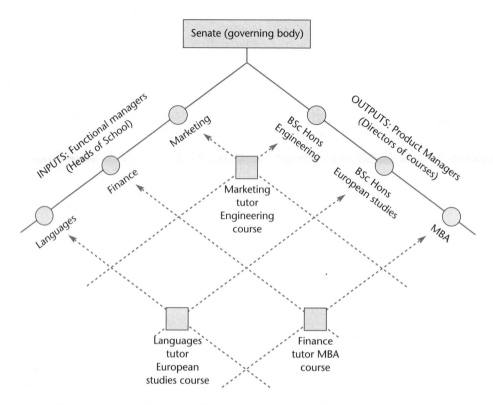

(a) What do you think the benefits of this structure might be?

(b) What communication problems would you envisage?

(c) How might these be resolved?

If possible, make contact with a manager who has experience of operating a matrix-type structure. See how far your assumptions prove to be correct in practice.

Case study G

Entrepreneurial networking – communication as organisation?

This case reviews some of the evidence on networking activity in entrepreneurial ventures and considers the implications for organisational communication. Recent research is contributing to a change in our view of the entrepreneur, from the individualistic and solitary 'hero' to the collaborative communicator, who makes skilful use of network connections. Entrepreneurial networks differ, in many respects, from those surrounding most other small firms. The discussion focuses on the ways that entrepreneurs make use of personal networks in order to generate new ventures.

Entrepreneurship and networks: diverse influences
Entrepreneurs are widely-regarded as playing a distinctive and often desirable role in the economy. An extensive research literature has built up, that seeks to understand

entrepreneurship, often with the explicit aim of encouraging its development. Research into entrepreneurial networks is a relatively recent phenomenon, emerging as part of the upsurge of interest in the 'enterprise cultures' of the 1980s (e.g. Aldrich and Zimmer 1986, Birley 1985, Johannisson 1998). Consequently, it has been influenced by the diverse and sometimes contradictory theories of entrepreneurship that had already developed in economics, sociology and psychology (Swedberg 2000).

No more heroes? Re-assessing the image of the entrepreneur

One of the traditional images of entrepreneurship is of fiercely independent individuals, characterised by egocentric attitudes and behaviours (Gray 1998). At first sight, this might appear to contradict the more collaborative concept of social networks (Johannisson 2000). The focus on individuals is seen in many popular biographies of successful entrepreneurs (e.g. Dyson 1997), which help to reinforce a particular image of the entrepreneur as hero. However, recent work on entrepreneurial networks has prompted a re-assessment, putting the actions of individuals into a wider perspective and challenging the view of entrepreneurs as isolated individuals (Donckels and Lambrecht 1995; Jones and Conway 2000). Research on entrepreneurial teams supports this challenge; empirical studies have linked several variables with the emergence and growth of firms, including the size of teams, the prior experience of their members and their heterogeneity (Birley and Stockley 2000). There are strong, yet largely undeveloped, parallels between the entrepreneurial teams and entrepreneurial networks literatures. These similarities are highlighted by recent attempts to probe beyond the artificial (i.e. legal/financial) borders of the firm, using a network perspective. The sharp distinction between internal and external connections is beginning to blur (Birkinshaw and Hagström 2000).

Entrepreneurial networking as a distinctive activity

Entrepreneurial activity is not synonymous with small businesses and start-up ventures. First, it is also found in other spheres, including large organisations (i.e. 'intrapreneurship') and community-based ventures (i.e. 'social entrepreneurship'). Second, most small firms display few entrepreneurial features (i.e. they are evident either to a very limited degree, or only intermittently). In terms of their activities, many firms are 'reproducers' rather than 'innovators', adopting well-established templates (Aldrich 1999: 80). In addition, most owner-managed firms harbour limited ambitions regarding growth and change, often choosing to remain 'micro' businesses (Johannisson 2000). Entrepreneurial ventures seek and exploit novel opportunities, often through some form of innovation, and under conditions of heightened uncertainty. They also tend to achieve higher levels of growth, relative to other ventures, often based on a modification of existing patterns of trade. Given these characteristics, it seems highly likely that entrepreneurial networks will also differ markedly from those of other small businesses.

Creating ventures: the role of personal contact networks

The process of *creating* a network is now identified as a key entrepreneurial activity, and has been the subject of many research studies (e.g. Birley 1985; Johannisson 1998; Larson and Starr 1993). One of the initial findings was that entrepreneurs rely largely on *informal* sources in their personal contact network (PCN) to mobilise resources before the formation of a venture (Birley 1985: 113). The unique connections between people in the PCN play an important communication role, enabling the entrepreneur to identify opportunities that are not evident to others. At the heart of this network, there are

▶

normally a small number of 'strong' ties that provide the entrepreneur with a shelter from the opportunism and uncertainty of the market. For example, one study found that most business owners reporting between three and ten strong ties, primarily business associates plus a few close friends and family members (Aldrich *et al.* 1989). The time and energy that entrepreneurs invest in these 'pre-organisational' networks appears to be converted into future benefits for their emerging firms. This includes 'human capital', in the form of relevant experiences, skills and knowledge, and 'social capital' (e.g. being known and trusted by others). Trust facilitates access to resources, through collaboration, and helps to overcome institutional barriers to entrepreneurial activity (e.g. local political resistance to a proposed development). However, the extensive personal ties used by entrepreneurs often lead a blurring of business and social life, with mixed consequences. For example, reliance on particular individuals can sometimes lead to sudden, unpredictable and potentially disruptive, structural changes. Furthermore, while all start-up businesses make some 'entrepreneurial' use of their personal networks, most small firms settle down into an established and fairly limited pattern of interactions. By contrast, entrepreneurs continuously develop their networks, with the more or less explicit aim of expanding existing ventures or establishing new ones. To achieve this, they maintain a broader 'latent network', parts of which are activated when required (Ramachandran and Ramnarayan 1993). Episodes of entrepreneurial networking can also be triggered by external events, such as the liberalisation of a market or the entry of new organisations into an industry (Blundel 2002). Figure 7.5 illustrates how an entrepreneurial network might develop, creating new connections (and breaking older ones) in response to changing industry conditions.

The shaded circle represents a manufacturing firm in a simplified supply chain. In the right-hand diagram, we can see three examples of entrepreneurial networking, where this 'focal' firm: (a) forms a new direct connection with a retailer; (b) forms a new alliance with another manufacturer; (c) encourages collaboration between two of its suppliers. The dotted lines in this diagram indicate network connections that have been discontinued as the firm pursues new opportunities.

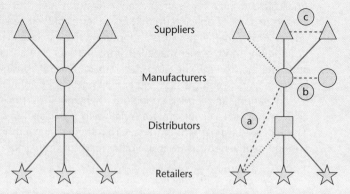

Figure 7.5 Entrepreneurial networks: changing connections over time
Source: Blundel (2002).

What are the implications for policy?
The research suggests that entrepreneurial networks develop in distinctive and often unpredictable ways. Some networks 'crystallise' in the form of an organisation (Larson and Starr 1993: 7), while others appear to thrive in a repeated cycle of re-invention

(Henry and Pinch 2000). Policy initiatives to support entrepreneurship need to recognise this inherent uncertainty and be flexible enough to allow for unanticipated outcomes. The implications for policy change once we start to look at entrepreneurial activity as an on-going process of communication. Turbulence at the level of an individual venture often masks a greater degree of stability at the level of the personal contact network (Johannisson 2000, Blundel and Smith (2001)).

Questions

1 Entrepreneurs are often regarded as important actors in regenerating deprived regions, including those attempting to recover from conflict. How could entrepreneurial net-working be supported, in order to encourage entrepreneurial activity in these situations?

2 How do you think the communication practices of entrepreneurs are likely to differ from those of other small business owners? For example, would particular com-munication channels be more heavily used when developing their PCNs?

3 Draft your own 'personal contact network', placing yourself at the centre and show-ing direct connections (or 'ties') and indirect ones (i.e. where the contact is through another person). Can you imagine a way of connecting members of your PCN as part of a commercial venture, or to provide an innovative service in the community (i.e. 'social entrepreneurship')?

Further reading

There are many general texts on organisations, including **Huczynski and Buchanan** (1997), on organisational behaviour and **Hatch** (1997), which reviews approaches to organisation theory. **Watson** (1994) is an interesting ethnographic study of managers in a UK-based manufacturing company. More specialised sources on organisation theory include **Morgan** (1986), **Aldrich** (1999), **Clark** (2000) and **Westwood and Clegg** (2001). **Andriof** *et al.* (2002, 2003) are edited volumes covering recent developments in stakeholder thinking; **Friedman and Miles** (2002) review theory development in this field. **Best** (2001), **Birkinshaw and Hagström** (2000) and **Ebers** (1999) tackle inter-organisational networks from various per-spectives. **Wenger** (2000) deals with networks of specialist practitioners, termed 'communities of practice', that may span organisational boundaries. **Nonaka and Takeuchi** (1995) is a widely-cited source on knowledge creation, while **Spender** (1996) offers a con-trasting view; **Newell** *et al.* (2002) is an accessible text on knowledge management. **Jay** (1987) is an entertaining and insightful commentary on the key issue of organisational poli-tics. **Swedberg** (2000) is a useful reader on entrepreneurship. Several of the contributions to **Jablin and Putnam** (2001) are also relevant to the themes discussed in this chapter.

References

Aldrich, H.E. (1999) *Organizations evolving.* Sage Publications, London.
Aldrich, H.E. and Zimmer, C. (1986) 'Entrepreneurship through social networks,' in Sexton, D. and Smilor, R. (eds.) *The art and science of entrepreneurship.* Ballinger, New York (3–23).

Aldrich, H.E., Reese, P.R. and Dubini, P. (1989) 'Women on the verge of a breakthrough: networking in the United States and Italy'. *Entrepreneurship and Regional Development*, 1, 339–56.

Andriof, J. and Waddock, S. (2002) 'Unfolding stakeholder engagement'. in Andriof, J., *et al.* (eds.) (2002) op cit. (19–42).

Andriof, J., Waddock, S., Husted, B. and Rahman, S. (eds.) (2002) *Unfolding stakeholder thinking: theory, responsibility and engagement*. Greenleaf, Sheffield.

Andriof, J., Waddock, S., Husted, B. and Rahman, S. (eds.) (2003) *Unfolding stakeholder thinking 2: relationships, communication and performance*. Greenleaf, Sheffield.

BT (2003) *Stakeholder dialogue: better world – BT's social and environment report*. British Telecommunications plc, London.

Best, M.H. (2001) *The new competitive advantage: the renewal of American industry.* Oxford University Press, Oxford.

Birkinshaw, J. and Hagström, P. (eds.) (2000) *The flexible firm: capability management in network organizations*. Oxford University Press, Oxford.

Birley, S. (1985) 'The role of networks in the entrepreneurial process'. *Journal of Business Venturing*, 1, 107–17.

Birley, S. and Stockley, S. (2000) 'Entrepreneurial teams and venture growth'. in: Sexton, D.L. and Landström, H. (eds) *The Blackwell handbook of entrepreneurship*, Blackwell, Oxford.

Blundel, R.K. (2002) 'Network evolution and the growth of artisanal firms: a tale of two regional cheesemakers – 1950–2000'. *Entrepreneurship and Regional Development*, 14, 1, 1–30.

Blundel, R.K. and Smith, D. (2001) 'Business networking: SMEs and inter–firm collaboration: a review of the literature'. Research Report RR003/01. Small Business Service, Sheffield (September).

Boulding, K.E. (1956) *The image: knowledge in life and society*. University of Michigan Press, Ann Arbor, Michigan MA.

Burns, T. and Stalker, G.M. (1961) *The management of innovation*. Tavistock, London.

Chandler, A.D. (1962) *Strategy and structure: chapters in the history of the industrial enterprise.* MIT Press, Cambridge MA.

Child, J. and Faulkner, D. (1998) *Strategies of co-operation: managing alliances, networks and joint ventures.* Oxford University Press, Oxford.

Clark, P.A. (2000) *Organisations in action: competition between contexts*. Routledge, London.

Climate Care (2003) 'About Climate Care'. (Available at: www.climatecare.org.uk (accessed: 19th August).)

Crane, A. and Livesey, S. (2003) 'Are you talking to me?: stakeholder communication and the rewards of dialogue'. in Andriof, J. *et al.* (eds.) *op cit.* (39–52).

Donckels, R. and Lambrecht, J. (1995) 'Networks and small business growth: an explanatory model'. *Small Business Economics*, 7, 273–289.

Dyson, J. (1997) *Against the odds: an autobiography*. Orion Business Books, London.

Ebers, M. (ed.) (1999) *The formation of inter-organizational networks*. Oxford University Press, Oxford.

Freeman, R.E. (1984) *Strategic management: a stakeholder approach*. Pitman, Boston MA.

Friedman, A.L. and Miles, S. (2002) 'Developing stakeholder theory'. *Journal of Management Studies*, 39, 1, 1–21.

Galbraith, J.K. (1967) *The new industrial state*. Hamish Hamilton, London.

Gray, C. (1998) *Enterprise and culture*. Routledge, London.

Hambrick, D.C. (1995) 'Fragmentation and the other problems CEOs have with their top management teams'. *California Management Review*, 37, 3, 110–27 (Spring).

Hatch, M.J. (1997) *Organisation theory*. Oxford University Press, Oxford.

Henry, N. and Pinch, S. (2000) 'Spatialising knowledge: placing the knowledge community of Motor Sport Valley'. *Geoforum*, 31, 2, 191–208.

Huczynski, A. and Buchanan, D. (1997) *Organisational behaviour: an introductory text*. Prentice Hall, Hemel Hempstead.

Jablin, F.M. and Putnam, L.L. (eds.) (2001) *The new handbook of organizational communication: advances in theory, research, and methods*. Sage, Thousand Oaks CA.

Jay, A. (1987) *Management and Machiavelli*. Hutchinson Business, London.

Johannisson, B. (1998) 'Personal networks in emerging knowledge-based firms: spatial and functional patterns'. *Entrepreneurship and Regional Development*, 10, 4, 297–312.

Johannisson, B. (2000) 'Networking and entrepreneurial growth'. in: Sexton, D.L. and Landström, H. (eds.) *The Blackwell handbook of entrepreneurship*, Blackwell, Oxford.

Jones, C., Hesterly, W.S. and Borgatti, S.P. (1997) 'A general theory of network governance: exchange conditions and social mechanisms'. *Academy of Management Review*, 22, 4, 911–45.

Jones, O. and Conway, S. (2000) 'The social embeddedness of entrepreneurs: a re–reading of "Against the Odds"'. Aston Business School Research Papers RP0023, Aston University, Birmingham.

Kitchen, P.J. and Schultz, D.E. (2001) *Raising the corporate umbrella: corporate communications in the 21st century*. Palgrave, Basingstoke.

Lado, A.A., Boyd, N.D. and Hanlon, N.C. (1997) 'Competition, cooperation, and the search for economic rents: a syncretic model'. *Academy of Management Review*, 22, 1, 110–41.

Larson, A. and Starr, J.A. (1993) 'A network model of organization formation'. *Entrepreneurship Theory and Practice*, 4, 5–15 (Winter).

March, J.G. (1991) 'Exploration and exploitation in organization learning'. *Organization Science*, 2, 1, 71–87.

Morgan, G. (1986) *Images of organisation*. Sage, London.

Newell, S., Robertson, M., Scarbrough, H. and Swan, J. (2002) *Managing knowledge work*. Palgrave, Basingstoke.

Nonaka, I. and Takeuchi, H. (1995) *The knowledge creating company: how Japanese companies create the dynamics of innovation*. Oxford University Press, Oxford.

Orlikowski, W.J. and Yates, J. (1994) 'Genre repertoire: the structuring of communicative practices in organizations'. *Administrative Science Quarterly*, 39, 541–74.

Pugh, D.S. (1997) *Organisation theory: selected readings*, Penguin Books, London.

Pugh, D.S., Hickson, D.C., Hinings, R. and Turner, C. (1968) 'Dimensions of organizational structure'. *Administrative Science Quarterly*, 13, 1, 65–105.

Ramachandran, K. and Ramnarayan, S. (1993) 'Entrepreneurial orientation and networking: some Indian evidence'. *Journal of Business Venturing*, 8, 513–24.

Schumacher, E.F. (1974) *Small is beautiful*. Sphere Books, London.

Skinner, A.S. (1987) 'Smith, Adam (1723–1790)' in Eatwell, J., Milgate, M. and Newman, P. (eds.) (1987) *The new Palgrave: a dictionary of economics*. [4 vols.] Macmillan, London (Volume 4, 357–75).

Smith, A. [1776] (1993) *An Inquiry into the Nature and Causes of the Wealth of Nations*. Oxford University Press, Oxford.

Spender, J.C. (1996) 'Making knowledge the basis of a dynamic theory of the firm'. *Strategic Management Journal* (Special Issue), 17, 45–62.

Swedberg, R. (ed.) (2000) *Entrepreneurship: the social science view*. Oxford University Press, Oxford.

Wenger, E. (2000) 'Communities of practice and social learning systems'. *Organization*, 7, 2, 225–46.

Watson, T. (1994) *In search of management*. Routledge, London.

Westwood, R. and Clegg, S (2001) *Point/counterpoint: central debates in organisation theory*. Blackwell, Oxford.

Yates, J. and Orlikowski, W.J. (2002) 'Genre systems: structuring interaction through communicative norms'. *The Journal of Business Communication*, 39, 13–35.

Part II

COMMUNICATION IN PRACTICE

CHAPTER 8

Letters, e-mail and text messages

A person who can write a long letter with ease cannot write ill.
Jane Austen, writer

Learning outcomes

By the end of this chapter you should be able to:

- assess the advantages and disadvantages of the letter as a communication channel;
- select and apply appropriate formats, including structure, content and style, and consider legal, practical and promotional aspects of letterhead design;
- review the traditional role of paper-based memoranda and comment on communication issues arising from the decline of this channel;
- assess the advantages and disadvantages of e-mail as a communication channel;
- select and apply appropriate e-mail formats, including headings, content and style, and consider related practical issues, such as the archive storage of e-mail;
- evaluate potential applications for emerging communication channels, such as text messaging.

8.1 Introduction

This chapter considers four text-based communication channels that are widely used in organisations. It begins with two traditional channels, letters and memoranda (or 'memos'). Letters have remained an important vehicle for internal and external communication, despite the expansion of electronic alternatives, while the use of paper-based memos and notes has declined in the face of e-mail, leading to some unexpected communication problems. This chapter then conducts a similar review of the role that the newer channels, e-mail and text messaging are playing in today's organisations. In each case, we assess the inherent advantages and disadvantages of the channel, note the different ways that it is used and highlight some of the major pitfalls. The examples given in this chapter illustrate British conventions regarding writing style and layout. More detailed advice on international usage, particularly in relation to letter-writing, can be found in larger dictionaries and specialist reference books, some of which are detailed in the Further reading at the end of this chapter. The companion website includes a more comprehensive set of sample letter formats, additional sources and useful links.

8.2 Business letters: principal uses and channel characteristics

For centuries, letters were the only practical form of long-distance communication short of dispatching an 'envoy' or travelling there yourself. Today, there are many faster and sometimes more reliable technologies for conveying text from one place to another, including fax, text messaging and e-mail. Given these alternatives, why do organisations continue to send so many letters? Table 8.1 summarises some common types of business letter, noting some of their varied message objectives.

Table 8.1 **Some examples of widely-used business letters**

Type of letter	Sender and receiver	Typical communication objectives
Promotional	Marketing department Prospective customer	Increase brand awareness, stimulate sales
Contractual	Purchasing department Supplier	Establish clearly defined contract terms
Credit control	Accounts department Customer (debtor)	Speed up customer payments – politely
Supplier payments	Accounts department Supplier (creditor)	Avoid conflict over firm's late payment
Adjustment/ complaints	Customer services Customer	Keep customer loyalty by prompt action
Recruitment	Human resources Prospective employee	Inform and attract applicants
Employment contract	Human resources Employee	Provide clear and accurate information on pay and conditions
Disciplinary	Human resources Employee	Inform, meet legal obligations and encourage behaviour change
Redundancy	Human resources Employee	Inform, meet legal obligations and provide appropriate support

This long-established channel of communication has three main characteristics. As you review them, consider which of these characteristics has the potential to offer advantages over other text-based channels. Having noted the advantages, try to identify the circumstances in which they are most likely to occur. For example, what kind of messages and what type of receiver are involved?

'One-way' and non-interruptible

In contrast to a telephone conversation, for example, the letter is a 'one-way' channel. This means that receivers cannot, in the short term, request clarification or additional information. Consequently, the written message must therefore be well thought out, clear and comprehensive. Try to predict likely questions and ensure that you have explained anything that the reader is unlikely to understand.

Asynchronous

The letter is an 'asynchronous' channel, involving a time delay between sending and receipt. This can make it unsuitable for urgent (as distinct from important) messages, unless you make use of a motorbike courier, or send an advance copy by fax or as an e-mail attachment. As a sender, you are also unaware of whether the receiver has read your letter. When a rapid response is essential, consider a combination of telephone, plus either fax or e-mail.

Provides a permanent record

The message contained in a letter can be retained by the receiver and reviewed at their leisure. This makes it more suitable than the telephone or face-to-face conversation when the message is long or complex. However, there is a down-side, since any hasty promises or 'spur of the moment' criticisms that you make in a letter cannot easily be retracted. This also applies to e-mail and text, where it is even easier to make a hasty remark that you may later regret.

Mini-case 8.1 illustrates some of the more common examples of bad practice in letter-writing.

| Mini-case 8.1 | **Letters and paper mail in a digital age** |

A research study by the University of Surrey's Digital World Research Centre (DWRC 2001), 'The future of paper mail in a digital age', reported that e-mail would not replace all of the functions of paper mail in the near future. The report was based on an ethnographic study, which involved observing the ways that people interacted with paper mail in a domestic setting. The research suggested that the letters have more than a simple communication function. Letters pass through a number of stages, from their arrival on the doormat until they are finally filed or thrown away. The researchers found that the progress of letters through these stages was dependent on the dynamics of family life in each household. For example, letters were left in prominent positions as visual 'reminders' (e.g. invoices awaiting payment); the parents of teenage children left mobile telephone bills outside their bedroom doors, with the intention of highlighting the costs or initiating a family discussion.

The visual characteristics of paper mail were also important at the initial stage in the process, when people skimmed through the incoming mail and sorted it intuitively. For

▶

example, they classified and prioritised letters by taking account of non-verbal cues, such as design and branding, as well as textual details such as the sender's address. The research suggested that the task of manipulating the flow of mail through the household was primarily undertaken by women:

> 'Women are the ones to first skim and sort the letters and it is women who actively position letters in strategic places in the home for other people to see. For example, they put bills in places where husbands will see them and then they keep track of whether the husband sees the bill. After a day or two the bill is taken away and paid by the women. In this way, men think they are in charge but in fact it is women who do all the work.' (Royal Mail 2001)

The researchers noted that e-mail technologies could not currently replicate these communication practices. As the lead researcher commented:

> 'Letter mail is inherently shareable and supports domestic interaction, but e-mail is inherently private, focused on the individual's screen. In fact when householders were using e-mail, they printed off the messages and used them like letters around the house to remind them to do things and to share the information.' (cited in Royal Mail 2001)

These findings reflect the concept of 'genre systems', in which patterns of communication and collaboration are shaped by the established technologies (Yates and Orlikowski 2002). It seems likely that developments in internet and e-mail technologies may transform these domestic behaviours in the coming years. However, for the time being, paper-based mail remains an important and influential communication channel. The Head of Future Technologies Group at Royal Mail commented on the implications of the study:

> 'Letters are used as an invaluable social tool. We have found fascinating relationships and roles that occur within the household when the mail arrives. Especially affecting women, these roles will be much more difficult in an increasingly digital age.'

Questions

1 Summarise the most important differences between paper mail and e-mail, in its current form, based on the findings of this study. Comment on these differences, noting any additional points from your own experience.

2 What are the implications of this study for organisations seeking to communicate with their various stakeholders:

(a) via conventional paper-based mail?

(b) via e-mail?

3 The research study reported in this case is an example of trying to find out how people really make use of a communication channel. Suggest how you might research the use of paper-based mail in organisations. Could a similar approach be adopted for other text-based communication channels (e.g. e-mail, text messaging)?

Sources: DWRC (2001), Royal Mail (2001), Yates and Orlikowski (2002). Written by the author.

8.3 The mysteries of page layout and structure

There has been a radical simplification of page layout in recent years, based on so-called *fully blocked* page layouts and *open punctuation*. Fully blocked layout simply means that all text, including dates, recipient's address and subject heading, is aligned with the left-hand margin. Traditionalists regard this layout as unbalanced, but it is quick and easy for anyone to reproduce, especially when using wordprocessing software. Open punctuation means that all of the commas and full stops are omitted in the address section, greeting and complimentary close of your letter. In a modern type font, open punctuation looks crisp and concise (see Figure 8.1). It also saves on the keystrokes required, saving time and reducing the risk of typing errors. Further examples of letter formats can be found on the companion website.

Herberts Herbs
West Hill Farm
Malvern
Worcestershire
WR7 1AB

Our Ref PA/AJR

3 February 2005

Prof E.F. Gustavson
Box 1234
SE-405 999
Göteborg
Sweden

Dear Prof Gustavson

HERBERTS HERBS CATALOGUE

Thank you for your letter dated 29th January regarding our advertisement in the *Financial Times*, and for your kind remarks about our products. I am pleased to enclose a copy of our new catalogue and look forward to dealing with your order.

Yours sincerely

Patricia Anderson

Marketing Manager

Telephone 01234 567890
E-mail enquiries@herbertsherbs.com   Website www.herbertsherbs.com

---

Figure 8.1 **A letter in fully blocked layout with 'open' punctuation**

The basic framework for a business letter is logical and straightforward (see Figure 8.2). However, it is worth considering in a little more detail the main functions of each element, reflecting on how that they may vary, according to the purpose of the letter and the cultural context in which it is sent and received.

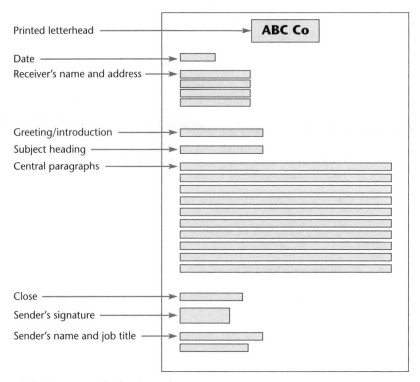

Figure 8.2 **Structure of a business letter**

The greeting/introduction

One of the first potential problems concerns the way that you address the person to whom you are sending the letter. There are many different local conventions regarding the way that you acknowledge a person's title and qualifications. For example, there is a British tradition of using a person's first name when writing to a Knight (e.g. 'Dear Sir John'), but most formal letters would begin with a person's surname (e.g. Dear Ms Patel). It is not always necessary to include the receiver's qualifications and professional memberships in the address section of the letter, but this can also cause problems for letter-writers. The normal order of precedence adopted in the UK is shown in Table 8.2. The following example shows how this works when addressing someone with a bachelor's degree, master's degree, doctorate and professional qualifications:

A.B. Starr PhD MSc BEng FRS

Local rules and practices of this kind may appear obscure and unimportant. However, in certain circumstances it can cause offence when conventions are broken, limiting the effectiveness of the message that is being conveyed.

Table 8.2 **Listing qualifications and awards: a conventional approach**

Order	Qualification or award	Examples
1st	Civil and military decorations and orders	OBE CBE VC DSO
2nd	Higher degrees	PhD MPhil MA MBA
3rd	Bachelor's degrees	BA BSc BEng
4th	Diplomas and similar	Cert Ed Dip M
5th	Professional memberships	MCIM ACA MIStructE

The central paragraphs of the letter have three main functions: to establish the context, deliver the main messages and state any action required by the receiver.

Establishing the context

It is always tempting to jump straight in with your main messages. Resist that temptation. Imagine your letter arriving on the receiver's desk. It may be half way down in a pile of other urgent correspondence. Three telephones are ringing and her marketing assistant has just poured a cup of coffee into his computer keyboard. How can you help this hard-pressed individual find her way into your letter in the simplest and most painless way?

- **Include a reference number**: If you have previous correspondence from her, copy that reference number onto your letter as 'Your reference: …'. Most reference numbers today refer to computer filenames, sometimes incorporating the initials of either originator or typist, such as 'SAL72/LJH'.
- **Include a short explanatory heading**: This should be in bold text and/or capital letters, identifying the purpose of the letter as concisely as possible. For example: LASER PRINTER MODEL EXL345A – PAPER TRAY FAULT
- **Provide a link to previous correspondence**: Use your opening lines to refer to the most recent contact with the receiver regarding this topic. Typical openers include: 'Further to your letter of 14th January …' , 'Thank you for your fax dated 5th March …' and 'I am writing regarding yesterday's meeting …'.
- **Explain your reasons for writing**: You can assist the receiver by telling her at the start your reasons for writing the letter! By providing a sound rationale, you can help to establish the importance or the urgency of your subsequent main messages.

Delivering the main messages

Business-related messages typically consist of a number of inter-related points. These need to be strung together in a logical order, with any significant changes of subject area identified by inserting a new paragraph (see Chapters 1 to 3 for further advice on structuring messages).

Stating any action required

Most business letters are written to achieve some kind of practical response from the receiver. However, letter-writers frequently under-emphasise or forget to include this essential section. The results of this are all too predictable:

- action not carried out at all;
- action carried out late, after numerous reminders;
- action carried out incorrectly, or in a different way to that envisaged.

In a hectic business world, your request for action must be stated clearly if it is to stand any chance of it being acted upon. You should also:

- Give a brief **explanation** of why the action is important and/or urgent.
- Include clear and realistic **deadlines**.
- Check that the receiver has the **authority** and **capacity** to act as required.
- But in all cases, even when chasing an unpaid bill, remain **polite**.

The close

The closing section of the letter is often used to highlight any action points, as noted above. It can also be used to express a positive, cordial and helpful impression. For example, a conventional closing sentence might be, 'Please do not hesitate to contact me, should you have any questions or require additional information.' The closing phrase varies between countries. For example, in Britain, the convention is to end a letter addressed to a named person with the phrase, 'Yours sincerely', while the phrase, 'Yours faithfully' is used when the person is not named (i.e. the letter begins with an expression such as, 'Dear Madam' or 'Dear Sir').

8.4 The style and content of a letter

The previous section provided an outline or skeleton, which we now need to flesh out in words. In doing so, it is useful to bear in mind the special characteristics of the letter. Receivers cannot easily question you about anything that they find ambiguous or unclear. They have to interpret your message based on the words used and what they already know about you and your organisation. The style of a letter is the product of a number of factors, including: vocabulary, grammar, overall length and appearance (Chapter 4). Ideally, the style should be adapted to suit both the receiver and the purpose of your message. However, since receivers are not visible and may often be unknown, writers are in danger of 'speaking' to them inappropriately. This can result in anger, confusion and less credible messages. An example of this occurs when 'Middleburg Bank' sends out its standard letter to a current account customer who has an overdraft (see Figure 8.3).

Middleburg Bank ®
Making money a pleasure ...

15th May 2005

Colonel JK Wilson
Dunmarchin
12 Castle Street
Avebury
Wiltshire SN99 PDQ

Dear Colonel Wilson

CURRENT ACCOUNT NUMBER: 78901234 – OVERDRAFT

It has come to our attention that this account is at present overdrawn by a sum of £104.46. This overdraft has not been authorised. Please note that in accordance with current regulations governing this account, an administration charge of £25.50 has been debited. Full details are available on our website at www.middleburg-bank.com. Please take immediate action to correct this situation. If you have any difficulty in making the necessary payment, please contact Middleburg's automated Financial Helpline on 01234 567890 as soon as possible.

Yours sincerely

IM Younger

Credit control assistant

www.middleburg-bank.co.uk

Figure 8.3 **Example of an ineffective letter**

Colonel Wilson is a retired soldier and respected magistrate. It later turns out that the bank overdraft was caused by a clerical error on this customer's standing order payments. He is therefore outraged at the tone of a letter that, 'totally ignores my unblemished record of loyalty and prompt payment'. After 38 years with the same bank, Colonel Wilson decides to move his account to one of Middleburg Bank's main rivals. He also uses his homepage to start a campaign, revealing other examples of the bank's incompetence and bad manners to the wider world. How might Middleburg Bank have avoided this upset, and the subsequent bad publicity?

In the following paragraphs, we highlight some of the more common pitfalls for the business letter-writer, and note the kinds of questions that need to be asked when drafting an effective business letter. These can be used in conjunction with the exercises at the end of the chapter, and on the companion website.

Initial questions about the receiver and subject matter

The first questions to ask concerns the person who is going to receive the letter. What is your relationship to this person or organisation (e.g. a long-standing customer, a key supplier, a charitable donor, an industry regulator or tax authority)? Are there related factors you should take into account? For example, any pre-existing issues between you and the receiver, or any known differences of culture and language.

Length, tone and use of words

In the light of these questions, consider whether your letter is of an appropriate length, assess the overall tone and check on any words that could be problematic. The following checklists can help to structure this assessment. Firstly, in relation to length:

- Does the letter contain any unnecessary information?
- Does it also include everything that is essential?
- Are the sentences clear and concise?
- Is there any repetition (other than intentional repetition for impact)?

Turning to the overall tone of the letter, as with other communication channels the aim should be to match it to the purpose of the message and the nature of the audience. One of the most important issues is the degree of formality. For example, you might write a letter to a friend or close colleague using informal expressions (e.g. 'Hi Mike', 'How's it going?' and 'Take care'), similar to those you would use in a conversation. This tone would be entirely inappropriate in other circumstances, such as direct mail letters distributed by organisations for promotional or campaigning purposes (see the case study at the end of this chapter and Chapter 10). The following questions may be helpful when assessing the letter at a draft stage:

- Does the tone of the letter appear appropriate? (Note: If you are unsure about the tone, it may be useful to read it out to a colleague.)
- What is the letter trying to achieve (e.g. is it seeking to inform, persuade, criticise or apologise)?
- Could the wording of the letter be mis-interpreted (e.g. could it appear either discourteous, unhelpful or over-familiar to the reader)?
- If the roles were reversed, how would you react to the letter?

It is particularly important to consider the use of words in a letter, including any technical language, specialist terms or abbreviations that might be unfamiliar to the reader. Decide whether it is better to explain these words in simpler language, or to replace them altogether with more common equivalents (see section 3.2). You should also avoid clichés and idiomatic phrases, which can be a source of confusion for readers who are unfamiliar with the language (see section 3.4). While expressions of this kind may be acceptable in face-to-face communication, they are generally perceived as unprofessional when incorporated into formal letters. For similar reasons, it is important to proofread outgoing letters, ensuring that spelling, punctuation and grammatical errors have been corrected. Many people rely on the grammar and spelling checkers provided with word-processing software. However, these are far from infallible, and often generate unsuitable substitutes. The final checking process should include a search for any factual errors, including incorrect dates, prices or contract terms. One of the other common pitfalls of wordprocessed letter writing, particularly in an organisational setting, is for someone to save the wrong version. Before posting any heavily revised letters, it is worth checking that the printed version is the *final* draft, and not an earlier one that has somehow remained on file.

8.5 Business stationery and letterhead design

Picture yourself in the process of opening a letter. What are the first things that you notice about it? Before reading the first word, you will have handled the **paper** and absorbed the graphic design of the **letterhead**. Business stationery conveys important first impressions about an organisation and gives you an opportunity to convey a positive, consistent image. This section considers some promotional, practical and legal issues regarding the design of business stationery.

Promotional and practical aspects

The letterhead contains factual information, including: company name, business address, telephone, fax and e-mail address. However, the receiver can also be influenced by design aspects, such as: the organisation's logo, use of colour, typeface and the overall visual impression that these elements convey (see Chapter 4). When preparing or selecting a letterhead design, it is important to keep some basic practical points in mind:

- Is adequate space left for the letter, especially when used with window envelopes?
- Is the font size large enough (i.e. are the address details still legible if a letter is scanned, photocopied or faxed)?
- Are the organisation's postal address, telephone, fax, e-mail or website details likely to change in the near future?
- Is the letterhead design consistent with other stationery and signage used in the organisation?
- Will the design look out-dated in five years' time?

It is also essential to consider printing costs. The key factors here are the number of colours used, size of print run and the choice of paper. Small print runs remain prohibitively expensive, despite advances in print technology. Against this, there is the danger of writing off large amounts of unused stationery when your address details change. Some large, multi-site organisations print only the corporate logo on their stationery, with all the other details being added when the letters are printed out. In some cases, this is a more flexible and cost-effective solution.

Statutory requirements

It is essential to ensure that business stationery meets the legal requirements of the countries in which it is being used. For example, much of the relevant British legislation can be found in the Business Names Act 1985 and the Companies Act 1985. The law covers business signs, letterheads and other formal documentation, including written orders, invoices, receipts and demands for payment. Similar legislation applies to registered charities. Regulations of this kind are designed to protect those who deal with an organisation from being misled or obstructed should they need to take subsequent legal action. For example, certain words cannot normally be used in the name of a business. These include 'Royal', 'National' and 'University'. There are also various disclosure requirements for business stationery and signs, depending on the business's legal structure (see Table 8.3):

- **Sole traders and partnerships**: If you trade under your own name, the Business Names Act 1985 does not apply. If using a different business name, your own name(s) and address must be included on all documentation. Large partnerships, with more than 20 partners, are allowed to omit names of partners from their stationery, so long as a full list is available for inspection. You cannot list some but not all of the partners.

- **Companies**: The Companies Act, 1985 requires that the following are disclosed on the letterhead: the full corporate name (indicating if it is a public or private limited company); the country or countries of registration; the company registration number (issued by Companies House); and the registered office address.

Directors are not usually listed on the letterhead. If this is done then, as for partnerships, all must be included. In practice, these details are normally printed, in a small font size, at the bottom of the letterhead page. The registered office address is often different from the business address. It may be the corporate headquarters or, in the case of a smaller business, the office of its solicitor.

Table 8.3 Statutory disclosure requirements: some practical examples

Sole trader	**Red Revolution Records** (proprietor: F Smith) 99 High Street Manchester M0 3QG
Partnership	**Lewis, Singh & Jones** (Dental Surgeons) (Partners: P Lewis, J Singh and K E Jones) 654 Market Street Manchester M0 8YP
Limited company	**Molto Bene Pasta Houses** Molto Bene House 56 New Lane Expressway Manchester M0 9LZ *ALSO, in smaller type at the bottom of the page:* Molto Bene Pasta Houses Limited Registered in England and Wales Registration Number: 1234567 Registered Office: 45 Lion Terrace, London SE44 2XY

8.6 The decline of the humble 'memo'

The internal memorandum, or 'memo', was once an important paper-based communication channel for short messages exchanged within organisations. This included written confirmation of agreed actions (e.g. dates of meetings, formal approvals, room bookings) and 'official' memos (e.g. setting out the organisation's health and safety policy). Though still in use today, the memo has been replaced for many purposes by e-mail messages, transmitted electronically over organisational intranets. The simple and concise format of the memo is reflected in the way e-mails are presented; it remains a useful model for clear and simple communication of this kind (see Figure 8.4). The apparent limitations of the paper-based channel, compared to its electronic replacement, relate to the speed and distance to which messages could be distributed, and the lack of immediate feedback. Memos had to be typed up, printed, copied and physically posted to the receiver, whereas e-mails can be typed and sent in a single action. However, in practice, many of the limitations could be readily overcome by combining the memo with other established channels, such as the telephone and face-to-face meeting. The essential format of the memo has been adopted in standard e-mail formats (see Figure 8.5 later), but it remains to be seen whether the new channel is really more 'effective' than its humble predecessor (see section 8.7).

MULTI-TECH SERVICES (ASIA) SA
Internal memorandum

To:	Cheung Yu Lo, AV Department	Date:	12 Nov 2005
From:	Adam Lee, Press Office	Copies:	Timo Scultz
Ref:	vidcon053/arl		
Subject:	VIDEO CONFERENCING EQUIPMENT LOAN: 17 NOV		

Following our telephone conversation today, this confirms our booking. As discussed, we will require the full videoconferencing suite (Rooms H327–2 and H327–3) and the standard technical assistance package. The international press briefing will take place at 11:00hrs. Please arrange for the suite to be set up and tested by 09:00hrs, to allow for a practice session. Call me on extension 1234 if you have any questions or anticipate any problems with the booking.

Figure 8.4 **Typical format for an internal memorandum**

8.7 E-mail: channel characteristics, formats and applications

E-mail is often referred to as a hybrid, a mixture of text-based and conversational communication. This is due to the characteristics of the channel, some of which are the same as paper-based alternatives, such as the letter or memo, and others which are the same as 'real time' channels such as the telephone. E-mail is like a letter in that it is non-interruptible (i.e. the receiver cannot ask for clarification mid-way through the message, as in a conversation) and leaves a permanent record of what has been said. It also relies on one form of coding (i.e. written words), so lacks the richness of verbal communication and the additional cues that come from face-to-face exchanges. However, the electronic nature of the channel does allow for a much greater degree of interaction between sender and receiver, so that exchange of messages can become effectively synchronous (i.e. they can happen in 'real time'), without the kind of time delay that occurs with an exchange of letters, for example. In many cases, these real-time exchanges might be better handled using other channels, such as the telephone, because speaking is generally quicker than typing. Indeed, one of the emerging 'folk tales' about dysfunctional e-mail interaction involves two people sitting in the same office, who type endless messages to one another, rather than speaking face-to-face.

E-mail can be very useful when used as an asynchronous channel. For example, it is now an important part of the tutoring process on e-learning courses. Students located in different time zones around the world can post queries on discussion boards, or e-mail them to tutors at any time of the day or night. Tutors can then respond relatively quickly and easily (i.e. in comparison with conventional airmail letters), and the response can, in turn, be read at a time convenient to each student. As is the case with letters and memos, there is also the option of sending out multiple copies (i.e. 'block e-mails'), of the same message to named individuals.

In this section, we consider the basic format of the e-mail, noting how it may be adapted for various purposes and highlighting a few common pitfalls, including the often-ignored social and cultural issues that surround this computer-mediated channel (see Figure 8.5).

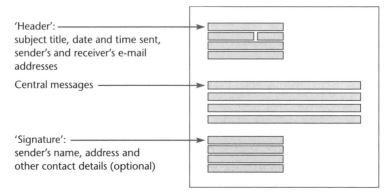

'Header':
subject title, date and time sent, sender's and receiver's e-mail addresses

Central messages

'Signature':
sender's name, address and other contact details (optional)

Figure 8.5 **Format of a typical e-mail**

E-mail subject heading: a useful cue, often ignored

E-mail subject headings serve the same purpose as those used in business letters. However, in an e-mail, they have particular value because the subject appears in the receiver's in-tray, along with the name of the sender and the date of sending. Many writers fail to include a subject line in their e-mails, an unhelpful habit that may result in their message being ignored or left until all of the other recent arrivals have been dealt with. A short but informative subject heading, usually written in capital letters, is all that is required. The original heading becomes the default that is inserted by e-mail software when the receiver replies to an incoming message. (e.g. 'AGENDA FOR MONDAY'S MEETING' becomes 'Re: AGENDA FOR MONDAY'S MEETING'). People rarely update their e-mail subject heading to reflect the way that the topic has changed following a series of exchanges, but doing so can help to clarify and emphasise the current message.

Specifying deadlines

If you require a response from the receiver, always state a reasonable, but specific deadline. This can be done politely, and may be re-inforced with a brief explanation or incentive. For example: 'To guarantee a place, please confirm before Wednesday 8th May whether you will be attending.' Avoid vague statements such as, 'when appropriate' or, 'in due course'; over-worked people are likely to read this as 'low priority' and your message may be forgotten. Setting your e-mail as 'high' priority and adding 'URGENT' to the subject heading might help to secure a response, but only if the claim is justified.

E-mail language, style and accuracy: unresolved issues?

E-mails tend to be used for short and relatively straightforward messages. They can be absorbed more readily if you make use of short paragraphs, rather than long stretches of text. It is also helpful to break up the text, particularly where it includes a list of items or an important item of information, such as a date or an address, making it easier to read on screen. The language used in e-mails tends to be concise and direct, as was the case with the internal memorandum (see section 8.6). However, e-mails are sent to a much wider range of people, including external stakeholders. The short and relatively informal language that is used in e-mails exchanged between close work colleagues and friends can sound over-familiar and discourteous if it is used in an e-mail to a senior executive or a customer. Consequently, your e-mail writing style needs to be very flexible, adapting itself to the needs of specific receivers. For example, informal e-mail messages are sometimes enhanced using improvised non-verbal cues, such as ;-) to signify knowingness and :-(for unhappiness, that would be regarded as unprofessional in more formal situations.

It is not easy to adapt writing styles in this channel, particularly when the conventional practice is to sit in front of a computer, responding to a large number of assorted e-mails one after another. Some people have interpreted the speed and relative informality of this channel as a justification for much lower standards of accuracy, in spelling, grammar and punctuation. Keying errors, or 'typos' may be left uncorrected and punctuation largely ignored. At a time when the channel is still without firm conventions, my own view is that accuracy in typing is as important in e-mails as it is in business letters, and for precisely the same reasons. Obvious errors are distracting to the reader, they can lead to mis-understandings and are also likely to give a poor impression of the sender, and the department or organisation that they represent. The counter-argument, that it saves time to leave the message uncorrected, is difficult to sustain. In practice, most keying errors could be avoided, and the whole process could be greatly accelerated if people invested some time in perfecting the skill of touch-typing.

Common e-mail problems and pitfalls

Perhaps the greatest problems for this communication channel, from an organis-ational perspective, are the rise of junk e-mail (or 'spam'), and the more general issue of overloaded in-trays. The sheer volume of e-mails received by many people in organisations has created stressful working practices, and an extension of workplace activities to any location where a person has access to the e-mail system. With the advent of mobile computing, this includes periods of business travel (e.g. dealing with e-mails during rail journeys or international flights) and a new intrusion into domestic life. For example, while it would have been unusual for employees to deal with work-related telephone calls at home during the weekend, it is becoming an established norm that people access work e-mails from a home computer. From the sender's perspective, the overload problem means that you cannot always be sure that your message will be spotted, amongst dozens of other messages, particularly in certain circumstances (e.g. when they have accumulated during the receiver's vaca-tion), of which you may be unaware. Many senders have unrealistic expectations of the channel, assuming that their messages will be read, understood and responded to in a very short period. This ignores the fact that synchronous communication is a *potential* but not an inherent feature of the channel. The only way to ensure syn-chronicity and instant feedback, is to select an alternative channel, such as the telephone or face-to-face meeting, where this characteristic is guaranteed.

Another problematic feature of e-mail has been highlighted by the practice of cir-culating supposedly humorous e-mail messages and attachments to friends and work colleagues. Recently, there have been several cases of disciplinary action taken against employees whose messages were interpreted as offensive by other work col-leagues. The seemingly informal and instantaneous nature of the channel seems to encourage spontaneous and often poorly thought-out messages, that would not have been sent when organisations relied on paper-based systems. This is illustrated by another common source of embarrassment, when someone inadvertently copies or forwards material to the 'wrong' people, including earlier e-mail exchanges that may still be attached to the current message. Again, this human error is facilitated by the technology, which makes it easy to press a key without a great deal of thought or preparation. In the worst case, it can lead to an escalating cycle of retaliatory e-mails. This begins when an already stressed person receives what they interpret as a dis-courteous or unreasonable e-mail message. Instead of allowing themselves to calm down, or checking their initial impression, the receiver responds immediately, send-ing a short and angry reply that provokes an even angrier response.

As this short review has indicated, e-mail is a relatively new and immature communication channel. As a consequence, there are still a number of teething-problems to be resolved. Mini-case 8.2 takes a wry look at one of the most troubling issues, how to end an e-mail message appropriately.

| Mini-case 8.2 | Anarchy in the world of e-mail sign-offs | |

So long, Yours sincerely. Farewell, Yours faithfully. These phrases, which helped us bring business letters to a courteous close for decades, are out of date. Finished. This distressing news is contained in a volume called *Perfect@E-mail – All you need to get it right first time* by consultant Steve Morris. According to Mr Morris, the perfect business e-mail is personal and informal. These two time-honoured endings are 'dusty' and won't do at all. Instead, the perfect e-mail should end: 'Kind regards' or 'Best wishes'. At a pinch it could end 'Regards' – though Steve (I hope he'll appreciate this personal form of address) does not altogether approve. He thinks it too cold. With letters, the rules were clear. If you started 'Dear Sir' you ended 'Yours faithfully'. If you started with a name, you ended 'Yours sincerely'. With e-mail there is no rule, which is good news for Steve, as there is money to be made in making a few up. It is also good news for me. If Steve can lay down the law, so can I. To help me produce my own definitive version of the perfect end to an e-mail, I have just spent an hour going through nearly 100 e-mails sent to me by perfect strangers. Each message I have looked at, made a note of the sign-off, then deleted if appropriate. This has been a thoroughly satisfactory exercise – I have a tidier in-box and some shocking survey results. My conclusion is that it is chaos out there.

The sample revealed no fewer than 20 different sign-offs. One woman sent me a message signed 'Thanks and best regards, Yours sincerely' – which shows how dire the confusion has become. I suspect people are spending ages over supposedly speedy messages because they don't know the right way of ending the things. In my sample, the most popular sign-off is – sorry Steve – 'Regards', which ended 22 of the e-mails. This strikes me as an acceptable farewell. Short but civil. 'Regards' is preferable to 'Best regards', 'Kind Regards' and 'Warm regards', which all sound false coming from someone you've never heard of. Yet they are better than 'Bestest regards' (false and ungrammatical), 'Warmest regards' and 'Kindest regards'. These, in turn, are superior to 'Rgds', with which 12 of my e-mail sample were finished. 'Rgds' conveys the information that the sender is very, very busy – too busy to waste three extra keystrokes on the recipient. 'Wishes' are a slightly less fitting alternative to 'Regards'. These are too friendly for me. Here there is also a range of options. 'Best wishes', 'With best wishes', 'Very best wishes', 'Bestest wishes' – none of them advisable for an e-mail to someone you do not know.

Moving still further away from an acceptable sign-off, there is 'Best', 'All the Best', and – ugh – 'Bestest'. Best what, you wonder. It gets worse. In descending order there is 'Take care', 'All the best', 'Cheers' and 'Enjoy'. These are familiar and vulgar and should not be allowed. A few FT readers are clinging to 'Yours sincerely'. Eight people sent me this sort of e-mail, with a further three using the just about acceptable 'Sincerely'. There was nothing dusty about these messages. The sign-off was polite and, well, sincere. At least, more so than a farewell that wishes the best to a stranger.

No doubt when people started writing 'Yours faithfully' and 'Yours sincerely' generations ago, there was much shaking of heads among the old guard – who clung to 'I remain, dear Sir, your obedient servant . . .'. Maybe that is all I am doing. Yet a change in greeting or farewell is more acceptable when it is brought on by a change in the medium. When telephones were fairly new, you picked up the phone and said your number – presumably as a signal to the lady who operated the manual exchange. As a child I was taught to say 'Gulliver 1741'. When the numbers got longer and the memory of switchboards distant, everyone started saying just 'hello' – except for the over-seventies. Now hardly anyone even says 'hello' – voice-mail does the job for us.

These changes in formal greeting have occurred because the technology has changed. And so it should be with e-mail. The problem with e-mails is that many of them should not be e-mails at all. Many of the ones that end 'Yours sincerely' are really letters, sent electronically. Anyone who has gone to the trouble of typing out a proper letter might take that little bit of extra trouble and print the thing out, sign it and put it in the mail. That way it is more likely to get noticed. But for e-mails that aren't letters at all, but messages that need the immediacy of the send button, the rule is different. The best ending for these messages is no sign-off at all. A brief, simple message, followed by the name of the sender. Quick, functional and characterless. Just like the medium.

Questions

1 What issues does the author identify regarding a lack of consistency in e-mails?

2 How do you begin and end your own e-mail messages?

3 Does your writing style vary according to the type of message and receiver?

4 What lessons can we draw about way this communication channel is being used at present and how it might be improved in the future?

Source: Kellaway (23 October, 2000). Copyright Financial Times Limited. Reproduced with permission.

8.8 Text messaging and beyond: emerging communication issues

Various commercial information providers are using text messages as a communication channel, for weather forecasts, sports results and traffic reports, for example. The channel has been used to provide online banking customers with immediate and automatic notification, when their current accounts either exceed or fall below a previously-agreed figure. It has also been adopted by household security firms, who can alert their customers when smoke or burglar alarms are sounded. In chapter 10, we review another recent application of text messaging, which provides potential customers with marketing information by interacting with their personal computers (see Mini-case 10.2). However, this section identifies some important limitations of the channel, when it is used inappropriately by organisations. Mini-case 8.3 opens with a reference to one of the more popular information services available via text messaging (i.e. supplying the latest football results). It goes on to report on a less attractive use for the channel, notifying people that they have been made redundant.

Texting redundancy: a communication perspective

You were promised Premiership goals on your mobile, but instead you learn you've been sent off. Staff at Accident Group, a Manchester-based personal injury specialist, were yesterday informed by text message that they had lost their jobs. The messages came from insolvency practitioners at accountants PricewaterhouseCoopers (PwC), administrators to Amulet Group, Accident Group's Luxembourg-controlled parent. Recipients were instructed to call a number, where a recorded message told them: 'All staff who are being retained will be contacted today. If you have not been spoken to you are therefore being made redundant with immediate effect.' While the growing popularity of text-sex is well documented, this example of text-sacking drew an angry response. 'Nobody should be given devastating news about their employment by text message. We desperately need more powerful provisions for proper workplace consultation,' said Brendan Barber, general secretary of the TUC. 'Sensitive matters of this nature should be carried out face-to-face.' The Department of Trade and Industry was equally critical, not least because PwC told employees to apply to the DTI to collect their May salaries, holiday pay, notice and redundancy pay. 'This shouldn't happen in future,' said the DTI, which later this summer plans to publish its proposals to incorporate the EU's information and consultation directive into UK law. While this is the first example of mass redundancies by text message, using alternative media to communicate bad news to employees is not new. Bill Morris, of the Transport and General Workers' Union, complained when Corus [a large steel-making firm] staff heard they had been made redundant on their car radios.

Questions

1 Why is text messaging an unsuitable channel for the purpose highlighted in this case?

2 What kinds of internal and external communication might be effectively undertaken using text messaging?

3 What are your own experiences of using this communication channel?

4 How do you think that existing texting conventions are likely to adapt, if this channel becomes more widely adopted in organisations?

Reflecting on new communication channels and practices

We have reviewed some traditional and emerging forms of text-based communication and noted the different ways that they are used – and abused – in organisations. It would be easy to stop our discussion at the level of the 'recipe', listing the best ways to exploit each of the channels that are addressed in this book. However, there are good reasons for reflecting more deeply on the impact that these channels, most notably those that exploit new technologies, are having on the overall quality and effectiveness of organisational communication. JoAnn Yates and Wanda Orlikowski have undertaken one of the most insightful research programmes addressing these questions (e.g. Orlikowski and Yates 1994, Yates and Orlikowski 2002). Their research shows how communication practices develop into established norms, structuring the way that we interact with one another. Their more recent work, on 'genre systems' has focused on the ways that technologically-mediated communication shapes the way that people collaborate at work. Details of these and other related studies are included in the Guide to Further Reading, at the end of this chapter.

Summary

- Letters remain an important communication channel for a variety of organisational purposes, and are associated with different communication practices than those of newer rivals, such as e-mail.
- Letters share three important communication characteristics: they are 'one-way' and non-interruptible; they are 'asynchronous' between sending and receipt; and they provide a permanent record of messages.
- Today, letters are normally prepared in a 'fully blocked' page layout with 'open' punctuation. They are typically structured around three tasks: ' establishing the context; delivering the central message; and stating any action required'.
- As with other channels, style and content of letters should reflect the receiver and the purpose of the message. This can be problematic in the case of standard letters, where a polite, clear and concise approach is generally most appropriate.
- The fusion of database and text-handling technologies offers the opportunity to create customised letters in large quantities. However, such letters require careful targeting and drafting.
- Stationery can convey a positive image of your organisation, but it is also important to consider promotional, practical and legal aspects of the design;
- The internal memorandum (or 'memo') has been largely superseded by e-mail, which has adopted aspects of its original format.
- E-mail and text messaging are powerful communication channels, combining characteristics of text-based and conversational communication. However, inherent limitations and a lack of consensus over communication practices remain problematic.

Practical exercises

1 Erskine Food Stores Limited

Consider the following exchange of correspondence between a customer and retailer. This is an example of a letter of complaint, followed up with a letter of 'adjustment' (i.e. seeking to resolve the complaint or dispute). First, consider the customer's letter.

(a) What do you detect from the style and tone of his letter?

(b) What do you think he expects the company to do?

Now, note how the reply is structured, its general layout, use of language, tone etc.

(c) How would you feel on receiving the retailer's letter?

(d) What messages do you think they have managed to communicate?

(e) What changes would you make to improve its effectiveness?

12th December 2004
Customer Services Department
ERSKINE FOOD STORES
545 Wroxeter Boulevard
Watlington
Herefordshire HE5 8WX

37 Wilson Street
Ickleston
Middlesex
UB22 8TX

Dear Sir/Madam

'ERSKWIK' BRAND SOUP: CHICKEN AND VEGETABLE WITH CROUTONS

I am extremely happy with our new Erskines branch in Ickleston, with its friendly staff and (generally) good products. However, the enclosed soup sachet comes as a big disappointment. Try it!

Having added your boiling water, see how rich and substantial it looks, a real improvement on the competition. Now sense the disillusion when you actually taste it. Regrettably, as I am sure you will agree, any initial flavour is overwhelmed by an excessive, lingering SALTINESS. On gastronomic and health grounds, your soup under-performs and does Erskine's a dis-service.

Do I have a duff batch, or do Erskine's have a duff Buyer?

Yours faithfully

Ronald Quincy-Smith

enc.
cc: Mr Bill Badger, *Consumer Watch*, Channel 7, XBC Television.

---

11 January 2005

ERSKINES FOOD STORES
545 Wroxeter Boulevard, Watlington HE5 8WX
www.erskines-food.com

Mr R Quincy-Smith
37 Wilson Street
Ickleston
Middlesex
UB22 8TX

Dear Mr Quincy-Smith

We thank you for your letter and your kind comments about the staff and general standards at our Ickleston branch. However, we were sorry to learn of the problem you experienced with the Quick soup and apologise for the inconvenience caused when the product was found to be too salty. We examined the sample you kindly returned and it was tasted by our Buyer who agreed that it did have an excess of salt and was not according to the specification. As we were not sure if this was an isolated instance or a more general problem, it was necessary to obtain further samples from stock for checking and we regret the delay this caused when responding to your letter. Although the salt level in the stock packs was not as high as the one you purchased, there was more than the specified amount and therefore the supply was removed from sale pending further enquiries with our suppliers.

Meanwhile, we were concerned that this could happen and escape detection during the strict quality control procedures and we are continuing to monitor the situation closely to ensure there is no further lapse in standards. May we say again how sorry we are that you had reason to complain in this way. Occasionally, in spite of all the care taken, things can go wrong and we are grateful to be alerted so that we can take any action necessary to correct any shortcomings.

We hope you will continue to shop with us without further disappointment and you will accept our apologies together with the enclosed voucher towards the out-of-pocket expenses you have incurred.

Yours sincerely

B V Kelly (Mrs)

Customer Services

Enclosed credit voucher: 970987 £5.00

Tel: 01999 876543 Fax: 01999 876321 E-mail: service@erskines.co.uk
KW Erskine Food Stores Limited Registered in England 6789101112
Registered Office: 34 Victoria Avenue, Farebury, Wiltshire SN00 2JK

2 Stationery and letterhead redesign: drafting an e-mail and letter

You are working for either a small high-technology manufacturing company or a voluntary organisation supporting children from deprived communities. Your manager has asked you to redesign the office stationery in order to meet current regulations and to project a more professional image of the organisation. She wants the work completed and the new stationery to be ready for use within the next eight weeks.

(a) Prepare an initial design to meet the promotional, practical and legal requirements discussed in this chapter. Invent a suitable business name and all necessary details, including your postal address, e-mail and website details. You may need to research the relevant legal requirements.

(b) Draft an e-mail to your manager, Sarah Brown, requesting approval of the design and dealing with any production issues, such as the cost of printing and paper to be used.

(c) Draft a letter to be sent to a number of companies, inviting quotes for printing your new design.

Case-study H

'Infant-plus' baby foods – direct marketing techniques

Many letters contain similar or identical information that needs to be reproduced for different receivers, including the routine letters sent out by banks, tax offices and education departments. Rather than redraft these each time, organisations used to generate standard (or 'form') letters, constructed from a series of model paragraphs. Inevitably, these letters sounded rather impersonal. As the 'Middleburg Bank' example in this chapter has indicated (see section 8.4), there are some obvious dangers in using standardised text, which ignores individual differences. However, by linking text handling and database software imaginatively (a technique sometimes referred to as 'mailmerge'), it is possible to generate relatively personalised letters in large volumes. Mailmerge is used in many types of organisational correspondence, but one of the most common applications is communicating with current and prospective customers. It is one of the basic techniques of direct marketing, where databases are used to target particular individuals about products and services, rather than broad market segments (see Table 8.4).

Consider, for example the imaginary food manufacturer, 'Infant Foods Inc', which specialises in bottled ready-meals for babies. The company wants to encourage new parents to trial *Infant-plus*, an up-market organic baby food brand. Several options are presented to the sales and marketing director. One suggestion is to run an extended series of adverts on breakfast television. However, the director points out that such a broad (or 'shotgun') approach would be largely wasted, since many of the viewers will not have babies, or have no interest in an organic product. After a long discussion, she decides to build the campaign around direct marketing. The first stage will be to purchase a list of prospects, the data set being captured from a competition, run in a specialist magazine for pregnant women. This data will then be combined with lists already held by the company, to create a new data set. The plan is to generate approximately 200,000 personalised letters with money-off vouchers and a brochure insert. She hopes that, with the help of a high-quality data set, this 'direct' approach will be very closely targeted on people who are likely to be interested in *Infant-plus*. The initial promotional letter will then be reinforced with other promotional tools, including a follow-up distribution of free samples and offers for related products and services.

Table 8.4 **Direct marketing terminology**

Term	Comments
Mailmerge	This facility is offered by most wordprocessing packages, linking a database file containing names, addresses and other information, to a text file containing a standard letter. Name, address and other data are drawn ('merged') into the standard letter in the appropriate locations, which are marked by keying in a code letter. The mailmerge is activated as the letters are printed out.
Database	A flexible electronic filing cabinet, often comprising a vast number of discrete items of data. Data can be sorted, filtered and extracted in ways that would be time-consuming and impractical using paper-based files. In addition to specialist software, spreadsheets and wordprocessing packages include useful database functions.
Dataset	Raw data loaded into a database for subsequent manipulation. Widely-used data sets include: publicly-available statistical data, commercial lists of prospective customer contacts and confidential results from an in-house questionnaire survey. All forms of stored data are subject to data protection legislation.
Field	Within a particular record (see below), a single (i.e. 'discrete') item of information, such as one line of an address, a surname, date of birth or nationality. In the case of survey data, a field may contain the response to a question.
List	Data set containing names and addresses of consumers, sometimes with lifestyle and purchasing behaviour. Lists are created from market research surveys, competitions, returned product guarantee cards, etc. Lists are purchased by organisations in order to undertake focused direct mailing (e.g. 25,000 paraglider pilots, or 43,000 charity donors).
Record	Within a data set, a block of information relating to an individual person or organisation. This is the electronic equivalent of a file placed inside a filing cabinet.

Many different types of organisations, including charities and campaigning groups, are making increasing use of direct marketing techniques for fund-raising and member recruitment, as well as in more traditional sales activity. Direct mail can be a powerful communication technique, but many people continue to dismiss it as 'junk mail'. Industry-sponsored research suggests that a high proportion of direct mail is opened, though this is not in itself a guarantee that the messages will be absorbed. When drafting communication in this form, it is essential to minimise the wastage rate. The following questions indicate some of the issues that need to be addressed:

- Have I targeted the recipients as closely as possible (e.g. filtering out existing customers when promoting introductory offers)?
- Is the style and content appropriate to all recipients? You may need to produce variants for different segments.
- Is the data set 'clean' and up-to-date? Have I considered using reply slips or other auditing techniques to assess the quality of the list?

One of the most important checks concerns the internal consistency of the dataset. Ensure that the data fields are in a correct sequence and that all of them are drawn from the same record. When an organisation gets its 'name' fields and 'address' fields out of sequence, absolutely everyone – perhaps many thousands of customers – receives a letter containing someone else's details, undermining the effectiveness of any message it contains.

Questions

1 Prepare your own direct marketing letters, using one of the scenarios below. Prepare two versions. In the first version, highlight each point in the letter where information would be merged from a database file. This will obviously include the recipient's name and address, but should also involve the main body of your letter. Try to be as creative as possible. Specify precisely the contents of each record and field. The second version of your letter should be addressed to a specific recipient, showing how a finished letter would look. Use the guidance on letter-writing contained in this chapter. Prepare a note to accompany the sample letter, suggest how you might capture the data that has been used.

(a) You are a charitable organisation, providing accommodation and support for young offenders, and helping them to escape a life of crime. You want to launch a long-term national fund-raising campaign, entitled *Youth Action 2020*.

(b) You are a conventional retailer, moving onto the internet to market your *Sandale* range of women's fashion shoes. You need to reach 20 to 35-year-old women in socio-economic categories ABC1.

(c) You are a government department, wanting to promote *Golden Age*, a new publicly-subsidised pre-retirement savings plan for 18 to 65-year-olds in regular employment. You want to reach both new and existing members of the workforce.

2 Comment on the potential advantages and disadvantages of direct mail as a communication channel, in areas *other than* sales promotion and marketing. Identify examples where it would be particularly effective, and those where it may be counter-productive.

3 Consider the potential applications for direct mail techniques using electronic media, including e-mail and text messaging. Outline your proposals in a short verbal presentation (maximum 5 minutes) or one-page summary.

Further reading

There are various guides to letter formats, giving 'model' examples of the major types of letter, including **Bond** (1998) and **Janner** (1989). Additional models and templates are available on the companion website. While it may be tempting to make use of popular guides to writing better letters and e-mails, the theme of this book is that the key to becoming a more effective communicator is to develop your own critical faculties, rather than relying too heavily on 'recipe book' solutions. Refer back to the reading recommended for Chapter 3, which deals more broadly with the use of language. Readers are also encouraged to consider recent research on the impact of emerging text-based channels, including work by **Minsky and Marin** (1999), **Yates and Orlikowski** (2002) and **Zack and McKenney** (1995). The broader implications for organisations are discussed in Chapter 7 of this book. **Newell** *et al.* (2001) provides a useful case-based analysis of intranet developments, while **Fulk and DeSanctis** (1995) explore the links between the new communication channels and organisational change. **Turban** (2003) is a good general introduction to e-business applications.

References

Bond, A. (1998) *300 Successful Business Letters*. Barron's Educational Series, Hauppauge NY.

DWRC (2001) 'The future of paper mail in a digital age'. Digital World Research Centre, University of Surrey, Guildford.

Fulk, J. and DeSanctis, G. (1995) 'Electronic communication and changing organizational forms'. *Organization Science*, 6, 4, 337–49.

Harris, C. and Orr, R. (2003) 'We rgrt 2 infm u yr fired. Hv nice day'. *Financial Times*, London edition, 1 (31st May).

Janner, G. (1989) *Janner's complete letter writer*. Century Hutchinson, London.

Kellaway, L. (2000) 'Never having to say goodbye'. *Financial Times*, London edition, 19 (23rd October).

Minsky, B.D. and Marin, D.B. (1999) 'Why faculty members use e-mail: the role of individual differences in channel choice'. *The Journal of Business Communication*, 36, 194–217.

Newell, S., Scarbrough, H. and Swan, J. (2001) 'From global knowledge management to internal electronic fences: contradictory outcomes of intranet development'. *British Journal of Management*, 12, 97–111.

Orlikowski, W.J. and Yates, J. (1994) 'Genre repertoire: the structuring of communicative practices in organizations'. *Administrative Science Quarterly*, 39, 541–74.

Royal Mail (2001) 'Paper mail is here to stay' (press release). Royal Mail Group, London (6th March).

Turban (2003) *Electronic commerce 2003: a managerial perspective*. Prentice Hall, Upper Saddle River NJ.

Yates, J. and Orlikowski, W.J. (2002) 'Genre systems: structuring interaction through communicative norms'. *The Journal of Business Communication*, 39, 13–35.

Zack, M.H. and McKenney, J.L. (1995) 'Social context and interaction in ongoing computer-supported management groups'. *Organization Science*, 6, 394–422.

CHAPTER 9

Reports, briefing papers and summaries

Perfection is achieved, not when there is nothing more to add, but when there is nothing left to take away.

Antoine de Saint Exupery, writer

Learning outcomes

By the end of this chapter you should be able to:

- contrast the different types of reports used in organisations, relating these differences to their audience and purpose;
- identify and apply the principles for preparing an effective written report;
- tackle the four main stages of report writing: briefing, preparation, drafting and completion;
- recognise the importance of summarising skills;
- develop these skills by drafting executive summaries and briefing documents.
- reflect on the characteristics of this communication channel and its application in technologically-mediated and multi-cultural contexts.

9.1 Introduction

This chapter considers reports and briefing documents, two text-based communication channels that are widely used in organisations of all kinds. As was the case with shorter text-based channels, such as letters, memos and e-mails (see Chapter 8), care and practice is needed to structure the content and refine the writing style in order to meet the needs of particular audiences and communication purposes. Our review of report-writing techniques includes a number of issues that influence the structure and content of a report. We trace the writing process, from the initial stages of obtaining a clear specification for the project, through to the final stages of editing and production. The final section of the chapter deals with an essential (and often under-rated) communication challenge, abstracting from complex source material and drafting concise summaries that focus attention on the most important evidence and argument.

9.2 Reports: principal types and purposes

Business reports come in all shapes and sizes. Our first task is to review the main options available, and consider which type of report best suits a particular purpose (see Table 9.1). One of the first issues to consider is how the report is to be delivered. This chapter focuses on written reports, but it is also possible to present an oral report, either in a meeting or as part of a presentation. (Chapters 12 and 13 deal with these channels.) Some reports are written in a very formal style, while others are relatively informal. They may range in scale from a single page of concise argument drafted by one author to a multi-volume report compiled by a large team of researchers and editorial staff. There is a significant difference between the task of preparing a routine report, where the content and format tends to be pre-determined, and an original, 'one-off' report, where there may be very little in the way of guidance from previous work. Many companies use standardised formats for routine internal reports, such as the 'Weekly Sales Update' produced by a sales department, or the regular 'Quality Monitoring Report' prepared by quality assurance staff in a manufacturing plant.

In the following sections, we focus on how to write an **original** report that makes use of relatively source-complex material, presented in a formal way. The subject matter might be, for example, a new strategy proposal, plans for an office relocation or an investigation into a recent industrial accident. The underlying principles of report writing are common to all types of document, so the advice can be adapted to suit your particular purpose. Whatever type of report you are writing, it is possible to identify four fairly distinct stages:

- obtaining a clear specification;
- research and preparation;
- drafting the report;
- editing and completion.

These stages are dealt with in sequence, beginning with the deceptively simple task of deciding what the report is about.

Table 9.1 **Types of report: some practical examples**

Type	Example of purpose
Executive briefing	The factory manager provides the managing director with a concise summary of the main issues and likely questions on health and safety prior to a shareholders' meeting when the issue is likely to be raised.
Research results	A market research executive at a medical charity is investigating the impact of a recent donor recruitment campaign. She presents the findings from a telephone survey to the charity's trustees and senior managers.
Regular update	On a weekly basis, the management accountant of a major retail chain advises regional managers of their profitability performances by branch and geographic area.
Business proposal	An entrepreneur contacts a venture capital company to offer a possible equity stake in her new leisure business. She provides them with a business plan to read before attending the presentation.

9.3 Obtaining a clear specification

A report is a kind of 'guided tour' through a jungle of ideas. It is important to plan your route in advance, but also to remain flexible; unforeseen changes are bound to arise once you get under way. To prepare successfully, it is worth asking some fundamental questions. Above all, clarify the report specification or 'terms of reference' and establish which items really need to be included to meet the needs of your audience. The questions are bound to vary from case to case, but they can be summarised under four main headings: audience, purpose, context and sources.

Audience, purpose, context and sources

Before putting pen to paper, there are four basic questions to answer regarding your prospective readers, the purpose of the report, the context in which the report will be read and the sources that you intend to use. These questions may appear simple and obvious, but they are frequently overlooked, resulting in a great deal of wasted effort on the part of the report-writer and a less effective end-product.

Audience

As with other communication channels, one of the most cost-effective ways of spending your time is to research and reflect on your 'target' audience. Find out as much as possible about the people who are going to read your finished report. Is it a specific person, a group of people with similar backgrounds or a more diverse readership (i.e. multiple audiences)? What is their existing knowledge and experience of the subject matter of your report? Will they be familiar with any technical language that you intend to use? Are they likely to hold positive, negative or neutral views on the issues that you are discussing? For example, imagine that you were preparing a report on 'marketing opportunities' related to genetically-modified (GM) foods, a subject that raises a great deal of emotional energy on both sides of the argument.

Purpose

It is also essential to consider why you are drafting the report, its primary purpose plus any secondary aims. For example: is it designed to consult readers; to provide information; to explain a novel concept; or to persuade them to adopt a particular course of action? These questions, in conjunction with your research on the audience and purpose, can then be used to inform decisions on the kinds of language used in the report. Consider the previous example, of the GM foods debate. While academic language, with full Harvard referencing, would be strict requirements of any scientific report on the subject, the same features would become serious distractions in a more popular document, designed as part of a public consultation exercise. Similar issues arise when considering the use of images in a report (e.g. are photographs appropriate? should data be presented in numerical or graphical formats?).

Context

Report writing does not take place in a vacuum; it is essential to consider the wider setting in which your report is being prepared. For example: Is there an urgent deadline for delivery, so that speed of delivery takes priority over perfecting the fine details of style and presentation? Is it a routine (e.g. weekly or monthly) publication that must follow a standard template, or – as we have assumed in this chapter – is it a bespoke piece of work that allows you to introduce a more original or distinctive style? Is the report designed to 'stand-alone' or is it designed to work with other communication channels, such as a series of oral presentations or an interactive website? Finally, if there are to be several channels, how will the authors ensure that the combined effect is both consistent and complementary?

Sources

There are always several preliminary questions to consider regarding the raw material that will form the basis of your report. Again, these questions appear very straightforward, but are easily ignored at the planning stages, leading to more serious problems later on. The most important questions concern availability and access:

- Where are the sources of secondary data that you will need to consult?
- Are they available in a compatible electronic format?
- If there are particular people that you need to interview, when are they going to be in the office, and are they willing to grant you a meeting?
- Is any of your source material likely to be either commercially or politically sensitive?
- Do any copyright regulations apply?
- Are there any other ethical issues regarding access or use of this information?
- Should sources be cited in the report?
- What is the quality of each available source (i.e. its credibility, accuracy, objectivity and currency)?
- Are there any information 'gaps' that need to be filled?
- If so, is it necessary to conduct additional research in order to provide a comprehensive coverage of the issues?

Failing to ask these questions, and to deal with any resulting issues, can result in costly and embarrassing delays at a later stage.

As the previous points have indicated, there is a lot of groundwork to do, before the writing can begin. In some cases, the organisation may decide that it is more appropriate to commission external consultants to prepare a report. However, even in these circumstances, managers need to become involved in the process of briefing the consultants, who will also need answers to the questions raised in this section. Mini-case 9.1 highlights some of the difficulties that can occur when inadequate attention is given to this initial stage in the report-writing process.

| Mini-case 9.1 | 'Nebulous Phones' and the under-specified reports |

One of the most common causes of bad report writing is failure to obtain a clear specification. Though you may need to *revise* them as the work proceeds, it is still important that the main requirements are agreed with those commissioning the report. As the following case suggests, people often find themselves struggling to extract a clear specification (or 'brief') from senior managers or external clients. Sergey Nebulous is the founder and chief executive of Nebulous Phones, a large and successful mobile phone retailer. Sergey is notorious for his vague instructions to staff, and he invariably complains whenever they produce something that fails to match his requirements. Here is a selection, taken from Sergey's recent requests to his hard-pressed employees:

'Klajdia!, sorry to interrupt your lunch. I need a report on the Blue Whale acquisition. Lots of graphs and things. You know, something impressive-looking; it's for the analysts ... don't you just HATE those people?!!! Anyway, enjoy the lasagne, I'll leave you to it.'

Subject: no subject
Date: Sun 12 July 2005 23:57:46 +0100
From: Sergey Nebulous <sergey@nebulous-elec.com>
To: Yusef Mugisha <ymugisha@nebulous-elec.com>
Priority: High
We need new supplier data interpreted. Include financial ratios etc. Sergey

'Is that Kay? Hello, Sergey here. Sorry to bother you at the weekend. Is it really that early? Anyway, have you seen that OUTRAGEOUS article in the 'Sunday Inquisitor'? Loads of media hype about radiation and handsets! Kay, I want the FACTS. Can you please draft me a full-scale report, showing just how 'green', you know, ' sustainable' we are? Thanks a million, got to go. Bye now!'

Questions

1 Review the above three extracts and note the main limitations in Sergey's specification for each report, including any missing or ambiguous information.

2 Based on the faults you have identified, what kinds of problems do you anticipate arising from the reports prepared by Klajdia, Yusef and Kay?

3 Re-draft Sergey's report specifications to overcome the problems you have identified, inventing and inserting any necessary details.

4 What would your response have been, in practice, if you had been one of these three employees?

Source: Written by the author. Nebulous Phones is a fictional organisation.

9.4 Researching and organising the source material

The second set of preparatory tasks is concerned with the research process and organising the source material you are going to use as the basis for your report. Research methods fall beyond the scope of this book, but detailed advice can be found in a number of specialist texts. Recent examples include Saunders *et al.* (2003) and Easterby-Smith, M. *et al.* (2002); additional recommendations are given in the Further reading at the end of this chapter.

For the purposes of this chapter, our interest in the research process begins at the point when the main data sources have been identified. In the era of internet search engines and electronic access to official statistics, academic journals, newspapers and technical publications, selecting relevant information from an ever-growing pile of possibilities is often the main problem. Diagramming can be a useful technique that helps the researcher to separate the 'forest' from the 'trees' (i.e. abstracting the main themes from the detailed background information that has been collected) (see section 2.5). By writing out the topics to be covered on a whiteboard or large sheet of paper, you can begin to identify the most important sources and uncover logical connections between major topic areas. These connections are the basis for the development of arguments (see Chapter 5). They should also help in developing an outline structure for the report. The structure of the report may be modified during the drafting stage, but this initial effort to organise the raw material can have a profound influence on the way that you think about the subject. Formulating a report is a creative process. It is generally advisable to draw on insights from a number of people, before committing to a particular approach. Much the same process occurs during the early stages of a student dissertation or thesis (Phillips and Pugh 2000).

There are generally several competing ways of tackling a research question and its associated body of evidence. The initial approach, which once seemed so promising, may reach a dead end. The prospective author becomes understandably downhearted at this point! However, students and supervisors often go through several cycles of proposals and counter-suggestions before the breakthrough occurs. As a result of discussion, someone stumbles upon the obvious 'solution', and the main stage of drafting the report can begin.

9.5 Report writing: drafting stage

How do you approach the task of writing? Some people can settle down and write out an extended piece of text from beginning to end. However, for most of us, writing is a more gradual process, with many corrections and a succession of drafts before arriving at the finished article. The task of writing a long report can be a source of concern, causing many writers to postpone the point at which they put pen to paper. In some cases, this is due to lack of prior experience and a fear of being exposed to external criticism (Ruderstam and Newton 2001). This, in turn, may flow from a person's lack of confidence in what they have to say.

However, as many authors have commented, the *activity* of writing is itself a source of learning, as you engage with the subject and really begin to *think* about the ways that your information sources are connected (Phillips and Pugh 2000). This insight is reflected in the wider field of knowledge management, which has highlighted the essential relationship between knowledge creation and human action (e.g. Nonaka and Takeuchi 1995: 58–9). In this case, it suggests that authors may need to remain flexible, adapting their initial outline structures to accommodate the new ideas generated during the writing process. It is also important to recognise that different cultures show distinctive preferences in the way that logical arguments are constructed (De Vita 2000: 172, Zaharna 1996: 80). The guidance presented in the following sections is influenced by British conventions for structuring and presenting material. While it is not possible to represent the full diversity of communication practices, the broader principles of successful drafting (i.e. organising the source material, making the structure visible and using graphics where appropriate) may be readily adapted and applied to most organisational and cultural contexts.

Organising the source material

A report is somewhat like a new building; a basic outline structure is required before you can work on the interior. In contrast to a building, report writers have some capacity to re-design the overall structure at a later stage. However, there is a close relationship between the way that the material is organised and the 'interior design' task of writing specific sections of text. Hence, it is advisable to draft an *initial* outline structure for the report as soon as the initial preparatory work is complete, but *before* drafting large amounts of text. There are two distinct elements to this process: identifying what the main sections and sub-sections are likely to be, and considering the order in which each topic should be placed. The first element is an extension of the activities outlined in section 9.4. At the drafting stage, we need to review the broad clustering of topics and loose connections that were identified previously, refining them into more concrete groupings of primary and secondary themes. For example, Whitley's (2000) text, *Divergent Capitalisms: the social structuring and change of business systems*, is divided into three distinct parts:

- the first gives an introduction to the concept of 'varieties of capitalism';
- the second outlines the 'comparative-business-systems' framework;
- the third applies the framework to business systems in East Asia and Eastern Europe.

While other structures may be conceived, the key point for the communicator is to ensure that there is an inherent logic, as indicated in this case. The actual order in which the sections are placed is always a matter of judgement. There are a number of logical alternatives to consider, as illustrated below (see Table 9.2). If you are unsure which order to adopt, it is worth experimenting with the alternatives; some are bound to work better than others. This choice should be guided by the standard concerns of the communicator. In other words, which sequence is most appropriate for the **material** being presented and which sequence is likely to be the most straightforward for the **audience** that has to absorb the message it contains?

Table 9.2 Getting a report in order: some alternative sequences

Logical sequence	Practical example
Importance	In a report entitled 'Ten challenges for the pharmaceutical industry', the most serious challenges are addressed first.
Urgency	The structural survey report for a newly-acquired building begins by identifying a leaky roof that needs to be repaired immediately and moves on to discuss longer-term maintenance work.
Date/Chronology	A progress report on computer system installation reviews events over the past month. Some reports, including the educational and employment sections of a CV, may be written in **reverse** chronological order, with the most recent items first.
Simple to complex	The documentation supplied with an accountancy training course begins with the basic concepts of book-keeping before explaining more advanced topics, such as accounting adjustments and ratio analysis.
Global to specific	A report into a company's absenteeism problems starts by looking at broad social factors, gradually narrowing down to causes within particular factories and departments. (Note: the opposite sequence, specific to global, may work equally well.)

The issue of structure raises questions regarding culture-specific approaches to writing. This can be a particular challenge for international managers and students, whose educational background has been in another national culture. For example, an Italian economist, now based in Britain, recalls the different expectations of British and Italian academics towards the essay format that is widely used in this discipline:

> 'In the Italian essay writing style, for example, a long and general introduction which illustrates the genesis of the issue to be examined and provides a retrospective analysis or historical overview of the issue is a must, regardless of the wording of the question. A British reader, however, as the author learned at his expense during the early stages of his undergraduate study in England, would see this as lack of "convergence" to the point, or even "waffling" [i.e. engaging in a long and irrelevant discussion], and it might not be until the second page of the essay that concepts expressed are regarded as being really pertinent, and aimed at answering the question.' (De Vita 2001: 172)

Experience with international students from many different backgrounds suggests that these kinds of cultural boundary can be crossed, given appropriate guidance and support. It also appears that there is a greater degree of convergence in the structuring of some text-based communication channels, including the academic dissertation and some varieties of business report, reflecting the internationalisation of the relevant organisations (e.g. universities, multinational companies and international consulting firms).

Table 9.3 compares the typical outline structure of an academic dissertation with that of a business report. This highlights two areas that tend to be downplayed in business reports. The first of these is the review of earlier and related research in the area, that helps to locate a particular piece of work in its broader context (i.e. the 'literature review'). Business reports tend to have a much narrower focus on the immediate issue at hand. Second, the dissertation always includes a discussion of the wider implications of the findings. Again, this broadening out of the findings is often seen as beyond the scope of a business report, due to its shorter-term and more managerial focus.

Table 9.3 **Structuring academic dissertations and business reports**

Academic dissertation	Business report
Title page	Title page
Abstract	Executive summary
Contents page	Contents page
Introduction	Introduction
Literature review	
Research methods	
Findings	Findings
Discussion	
Conclusions	Conclusions
Recommendations	Recommendations
References	
Appendices	

The following headings review the main sections of the business report, commenting on their main characteristics and some of the more common issues that can arise when drafting them.

Title page

Like the rest of the report, the title should be clear, concise and unambiguous. Writers commonly use a short 'main' title, followed by a colon and a more explanatory sub-title (e.g. 'Project Equinox: progress report for the period 2005–07'). The title page typically includes the author's name, organisational affiliations and the date of publication.

Executive summary

This should distil the *entire* contents of the report into a few words, providing busy executives with the essence of the report 'at a glance'. It serves the same purpose as the abstract in an academic article, allowing the reader to make a rapid assessment of whether the report is relevant to their needs. Executive summaries usually emphasise the key recommendations of the report, which may be presented in bullet point format. A common error in report writing is to confuse the executive summary with the introduction; the latter serves an entirely different purpose.

Introduction

The purpose of an introduction is to lead the reader into the main body of the report. Like all reception areas, it should be welcoming to the new arrival. It may include the terms of reference, or state the reasons for writing the report and establish its importance. Introductions often contain a 'chapter summary', outlining how the topic is to be tackled in the following chapters. However, this should be brief, otherwise it could pre-empt the rest of the report.

Main section(s)

This comprises a number of sections and sub-sections, with appropriate titles, which may take the form of chapters. Authors can help their readers to navigate a way through the body of the report, by inserting some linking text at the end of each main section or chapter. This text should summarise what has been discussed and indicate how this relates to the next theme or argument.

Conclusion

This is where the key arguments and/or findings of the report are drawn together and put in context. The concluding section should also relate back to the original objectives of the report. (Note: Writing the conclusion provides the author with a useful check that everything has been addressed.) The conclusion should not include any new, previously undiscussed material. Late findings or last-minute ideas should be either fully integrated into the text, or reported separately. It may be tempting to simply 'tack them on' to the rest of the conclusion, but it is an unwise tactic. Audiences find it very confusing, and the resulting irritation can help to undermine the credibility and persuasive power of the report.

Recommendations

This section is sometimes combined with the conclusion. In any event, the recommendations should always flow logically from the points made in the conclusion, and the preceding argument. For example, this section might be used to suggest a preferred option from a range that was under consideration. Alternatively, it might make new proposals or recommend further research, based on the findings of this report.

References

Most business reports provide minimal referencing, the aim being to make the document as short and focused as possible. However, there is a trade-off between concision and evidence-based argument. Where external information sources are used, it may be helpful to provide some supporting details for the reader. Academic dissertations and research papers tend to have much fuller referencing, listing all of the sources. This is combined with extensive referencing in the text. Again, this reflects the trade-off between needing to substantiate the evidence, and word length and readability. For example, the 'Harvard' system of referencing (e.g. 'Kropotkin (2002) states that...' or, '... as suggested by recent studies (Schmidt

1999a)...'), has been widely-adopted in academic writing. However, heavy use of referencing in this format can 'clog up' the text, making it cumbersome to read. Where business reports do include references, the simpler 'Vancouver' numbering system is commonly adopted (e.g. '... as suggested by recent studies[23], ...'), and the number of references is also kept to a minimum.

Appendices

These are used for detailed data and analytical material that some readers are likely to need, but which would obstruct the flow of your argument if inserted earlier. In practice, they are rarely included in business reports, other than those presented as part of a detailed inquiry, involving large amounts of technical or statistical data. Appendices should never be used to 'pad out' a report or simply to indicate the amount of research material that has been collected; unlike the *human* appendix, they must serve a useful purpose!

Make the structure visible – 'signposting' the report

One of the most useful mental exercises for any report-writer is to consider how an audience is going to approach the task of *reading* the report. Most authors find it hard to accept that readers are unlikely to be sitting down with a nice cup of tea, working their way steadily from the opening sentence to the final full stop. In practice, a busy manager will begin by 'scanning' your report, absorbing the over-all look of the piece and pausing over the occasional heading, paragraph, bullet point or illustration that catches their eye (see Chapter 4). You can increase the impact of your report, and assist the reader, by bearing this behavioural pattern in mind. Concise, informative headings, sub-headings and labels act as well-lit sign-posts, guiding the reader through the report. They also make a positive impression in the mind of the reader, suggesting that this is a competently drafted and valu-able document. By contrast, poor signposting gives readers a poor initial impression of your report, even where the underlying content is strong.

The contents page, index, glossaries, section numbering and typography are also important signposting devices. Graphical items, such as charts and photo-graphs, can help to identify the main subject areas, as well as being informative in their own right.

Contents pages and indexes

The contents page provides an overview of the entire report and is essential in all but the shortest documents. The conventional formats list section numbers and headings, with their respective *opening* page number indicated in a column on the right-hand side. Sub-section details may also be included. Accurate and detailed indexing is a fairly specialised skill, which tends to be restricted to longer reports and book-length publications. However, both tables of contents and more straightforward indexes can now be generated relatively easily with the help of standard wordprocessing software.

Section headings and numbering

The conventional approach is to keep headings short and to the point, the aim being to make the contents of that section or sub-section clear to the reader. In more formal reports, decimal numbering systems are normally used alongside the heading. Some legal and scientific reports may use up to four levels of sub-section, so that 'Section 1.9.3.1' is followed by 'Section 1.9.3.2', etc. This can be useful when it is necessary to refer to specific sections of text. However, multiple sub-sections can be confusing, for both the report writer and the reader. In business reports, numbering is best kept simple, using no more than three levels. If further levels are required, you can switch to bullet points or lists based on either lower case letters or Roman numerals (i.e. sequences running, 'a, b, c, d ...' or, 'i, ii, iii, iv ...').

Changing type

Bold text and larger font sizes can be used to identify the main section headings. You can also use upper case and lower case letters to create a logical hierarchy of headings and sub-headings. This hierarchy normally descends from larger font sizes to smaller, upper case to lower case and bold to ordinary text. It is important to use the structure consistently throughout the report, a task that is made easier by creating a template, or making use of those provided with your word-processing package. (Note: These are usually available as a 'drop-down' menu on the toolbar, or as part of the 'tools' menu). In the days when most reports were produced on a typewriter, underlining was commonly used in titles and sub-titles. However, in wordprocessed reports this has been largely replaced by bold text, as illustrated in the following example (see Figure 9.1).

Chapter title (20 pt bold, title case)	**12 Field Research**
Main headings (12 pt bold, upper case)	**12.1 INTRODUCTION** **12.2 REGIONAL BREAKDOWN**
Sub-headings (12 pt, bold, title case)	**12.2.1 South Asia region** **12.2.2 East Asia region**
Lower levels (12pt, title case)	Consumer sample Producer sample
Bullet points (10 pt, title case)	● Increased demand for premium products ● Dynamic new segments emerging ● Limited impact of promotional campaign

Figure 9.1 **Consistent use of typography: sample hierarchy of headings**

Incorporating tables and figures

Wherever possible, summarise your analysis or findings in the form of tables or figures. Tables generally refer to numerical data, set out as labelled rows and columns, while figures can include anything from a photograph or line drawing to a pie chart, summarising statistical data. A table is more concise than the same data presented as continuous text. However, a well-designed graphic and can be even more focused and revealing (see Chapter 4). Tables and figures should be positioned as closely as possible to the relevant section in the report. However, to avoid confusing the reader they should always follow rather than precede the text to which they refer. The connection between them is made by including a brief reference in brackets at the end of the relevant sentence. For example, the text might state that, 'An artist's impression of the new headquarters building indicates where the solar heating panels will be installed (Figure 18.3) ... .' By connecting text of your report to the correct figure or table, you can assist the reader and reinforce your main arguments. (Note: Further advice on business graphics is included in Section 4.5.)

9.6 Report writing: completion stage

When you have been working on a report for a long time, it is difficult to judge it objectively. Be sure to get an independent opinion of the contents and format of your report before it is finalised. Ideally, you should ask a number of colleagues or friends to read it and make comments. If possible, your choice of reviewers should reflect the kinds of people that are going to be reading the final version. Your reviewers can provide constructive criticism on the content and advise on whether the writing style is readable and appropriate for the intended audience. One of the leading US software companies has described this review process, in somewhat patronising terms, as, 'checking with Brad's mom'. In other words, the report authors ask themselves whether the mother of one of their executives would understand it. The next best alternative is to reread the report for yourself. Indeed, this rereading remains essential, even if the report has gone to external reviewers. Try to put it aside for a week, or at least a few days, since a period away from the material will give you a more realistic perspective. Some writers take it a step further, find themselves a secluded location and read out sections of the report to an imaginary audience. This simple, if potentially embarrassing, technique is very effective at highlighting any unclear or long-winded passages.

Finalising a printed report

In some situations, the wordprocessed text of a business report may be typeset, in order that it can be printed professionally. For example, annual reports and other publications designed for external audiences may require this additional treatment. Copy editors use a standard set of symbols for correcting the page proofs that are returned by the typesetter (see Figure 9.2). These comprise marks that are made in the text, and a corresponding mark to be made at the same point in the margin. The symbols can also be helpful when editing your own wordprocessed printouts.

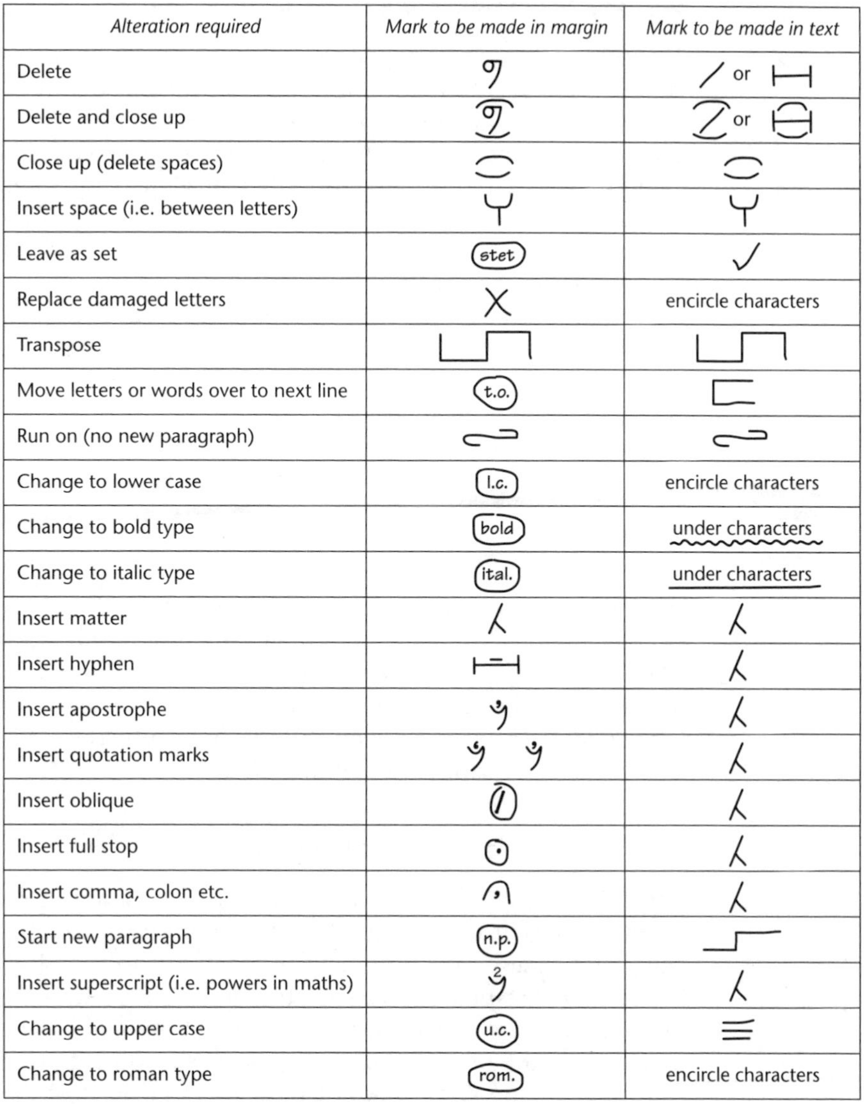

Alteration required	Mark to be made in margin	Mark to be made in text
Delete	⑨	/ or ⊢⊣
Delete and close up	⑨	Ɀ or ⊖
Close up (delete spaces)	⌒	⌒
Insert space (i.e. between letters)	Ƴ	Ƴ
Leave as set	(stet)	✓
Replace damaged letters	✕	encircle characters
Transpose	⌐⌐⌐	⌐⌐⌐
Move letters or words over to next line	(t.o.)	⊏
Run on (no new paragraph)	�	�
Change to lower case	(l.c.)	encircle characters
Change to bold type	(bold)	under characters
Change to italic type	(ital.)	under characters
Insert matter	⋏	⋏
Insert hyphen	⊢−⊣	⋏
Insert apostrophe	⸌	⋏
Insert quotation marks	⸌ ⸌	⋏
Insert oblique	(/)	⋏
Insert full stop	⊙	⋏
Insert comma, colon etc.	(,)	⋏
Start new paragraph	(n.p.)	⌐
Insert superscript (i.e. powers in maths)	⸌²	⋏
Change to upper case	(u.c.)	≡
Change to roman type	(rom.)	encircle characters

Figure 9.2 **Proof correction symbols**

Finalising multi-authored reports

Many of the reports written in organisations draw on the expertise of several authors. There are some intrinsic challenges to face when working on a large multi-authored report of this kind. For example, there is the task of co-ordinating the contributions of authors who may be located in different buildings, countries or continents. Above all, it is extremely difficult to produce a clear and consistent approach when the authors have different technical and cultural backgrounds. The following headings identify some common symptoms of this problem and suggest practical ways that they can be resolved or mitigated.

Variable grammar and writing style

Authors are likely to adopt the style with which they are most familiar. Such variation has its attractions, and may be encouraged in some cases (e.g. where the purpose is to explore a range of views on a subject, held by a diverse group of people). However, if the report is aiming to express a collective voice (e.g. a statement setting out the organisation's ethical policy), it needs to be expressed consistently throughout. By anticipating this requirement at the planning stage, it is possible to minimise this variability, and the need for excessive editing at the final stage. The authors should agree on grammatical and stylistic issues at the outset. For example, it is important to decide on using the present or past tense and the active or passive voice (see section 3.2). There also needs to be some agreement on the terminology used, and any assumptions about the readership, including their level of understanding of such terms. As the writing proceeds, it is also advisable to exchange initial drafts between the authors, to ensure that everyone is following the agreed guideline.

Incorrect cross-references

When a section is added or deleted during the drafting process, it is easy to forget to change earlier references to numbered sections in the text. This becomes even more problematic in multi-authored documents. Most wordprocessing software includes facilities for sharing of files, within an overall 'master document'. The alternative is to leave the cross-referencing until the latter stages, though this can become a very time-consuming task.

Inconsistent headings and labelling

This is another topic to address during the planning stages. The co-authors should adopt an agreed template, specifying variables such as the number of levels of heading and the relevant typefaces. In practice, many organisations have adopted standardised templates for their reports, minimising any potential for inconsistency. However, even where this software is being used, it is advisable to appoint one of the co-authors, or a third party, to act as the overall editor, tidying up any remaining differences in the heading formats, labelling of figures and tables, referencing and so on.

Grammatical and spelling errors

Today's wordprocessing packages contain very powerful spelling and grammar checkers. However, the editor cannot rely on these tools exclusively, since they are not yet intelligent enough to identify words where the spelling is correct, but the word itself is wrong (e.g. 'soul trader' would not be corrected to 'sole trader'). Allowing a spellchecker to correct the text automatically is always a mistake, as the software is free to replace mis-keyed and unrecognised words with meaningless substitutes.

Mini-case 9.2 reviews how one application of technology, the use of editing tools, is influencing the drafting of business reports.

Using editing tools in report-writing: a critical assessment

Software packages, such as Microsoft Word®, include a number of tools that can help with the editing process. These can be particularly useful in the case of multi-authored reports. In the past, the typical practice has been for authors to print out a paper copy of their report, with wide margins (i.e. 4 centimetres) on either side. The copy editor then annotated the printed version, using a coloured pen. By contrast, the software-based tools enable editors to insert their comments directly into the text, while it is still in electronic form. This means that the file containing this annotated text can be circulated by e-mail to several authors for further comments and revision, whereas the paper version would need to be photocopied before distribution.

The following extracts illustrate: (a) how report text may be annotated, and (b) the revised text.

6.31.1 ~~*Predictions of future effects of climate change*~~ *From the regrettable to the tragic: predictions of future effects of climate change...(?)*

The IPCC's projection, published in 2001, is that the world's temperature is likely to increase by 1.4° C to 5.8° C over the period 1990 to 2100, depending on ~~the emissions scenario followed~~which forecast is closest to the truth . However, as this is a project **ion** for the average global surface <u>temperature</u> (which includes sea surface ~~temperature~~), it is very likely that nearly all land areas will warm to a greater extent, particularly in northern North America and northern and central Asia, where land temperatures could rise by 10°C. Although these temperature differences may not sound very serious, the global temperature difference between the last Ice Age and the present time was around 5° C – 6° C. ~~Six~~ Ten(?) degrees of warming is therefore a ~~frightening~~ terrifying prospect.

The likely effects on humans and the natural environment of the high emissions scenarios range from the death of coral reefs to the creation of millions of environmental refugees. ~~Some~~ Many???? species will become extinct: it is expected that by 2060 Arctic pack ice will have melted so much that all polar bears will starve because the animals they feed on, such as seals, will be<u>come</u> scarce. Infectious diseases will rise as the world gets warmer and, in addition, ~~diseases~~ they will sweep north into higher latitudes, infecting people and disrupting fragile ecosystems <u>(this seems odd: are you talking about diseases that will affect animals and plants? In which case you should broaden the scope of 'Infectious diseases' at the beginning of the sentence.</u>– Many countries will be under threat from rising sea levels, drought, storms, heat waves and extreme economic and social disruptions. Sea levels are predicted to rise by a metre over the next century, leading to huge delta areas of Bangladesh, Egypt and China ~~being inundated~~becoming submerged ????. The consequences of allowing the higher emissions scenarios to become reality are global, irreversible and ~~highly damaging~~catastrophic????. ~~It should be unthinkable when the cause can be attributed to the inadequacy of our current action and the lack of urgency in attending to it.~~<u>(Make this blunter): How can we allow this to happen given that we know what needs to be done? Our lack of action and urgency are criminal and will be cursed by future generations.. (??)</u>

(a) **Extract from a draft report: text annotated by an editor**

1.2 From the regrettable to the tragic: predictions of future effects of climate change

1.2.1 Higher temperatures

The IPCC's projection, published in 2001, is that the world's temperature is likely to increase by 1.4° C to 5.8° C over the period 1990 to 2100, depending on which greenhouse gas emission forecast is closest to the truth. However, as this is a projection for the average global surface temperature (which includes sea surface), it is very likely that nearly all land areas will warm to a greater extent. This is particularly true in northern North America and northern and central Asia, where land temperatures could rise by 10°C. The latest reports show that the effects of greenhouse gas emissions on temperature could be even more extreme than this. A new climate modelling approach, developed at the UK's Hadley Centre for Climate Prediction and Research, suggests that the twenty-first century could see more and faster warming than that estimated by IPCC. It is important to put possible temperature changes in perspective. The global temperature difference between the last Ice Age and the present time was around 5° C – 6° C. An increase of 10°C would turn the south of England into the Sahara desert. Five to ten degrees of warming is therefore a terrifying prospect.

1.2.2 Global impacts

The likely effects on humans and the natural environment of the high emissions scenarios range from the death of coral reefs to the creation of millions of environmental refugees. Many species will become extinct: it is expected that by 2060 Arctic pack ice will have melted so much that all polar bears will starve because the animals they feed on, such as seals, will become scarce. Researchers at Bristol University have shown that 6° C of global warming was enough to wipe out up to 95% of the species which were alive on earth at the end of the Permian period, 250 million years ago. Therefore, a huge wave of extinction could be set in motion before the end of the century. Human infectious diseases will rise as the world gets warmer and, in addition, they will sweep north into higher latitudes. Humans may not become extinct, but many more of us will die prematurely and we will run out of comfortable climatic zones in which to live. Many countries will be under threat from rising sea levels, drought, storms, heat waves and extreme economic and social disruptions. Sea levels are predicted to rise by a metre over the next century, leading to huge delta areas of Bangladesh, Egypt and China becoming submerged. The consequences of allowing the higher emissions scenarios to become reality are global, irreversible and catastrophic. How can we allow this to happen given that we know what needs to be done? Our lack of action and urgency are criminal and will be condemned by future generations.

(b) The same extract with the editor's comments incorporated

Questions

1 Review the editor's annotations and try to classify the kinds of changes that have been requested.

2 Compare the two extracts. Do you think the revised version is an improvement over the original? What criteria did you use to make this judgement?

3 When editing your own written work, what are the most common changes that you need to make?

4 What do you see as the potential advantages and disadvantages of software-based editing tools, as outlined in the case.

9.7 Summarising written material: the vital art

One of the defining characteristics of successful managers is their ability to get to the heart of a complex issue and to make informed decisions. To achieve this, they must have a capacity to select and focus on key arguments and information. This has always been a demanding task, but it has arguably become more difficult, due to the rapid diffusion of information and computing technologies (ICTs). Access to potential data sources has expanded enormously, broadening the possibilities for research, but leaving people vulnerable to 'information overload'. In large organisations, strategic decisions are often informed by heavily summarised material, prepared by more junior staff or external consultants. Rather than finding time to read the full report, senior managers may rely on a combination of executive summaries and briefing papers, complemented by short presentations and skim-reading of material that they see as requiring further attention. Consequently, converting long pieces of text into concise yet accurate summaries has become a vital art. It is essential that organisations develop this capability, given their reliance on highly-summarised documents in strategic decision making. For similar reasons, it is also an essential skill for anyone making their career in a large organisation. Like any art, it can only be learned through practice and reflection (see the Practical exercises later in this chapter). However, the following checklist provides some initial guidance on drafting concise but accurate summaries:

- **Be sure of your brief**: Do you need to summarise everything in a document (or collection of documents)? Does your recipient have a particular focus or topic of interest that might influence the way you select and present material from the original source? What level of knowledge is assumed?

- **Read the source material thoroughly**: Do you understand the main themes and the structure of any arguments? Are you able to distinguish between reliable sources and more dubious ones (e.g. an objective, validated research study versus the unsubstantiated opinion of 'a person on a bus').

- **Identify the key points in the original text**: If the material is well-written, each paragraph should contain a number of clearly identifiable key points. Separate each major point from the supporting material (i.e. additional evidence or elaboration, often found in the following sentences); a coloured 'highlighter' pen is a useful tool for this task. Mark only those points that are relevant to your brief. Consider using several colours to help you isolate different themes. Some of the material may be incredibly interesting, but if the person reading your summary does not require this information, leave it out. If you have several source documents, prepare 'key point' summaries of each, before moving to the next stage.

- **Compose a rough draft of the summary**: Prepare the text in plain English, based around the key points and cutting out any supporting material (see section 3.2). This includes sentences beginning, 'For example ...', detailed statistics and other data sources. Consider using simple graphics to illustrate the main arguments or evidence; this is a useful form of 'shorthand' that reduces the word length and makes material easier to assimilate (see section 4.5).

- **Check the rough draft against the source material**: Double check any facts and figures that you have copied from the source documents. Ensure that you have covered all of the areas specified in the brief and omitted any topics that were not specified. Reread the whole draft summary. Does its overall 'balance' reflect that of the original source document(s)? In other words, have you reflected the underlying arguments or perspectives equally?

- **Prepare a final version of the summary**: With careful editing you may be able to shave off a few more words, omitting any repetition or non-essential text. This process is much the same as that outlined for any report, but in this case you are paying even more attention than usual to the word length. It may be appropriate to present parts of the summary in 'bullet point' format. However, unless your audience has specified otherwise, it is advisable to retain full sentences – note format may be concise, but it is less readable than normal text and can be rather difficult to interpret. As a final check on readability, you may consider reading the summary out loud, to ensure that it 'flows' smoothly.

9.8 Reflecting on the process of report writing

This chapter has presented an approach to report writing that is grounded in the cultural assumptions of Western, and specifically British, thought. While there is a good deal of common ground in some areas of international report writing, such as the structure of academic conference papers, and the official reports of the United Nations and its various agencies, there are also local variations. For example, despite the introduction of international standards, there are still significant differences in approach to financial reporting in various parts of the world. This closing section asks you to reflect on the kinds of adaptations – or transformations – that may be required if written reports are to meet the needs of today's diverse audiences. Though it might seem like a good idea to 'customise' reports to the needs of different readers, organisations face considerable practical problems, including resource constraints, in making their published reports accessible. Mini-case 9.3 develops the theme. It describes how a leading international company has approached the challenge of presenting various types of company report on its website:

Mini-case 9.3	**Incorporating reports onto a website: the case of Nokia**

Nokia is one of the world's top companies in the field of mobile communications; it is also a major global brand. The company's origins are in Finland, but by the end of 2002 it was operating 17 production centres in nine different countries, and was conducting research and development in a total of 14 countries around the world. Nokia has net sales of €30.0 bn and a pro-forma operating profit of €5.4 bn (based on 2002 year-end). The company employs almost 52,000 people worldwide. All of the material on Nokia's international website (www.nokia.com) is in the medium of English, with a simple drop-down menu ('select a country') providing links to a number of national sites that display material in local languages. Nokia has made many different types of report freely available on its websites, including financial reports, environmental reports and 'white papers', each of which are reviewed briefly:

- **Financial reports:** it is possible to download the most recent annual and quarterly reports, plus those for previous periods, as pdf files. This part of the site also includes an interactive 'Guide to understanding financials', which is presented as a series of linked webpages. This provides information on each of the main financial statements, with hypertext links providing clear explanations of key terms, such as 'minority interests' and 'diluted earnings per share'.

- **Environmental reports:** Nokia has made a number of reports available concerning its efforts to take care of the environment. These are generally in the form of pdf files, reproduced to a high standard with extensive use of colour, photography, etc. Another part of the site details the company's approach to dialogue with its internal and external stakeholders regarding environmental issues. There are also several case studies, accessible via hypertext links.

- **White papers:** these are commissioned research reports on a variety of current technology and product-related issues (e.g. 'Next generation mobile browsing' and 'Mobile video services'). These reports are also presented as pdf files and are freely available to download. As with other lists of pdf files, there is a short piece of explanatory text, with an icon that links to the website of Adobe, where users can download Acrobat® Reader® for free.

Nokia's various national websites carry a large amount of textual and graphical material, covering topics that are likely to be of interest to various audiences, including: product details, support services, investor relations, career opportunities and contact information. Almost all of the text on the national sites is in a local language. However, links to some of the more detailed reports indicate that some of these items are only available in an English language version.

Questions

1 Some reports are presented on websites in html format, while others are available as pdf files. What kinds of communication issues would influence the choice between these formats?

2 Review some sample reports in html format, from the Nokia site or that of another international organisation. In what ways would you need to adapt a 'conventional' approach to report writing in order to produce reports in this format?

3 Consider the main challenges and opportunities for international organisations like Nokia, in providing reports on their websites for diverse audiences around the world. Prepare a short (400-word) briefing document, outlining the opportunities and suggesting how the challenges might be overcome.

Source: Nokia (2003), Turban (2003). Case written by the author.

Summary

- Reports are an important text-based communication channel for complex and extended investigations and arguments. As a consequence, they require careful preparation and design.

- The key tasks at the preparation stage are to seek or develop a clear specification (or 'brief'), covering issues such as the nature of the audience, the intended purpose, context and sources.

- At the drafting stage, authors need to consider logical sequence, ways of making the structure visible and use of figures and tables to summarise material.

- The process of writing can be a source of learning. Authors often make new connections as a result of engaging with the material, and may therefore need to remain flexible in response to emerging ideas.

- Proof-reading and an independent perspective are important at the completion stage. Authors and editors need to ensure that grammar and writing style are consistent and check cross-referencing, a particularly challenging task in the case of multi-authored reports.

- Organisations make regular use of summaries and briefing papers. It is important to practise the art of summarising text, which involves the identification of key arguments, elimination of superfluous detail and tailoring material to particular audiences.

- Organisations face new challenges in providing reports that are suitable for more diverse groups of stakeholders and for delivery using multiple channels, such as print and web-based formats.

Practical exercises

1 Reports, briefings and bullets – summarising skills

Select a current organisational issue, one of the chapters of this textbook, or a topic provided by your tutor. Prepare the following documents, based on this topic:

(a) A 2,000-word 'long' report, with contents page, executive summary, referencing and bibliography. Include tables and figures where appropriate.

(b) A 500-word 'short' report, suitable for use as a briefing document. Imagine that your boss has to give a public talk on the topic and needs some background material.

(c) A five bullet-point summary, suitable for use as an OHP transparency.

Seminar option: Compare the three versions of your report with those produced by other students. Run a discussion around the following topics: What was the most difficult aspect of the task? What kind of information is omitted in the shorter versions of the report? What assumptions did you make about the audience in each case?

2 Presenting data – images replacing words

(a) Obtain sufficient raw data for a short report from one of the following sources: results from a statistical survey (e.g. data from the UK's Office of National Statistics, which can be downloaded in pdf format); financial accounts from a company report (these are also available from many company websites in pdf format); technical data from a scientific report.

(b) Write a short report (maximum 1,000 words, include a word count), summarising the data. The report should contain words and numbers, but no graphics or data tables.

(c) Prepare a second version of the report, editing the text down to 500 words and inserting suitable graphics (e.g. bar charts, flow diagrams) to illustrate your main arguments. (Note: The Further reading in Chapter 3 suggests a number of suitable texts on statistics and data presentation.)

(d) Prepare a third (and final) version of the report, containing only graphics, with explanatory titles.

Seminar option: Compare the three versions of your report with those produced by other students. Run a discussion around the following topics: What was the most difficult aspect of the task? What options did you consider for representing the data graphically? Which version do you think would be most effective in communicating your arguments?

Case study

Getting the message across: annual reports in the internet era

This newspaper article reviews recent developments in the world of investor relations. One of the traditional communication channels, the paper-based annual report, is being transformed by technological innovation and changes in the communication needs of investors, analysts and other stakeholders.

When you want to review an investment, do you reach for the glossy annual report sitting on your shelf? Or do you power up your computer and click your way through the same document online? If print is your preference, you are not alone. Technology evangelists may have predicted otherwise but shareholders and analysts continue to favour printed material as a source of corporate information. The enduring popularity of print is, however, only one side of the shareholder communications story. The web is coming into its own not as a replacement for traditional investor material but as a source of additional, richer, more frequent and more time-sensitive information. As a result, investor relations are gradually being transformed.

There is plenty of evidence pointing to the continuing popularity of print among investors and analysts. Seventy-four per cent of sell-side and 63 per cent of buy-side analysts expressed a preference for printed annual reports over online equivalents in a recent survey by *Investor Relations* magazine. Furthermore, UK companies with large private shareholder bases think that 80 per cent of private shareholders would continue to ask for a printed annual report even if offered an online alternative, according to an October 2002 study by London-based consultancy Pauffley Creative Communication. 'The internet is simply not a good medium for large chunks of text,' says Roger Burgess, a director at Pauffley. Indeed, the web is proving most popular as a distributed printing mechanism for annual reports, rather than a stand-alone medium: the Pauffley survey found that 96 per cent of companies that publish annual reports online do so in 'printer-friendly' PDF format rather than in the website language of HTML or a spreadsheet format such as Excel.

However, companies are finding the internet to be a powerful complementary medium for investor relations, one that is slowly shifting companies' relationships with them. BP, the energy company, was an early adopter of online shareholder communications. 'The internet helps us to disseminate information more rapidly and more

▶

cheaply on a completely global scale and opens up new opportunities to establish a dialogue with our shareholders,' says David Bickerton, head of external communications. The company uses the internet to provide online broadcasts of presentations and speeches, corporate news announcements, electronic voting and other 'interactive' features. 'Print remains the best medium for reference material such as annual reports but the web brings wider coverage and greater efficiency,' says Mr Bickerton. 'In particular, it allows us to provide private investors with information and assistance in ways that simply wouldn't be possible off-line.' In 2001 the company launched New2BP.com, an online service for UK citizens unfamiliar with the stock market.

BP is seeing clear evidence that the web is bringing the company's corporate information to a larger audience: its *Statistical Review of World Energy* has a print run of 60,000 but is now downloaded electronically 300,000 times a year. With financial authorities and legislators in the US and Europe placing increasing demands on companies to provide greater transparency for all types of investors, the use of the internet in shareholder communications is set to grow. For example, 'web-casting' – the online broadcast of corporate meetings, presentations and speeches – is already being used as a means of complying with tighter disclosure rules.

Many believe that this is good news for investors and other stakeholders. 'Web-casts allow investors to see corporate management perform in front of a real, sometimes hostile audience, something that has previously been impossible for shareholders unable to attend physical meetings,' says Donald Nordberg, former financial editor at Reuters and current director of strategy for Raw Communications, an investor communications company. 'Downsizing has meant that many analysts now have far more stocks to cover,' adds Mr Burgess. 'Web-casts are extremely useful for them, since they cannot be in two physical meetings at the same time.'

Others believe that web-casts can also help companies to cultivate greater confidence and trust among their shareholders: 'As a species, humans are very receptive to audio and visual communications,' says Craig Moehl of Groovy Gecko, the London-based streaming media company. 'As such, web-casts allow companies to convey information in a far more personal and contextual way than text.'

Corporate web-casts are widely established in the US, where 83 per cent of the Fortune 100 companies now use them. They are also proliferating in the UK, where 30 per cent of FTSE 250 companies provide them, according to a July 2002 survey by *Investor Relations* magazine and European streaming media company Simplywebcast. The recent UK Company Law Review is likely to accelerate this trend: it recommended that annual reports should be made available online as soon as they are signed off – and at least 15 days before they are sent to shareholders – to allow investors to formulate and circulate questions before their annual general meeting.

Just over the horizon lies a more radical use of the internet for serving professional investors. A new online standard for financial information, called 'eXtensible Business Reporting Language' (XBRL), promises to allow investors and analysts automatically to extract corporate performance data from multiple websites in a compatible format and compare, contrast, process and model it in any way they choose. A handful of companies, including Reuters and Microsoft, have already published financial statements in XBRL but the true value of the standard will be reaped only when – or if – it becomes widely established. 'At present, many buy-side analysts need to go to more than 100 different websites to keep track of information presented in a variety of different formats,' says Mr Nordberg. 'When XBRL becomes widespread, investors and analysts will be able to conduct automatic, global, real-time ratio analysis for the first time. And that really will be exciting.'

Questions

1 Prepare two tables, summarising the potential advantages and disadvantages of annual reports, first for users and second for investor relations departments. The lists should compare the following formats:

    (a) conventional 'hard copy' (i.e. full colour printed brochure);

    (b) downloadable pdf file available via a website;

    (c) HTML (i.e. hyper-linked web pages).

2 What do you consider to be the main factors driving the move to online reports in this area? Identify two other areas of organisational activity where online report writing is likely to become more important.

3 Sample an investor relations web-cast, either at the BP website, or that of another large corporation. Comment on the effectiveness of this channel, in comparison with a text-based report, noting any significant advantages or limitations.

4 The article contained in this case study comprises approximately 980 words. Referring to the section on summarising in this chapter, prepare the following documents. Give each document a title and include a word count:

    (a) an executive summary/abstract (250 words maximum);

    (b) an outline (50 words maximum);

    (c) a list of key words (five words maximum).

Source: Payton (2002). Copyright Scott Payton.

Further reading

For many students, the most demanding text-based document is the dissertation or thesis, written towards the end of a course of study. There are several useful guides to preparing dissertations and the broader issues of research, including **Easterby-Smith** *et al.* (2002), **Ruderstam and Newton** (2001) and **Saunders** *et al.* (2003). **Phillips and Pugh** (2000) is designed for PhD students, but contains some helpful advice for those preparing undergraduate or masters dissertations. **National Audit Office** (2003) discusses the challenge of communicating in commissioned research projects. Students may also be interested in drafting business plans, specialised reports used to present a new business venture to prospective financiers. There are many texts setting out typical formats for business plan reports, including several published in conjunctions with major banks and newspapers. Additional references on writing style can be found in Chapter 3.

References

De Vita, G. (2001) 'Inclusive approaches to effective communication and active participation in the multicultural classroom'. *Active Learning in Higher Education*, 1, 2, 168–80.

Easterby–Smith, M., Thorpe, R. and Lowe, A. (2002) *Management research: an introduction* (2nd edn.). Sage, London.

National Audit Office (2003) *Getting the evidence: using research in policy-making.* Report by the Comptroller and Auditor General HC 586–1 Session 2002–2003 (16 April). The Stationery Office, London [also available at www.nao.gov.uk].

Nokia (2003) 'About Nokia'. (Available at www.nokia.com (accessed 20th August).)

Nonaka, I. and Takeuchi, H. (1995) *The knowledge creating company: how Japanese companies create the dynamics of innovation.* Oxford University Press, Oxford.

Payton, S. (2002) 'Getting the message across: shareholder communications'. *Financial Times*, London edition, 14 (4th December).

Phillips, E. and Pugh, D. (2000) *How to get a PhD* (3rd edn.). Open University Press, Milton Keynes.

Ruderstam, K. and Newton, R. (2001) *Surviving your dissertation* (2nd edn.). Sage, Newbury Park CA.

Saunders, M.N.K., Lewis, P. and Thornhill, A. (2003) *Research methods for business students* (3rd edn.). FT Prentice Hall, Harlow.

Turban, E. (2003) *Electronic commerce 2003: a managerial perspective.* Prentice Hall, Upper Saddle River NJ.

Whitley, R. (2000) *Divergent capitalisms: the social structuring and change of business systems.* Oxford University Press, Oxford.

Zaharna, R.S. (1996) 'Managing cross-cultural challenges: a Pre-K lesson for training in the Gaza Strip'. *Journal of Management Development*, 15, 5, 75–87.

CHAPTER 10

Advertisements, promotions, news releases and exhibitions

Advertising is the cave art of the twentieth century.
Marshall McLuhan, media commentator

Learning outcomes

By the end of this chapter you should be able to:

- recognise how principles of persuasive communication are applied in the fields of advertising, public relations and campaigning;
- develop communication skills in commissioning advertisements, managing promotions, drafting news releases and designing exhibitions;
- consider how emerging technologies such as text messaging may be used to communicate promotional and campaigning messages;
- locate each communication channel in the wider context of a co-ordinated promotional or campaigning strategy;
- reflect on cultural and ethical issues raised by the persuasive communication practices in these channels.

10.1 Introduction

All types of organisation become involved in some form of promotion, whether it is to sell their products and services, attract funding from donors, campaign for a change in legislation or simply to improve their 'image' in the minds of key stakeholders. As a result, most managers become involved at some point in their careers in preparing promotional materials. For example, they may be commissioning a newspaper advertisement, drafting a news release or helping to design an exhibition stand. Together, they form part of the 'promotional mix', the ways that an organisation communicates with the world around it. It has always proved difficult to categorise the various channels for promotion, but the following components are identified in most of the literature:

- advertising
- direct marketing
- public relations

- exhibitions and displays
- corporate sales promotion
- personal selling.

In the late twentieth century, there were strong trends towards integrating the various elements of *marketing* communication, with the aim of maintaining strong and coherent brands. This has been reflected in the promotional services industry, which has restructured to bring specialist services together and to offer them across broader geographic markets, reflecting the changing demands of their corporate clients. Some commentators have argued that the process of integration needs to continue, making closer connections between product-related messages and the kinds of internal and external communication taking place at an organisational level:

> 'Corporate performance is not just a function of how well its brands are doing, but also of how well the company as brand is doing. In our view it is insufficient to integrate all communication activities at brand level only. All communication activities at the level of the business or corporation must be integrated as well. [...] Moreover, there must also be interaction between the two forms of communication in an ongoing, interactive, interdependent, and synergistic manner. There should be no walls or barriers, despite their often different functions, between these types of communication, for both ultimately are needed to drive the business forward.' (Kitchen and Schultz 2001: 95)

This is an ambitious goal, given the kinds of barriers to communication discussed in previous chapters. If organisational managers are to have any chance of achieving the kind of integration proposed in the literature, they will need to have a sound understanding of the wide range of communication channels that are used to promote the 'brand', whether these are operating at the level of specific products, strategic business units, or the organisation as a whole. The practical tasks required to *produce* promotional and campaigning materials are often contracted out to specialists, such as advertising agencies, public relations (PR) firms and exhibition consultants. However, experience suggests that it is very useful to gain an understanding of what these professionals are up to. Furthermore, in many smaller organisations, including some charities and campaign groups, managers may have a more direct involvement in these activities, perhaps as part of a small in-house team.

This chapter focuses on three communication channels that often form part of the promotional mix – adverts, news releases and exhibition stands. We concentrate on assessing the ways that persuasive messages are conveyed in each channel. This allows you to apply many of the underlying principles of persuasive communication that are discussed in Chapter 5. (Note: Direct mail, another important element in the 'promotional mix' of many organisations, is considered in Chapter 8.) However, there is also practical advice and exercises that will help you to prepare your own promotional materials. These activities are designed to make you better informed when preparing 'briefs' (i.e. project specifications) for an agency, comparing the sales 'pitches' of competing firms or simply working with specialists from one of these areas. Vast amounts of money can be wasted if clients fail to communicate their requirements clearly to external agencies or in-house teams. These initial communication breakdowns have a knock-on effect, in the form of over-priced and unsuitable advertising, PR and exhibition materials. By taking a 'global' view of promotion, managers are also able to assess the overall effectiveness of the existing promotional mix, and to take action to reconfigure and enhance specific channels where necessary. We begin our review with the role of advertising, and its close relationship with techniques of sales promotion.

10.2 Advertising and sales promotion: an overview

Markets have existed from the earliest times, and wherever people have sold goods or services, they have advertised. However, the advertising *industry* is a more recent phenomenon, a mid-nineteenth century response to mass production (creating products and markets) and mass literacy (creating the books and magazines in which adverts were placed), which has become a global industry. Most of the expenditure is on 'display' advertising, mainly commissioned by organisations to promote their goods and services. Other important categories include: recruitment advertising; financial and legal notices; and classified advertising (i.e. 'small ads', which are mainly placed by individuals). All this activity means that adults and children are exposed hundreds of advertising messages every day. Many of these are both highly sophisticated and expensive to produce. However, there are less expensive forms of advertising, through regional newspapers, for example.

Advertising can serve a variety of communication objectives, including:

- creating or increasing awareness (e.g. informing the target market of a new service, brand name or social issue);
- informing or educating (e.g. explaining how to make better use of a service, advising members of risk groups of potential health threats);
- stimulating various types of 'purchase' decision (e.g. encouraging people to buy a product, switch between competing brands or donate to a particular charity).

Success in advertising requires the organisation to present persuasive messages to specific audiences. Individual advertisements can be very striking, but they rarely operate in isolation (see Figure 10.1). They are usually run alongside a number of related advertisements, plus other promotional devices, as part of a co-ordinated 'campaign'. This combined effort is designed to reinforce the core messages through repeated exposure in various formats.

Figure 10.1 *Financial Times* **advertisement for Chinese New Year 2003**
Source: Financial Times (2003).

10.3 Planning an advertising and promotional campaign

Advertising is all about exposure and impact. An isolated advert, however well-crafted, is unlikely to have any lasting impact because it is unlikely to reach sufficient receivers, and those that are exposed to it may not absorb the message on the first occasion. Therefore, advertisers develop integrated 'campaigns' that run over an extended period. Promotional campaigns have some similarities with those conducted by the military. They employ a vocabulary that refers to 'strategic targets', 'hit rates' and 'pre-emptive strikes'. To illustrate some of the key elements of a campaign, imagine that you are the product manager responsible for launching *Vegetale* in your organisation's Northern European sales territory. It is a new, vegetable-based, high-protein food that is being positioned as an attractive alternative to meat. How would you develop an advertising campaign, as the product moves from the development stage to its initial launch in this market?

Marketing research

You could begin by investigating the market, its principal characteristics and long-term potential. The following questions are indicative for the *Vegetale* case. Who buys food for the household? What are the recent trends in meat consumption? What are the existing alternatives to meat, and how are they perceived by both consumers and non-consumers? What do people already know and think of *Vegetale* and the company's other products?

Identifying target market(s)

Market research, together with your own instincts, should suggest how the market is segmented, and indicate the nature of your target customer. In the case of a product launch, the initial focus is likely to be on so-called 'innovators' and 'early adopters', the sub-groups who are first to experiment with an innovative product (Rogers 1995). In the *Vegetale* example, your research suggests that the demographic profile is likely to comprise females aged 20 to 35 from socio-economic groups A, B and C1 (professionals and skilled workers). It may also be possible to obtain segmentation data, based on psychographics (i.e. related to the ways that people think), lifestyle and type of residential area (e.g. Trout and Rivkin 1997).

Developing campaign objectives

It is important to establish what the organisation is trying to achieve through its advertising campaign. Objectives are usually quantified, so that the success (or otherwise) of the campaign can be measured. Advertisers are particularly interested in the level of awareness of a product, and how far this is converted into trial purchases. In this example, you have decided to aim for a 25 per cent unprompted recall of *Vegetale* in your target market, by the end of a three-month media campaign. Unprompted recall means that, in a follow-up survey of the target group, respondents can describe the advertisement without being given a brand name or a similar prompt by the interviewer.

Planning and budgeting

In most organisations, budgets are tight, and campaigns have to be designed within these constraints. Planning decisions include the channels to be used (e.g. newspaper and television adverts, direct mail, in-store promotions), and the timescale of the campaign. Project management techniques are used to schedule and co-ordinate the different activities. The budget for *Vegetale* is sufficient for you to run the following: full-colour adverts in six women's magazines, with accompanying 'advertorials' (i.e. sponsored editorial articles that are used to provide more detailed information on the product); a series of radio adverts on a regional music station that caters for the target age group; and a month-long programme of in-store tastings, run in conjunction with the three largest multiple food retail chains. In the second phase of the campaign you plan to run a 'buy one, get one free' (or 'BOGOF') promotion, supported by additional magazine advertising. You are considering whether to deliver single-portion samples of *Vegetale* to selected addresses, as part of an on-going market research survey (a technique sometimes referred to as *knock and drop*).

Drafting material – key messages

Alongside the campaign planning, you need to recruit people to create the advertising materials. Individual adverts are built around 'key messages', and the real skill of advertising agencies is to convert these messages into memorable words, sounds and images. For example, your key messages might be that *Vegetale* is a new, nutritious, low-fat product, derived entirely from natural vegetable ingredients, which can be prepared much like meat and which has a similar texture to veal. How do you convey this to your audience?

10.4 Communicating with an advertisement

An effective advertisement is likely to have to two distinguishing features: messages summarised briefly, and messages reinforced using more than one medium. With an emphasis on the target audience and their creative approach, advertisements display many of the best features of effective communication, many of which can be applied in other aspects of organisational life. Advertisers can select from a wide range of possible formats, matching the style of delivery to the specific needs of the audience and the nature of the message (see Table 10.1).

The ways that advertising messages are formulated raises many interesting communication issues, with broader social and cultural implications. For example, Carlson (2001) conducted a cross-cultural comparison of televised political advertising in Finland and the US, focusing on the role of gender. The following quotation summarises one aspect of the findings, relating to the differences in non-verbal communication (see section 4.7).

> 'Concerning the kinetic aspects, the US female candidates' ads differ in a way that is statistically significant from the ads of their male colleagues. Thus, the female candidates project a "softer" image than the male candidates by assuming smiling facial expressions and making eye contact with the viewers more frequently. In Finland, eye contact is the rule for the candidates of both genders. However, this can be explained by the fact that the "candidate head-on" production technique – denoting that the candidate talks directly into the camera – is clearly dominant in Finnish candidate advertising. In the US, the production techniques are more varied. Regarding facial expression, the Finnish female candidates, as their US colleagues, smile more frequently than their male counterparts. This finding is statistically significant.' (Carlson 2001: 147)

The findings of this study appeared to go against the expectation that communication styles would differ between the two countries due to factors such as the higher proportion of female politicians in Finland. However, it did offer support for the view that female politicians continue to face the dilemma of balancing 'male' and 'female' styles in their advertising messages.

Table 10.1 **Some popular advertising formats**

Slice of life	This traditional format has been commonly used on television adverts for fast-moving consumer goods and domestic appliances such as washing machines. Short dramatised excerpts can be used to link a product with a lifestyle that is familiar to the target audience. They can also provide opportunities for the use of other formats, such as humorous, aspirational and demonstration.
Humorous	Visual and verbal humour secures audience attention and generates positive reactions. Humour is used for all kinds of products, including very 'dry' ones, such as financial services. For example, in the 1990s, the UK electricity industry ran a campaign called 'Creature Comforts', which combined the voices of ordinary customers with an animated film featuring a 'family' of cuddly animals. The campaign was a response to research suggesting that people perceived electric power as less 'friendly' than gas.
Aspirational	This is commonly used for premium and heavily-branded products. Imagery is used, either to enhance a brand identity, or to suggest that consumers can obtain some element of a fantasy lifestyle by purchasing the product. However, the credibility of aspirational messages can be undermined if they are not applied consistently, or where there is too stark a contrast between the aspiration and the actual experience.
Endorsement	This can work at various levels. At its simplest, the receiver is given an assurance regarding the message, because it is delivered by someone that they know and trust. Celebrities can also be perceived as 'humanising' a product or corporate brand. For example, in the early 1990s, the brewer Guinness used actor Rutger Hauer (star of the film *Bladerunner*) to re-position an 'old man's drink' for a new generation. Dressed in black and with bleached hair, he literally 'embodied' a younger and more sophisticated image of the product. Celebrities do not even have to be alive! Computer animation has been used to revive former celebrities, including Alfred Hitchcock, to promote products. Along with animated cartoons, these celebrities have three advantages over their living counterparts: they are immortal, they cannot become embroiled in a scandal and they do not demand repeat performance fees.
Demonstration	One of the most effective ways of introducing novel or difficult to understand products is to show them in use. Demonstrations are often used on television, but with some imagination they can be applied to other channels, such as newspaper advertisements. They can educate potential consumers, and reduce their fear of the unknown. For example, innovative technological products are often shown in the hands of non-specialists, highlighting their apparent ease-of-use.
'Postmodern'	There has been a recent increase in bizarre and self-parodying advertisements, sometimes given the inaccurate title 'postmodern', where the promotional message appears obscure, if not unintelligible. Tobacco companies pioneered this format when regulators began to restrict the content of their adverts. Over many years, the 'Silk Cut' campaign played on the brand name 'silk' and 'cut' in many different ways. Surreal advertising has been introduced because audiences are now so 'visually literate' that they can see through, and 'de-construct' traditional adverts. Hence, more sophisticated and puzzling content is needed to secure their attention.

The best way to explore the various options available to advertisers, and to reflect on the wider communication issues that they raise, is to gain some practical experience of creating your own advertisement (see the Practical exercises section later in this chapter). When selecting the preferred treatment, it is essential to keep the target audience in mind, and to construct messages in ways that they are likely to find both meaningful and attractive. Perhaps the easiest trap to fall into is in developing material that appeals to *you*, the designer, rather than to those with whom you are seeking to communicate.

The power of display advertising in an era of mass communication is also reflected in the way that this communication channel has been subverted. Perhaps the simplest and most long-established method has been where graffiti (i.e. hand-written messages) are added to advertisements displayed in public venues, transforming the meaning of the original slogan. Mini-case 10.1 concerns the activities of an organisation that has refined the technique, using the power of the Internet.

**Mini-case
10.1**

Adbusters: challenging corporate advertising?

Adbusters describes itself as 'a global network of artists, activists, pranksters, students, educators and entrepreneurs who want to advance the new social activist movement of the information age'. Adbusters is probably best known for its professionally-designed parody (or 'spoof') advertisements, which reinterpret images and slogans associated with major global brands, such as Nike, Calvin Klein and McDonalds, in ways that subvert the original message. The advertisements form part of a wider array of persuasive and informational messages, supporting Adbusters' key stated aims, 'to change the way we interact with the mass media and the way in which meaning is produced in our society.' Adbusters Media Foundation publishes a 120,000-circulation magazine from offices in Vancouver, Canada. Two-thirds of its magazine readership is based in the US, but the organisation reports having a diverse readership in 60 other countries. Adbusters also operates its own full-service advertising agency, which is promoted for use by not-for-profit organisations wishing to develop a social marketing campaign.

The most important communication channel for Adbusters is probably its website (www.adbusters.org), which provides information on the organisation and its campaigning activities, contact details, useful links, magazine extracts, sample advertisements and materials that can be downloaded, including stickers to promote its annual campaigns, 'Buy Nothing Day' and 'TV Turnoff Week'. Most of the textual material on the website is in the medium of English, though the organisation's aims are also summarised in Spanish and French, under the headings: 'Cultural revolution is our business'; 'La revolucion cultural es nuestro negocio'; and 'Notre affaire, c'est la revolution culturelle'.

The Adbusters campaigns are an example of 'cultural jamming', a phrase coined by a San Francisco-based band called Negativland, who saw a skilfully reworked billboard as a way of encouraging viewers to reconsider original corporate strategy of the advertiser. Culture jamming has a long history that can be traced to the activities of French 'situationists' in the late 1960s, and many previous generations of graffiti artists and humorists. Naomi Klein, author of 'No Logo', suggests that jamming has been enjoying a recent resurgence, resulting from a combination of technological advances and an underlying popular resentment against the overpowering commercialism of the leading corporate brands. This has stimulated a demand for counter-messages:

> 'The most sophisticated culture jams are not stand-alone ad parodies but interceptions – counter-messages that hack into a corporation's own method of communication to send a message starkly at odds with the one that was intended. The process forces the company to foot the bill for its own subversion, either literally, because the company is the one that paid for the billboard, or figuratively, because any time people mess with a logo, they are tapping into the vast resources spent to make that logo meaningful.' (Klein 2000: 281)

However, culture jammers also face challenges in conveying their persuasive messages. For example, Adbusters had to reconsider its promotional strategies after it was attacked for merchandising products associated with the 'Buy Nothing Day' campaign; the organisation has also been criticised for what some people regard as a patronising and puritanical tone in its 'adbusting' attacks on alcohol, smoking and fast food. A more fundamental challenge to culture jamming is demonstrated by the ease with which corporate advertising and branding has been able to appropriate jamming techniques for its own purposes. Klein (2000: 298) cites the example of Nike's 'pre-jammed' advertising campaign, which carried the slogan, 'I am not/A target market/I am an athlete.'

Questions

1 Review some examples of culture jamming, from Adbusters or similar sites. What are these messages seeking to achieve, and what persuasive techniques do they employ? How might they respond to the appropriation of jamming techniques by corporate advertisers?

2 Consider the implications of culture jamming from the perspective of a large corporation, such as Nike. What communication strategy would you recommend in the event that key promotional messages were being 'jammed'?

3 Select several examples of current corporate advertising. Analyse the material, identifying the key promotional messages and noting how these are reinforced (e.g. using words and visual signals). Suggest how a culture jammer might subvert these messages.

Source: Adbusters (2003), Klein (2000). Written by the author.

We close this section with a brief reflection on the complementary role of sales promotion, and the unique communication challenges presented by this channel.

Reflecting on sales promotion: when the 'receiver' bites back

In the introduction to this chapter, we noted that advertising and sales promotions are often closely connected channels. Conventional approaches to advertising reflect a 'one-way', linear model of communication, in which the primary aim is to code the persuasive message in a way that minimised the scope for noise (see section 1.3). While the advertising message may be thoroughly researched (e.g. by securing feedback from 'focus groups'), the mode of delivery through mass media appears to leave the 'receiver' in a relatively passive role. As we have seen, the underlying assumptions of the linear model are challenged by interpretivist and postmodern perspectives (see section 1.7). These emphasise that any communication activity is based on active engagement, requiring the negotiation of meanings with intended audiences (see section 1.7). In other words, it is their interpretations, rather than the intended goals of the advertiser, that determine the impact of a campaign. The importance of this insight is highlighted by the case of sales promotions, such as product samples and special offers. These are widely-used promotional techniques, which do seek a direct engagement with the receiver. Typical applications of the product sample include 'trial size' shampoos, attached to magazines or delivered to the door, and cut-down versions of computer software packages, supplied as a CD-Rom or downloaded via the internet. However, once the receiver becomes an active participant in the process, there is considerable scope for unanticipated effects, which can prove disastrous for the unwary communicator. In an example dating from the 1960s, a company was forced to discontinue its new promotional campaign for razor blades. There was a fundamental flaw in its approach to product samples, demonstrating an astonishing lack of imagination when it came to assessing its audience. The miscalculation was revealed when inquisitive children across the country began opening product samples that had been dropped through their letterboxes.

Miscalculating the response of consumers has also been a common feature in several disastrous promotional campaigns. In one high-profile example from the early 1990s, the domestic appliances company, Hoover, offered its UK customers two 'free' flights to European or US destinations if they spent more than £100 on its products. Many of the people who saw advertisements for this offer made the simple calculation that it was worth purchasing a Hoover product, simply to secure the two free flights. However, it appeared that the people responsible for promoting the offer had simply failed to envisage this response. Consequently, the offer was massively over-subscribed, leading to legal actions by disappointed customers, a public relations disaster, multi-million pound losses and the subsequent departure of several senior executives.

There is a general lesson from these cases of 'bad practice'. There is considerable scope for error when organisations seek to engage with 'receivers'. Communicators need to consider their outgoing messages very seriously, and have an imaginative grasp of the way that people are likely to respond. The theme of interaction is continued in the next section, which considers the role of public relations. Linking the two sections, Mini-case 10.2 outlines how an emerging communication channel, text messaging, is being used to facilitate more customised and responsive relationships between organisations and customers.

| Mini-case 10.2 | RSVP*i*™: Managing customer relationships via text | **RSVP*i*™** |

RSVPi Limited (www.rsvpi.co.uk) was founded in 1999 to develop innovative technology-based marketing services. The company's RSVP*i*™ system has combined SMS (text) messaging and e-mail technologies, allowing organisations to respond to customer requests in a flexible and cost-effective way. In effect, it offers the opposite of 'junk mail', because the customer receives only information that has been requested specifically, via an initial text message.

Imagine, for example, that you are reading a newspaper or magazine. You may be sitting at home, with friends at a local bar, or travelling to work on the train. A travel advertisement catches your eye and you decide to request some additional information. Rather than trying to telephone a customer call centre or searching for the material on a website, you simply text a short keyword, such as HOLIDAY, to the RSVP*i*™ number. Once your mobile phone number and e-mail have been registered, the system acts as a kind of sorting office, selecting the relevant material and sending it to your specified e-mail address. Text messages are used to reassure you that your e-mail address will not be passed on to other organisations and to confirm that the requested information has been delivered to your e-mail address. The follow-up e-mails may be in basic text or the more information-rich html (i.e. web page) format, with the option of including file attachments, such as forms and brochures in pdf (portable document file) format. The information can then be viewed on screen or printed out at your leisure, using a personal computer. Following this initial transfer, from an off-line communication channel (i.e. the newspaper or magazine), you may opt to continue your relationship with the organisation, using on-line channels, making use of their website and exchanging e-mails or text messages.

Ecover

Ecover is a major European ecological FMCG (fast-moving consumer-goods) company, which has been working for over 20 years in the field of sustainable cleaning products and manufacturing processes (www.ecover.com). Its 'ecological factory' is a pioneer plant, designed to run with minimum energy requirements, and to recycle much of its waste material. The company's UK subsidiary was one of the first organisations to make use of the new communication channel, under the keyword CARE. It was seen as a way that Ecover could develop its brand in the UK, enabling consumers to learn more about the company's products and its ethical and environmental policies. The company's UK brand manager commented that the system, 'lets people respond to our promotions instantly and enables us to deliver detailed follow-up information by e-mail – a medium which is environmentally friendly itself'. With the expansion of broadband access, it is anticipated that e-mail will become a much richer communication channel, improved graphics and video images replacing the very simple text-based messages that have characterised its early development.

Questions

1 Prepare two diagrams to illustrate the information flows using this technology, compared to a conventional telephone call centre. For example, how are the messages encoded and which communication channels are being used at each stage?

2 What do you see as the advantages of the new communication channel from the customer's perspective?

3 What are the advantages for the organisation that is using this system as part of its customer relationship management (CRM) strategy?

4 Can you identify any potential issues that might influence the long-term effectiveness of this channel? If so, how might these be resolved?

10.5 Public relations – an overview

Public relations (PR) did not develop into a unified profession until the second half of the last century (Miller and Dinan 2000, Kitchen and Schultz 2001). It draws on several specialist fields, involving people as varied as publicity agents and promoters from the entertainment industry, political lobbyists, analysts and advisors, newspaper and broadcast journalists, management consultants and advertising copywriters. Commentators have often noted, with some irony, that the PR profession seems unable to escape its reputation for engaging in disreputable practices. The main criticism is that PR is used to create a false impression of an organisation, individual or issue in the minds of the public. It is also criticised for the kinds of activities that take place, the assumption being that it is all about 'corporate hospitality', meaning the provision of lavish, free entertainment for important clients and sleazy politicians. In reality, while it is possible to identify many examples of bad practice, PR can be a valid form of persuasive communication. It is used by all kinds of organisations, including charities, pressure groups and political parties.

The language of today's PR professionals reflects the concept of multiple stake-holders (see section 7.3). They talk in terms of developing a long-term dialogue with their various 'publics' (see Figure 10.2), each of which has different information needs. The UK's Institute of Public Relations (IPR) has defined this communication role as: 'The planned and sustained effort to establish and maintain goodwill and mutual understanding between an organisation and its publics' (IPR 2003). In the next section, we consider how this mutual understanding can be achieved and some of the potential pitfalls in communicating the relevant messages.

Figure 10.2 **An organisation's dialogue with its stakeholders**

10.6 Successful PR: long-term commitment v short-term fix

The following discussion applies many of the principles of stakeholder theory, raised as part of our review of organisational communication. In particular, it draws attention to the concepts of stakeholder communication, including the distinction between asymmetrical and symmetrical dialogue (Crane and Livesey 2003) (see section 7.3).

For example, imagine that your organisation is running a large manufacturing site in a rural area. It is very scenic (i.e. is regarded as having high 'amenity value'), but there are also few local employment opportunities and public services are in decline. The directors have agreed to an investment strategy that involves a major expansion of this factory site. It seems like 'good news' for stakeholders in the local community. However, if the company has a poor record, with a series of pollution incidents, safety scares and arguments over planning controls, the local community may be unsympathetic to the expansion plans. This could turn to hostility and active resistance if, for example, a programme of automation at the factory is likely to result in local job losses. In such a situation, a typical short-term PR exercise, such as sponsorship of the local village carnival, would clearly be counter-productive. Everyone in the community would interpret it, quite correctly, as a cynical and 'cosmetic' (i.e. superficial, surface-level) exercise.

Long-term PR requires a much greater commitment of time and effort, in communicating with a particular 'public'. In practice, it would involve the organisation in a variety of activities, such as: hosting regular 'open days' for local schools, residents and other interested parties; setting up consultative groups with representatives from the community; introducing planned and sustained initiatives to keep all members of the workforce informed and able to voice their opinions; and making a genuine and sustained investment in community activities. The investment is substantial, but long-term PR can also lead to significant benefits, as the organisation builds a kind of 'equity' in its employees and local community. The accumulated goodwill can provide it with a degree of protection during short-term crises, like a factory fire or a financing problem. However, this more substantial and ultimately more effective form of PR can only be successful if it addresses the following key principles.

Senior management commitment is essential

PR must be seen as a strategic concern, which rests ultimately with the chief executive or equivalent. Without top-level support, it is unlikely that the organisation will have the resources to make substantive changes in its day-to-day operations. The resulting lack of commitment, and competing pressures for resources, will lead to cynicism amongst stakeholders, including employees, and the often-criticised symptom of PR as a meaningless and cosmetic 'gloss'.

PR activity must be linked to strategic aims

This follows from the previous argument, regarding senior management commitment. Communication strategies must interact with the organisation's business and corporate strategies. However, few have grasped the radical implications of engaging in a real dialogue with stakeholders, in a way that informs strategic decisions, as opposed to a 'monologic' dialogue, that is simply designed to control the area of debate in order to achieve pre-determined objectives (Crane and Livesey 2003: 47–8).

Organisations must understand and engage with its publics

The organisation must research and listen to its various publics or stakeholder groups. It is not simply a matter of seeking to express its messages in their terms; this may be a fundamental communication principle, but it remains rooted in the linear, 'one-way' model of communication. There is also a need to engage with their perspectives, and allow these to be reflected in public arenas, as part of a genuine dialogue.

PR strategies require plans, budgets and resources

Effective PR activity is an on-going managerial task, rather than simply a short-term project, to be introduced in a crisis. As a consequence, it must be organised effectively, with a degree of planning (e.g. allocation of roles, preparation of budgets and monitoring). In addition, senior management commitment must be reflected in the allocation of adequate resources to support these activities over the long-term.

Feedback from PR activity should inform strategic change

PR activity should provide the organisation with a continual monitor on the environment within and beyond its administrative boundaries. By following these broad principles, it can be of great value to the whole organisation, helping it to interpret and adapt to changing situations. In this role, PR becomes much more than an exercise in presenting an 'image' to the outside world.

PR activities and communication channels

Organisations engage in many types of PR activity, which make use of particular combinations of communication channels. The choice of channel should be based on a combination of research into the needs of the various publics and an awareness of the organisation's objectives. Practitioners are also experimenting with emerging channels, notably the internet and the new breed of transnational television channel, such as MTV, CNN, Eurosport and BBC World. However, research evidence suggests that professional communicators have yet to fully-grasp the nature and implications of these new channels (Aldísardóttir 2000, Chalaby 2002). The following summarises some of the more popular PR channels in use today.

Corporate advertising and brochures

Organisations sometimes promote themselves, rather than specific products or services. Brochures and annual reports are sent to major customers, suppliers, financiers and shareholders. These are often made available on corporate websites, either in an html version, as a series of hyperlinked pages, or retaining the original hard copy features by encoding it in 'pdf' (portable document file) format.

Sponsorship

This can involve the organisation in supporting anything from an opera company to a baseball team, with the added incentive of prime seats for corporate hospitality (i.e. entertaining important clients). However, sponsorship can also take the form of a simple donation, based on employee interests or charitable activities, such as sponsoring a company team that is taking part in a fund-raising half-marathon or cycle race. Large corporations sometimes offer sponsorship to organisations with higher status or a perceived ethical stance (e.g. universities, schools, hospitals, charities), in the hope of enhancing a poor public image. However, if the contrast between donor and beneficiary is too stark, such initiatives can generate unwelcome media coverage for both parties. This is particularly likely if the funding is resisted, either by employees or other stakeholders of the beneficiary organisation.

Lobbying

Lobbyists have an important role, providing decision-makers with well-researched briefing materials, technical advice and arguments in support of their respective positions. Governments often make use of these 'expert' briefings when drafting complex legislation. However, the activities of some lobbyists are highly suspect. For example, rewarding politicians for raising specific issues in parliamentary debates, or in specialist 'select' committee meetings, is a morally dubious activity that has prompted several public controversies (e.g. the UK's 'cash for questions' scandal of the early 1990s), while bribing politicians to vote in a particular way is generally regarded as a corrupt and illegal practice.

Internal communication

It is essential to keep employees informed, involved and motivated, not only for the internal health of the business but because employees are an important channel to the outside world. Proud, satisfied employees will tell relatives and friends what an excellent organisation they are working for, whilst disgruntled ones will do the opposite. The views of 'insiders', whether positive or negative, will always carry considerable weight. Research into the use of employee communication has shown that it both increases the perceived external prestige of the organisation and is an important factor in explaining the extent to which employees identify themselves with their employer (Smidts *et al.* 2001).

Day-to day procedures

Seemingly routine activities, such as the time taken to answer an external telephone call, can have a big impact on the way that an organisation is perceived. For example, if in-coming callers with simple queries are passed from department to department, they are likely to share their experiences with others; if these 'stories' accumulate, the organisation may find itself with a poor public image that is difficult to counteract. In this case, improved staff training programmes and better-constructed computer databases could reduce the problem. More generally, the lesson for all organisations is to monitor the effectiveness of all communication channels, however humble they might appear. Take complaints seriously, particularly where a pattern is detected, and ensure that routine procedures are operating satisfactorily.

Other methods – briefings, news releases, exhibitions and events

Public relations practitioners make extensive use of press briefings and news releases, which are considered in the next section. They also communicate directly with stakeholders at exhibitions and by hosting special events (see section 10.8).

In the next section we experiment with drafting a news release, one of the most widely-used and cost-effective communication channels, with applications to public relations and other areas of promotional activity.

10.7 Media relations – planning a news release

The media, which in this context means television, radio, newspapers and magazines, can be seen as a kind of indirect route to the public. Journalists research your business and listen to your briefings, then report their findings to a wider audience as news stories. These stories can deliver powerful messages, since much of the media, and the trade press in particular, are perceived as relatively impartial and fairly well-informed. Because of this, their reports and editorials tend to be accepted more readily than material that an organisation issues directly. The other advantage of this communication channel is its cost-effectiveness. You have to pay for advertising, but any messages that a journalist communicates are essentially free. There is only one catch; the PR practitioner has to deliver the kind of stories that make news. So what makes a story newsworthy? One popular definition of a non-story is 'Small earthquake, nobody hurt'. Similarly, as a nineteenth century commentator, Charles Anderson Dana noted, 'When a dog bites a man that is not news, but when a man bites a dog that is news.' In other words, the best stories go beyond everyday experience, or include at least some element of originality. It is also the case that the potential coverage of a story depends on whether it is being presented to international, national, local or specialist media, each of which has its own distinctive agenda and practices.

National and international media

Only the largest organisations are likely to be in a position to secure national or international media coverage on a regular basis. For example, the major publicly-quoted companies are of interest to the wider public as consumers, investors or employees. This would not be the case for a small enterprise with a limited client base, other than in exceptional circumstances. For this reason, it is not worthwhile issuing news releases to this audience, unless your story has a wider resonance (e.g. where a team of employees has made a major discovery, or the organisation has become involved with a more newsworthy partner). The national media tend to take a pro-active role, telephoning for comments on a particular issue and sending out their own journalists and photographers. This means that organisations generally have a very limited influence on the end product. PR managers are often horrified to see a relaxed 45-minute interview with a broadcast journalist turned into what they regard as a, 'wholly unrepresentative' 10-second 'clip' that is inserted into a television news story. To overcome this problem, interviewees and writers of press releases often structure their words into 'sound bites', short and memorable phrases that the journalist is more likely to use in an uncut form. The international and national media also monitor local media for suitable stories (see Figure 10.3 later). For example, the leading national newspapers make use of news agencies and local representatives (i.e. 'stringers'), to ensure that they have coverage around the world. These sources are ready to feed back any interesting news items, which may occasionally turn into major stories. These offer additional points of entry for organisations seeking more extensive coverage.

Local and regional media

The newspapers, television and radio stations that serve a local area may be 'hungrier' for stories than their national counterparts. However, they do have strict selection criteria. For them, the main factor is the 'local angle'. For example: Does the story, irrespective of where it takes place, concern people from this area? Does it refer to famous people who are visiting the area? Does it provide information on local events, proposals or controversies? Due to their limited resources, local newspapers may be more likely to reproduce the content of a news release, probably in the form of extracts, rather originating their own story. They may also make use of photographs that are supplied to accompany a story.

Specialist media

Even the smallest organisations may be able to get into one of the many specialist media, including broadcast programmes, publications and websites. Consumer-oriented publishers cover a vast number of leisure and lifestyle interests such as yachting, football, music and cookery. There is also an extensive business or 'trade' press, which serves all kinds of industrial and professional interest groups (e.g. catering, quantity surveying, social work, mechanical engineering, medicine, farming). The main advantage of specialist media is that it enables an organisation to target messages at well-defined audiences, and to obtain informed feedback on subject-specific issues. However, for the same reason, these media may not be suitable for more general messages.

Figure 10.3 illustrates a typical format for a news release. The message content demonstrates a number of 'good practice' features, including:

- the provision of many concise and relevant facts, addressing the six fundamental news questions (i.e. who? what? when? where? why? how?);
- placing the most important facts at the beginning, so increasing the chances that they will be included in an edited version of the story;
- presenting the information in a clear and simple format;
- providing relevant contact details for journalists wishing to clarify points, plus background notes for editors.

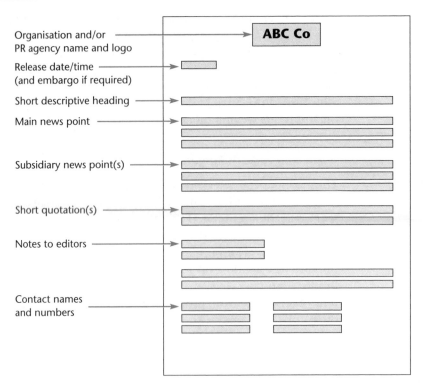

Figure 10.3 **The structure of a typical news release**

10.8 Exhibitions and events

Exhibitions and events enable organisations to interact intensively with various audiences. As such, these channels have great potential for persuasive communication. Organisations can attend a wide range of 'business to business' trade fairs and regular events, such as the film industry's international festival at Cannes. There are also many consumer-oriented exhibitions, covering industries such as house-building, food manufacturing and travel. Venues can range from 400 square metre meeting rooms to the 158,000 square metres of floor space at the UK's National Exhibition Centre (NEC), near Birmingham. Many organisations invest in expensive exhibition stands, which require considerable staff time, both in setting-up and to maintain the exhibits. So is this an effective channel for promotional messages? Exhibitions do offer unique communication opportunities, arising from direct and simultaneous contact with many existing and potential customers (see Figure 10.4). For example, academic book publishers attend many international conferences, enabling their representatives to interact with customers, discuss book proposals with potential authors and monitor developments in research and practice.

Exhibitions are also a popular venue for new product launches. In some sectors, such as car manufacturing, companies sometimes invest in dramatic 'roll outs' of their latest product, with musical fanfares, dry ice and laser displays.

Figure 10.4 **Stands at an international trade show**
Source: PA Photos/EPA.

However, these high-budget performances have become something of an industry cliché, and there is an increasing interest in more focused and interactive alternatives. For example, the organisation may arrange a series of regional 'open days' for an invited audience, drawn from its network of distributors or agents, existing customers and journalists. Exhibitions are also used to entertain key clients and suppliers, monitor competitor activity, build lists of prospective customers (or 'prospects'), obtain media coverage and foster relationships with journalists and commentators.

Staging 'events' – an alternative approach to persuasion?

Exhibitions are one form of 'event', which may engage the interest of the media, along with others. An alternative way to obtain media coverage is to stage an event that is designed solely for the purpose of creating a compelling news story. There is a long tradition of political protest, which has made use of this approach to overcome social and cultural barriers and ensure that marginalised voices are heard. For example, the civil rights activist Mahatma Ghandi led a number of protests, including the famous salt march, which highlighted inequitable trading conditions in colonial India (Ghandi 1993). More recently, the environmental campaign group, Greenpeace has perfected the technique with carefully-staged events that attract the world's media (e.g. abseiling down tall buildings, unfurling colourful banners and making appearances in unusual costumes). Greenpeace and other campaigning organisations also ensure that journalists are given access to photo-opportunities, increasing the potential for high-profile media coverage.

Managing exhibitions: a communication perspective

There is very little coverage of this topic in the advertising and marketing literature, but the principles appear similar to those outlined in our discussions of advertising and public relations. Exhibitions and events should be part of a coherent promotional strategy. The organisation's objectives need to be clear, and the whole exercise requires careful planning and budgeting. Mini-case 10.3 is a fictionalised example of the problems that can arise if these factors are not addressed.

Mini-case 10.3

'DozeyToys' – communicating at an international exhibition

The directors of DozeyToys, a new company specialising in wooden toys for young children, decided that it was the right time to start promoting their products to a wider audience. Jean-Paul Dozey, the chief executive, had spotted an advert for SuperCadeaux 05, a major international trade fair for the children's toy industry, which was to be held in Marseilles in two months' time. The company was pleased to secure the last available exhibition space and set to work constructing a world-beating stand. Arriving in Marseilles two days before the opening, DozeyToys' marketing assistant was horrified to find that its display stand was 15 cm wider than the allocated space, so the stand had to be hastily re-designed. It was located in the centre of a section labelled *loisir-sportif*, which was devoted to children's sports equipment. This was unfortunate, given that the company's speciality was small wooden toys. On the opening day, there was no sign of the newly-translated product brochures. There were several frantic telephone calls to the printers, who claimed that the delivery deadline was not specified in the original order. When the courier finally reached Marseilles, the marketing assistant found a number of embarrassing spelling errors in the German and English translations; it was now too late to get them corrected.

For the first two days of the Fair, the DozeyToys stand was very quiet. This was not surprising, because none of the key retail buyers for this product area had been contacted or invited to the stand. Day three was a complete contrast, and life on the stand became very hectic. The exhibition had opened to the public and a large army of school children descended onto the stand. They scooped up the entire stock of promotional literature, including 10,000 brand new, full-colour French, German and English language brochures. The sales manager calculated that each brochure had cost approximately E3.50 to produce. At last, the fair was over and the display stand was dismantled. The managers of DozeyToys returned home sadder and wiser.

Questions

1 Review the case and identify the main strategic and operational errors that were made by the managers of DozeyToys.

2 Take each error in turn and analyse it from a communication perspective. What messages were sent and received? What were the main sources of noise?

3 Prepare a 500-word briefing document, consisting of practical advice for organisations attempting to stage their first international exhibition. Specify which items you think are most important, and which problems are most likely to arise.

4 Suggest how the company might recover the situation without a large amount of additional spending, by exploiting other promotional communication channels discussed in this chapter.

Source: Case written by the author; 'DozeyToys' is a fictional organisation.

Summary

- Organisations engage in various forms of promotion and campaigning, using traditional channels, such as news releases and exhibitions, and emerging technologies such as text messaging. These activities often involve outside agencies, such as designers and media companies.

- Advertising messages are generally reinforced by other elements of a co-ordinated promotional/campaigning strategy. Strategies include well-defined objectives, reflecting organisational values and addressing the characteristics of target audiences.

- In promotional or campaigning activities involving direct interaction with customers or other stakeholders, there are more complex patterns of communication and an increased risk of failures.

- The concept of stakeholder dialogue is increasingly important in the field of public relations, challenging conventional views and practices.

- The news release remains an important communication channel, which needs to be seen as part of a broader public relations effort, involving other activities such as corporate advertising, sponsorship, lobbying and consultation.

- News releases, and the stories they contain, must be matched to the agenda, priorities and practices of the relevant local, national or specialist media organisations.

- Exhibitions and events provide organisations with an opportunity to interact directly with customers, or other stakeholders. However, they are also complex communication channels that demand careful planning and implementation.

Practical exercises

1 Creating the *Vegetale* campaign

1 Take up the role of the advertising agency designer (sometimes called a 'creative'), working on the promotional campaign for *Vegetale* (see section 10.3). Your brief is to address the following issues:

(a) Suggest a more appropriate alternative to the client's current product name, bearing in mind its target market and the benefits that the product offers to the consumer. Give reasons for your choice, identifying any important communication issues.

(b) Convert what you see as the key messages about the product into a concise and attention-grabbing slogan that can be used as the campaign develops. Again, give reasons for selecting this slogan, based on relevant communication issues.

(c) Draft an e-mail to your client, explaining your proposals and requesting a response.

2 The first phase of the *Vegetale* campaign has gone well, and the product is now in the shops, with a growing consumer base consisting predominantly of young ABC1 women. (Note: Insert your replacement product name for *Vegetale*, as selected in part 1(a). The advertising agency has now been asked to design a new advert, targeting health-conscious, recently-retired people. The key messages are unchanged, but the client's own research suggests that there will be greater resistance to a novel food product amongst older people.

(a) Select a treatment from those outlined in Table 10.1. Prepare a short (maximum 200-word) justification for the client, explaining this choice. Feel free to combine two or more of these formats, or to introduce novel approaches of your own.

(b) Sketch out a 'rough', a hand-drawn design for the proposed advertisement. Figure 10.5 identifies the main elements you are likely to find in a typical 'display' advertisement, but these can appear in many different guises, so feel free to adapt it to meet your needs.

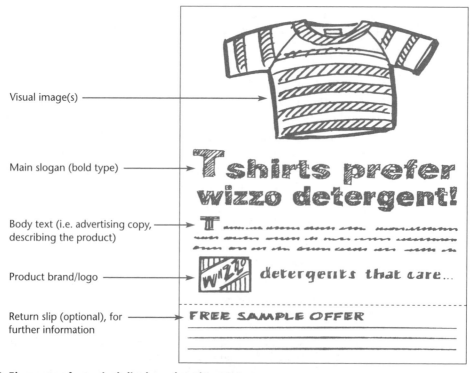

Figure 10.5 Elements of a typical display advertisement

2 Making news – drafting a news release

Based on the advice given in section 10.7, select from the outlines provided below, material that can form the basis for a news story that is likely to interest:

(a) international/national media

(b) local media

(c) specialist media.

Draft different news releases for each story. The outlines are deliberately brief and mundane. However, in this exercise you have the great luxury, which is unavailable in real life, of inventing whatever additional details are necessary to turn something rather ordinary into a really newsworthy story. Follow the news release layout presented in Figure 10.3.

Outlines for the potential news stories

- Museum hosts a travelling exhibition
- New shop opens in city centre
- Company chief executive resigns
- Canteen manager retires
- Company launches a new product line
- Charity begins a new fund-raising effort
- Hospital expands (or threatens to close) a paediatrics unit
- Regional tourism strategy unveiled

Case study J

Communicating sustainability in tourism – 'sticking your head above the parapet'

Background to the study

This case investigates the ways that sustainability messages are communicated in the travel and tourism industry. It draws on a research study conducted in six organisations, including in-depth interviews with the environmental managers at each company. These six travel and tourism operators host over 8.5 million leisure-focused visits (or 'trips') per year, including traditional sun and sea overseas package tours, long-haul cultural tourism, and all-inclusive resort breaks. Many tourism businesses are aiming to build sustainability into consumer perceptions of product quality and, over a longer time period, as a value associated with their corporate brand. In order to achieve this, communication to stakeholders is essential. Research into 'green' communication has focused on the micro, or managerial level, with green advertising as arguably the dominant topic (e.g. Banerjee *et al.* 1995, Carlson *et al.* 1993, 1996, Obermiller, 1995, Polonsky *et al.* 1998). One of the common themes running through this research literature is consumer disillusionment. It seems that there is considerable confusion, and scepticism surrounding green communication (e.g. Kilbourne 1995, National Consumer Council 1996). Indeed, green communication from industry sources has been pin-pointed as the least credible with consumers (Coddington 1993, Linnanen *et al.* 1999). This is reflected in expressions such as 'greenwash', a play on the term 'whitewash', suggesting that the sustainability messages represent a

▶

superficial attempt to paint over a largely unchanged core product. However, from the perspective of the tourism businesses, engaging in green communication was perceived as generating significant risks for the company. This can be seen in the following quotations, which are from different tour operators, both large and niche, all with official awards and recognition for their programmes of environmental practice:

- 'We want to avoid putting our head above the parapet really ... It's a bit like health and safety. We don't publicise that much at all either.'
- 'Once you start shouting about it, of course, you are sort of looking to be shot down because there is so much that you should be doing.'
- 'Building up credibility, but also to a certain extent it was based on the philosophy that if you stuck your head above the parapet and said we're environmentally friendly – say, for example, like the Body Shop did as a good example – you get your head shot off. Not for the hundreds and thousands of good things that you were doing, but for that one little thing that you weren't doing.'

Green communication can involve interaction with many internal and external stakeholders. In this case, we focus on communication with the consumer, the arena of marketing communications. Given the inherent problems, how are tourism businesses attempting to convey their messages on sustainability to consumers?

Communication in the tourism industry
The traditional framework for marketing communications comprises advertising, public relations, personal selling, and sales promotions. As they faced the credibility, or 'sticking your head above the parapet', problem, tourism businesses might be expected to exploit most of these communication channels in order to get their message across. However, the research found that, with the possible exception of public relations, the companies made limited use of traditional approaches when seeking to communicate with consumers about sustainability. So how did they approach the communications task? The secret lies in the inseparable nature of the tourism product, a characteristic shared with many other service sectors. The product is inseparable because the consumer is a part of the production process. This connection lasts for the duration of the holiday, as the holiday-maker enjoys a 'product' that is rich in experiences, including their interactions with staff and with other features of the service environment that are created (or sub-contracted) by the tour operator. Inseparability provides the tourism businesses with an exploitable communication advantage that is not readily available to the manufacturer of goods, green or otherwise (Middleton and Clarke, 2001)

A blueprint of the customer journey
It is possible to construct a flow chart, representing the main consumer/provider contact points throughout the service consumption process. This analysis, sometimes termed a 'blueprint' in the services marketing literature, provides the skeleton onto which physical evidence and other communication devices related to sustainability can be attached (Lovelock 2001). Figure 10.6 presents the different stages of what one of the interviewees termed, 'the customer journey', as analysed from the research interviews.

Each of these stages provides opportunities for consumer contact and communication, as mapped out and utilised by the tourism provider. Table 10.2 presents the actual communication channels and techniques used by the case study companies at each stage of the 'customer journey'.

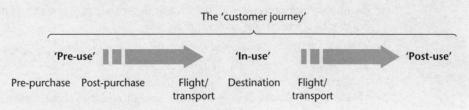

Figure 10.6 **Mapping the customer journey**

Table 10.2 **Communication during the 'customer journey'**

Stage in the 'customer journey' (Figure 10.6)	Communication channels and techniques
Pre-use Pre-purchase Post-purchase	Brochures, website (traveller's tips, trip notes). Codes of practice, slide shows, newsletter, travel documentation and inserts, other printed documents (e.g. holiday hints guides/essential holiday guide/'making the most of your stay' leaflets, trip notes).
Transportation/flight To destination From destination	In-flight magazine, in-flight video. In-flight magazine.
Destination/resort	Resort magazine/guide, participation in environmental initiatives, in-room TV channel, room information and folders, noticeboards, posters (e.g. environmental statement, codes of practice), display of environmental awards, staff (e.g. representatives, tour leaders), welcome meetings and welcome information print, resort-based customer survey.
Post-use	Survey, newsletter.

Channels available at one or more stages in the journey
Annual reports, environmental reports, website (e.g. summary of environmental policy, environmental mission statements), newsletter, public relations (including media relations and sponsorship).

The communication methods adopted by these tourism companies emphasised the importance of physical evidence in the form of standardised literature. This counterbalanced the highly variable nature of the particular service product (e.g. experiences can vary due to changes in the weather, local travel problems, etc.). The communication strategies also made considerable use of front-line employees interacting directly with the consumer throughout the holiday (i.e. 'the personal touch'). According to one interviewee, 'the most effective way of getting all the information across is really through the [tour] leaders, because they have face-to-face contact with people and people listen to what they say ... let's say they have a bigger role, which is why we're really concentrating on having the right people doing that job who understand the issues.' It is this direct staff/customer contact, so vital a communication tool during service usage, that is not generally available to most goods manufacturers.

Other applications?
A similar 'customer journey' or blueprinting approach could be used by other categories of service providers, to convey sustainability messages to pursue other

communication objectives. Based on the experience of these companies, there are a number of guidelines for achieving this aim:

- Set the parameters in terms of customer segment, product, location or brand.
- Map or flow chart the different stages of the 'customer journey', from initial decision process through to post-use feelings.
- Identify all points of contact, both human and inanimate, between the provider and the customer. Information can be gathered by observation, or from key customer groups and employees.
- Identify the existing methods of communication at each point of contact, including any gaps, and consider appropriate ways to strengthen communication at each point.
- Assess the overall package of communication methods for consistency in presentation and reinforcement of the brand (i.e. beyond any immediate communication objectives), as well as for costing purposes and to deal with relevant issues such as staff motivation and training.
- Monitor and review the success or otherwise of the different communication methods post-implementation.

Questions

1 What do you see as the main communication challenges facing the case study companies?

2 Why do you think printed literature has proved to be such a popular communication tool for this and other service products?

3 Why might public relations activity, including the role of front-line staff, be more successful than advertising in communicating messages about sustainability?

4 What other messages might be communicated to consumers through use of flowcharts/blueprints of the 'customer journey' and physical evidence at the points of contact?

Source: Written by Jackie Clarke.

Further reading

Packard ([1957] 1997) is the classic study of mass market advertising, which is still in print. Another useful source of insights into advertising is the work of **Ogilvy** (1995), a leading twentieth century practitioner, and **Klein's** (2000) journalistic critique. **Carlson** (2001) is an interesting example of cross-cultural research in advertising, which also addresses gender differences, while **Carson** (2002) addresses ethical issues in this field. **Miller and Dinan** (2000) is a brief account of the rise of the public relations industry. **Olins** (1989, 2003) addresses corporate visual identity. The debate between integrated corporate communications and the more open approach of stakeholder engagement can be captured by comparing **Kitchen and Schultz** (2001), who promote the integration, and contributions, such as **Crane and Livesey** (2003) in the edited volume by **Andriof *et al.*** (2003), which present leading ideas from stakeholder theory. **Charter and Polonsky** (1999) is a useful edited text on product marketing and other forms of promotion, from an environmental perspective.

References

Adbusters (2003) 'Information: the Media Foundation'. Adbusters Media Foundation, Vancouver BC. (Available at www.adbusters.org/information (accessed 19th August).)

Aldísardóttir, L. (2000) 'Research note: global medium, local tool? – how readers and media companies use the Web'. *European Journal of Communication*, 15, 2, 241–51.

Andriof, J., Waddock, S., Husted, B. and Rahman, S. (eds.) (2003) *Unfolding stakeholder thinking 2: relationships, communication and performance*. Greenleaf, Sheffield.

Banerjee, S., Gulas, C.S. and Iyer, E. (1995) 'Shades of green: a multidimensional analysis of environmental advertising'. *Journal of Advertising*, 24, 2, 21–31.

Carlson, L., Grove, S.J. and Kangun, N. (1993) 'A context analysis of environmental advertising claims: a matrix method approach'. *Journal of Advertising*, 22, 3, 27–39.

Carlson, L., Grove, S.J., Kangun, N. and Polonsky, M.J. (1996) 'An international comparison of environmental advertising: substantive versus associative claims'. *Journal of Macromarketing*, 16, 2, 57–68.

Carlson, T. (2001) 'Gender and political advertising across cultures: a comparison of male and female political advertising in Finland and the US'. *European Journal of Communication*, 16, 2, 131–54.

Carson, T.L. (2002) 'Ethical issues in selling and advertising' in Bowie, N.E. (ed.) *The Blackwell guide to business ethics*. Blackwell, Oxford (186–205).

Chalaby, J.K. (2002) 'Transnational television in Europe: the role of pan–European channels'. *European Journal of Communication*, 17, 2, 183–203.

Charter, M. and Polonsky, M.J. (eds.) (1999) *Greener marketing: a global perspective on greener marketing practice*. Greenleaf, Sheffield.

Coddington, W. (1993) *Environmental marketing: positive strategies for reaching the green consumer*. London: McGraw–Hill.

Crane, A. and Livesey, S. (2003) 'Are you talking to me?: stakeholder communication and the rewards of dialogue' in Andriof, J. *et al.* (eds.) *op cit.* (39–52).

Ghandi, M.K. (1993) *An autobiography: the story of my experiment with truth*. Beacon Press, Boston MA.

IPR (2003) 'Fact file'. Institute of Public Relations, London. (Available at: www.ipr.org.uk/news/factfile.asp (accessed 15th December).)

Kilbourne, W.E. (1995) 'Green advertising: salvation or oxymoron?' *Journal of Advertising*, 24, 2, 7–19.

Kitchen, P.J. and Schultz, D.E. (2001) *Raising the corporate umbrella: corporate communications in the 21st century*. Palgrave, Basingstoke.

Klein, N. (2000) *No logo*. Flamingo, London.

Linnanen, L., Markkanen, E. and Ilmola, L. (1999) 'Building environmental credibility: from action to words'. in Charter, M. and Polonsky, M.J. (eds.) *op cit.* (207–23).

Lovelock, C. (2001) *Services marketing: people, technology, strategy* (4th edn.) Prentice Hall, Upper Saddle River, NJ.

Middleton, V.T.C. and Clarke, J. (2001) *Marketing in travel and tourism* (3rd edn.). Butterworth–Heinemann, Oxford.

Miller, D. and Dinan, W. (2000) 'The rise of the PR industry in Britain, 1979–98'. *European Journal of Communication*, 15, 1, 5–35.

National Consumer Council (1996) *Green claims: a consumer investigation into marketing claims about the environment*. NCC, London.

Obermiller, C. (1995) 'The baby is sick/the baby is well: a test of environmental communication appeals'. *Journal of Advertising*, 24, 2, 55–71.

Ogilvy, D. (1995) *Ogilvy on advertising*. Prion, London.

Olins, W. (1989) *Corporate identity: making business strategy visible through design*. Thames and Hudson, London.

Olins, W. (2003) *On brand*. Thames and Hudson, London.

Packard, V. ([1957] 1997) *The hidden persuaders: the classic study of the American advertising machine*. Penguin, London.

Polonsky, M.J., Bailey, J., Baker, H. and Basche, C. (1998) 'Communicating environmental information: are marketing claims on packaging misleading?' *Journal of Business Ethics*, 17, 3, 281–94.

Rogers, E.M. (1995) *Diffusion of innovations* (3rd edn.). Free Press, New York.

Smidts, A., Pruyn, A.H. and van Riel, C.B.M. (2001) 'The impact of employee communication and perceived external prestige on organisational identification'. *Academy of Management Journal*, 49, 5, 1051–62.

Trout, J. and Rivkin, S. (1997) *The new positioning*. McGraw-Hill, Maidenhead.

CHAPTER 11

Interviews, questioning and listening

Knowledge speaks, but wisdom listens.
Jimi Hendrix, musician

Learning outcomes

By the end of this chapter you should be able to:

- compare the various ways that interviews are used in organisations, noting the differing requirements of each situation;
- make appropriate practical arrangements for successful interviews;
- enhance your listening skills and develop appropriate questioning techniques, reflecting the needs of the situation;
- prepare more effectively when attending interviews;
- appreciate related techniques, including those adopted in counselling interviews.

11.1 Introduction

Interviews have been usefully described as 'a discussion with a purpose'. They serve various purposes in organisations, ranging from recruitment and employee appraisal to marketing research and public relations. In communication terms, interviews are particularly rich in messages. The words spoken are often less important than the non-verbal signals that are exchanged. These include facial expressions, eye contact, gestures and posture (see section 4.7). As a result of this complex mixture of stimuli, interviews also offer considerable scope for misunderstanding and confusion. Hence, it is important for all managers to develop strong interviewing skills. Fortunately, there is considerable overlap between the knowledge and capabilities required by an interviewer and those that are needed to be a successful interviewee. Most people have had some experience of being interviewed. We will draw on these experiences as a useful starting point when discussing how to develop or enhance communication skills as an interviewer.

The chapter begins with a brief review of the main types of interview, which describes their distinctive characteristics. Two practical sections deal with the essential, yet infrequently practised, skills of listening and questioning. These are followed by suggestions on how best to prepare for an interview, looking from the interviewee's perspective. Finally, there is a short discussion on the role of counselling techniques at work.

11.2 Types of interview

Organisational managers and employees are routinely involved in the four broad categories of interview (i.e. recruitment and promotion, appraisal, coaching and mentoring, and disciplinary and grievance) that are reviewed in this section (see Table 11.1). In some cases, they may also find themselves being interviewed as part of the organisation's public relations, marketing or campaigning activities, which were the subject of the previous chapter. While it is possible to identify some 'ideal-typical' patterns of communication, each interview is a unique and dynamic situation, so that the results of a particular interaction may be difficult to predict at the outset. The level of formality (i.e. the degree to which the interview follows established procedures, with the associated paperwork) is likely to vary depending on the organisation and the individuals involved. However, some common features can be identified in each interview type.

Table 11.1 **Main interview types and related communication practices**

Type	Typical interviewer	Typical interviewee
Recruitment and promotion	Clarifies factual information regarding application; assesses inter-personal skills; makes conscious or unconscious subjective assessments of candidate; engages in persuasion.	Seeks to persuade interviewer(s); obtains additional factual information; makes conscious or unconscious assessments of organisation.
Appraisal	Listens to employee's self-assessment; probes for related problems and possible solutions; should be open, seeking to establish shared understandings and encourage employee.	Clarifies and reflects on challenges and achievements; raises outstanding issues and concerns; expresses preferences for future activity; should be open and not attempt to mislead employer.
Coaching and mentoring	Supportive questioning; clarifies employee's next phase of activity; encourages employee to reflect on previous phases of work experience and to generalise.	Identifies perceived needs; reporting on work experiences; responds to mentor's questions; reflects on previous phase of work experience.
Discplinary and grievance	Clarifies the problem and outlines any formal procedures; maintains objectivity and avoids personalising issues; seeks employee's agreement and commitment.	Explains the problem and/or mitigating circumstances; maintains objectivity and avoids personalising issues; may either seek agreement or engage in further persuasion.

Recruitment and promotion interviews

Interviews are normally used at the second or third stage of a recruitment process. Prior to this, applicants are 'screened' on the basis of information provided in *curriculum vitaes* (CVs) and application forms. Screening is essentially a *rejection* process. It is used to produce a 'shortlist', reducing the initial numbers to a more manageable size. Some larger organisations then ask shortlisted candidates to take part in psychometric tests, 'in-tray' exercises, etc. The final stage, where *selection* takes place, is almost always a personal interview. Selection, unlike screening, is about choosing the most suitable candidate from a shortlist, most of whom could probably do the job very well. Interviews can also be used to clarify and check up on the candidate's achievements and interests, as they are recorded on application forms or in a CV (e.g. 'So tell me, did you really cycle all the way from Moscow to Beijing?'). However, for many managers, the principal function of a face-to-face interview is to see whether the candidate would make a suitable colleague. In many cases, this draws on a more informal assessment, which seeks to establish whether the person would 'fit in' with existing members of the department or team. As a result, recruitment interviews can become highly subjective exercises, no matter how objective the rest of the process has been.

Recruitment interviews involve both parties in various forms of persuasive communication (see Chapter 5). Interviewees make use persuasive techniques with the obvious intention of getting themselves selected. However, prospective employers are also engaged in a more complex task of persuasion. First, they will be trying to ensure the most promising candidates accept their job offer, knowing that these people may have attractive offers from rival firms. Second, recruitment interviewers should be ensuring that *all* interviewees, successful and unsuccessful, are left with a positive impression, perceiving the organisation as an efficient, fair and decent place to work. After all, it may be that the organisation wants to recruit some of the unsuccessful candidates on another occasion. They also have the potential to become important customers, suppliers or partners in the future. In any event, having had a direct experience of the organisation, they are bound to share their impressions with others. This kind of informal communication can contribute powerfully to the organisation's external image, particularly where there is a relatively small community of interest (see section 10.5).

Promotion interviews operate in a similar way to recruitment, with internal candidates competing for a more senior post. The key differences are that interviewees are bound to know some members of the interview panel quite well, and that the applicants will continue to work for the organisation, whether or not they are successful at interview. Organisations also conduct interviews when employees are applying for changes in work task or location, which do not involve an increase in salary or status (i.e. a transfer or 'sideways move').

Appraisal interviews

Most large and medium-sized organisations operate a system of appraisal interviews. An appraisal interview should provide an opportunity for employees to review with their line manager performance and progress. An open and honest discussion can highlight the person's achievements, probe the reasons behind any 'problem areas' and identify training or work experience needs. The interviewer prepares a summary of the discussion and outcomes, and both parties agree an 'action plan' for the next period. If the manager ensures a climate of openness and trust, the appraisal interview can be highly motivating. By reviewing the results of a number of interviews, underlying structural or procedural problems in the organisation can be identified and corrected. However, some organisations continue to link appraisals to performance-related pay schemes or bonuses. This combination is unlikely to encourage an open or self-critical approach in the employee, limiting the effectiveness of the appraisal as a feedback mechanism. Chapter 6 includes a more detailed discussion of the role of appraisal systems, including the technique known as '360-degree' feedback (see section 6.3 and Mini-case 6.2).

Coaching/mentoring interviews

Coaching and mentoring interviews are a form of on-going developmental appraisal, which are often used with newly appointed and recently promoted staff. The coaching model derives from the world of sport, where personal and team coaches help athletes to enhance their performance. It has become increasingly popular at board level (i.e. 'executive coaching'), where senior staff may be allocated a coach, normally recruited from a specialist consultancy. In a coaching interview, the emphasis is on making the person more self-aware, encouraging them to discuss work-based projects, evaluate progress since the previous meeting and look forward to future challenges. Here, the role of the interviewer is not primarily to instruct or to give detailed advice, but to develop the interviewee's confidence and capabilities by agreeing targets and encouraging reflection upon what has been learned.

Disciplinary and grievance interviews

Disciplinary and grievance interviews are both concerned with responding to problems. Disciplinary interviews are normally a response to the problematic behaviour of an employee, while grievance interviews deal with problems that an employee has raised. Both raise considerable challenges in balancing the need for formality and objectivity with a degree of human empathy and persuasive communication. Ideally, problems should be identified and remedied at an earlier stage (e.g. arranging an employee meeting to air and resolve a grievance, or tackling a disciplinary problem as part of the employee's appraisal or coaching session). In the case of disciplinary issues, isolated, minor incidents should be dealt with quickly and with minimal formality. In the case of a more serious, complex, or long-running problem, a more formal interview may be necessary.

Procedures for this type of interview should be clearly stipulated in the individual's employment contract, and these must be closely followed. In the worst case, you might subsequently need written evidence to defend against an unfair dismissal claim before an employment tribunal. During a disciplinary interview, the interviewer's main priorities are to establish the facts and to remain calm and objective. Both parties should avoid personalising the discussion, even if provoked. The employer is normally trying to secure some kind of commitment from the employee to acknowledge the problem and to overcome it voluntarily. Where the interview has been prompted by an employee's grievance (e.g. a junior member of staff has made a complaint about the behaviour of a manager), the interview follows a similar pattern, in which a participative, problem-solving style is generally the most appropriate. Though regulations vary between countries, there may be a legal requirement or a code of practice governing the way that the interview should be conducted (ACAS 2003). Disciplinary and grievance interviews raise questions concerning the relative power of employee and employer, which also influence the nature of the communication process. For example, research evidence suggests that supervisors and managers do not always adopt the most appropriate style to achieve a desired change in behaviour, with many of the disciplinary cases that are perceived as 'less serious' being handled in an autocratic manner (Hook *et al.* 1996, Rollinson *et al.* 1996).

Mini-case 11.1 considers another important application of interviewing, where it forms one of the data collection methods adopted for an organisational research project. The case distinguishes between three types of research interview:

- 'structured' interviews, where interviewers follow a carefully worded script;
- 'semi-structured' interviews, where they typically make use of a checklist of topics to be covered, but are more flexible in the way that the questions are worded and the order in which they are raised; and
- 'unstructured' (or 'in-depth') interviews, where there is minimal formality and the interviewee is encouraged to speak freely.

This allows the researcher to explore issues in greater depth, and is based on a less directive style of interaction, which is guided by the interviewee's perceptions, rather than the interviewer's pre-determined plan (Saunders *et al.* 2003: 246–7).

| Mini-case 11.1 | Using interviews in an organisational research project |

During a research project to survey employee attitudes in a public sector organisation, the use of interviews was considered for each stage of this undertaking. The first stage of data collection consisted of a series of unstructured interviews, which were undertaken with a representative cross-section of employees, to reveal variables to be tested empirically at the second stage of the research project. A number of decisions were made about these interviews during the initial planning phase:

- to obtain personnel data relating to job categories and grades, gender, age and length of service in order to select a representative sample;
- to combine similar employee categories and to use group interviews in order to overcome time constraints and assist the researcher's capacity to handle the data to be collected. As a result, six group interviews were arranged, consisting of about ten participants in each group, in order to cover all employee categories;
- not to mix managerial and non-managerial participants within a group because this could have meant that non-managerial employees would be reluctant to take part.

▶

At the next stage of the research project a decision had to be taken about whether to use a questionnaire or structured and standardised interviews. Because the number of employees in the organisational sample to be surveyed exceeded 30, it was decided that it would be more efficient to use a questionnaire rather than interviews (Wass and Wells 1994). After the analysis of the questionnaire data, a further stage used a series of semi-structured interviews in order to explore and explain the findings obtained through the survey. These were also conducted as group interviews. Care was again taken in relation to the representativeness, size and composition of each group, as well as in relation to choosing the setting for the discussion to occur.

Questions

1 What kinds of information were the researchers seeking to obtain from the interviews that were conducted:

   (a) at the first stage of data collection?
   (b) after the analysis of the questionnaire?

2 Try to develop three or four of your own sample questions, in a format that might be suitable for each of these interviews. (Note: Review the content and format of these questions once you have completed the chapter, redrafting as necessary.)

3 In 'unstructured' interviews, the interaction is sometimes described as 'non-directive' (i.e. the researcher does not specify the questions). Can you identify other interview situations where a non-directive approach might be appropriate?

Source: Case based on an extract from Saunders et al. (2003: 249). Reproduced with permission.

11.3 Listening techniques

Our ears play an important role in the communication process, and as the opening quotation of this chapter suggests, listening underpins many forms of human interaction. (There is a long-established saying, to the effect that there was a good reason for providing us with two ears yet only one mouth.) However, anecdotal evidence suggests that society places a relatively low value on the art of listening. For example, there is considerable coverage of 'effective speaking' in the popular communication literature, but very little material on 'effective listening'. Despite this, one of the best ways of enhancing inter-personal communication in interviews and other channels, such as meetings, is to invest some time in developing better listening skills. This section reviews six general characteristics associated with being a more 'active' and effective listener.

1 Avoiding prejudice

Prejudice acts as a perceptual filter on the ear, cutting out those things that do not fit in with a person's original viewpoint and reinforcing anything that does. In order to cope with a complex world, we try to fit our experiences, and the people we meet into pre-existing categories (see section 2.3). However, these rough and ready categorisations can become an obstacle to communication, distorting the more detailed information that we subsequently receive. In order to deal with our prejudices, they need to be recognised. One way of increasing awareness is to consider previous occasions when you have formed an inaccurate impression, based on an initial reaction to a personal characteristic, such as ability, accent, age, educational qualifications, gender, height, nationality, occupation, religious background or sexuality. The aim is to resist any simplified and pre-determined categorisation, and to pay greater attention to the individual person, and what they have to say.

2 Signalling interest in the person speaking

Interviewers and other listeners need to do more than simply pay attention. They need to *demonstrate* that they are receptive to the other person, showing that they are actually interested in what is being said. Interest can be signalled in a number of ways, mostly through non-verbal cues. For example, interviewers should adopt an 'open' posture with arms *unfolded*. They should also be facing towards the person speaking, and may also lean forwards slightly. Other non-verbal signals, such as degree of eye contact and facial expression can be influential. Skilled interviewers combine these with verbal and paralinguistic cues, adjusting their tone of voice and using prompts (e.g. 'yes', 'I see ...', 'good', 'mmm ...', 'uh-huh'), reinforcing their support and encouraging the speaker.

3 Being aware of feelings

Good listeners can operate simultaneously at two levels, picking up both cognitive and affective messages. At a 'surface' level, they need to extract and process information that the other person injects into the conversation (e.g. 'Yes, I have completed the report', 'No, we did not receive the training materials'). However, they also need to be alert to messages that are concerned with personal feelings and emotions. In some cases, national, organisational or departmental cultures discourage people from expressing their feelings in conversation, so that listeners are forced to interpret the messages more indirectly (i.e. they have to 'read between the lines'), in order to interpret the implicit meanings. National cultures are also thought to influence the extent to which people rely on cues from the overall situation when communicating. These range from 'high context' cultures, that draw a great deal of meaning from non-verbal cues, to 'low context' cultures, that rely more explicitly on the actual words that are used (Hall and Hall 1990) (see section 2.3). As we noted, the situation is rather more complex in today's more culturally diverse international organisations, which are often populated by people with several overlapping cultural identities. However, it remains the case that cultural factors can undermine communication during interviews (see Mini-case 11.2).

| Mini-case 11.2 | Jean-Jacques and the appraisal interview |

Jean-Jacques and the appraisal interview

It is 5.30 pm on a hot summer's day. We are in the administrative offices of a large city teaching hospital in northern Germany. Jean-Jacques, a talented computing technician, is in the middle of his six-monthly appraisal interview. He is trying to explain a series of problems to Petra, his immediate line manager. The main problem appears to relate to the contractors being used to install new computer cabling in part of the main teaching block, a nineteenth century building in the centre of the hospital grounds. Petra asks Jean-Jacques to explain what is wrong:

J-J: (Folds arms across chest and sits back in the chair) You see, the contractors we hired have still not finished. I have spent *five* hours today trying to chase them up and the cabling is still not completed. (Sighs)

Petra: Will the computer suite in the teaching block be ready for the conference next week?

J-J: I hope so, but you know, it is not acceptable for private contractors to treat a customer in this way, simply because we are a not-for-profit organisation. I feel that hospitals like ours should make more intensive efforts in this direction.

Petra: But will the cabling be completed in time?

J-J: (Looks at the ceiling) I am not sure that I am making myself clear. We are experiencing a problem which is …

Petra: No, I do not understand. We just need to be sure that the work will be completed in time.

J-J: You *should* understand that I am doing everything possible to ensure that the work will be finished, (gestures with open hands and raised eyebrows), but I think perhaps there are wider issues here?

Petra: Good, so I will not expect a problem next week.

Petra continues with the appraisal interview, moving on to set Jean-Jacques' performance targets for the next six months. She is pleased to finish the interview on time, at 5.45 pm. Jean-Jacques is much less happy with the outcome. On the way home, he picks up a copy of his favourite newspaper and sits down at a pavement café to read through the job advertisements.

Questions

1 Review the case and the extract of dialogue. What do you think that Jacques is trying to communicate to Petra? Consider both cognitive and affective aspects of the messages.

2 What are the most likely barriers to communication operating in this interview? Consider the question from the perspective of both individuals.

3 Prepare a revised version of the dialogue, in which both Jacques and Petra have taken account of the issues you identified in the previous question.

Source: Case written by the author. The characters and organisation are fictional.

4 Avoiding interruptions and distractions

One of the most difficult challenges for an interventionist (i.e. 'hands on') manager is to avoid interrupting other people while they are talking. By starting to speak, you will generally cause the other person to stop, and possibly lose their line of argument. Repeated interruptions are likely to cause irritation. In effect, the interruption signals that, 'I no longer want to listen to what you are saying'. Consequently, interviewers should only interrupt when there is a good reason to do so. For example, it may be appropriate if the interviewees are either repeating themselves or digressing from the subject matter of the interview. Other gestures, such as shuffling paperwork or reading while an interviewee is speaking, are also distracting and should be avoided. However, interviewers may sometimes make use of non-verbal cues in a deliberate attempt to encourage the person speaking to be more concise, or to signal that they are bringing the interview to a close.

5 Signalling encouragement

There are various ways to maintain the momentum of a conversation without distracting the interviewee. As we have already noted, occasional nodding of the head, eye contact, smiling and the use of vocal cues, can act as strong signals of encouragement. However, the reverse is also true. If the interviewer either fails to provide these cues, or stops using them during the course of the interview, the effect can be dramatic. This is particularly apparent in situations where the interviewee is nervous or has other reasons for being a reluctant speaker.

6 Clarifying and summarising

If an interviewee is having difficulty expressing ideas coherently, the interviewer can assist by seeking confirmation, checking for a correct understanding of what has been discussed or agreed. One option is simply to ask the interviewee to clarify what they have been saying. Alternatively, the interviewer can attempt to paraphrase the discussion, and ask the interviewee whether this was an accurate representation. A similar interaction is required towards the end of an interview, when the interviewer draws the various points together in the form of a summary. Summaries are concerned with shared meanings. They help to ensure that all parties have a similar understanding of what has taken place during the interview. They also provide an opportunity to specify any agreements, decisions or actions. However, there is the danger of creating a false sense of agreement, particularly where the interviewer is overly-directive, or where the interviewee feels unable to challenge the way that the summary has been framed. 'Active listening' requires interviewers to reflect carefully at this point, checking whether their clarifications and summaries accurately reflect the other person's contribution (Rogers and Farson 1976).

Effective interviews: the importance of practical arrangements

The practical preparations for an interview can make a significant difference in its effectiveness. These arrangements include the way the room is set out, avoidance of interruptions, and the way that interviewees are treated before and after the interview. It is also important to consider who is to do the interviewing, an individual or a panel.

● **Seating and room layout**: Layout does affect the atmosphere of the interview. It is often better to move away from your desk, with its distracting piles of work. Putting your interviewee in a lower or less comfortable chair sends out a message of superiority and distance. However, if you are aiming to retain some degree of businesslike formality, relaxing armchairs are best avoided (Figure 11.1).

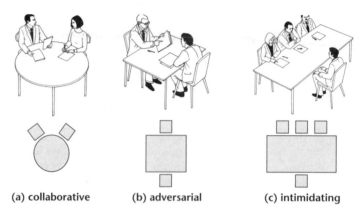

(a) collaborative   (b) adversarial   (c) intimidating

Figure 11.1 **Seating layouts for interviews**

● **Interview panels**: Some interviews are conducted with a panel, comprising several people who may be from different parts of the organisation. For example, a recruitment interview panel may include a representative from human resources (HR) and one or more line managers. Panels are used in this case to ensure that different interests are represented, and to enable the interviewers to discuss the candidates after the interview. Panels can be particularly daunting for the interviewee, so seating arrangements become even more important. Panel members should remember to introduce themselves carefully at the start of the interview. It may also be appropriate to explain who will be asking questions first and what areas each will cover. These courtesies help to put the interviewee at their ease, and therefore enable the interviewers to make a more realistic assessment of their abilities.

● **Minimising interruptions and distractions**: Managers tend to have frequent telephone calls and visitors, so it is advisable to divert calls, switch off mobile phones and place a 'do not disturb' sign on the door. If the organisation's offices are open-plan, it is important to book a more private meeting room for the interviews. Interviewers often ensure that they are sitting in sight of a wall clock, so that they can keep track of time without glancing at their wristwatch, a gesture that is bound to disturb the interviewee.

● **Before and after the interview**: Especially in the case of recruitment interviews, where the person is a visitor, some basic courtesies convey a positive image of the organisation. For example, it is bad practice to leave people waiting in a busy corridor, fail to provide refreshments or leave them unaware of where the toilets are located. It should be reasonably easy to obtain a suitable waiting room, offer the interviewees a coffee, keep to stated times if possible and ensure that any agreed follow-up action is taken.

The next section takes us into the interview room and considers how questioning techniques and other aspects of behaviour might affect the quality of interaction between interviewer and interviewee.

11.4 Questioning techniques and related behaviours

An interview is punctuated by questions and answers. The same question can be asked in many ways, and each of these can actually generate a *different* response. By considering the types of questions people ask, and the related behaviours that they employ, it is possible to improve your questioning technique and encourage more useful interaction.

Open and closed questions

One of the most important distinctions is between 'open' and 'closed' questions. Closed questions demand a short pre-determined response, often a simple 'yes' or 'no' (e.g. 'Have you called the office this morning?'). Open questions, by contrast, encourage the respondent to think for themselves and thus allow for a wider range of responses (e.g. 'How should we tackle this production problem?'). Consider how using a closed question limits communication in the following dialogue:

Peter: So anyway, Helen, was that training course OK?

Helen: Yes, I suppose so, though ...

Peter: Excellent, see you later!

An 'open' version of the same basic question produces a much more informative (and therefore useful) answer from the interviewee, since it encourages them to speak for longer, and to give a more considered response:

Peter: So, Helen, how did you feel about the training course?

Helen: Well..., the tutor was excellent, but she was repeating a lot of the material we covered during our induction sessions in September.

Peter: Ah, that's unfortunate. Looks like we may need to revise the programme before the next run.

Closed questions are useful for establishing the basic facts (e.g. *'How many people do you employ?'*). You can also use them to 'close down' an overly wordy or rambling interviewee, forcing them to give more concise responses. Open questions, with occasional closed questions for clarification, are a very useful way to investigate complex issues, especially where your own knowledge of the area is limited.

Probing questions and clarification

Probing questions may be open or closed, and ask for additional information, based on the interviewee's previous responses. Clarification can play a similar role, but its primary purpose is to confirm that the questioner has understood the previous response correctly, rather than to ask for more. Probing and clarification need to be tackled carefully. These questions can easily sound aggressive, which typically prompts a defensive reaction from the 'victim', closing down the possibilities for further communication:

Peter: So, Helen, how did you feel about the training course?

Helen: Well, the tutor was excellent, but she was repeating a lot of the material we covered during our induction sessions in September.

Peter: Oh really, so which topics were repeated?

Helen: The presentation skills, and the session on company organisation.

Peter: And did you tell the tutor about this?

Helen: No, actually ...

Peter: Was there a feedback session for the trainees?

Helen: Well, yes, but I wasn't about to say anything about it there.

Peter: So, what your're saying is, you could have spoken out at the feedback session, but you didn't?

Helen: Hey, don't blame me, it wasn't my fault they got it wrong!

Encouraging and summarising

These behaviours are useful tools that the interviewer can use to maintain momentum in the interview and to ensure that it achieves a degree of shared understanding. The interviewee may be encouraged by non-verbal signals, such as when the interviewer is nodding, smiling or displaying an open posture while the interviewee is talking. This is where the interviewer can make use of paralinguistic cues to signal encouragement (see section 11.3). However, as we saw in Chapter 4, many of these signals have highly culture-specific meanings. For the same reason, they are learned behaviours, so that people may be largely unconscious of making them (see section 4.7). Consequently, interviewers need to be particularly flexible and sensitive to the potential for mis-interpretation in crosscultural contexts. We have also discussed how summaries can be used to restate and encapsulate the interviewee's responses up to that point. They can clarify the interviewer's interpretation and enable the interviewee to confirm or challenge that interpretation. Both clarification and summarising are simple techniques, yet many interviewers make limited use of them, resulting in a less effective and more error-prone exchange.

Hypothetical questions

Hypothetical questions are an excellent way to make your interviewee reflect on things. This type of question is often used to test the mental agility and creativity of prospective employees (e.g. 'Imagine you're in charge of our Japanese export marketing operation. The local stock exchange has just collapsed. What would you do?'). Hypotheticals are also used in coaching and counselling, to help a person explore previously unconsidered options (e.g. 'So, if we could arrange that extra language tuition and the travel leave, how would you feel about spending two years in the Columbian regional office?').

Leading questions and interruptions

Leading questions direct the interviewee to respond with the answer that you either desire or expect. Leading questions are probably the interviewers' most common fault. They are always communication failures, because they represent one-way messages masquerading as an exchange of views. They are often compounded by the use of frequent interruptions, so that the interviewee is unable even to complete the response to a question. An extreme example of both tendencies illustrates these dangers:

Peter: So what did you think of our 'so-called' training course?

Helen: Well, it's difficult to say ...

Peter: That tutor!; a complete waste of space, don't you think?

Helen: I'm sure she ...

Peter: Means well?

Helen: No, not really. It's ...

Peter: Helen, I couldn't agree more. Be seeing you!

Leading questions are sometimes disguised, but they can be readily identified. Review the question and simply look out for any kind of prompt that would have the effect of directing the interviewee towards a particular response. In the first of the practical exercises at the end of this chapter, you are asked to monitor a 'live' interview. It is also possible to learn more about questioning techniques by analysing a recording of an interview, taken from a television or radio broadcast. The analysis grid illustrated below (see Table 11.2), can be used to record the type of question used, noting other interviewer behaviour, such as encouraging, clarifying and summarising. The use of an analysis grid allows for comparisons to be made between the performances of different interviewers, based on these or related criteria. It is only by exploring and practising these skills that you will discover whether, for example, you ask too many closed questions, fail to use clarification questions when faced with ambiguous responses, or have a tendency to ask leading questions. In any event, the key to more effective interviewing is to make a conscious effort to listen to the interviewee, focusing on their responses and trying to keep your opinions to yourself.

Table 11.2 **Sample grid for analysing interview questions**

Questioning techniques							
Open							
Closed							
Probing							
Hypothetical							
Leading							
Related behaviours							
Encouraging							
Clarifying							
Summarising							
Interrupting							

The process of questioning can be expensive and time-consuming, requiring specialist staff. Some organisations are experimenting with the use of web-based technologies in order to manage some questioning activities, including those used as part of the recruitment process. Mini-case 11.3 investigates how 'online recruitment' (OR) technology is being applied.

Mini-case 11.3

Online recruitment: an effective communication channel?

Online recruitment (OR) is a rapidly-developing activity that is beginning to challenge conventional recruitment practices, such as newspaper advertising and the use of local recruitment agencies to attract and screen potential candidates. Online agencies claim to be more efficient than their 'bricks and mortar' rivals. The chief executive of the new breed of online recruiters has argued that, 'A face-to-face interview is often not necessary for temporary positions. More important is checking a candidate has the right experience' (cited in Ward 2000: 25). Meanwhile newspapers, who often depend heavily on this form of advertising revenue, are responding to the threat by providing customers with a combination of print and website advertising. Established recruitment agencies are also moving online, arguing that their combination of virtual presence and physical support services provides an advantage over the newer operators.

There are three main segments of the OR industry: the addition of recruitment pages to existing corporate websites; the creation of specialist web-based recruiters; and the extension of recruitment advertising onto the web. The early users of OR included the IT industry and universities, but this practice is now developing in many sectors. One recent estimate suggests that the OR industry in Europe will grow from just over £50m (€75m) in 1999 to around £3.8bn (€5.7bn) in 2005 (cited in Galanki 2002: 243). Researchers have identified a number of advantages in OR as a communication channel, including:

- cost savings over conventional recruiting methods;
- more rapid responses and shorter recruitment cycles;
- access to a wider pool of potential applicants;
- access to higher-quality applicants (e.g. 'passive' job-seekers);
- access to highly specialised 'niche' markets;
- overcoming geographic constraints of international recruitment.

However, there are also possible disadvantages and dangers in adopting this communication channel for recruitment purposes, including:

- excessive response to website advertisements, requiring costly screening;
- under-representation of individuals and groups that are less familiar with web-based technology;
- poorly-designed or maintained websites/interfaces, resulting in the loss of good candidates and damage to corporate reputation;
- costs involved in implementing an effective system;
- ethical concerns arising from transfer of CVs and other personal information in electronic format (e.g. reselling of CVs to other organisations, potential for disclosure to existing employers, etc.).

The limited research conducted to date suggests that for most organisations, the attractions of OR, notably its cost-effectiveness, are beginning to outweigh the disadvantages (e.g. Galanki 2002, Pearce and Tuten 2001). Furthermore, most of these negative factors can be addressed by careful preparation of web-based materials, for example, by providing realistic information in the job and candidate descriptions, and by using interactive tools to encourage self-screening by potential applicants. Some have questioned the ability of online tools to facilitate interviews. However, it is likely that the spread of higher-quality video connections will encourage a greater use of on-line interviewing, particularly in the initial stages of candidate selection (i.e. replacing existing practices, such as the use of telephone interviews for candidates located a long distance from the interviewer).

OR also offers a number of advantages for the job-seeker, including rapid access to a wider range of job opportunities. The switch to electronic media may also signal an end to the tedious and time-consuming task of filling out hand-written application forms. However, candidates would also benefit from learning about the way that organisations are using OR, and to develop appropriate skills in using this channel persuasively.

Questions

1 Review the advantages and disadvantages of OR, as discussed in the case. Comment on how this technology could either enhance or limit an organisation's ability to communicate in each of the following cases:

   (a) A small or medium-sized enterprise (SME) that is not well-known, seeking to recruit someone with very rare and specialist technical skills and knowledge.

   (b) An organisation seeking to ensure that its recruitment policies provide fair and equal opportunities, irrespective of age, gender, ethnicity and (dis)ability.

2 Find examples of the following:

   (a) a corporate website with OR pages;
   (b) an OR website;
   (c) a media website with OR advertisements.

   Compare the OR facilities on each site, assessing characteristics such as the quality of information provided, whether the site is easy to navigate, visual attractiveness and degree of interactivity (e.g. online screening questions).

3 Practice completing an OR application. Compare your experiences with those of colleagues or other students.

Source: Galanki 2002, Pearce and Tuten 2001, Ward 2000. Written by the author.

11.5 The interviewee's perspective: making the best of it?

Interviews can be nerve-wracking occasions. However, from the interviewee's point of view, they are best viewed as just another channel of communication. Given practice and preparation, interviews can be handled more effectively. In this section we consider everyone's favourite nightmare, the job interview, noting how communication principles can be applied to enhance the impression made by an interviewee. There are a number of things that can be done, both in advance of the interview and on the day itself.

Practice and review

It is worthwhile attending as many interviews as possible, in order to rehearse your interview technique. Mock interviews, ideally with a video recording, are also a useful technique for reviewing your own performance and that of other 'candidates'. The review should cover both the verbal interaction and any non-verbal signals. For example, the camera may pick up nervous habits, such as hand-wringing and ear scratching. There are also many interesting 'fly on the wall' documentaries that follow applicants through the job interviews process. Though the subject specialism may be different (e.g. many documentaries concentrate on the recruitment of doctors and veterinary surgeons), the basic principles are much the same. Use each interview that you go through as an opportunity for learning. This means reviewing your performance objectively. Do not waste time complaining about the way you were treated, but focus on how well you responded to the questions that were asked. If possible, try to get some informal feedback from the interviewer.

Prepare and organise

In a job interview, you are clearly involved in a process of persuasive communication (see Chapter 5). The interviewers are going to be looking for a range of personal attributes (e.g. enthusiasm, social skills, creativity, decisiveness), plus evidence to support your application. Prepare by finding out as much as possible about the subject of the interview, in this case the company and the job itself. Ensure that you are ready to reinforce the information contained in your written application. For example, if your form mentions that you are a keen mountaineer, be ready with anecdotes from expeditions that you have organised. If you have stated a particular ambition, be prepared to explain how you intend to realise it. There are also more practical aspects to consider:

- Do you know how to get to the interview address?
- Have you left sufficient time to cover a delayed train or traffic jam?
- What clothes are going to give the right impression?
- Have the interviewers asked you to prepare a short presentation (see Chapter 10).

On the day

Always arrive in good time; you may pick up some useful information while waiting for the interview, or simply have a chance to chat to other candidates. When you enter the interview room, always remember to smile at the interviewer(s) and try, if possible, to shake hands. You should be aiming for that difficult combination of calmness and focused attention. When you are asked a question, take a few seconds to consider your answer; that pause always seems far longer to you than it does to the interviewer. Always answer honestly but concisely. At an appropriate moment, try to insert a few questions of your own. Asking questions about the role for which you are being interviewed and the organisation is essential as it shows you have genuine interest. Make sure that you have some prepared questions; it is perfectly acceptable to have them written down to use as a reference. Good questions to ask of an organisation include: 'What sort of training can I expect to undertake in my first year?'; and at later stages of the interview process, 'How will my performance be assessed?' This kind of question demonstrates your interest, but also provides you with an opportunity to assess the organisation, and how seriously it is taking your recruitment.

If there is good dialogue during the interview, you will probably find that most of your questions have been dealt with. However, a good interviewer will usually close the interview by asking if you have any more questions, so it is a good idea to have another one in reserve; this ensures that you finish the interview with the last question. All the important areas should have been covered by this point, so your question may be something more straightforward (e.g. 'Please can you tell me what the next stage in the interview process is?'). When the time comes to leave, do so with another smile and handshake. Avoid the temptation to scramble for your coat and make an undignified rush for the door.

Job interviews as two-way communication: 'taking control'

The idea of an interviewee 'taking control' of the process may sound aggressive and unlikely. However, it is important to see interviews as channels for a genuine two-way exchange of information. In this context, interviewees benefit by recognising that they are in control of their own responses. Interviewees who adopt this view often report that they feel less nervous about the process, and are therefore able to present their case more effectively on the day. Remember that interviewers are also human beings, and that most of them are not actively seeking to 'catch you out'. Taking control means trying to 'help' interviewers to feel more positive about your application. Since they are likely to be meeting a number of other candidates, it is important to give them something – or ideally, several things – that make you stand out from the crowd. With suitable practice and preparation, plus a better understanding of the interviewer's task (see the case study at the end of this chapter), the whole process of attending an interview can become more enjoyable as well as producing more successful outcomes.

11.6 Counselling techniques and the manager

Counselling techniques are now widely used in organisations, with many courses aimed at both personnel 'professionals' and those with a general interest in people. Managers are often criticised for taking insufficient interest in the problems faced by their staff, either due to time pressures or a reluctance to become involved in the private lives of their employees. While these objections are understandable, human resource specialists are keen to promote 'workplace counselling' as a positive development, benefiting both the individual concerned, the manager and the wider organisation.

Person-centred counselling: the interviewer as facilitator

In what is known as a 'person-centred' counselling interview, the role of the counsellor is simply to listen and to 'facilitate'. Above all, this means that a counsellor should *not* give advice (i.e. telling the interviewee how to solve the problem). Instead, the primary objective of counselling is to provide a climate in which the person is able to resolve problems for themselves. However, there are some important obstacles to successful counselling at work. Employees are understandably unwilling to share personal problems with line managers, whilst managers often find emotions difficult to handle, and (as professional 'problem-solvers') are unable to avoid giving advice. Hence, for many practical reasons, the following areas need to be distinguished:

● advice and instruction,

● befriending,

● workplace counselling,

● professional counselling.

During a counselling interview, the counsellor may make use of a range of 'active listening' techniques, of the kind outlined in this chapter. These have been summarised within the counselling field as displaying 'empathy', 'acceptance' and 'congruence' (Rogers and Farson 1976). In other words, the counsellor seeks to understand the problem from the other person's perspective (i.e. 'empathy'); they also avoid making judgements about the person's past actions or intentions (i.e. 'acceptance'); and they aim to show genuine concern for the person's interests, above those of the organisation for example (i.e. 'congruence'). Each of these actions implies particular styles of questioning and other aspects of communication that we have addressed. However, these may not always be present in a manager's repertoire of skills; they may also conflict with the political, economic and cultural climate of the parent organisation.

Counselling and the limits of work-related communication

Counselling is clearly different from giving advice or instructing employees. In practice, it is extremely difficult to switch between these roles, so managers may find their counselling sessions reverting to one of the other standard forms of interaction with employees. Counselling is also a different role to that played by a close friend who takes time to share personal problems, acting as a 'shoulder to cry on'. Perhaps the key distinction for the organisational manager is between workplace and professional counselling. It is essential for all concerned to recognise the dividing line between work-related personal issues, where the manager or human resources department has the relevant skills and experience to handle things, and those more serious problems (e.g. drug and alcohol abuse, clinical depression), which require urgent and professional support. Managers need to recognise the limits of work-related communication, referring cases of this kind to outside agencies.

Summary

- Interviews are a popular two-way communication channel that can help to create shared meanings, but their rich messages are open to misinterpretation. Interviewers can draw on their own prior experience as interviewees.

- Interviews are used within an organisation for a variety of purposes, including: employee recruitment, promotion, appraisal, coaching and mentoring. They are also used to deal with disciplinary problems and grievances.

- Listening is a skill that can be improved with practice. It is important for interviewers to focus attention on what is being said, avoid prejudice, signal interest and encouragement, be aware of feelings and emotion, clarify issues where necessary and summarise discussions.

- It is essential to recognise the differences between open, closed, probing, leading and hypothetical questions, and to make appropriate use of them during interviews. Interviewers should also be aware that interactions and responses are altered by the way they frame and express their questions.

- Interviewees can reduce the inevitable tensions associated with interviews by practising with this channel, and by exploiting its two-way features. This involves taking time to consider and respond to the perceived needs of the interviewer.

- Workplace counselling can be a helpful activity, using many of the listening techniques discussed in this chapter. However, it requires specialist skills and its use in an organisational setting demands careful consideration.

Practical exercises

1 The recorded interview

With the help of a video camera, tripod and recorder, you can practise the roles of interviewer and interviewee. Try to make the setting as realistic as possible by setting up desks and chairs, and by wearing appropriate clothes. Select one of the following scenarios, inventing any incidental details:

- a job interview,
- a promotion interview,
- an appraisal interview,
- a disciplinary interview,
- a research interview,
- a media interview.

Allow five minutes for the interview, play it back and discuss the outcomes with colleagues. Try to identify specific strengths and weaknesses. The interview grid provided in Table 11.2 can be used to record what occurred during the interview.

2 Where does it hurt?

The interviewer takes the role of a placement student or volunteer visitor in a hospital. The interviewee is a patient being visited, and takes one of the following roles, or others developed by the group:

- You have suffered a mild stroke.
- You have just had a baby prematurely.
- You are undergoing tests, having had repeated stomach pains.
- You have suffered concussion in an accident and have lost your memory.

The objective is for the interviewer to discover as much as possible about the patient's condition, without upsetting or annoying the 'patient'. Of course, the interviewee should try to be as reticent and unhelpful as possible, providing ambiguous answers or straying from the question. Observers should pay particular attention to the interviewer's use of open, closed, probing, hypothetical and leading questions.

Case study K

'A day in the life of a headhunter': selection interviews

This case study is based on a 'real-life' assignment conducted by an executive recruitment consultancy (i.e. a 'headhunter') on behalf of an international client. Some of the incidental details have been changed to protect identities.

Setting the scene
My client is the Dutch subsidiary of, 'Leisure Shops Europe' a British company looking to recruit an Area Operations Manager. The role is based in the Netherlands and covers a wide geographical area, containing 25 retail outlets and leisure clubs, across

Northern Europe. The company is going through a major cultural change as it seeks to enhance the profitability of its retail and leisure portfolio. Consequently, it is in the process of bringing in experienced professionals across all functions. The initial recruitment, at board level, has recently been completed. Apart from the essential requirement of operations management experience in retail/leisure sectors, the candidates will need to show excellent people management skills and an ability to be flexible while the organisation goes through inevitable pains of change. Today I have three candidates for face-to-face interviews. The fourth candidate is currently living abroad, so I will also be conducting a telephone interview this afternoon. We have used a combination of advertising – placed on a recruitment website – and executive search techniques to identify these candidates. I have already reviewed their CVs, which were either sent electronically or by post. Each candidate has been sent a detailed brief about the organisation and the role in advance of the interview. They have also received an ideal candidate profile, reproduced below.

Extract from the ideal candidate profile

Leisure Shops Europe

Area Operations Manager, Netherlands

The successful candidate will have a minimum of five years multi-site experience of operations management in retail and/or leisure organisations, ideally both. In addition to strong leadership and people management skills, they will be effective in motivating local managers to achieve high standards of customer service. Their personal maturity will enable them to be completely comfortable with the changing nature of the business, drawing on their own previous experience to implement change. They will also be conversant with computerised management information and budget planning/monitoring systems. Food experience (i.e. awareness of food hygiene, health and safety standards and regulations) is not essential, but would be preferred. While there is no requirement to speak Dutch, some language ability would be an advantage. A wide range of development opportunities are available including free language courses and on-job coaching from language specialists.

One of the key challenges of this assignment is to find people who are prepared to relocate. There is an attractive benefits package and the company will pay for housing and schooling but I wonder whether the location will put off good candidates. There is no requirement to speak Dutch, but it will help if they have some knowledge or, at least, are prepared to learn.

The interviews begin
Candidate 1: David

David replied to the advert that we placed on the website. He has a background in retail operations together with some food service/catering experience.

▶

David arrives on time at 9.30am. He is smartly dressed, well groomed and is carrying a fairly new leather briefcase. He has a firm handshake and looks me directly in the eyes. He responds to my questions about his work experience by giving clear examples of situations he has faced and how he has dealt with them. He gives enough detail but appears to be careful not to go on talking, preferring to wait for another question. One of our associates used to work with David's boss and we have been told that a potential area of weakness is in his people management, so I intend to probe this deeply.

He responds well to questions about his management style, dealing with poor performers and redundancy situations and I am reasonably assured that there is no big hole in this area. Our dialogue is easy and relaxed and he tells me that he is very excited about this job opportunity. He asks me questions about something he has seen on the company's website and about the new strategy which he has read about in an article in a trade magazine. Finally he asks about the next stage of the interview process and I tell him that I have several other candidates to see and will get back to him at the end of next week. The interview has taken one hour and 20 minutes.

Candidate 2: Maeve

Maeve was identified through our executive search process. She has a strong leisure background and has held managerial roles in several international companies.

It is now 11.35am. Maeve arrives a few minutes late and is rather flustered having got caught up in bad traffic. She is smartly dressed and is carrying a *BlackBerry* organiser, which she places in front of her on the interview desk. She speaks clearly and enthusiastically about her background and previous roles and enjoys telling me in great detail about the development project she is currently working on – how she identified the opportunity, hand picked the team of people she wanted to work with, developed good team spirit and set out innovative ways to set individual targets and incentives for each member.

She appears slightly concerned about the issue of moving her family to Holland, but is keen to stress that her partner, who is German, is very excited about the prospect. She asks a lot of questions about the location and, at the end of the interview, says she is very interested in being put forward to meet the client. I close the interview at 12.45pm. Maeve sends me an e-mail the next day to thank me for seeing her and to confirm an interest in the role.

Candidate 3: Thor

Thor appears to be the perfect candidate on paper. He has both retail and leisure experience gained in large, well-respected organisations. He is German and speaks five European languages including Dutch. He is married to an English woman who also speaks Dutch, is available for immediate work and happy to relocate.

Thor arrives on the dot of 2.30pm, our appointed hour. He is dressed in a three-piece heavy wool suit and shirt with a stiff starched collar. He is very well groomed and his hair is immaculate. He has a strong (*very strong!*) handshake and asks for a cup of English tea (black). In asking him to tell me about the jobs he has held and why he moved from the leisure sector into retail, he responds in very short sentences preferring not to expand on any aspect unless I specifically ask him to. When I ask what has been his favourite job and why, he says he has liked all of them. His CV says that he left his last job two months ago. When I ask why (he has already told me he has a wife and four children under the age of five), he says, 'The role was not fulfilling and I needed the space to consider other options.' He also tells me this is his 'perfect job'. However, what he omits to tell me – and I find out later from the human resources manager – is that he has already applied for a different role with my client's organisation and has been rejected due to poor perceived cultural fit. We shake hands at 3.35pm. I take a short coffee break and check my e-mails.

Candidate 4: Sasha

Sasha replied to the advert we placed on the website. She has a managerial background in retail operations and specifically food service experience.

My telephone interview with Sasha lasts about one hour and ten minutes. She tells me about her background, highlighting why she has made certain career decisions in the past. She is very keen to point out that she enjoys working outside the UK and is looking to find another such position. She says that her current role in Istanbul is coming to an end because the division she heads up is merging with another and the entire management team is being made redundant. Sasha also tells me she is very happy to fly to the Netherlands for an interview at her own expense. She does not appear particularly concerned about the benefits package, which I mention briefly towards the end of the conversation. It is now just after 5pm, time to write up my interview notes and prepare a report for the client, proposing a shortlist of candidates.

Questions

1 What do you think is the headhunter's impression of each candidate?

2 Identify which candidates more accurately match the job specification and suggest who should be put forward on the shortlist to the client.

3 How well do you think each candidate has prepared for the interview? Refer to the chapter and support your assessment with examples from the case.

4 Select one of the candidates and, based on what you know about the headhunter's requirements, prepare guidance notes covering the following points:

   (a) Preparing for the headhunting interview.

   (b) Conduct during the interview.

   (c) Any follow-up actions after the interview.

Source: Written by Linda J Clark.

Further reading

Burley-Allen (1995) is one of the few straightforward guides to enhancing your listening skills. Most of the leading human resource management texts, including **Torrington *et al.*** (2002), deal with the operational aspects of recruitment, appraisal, mentoring, disciplinary and grievance interviews. **Healey and Rawlinson** (1994) is a recommended contribution on the use of interviews in organisational research. **Galanki** (2002) reports an exploratory study into online recruiting in the IT industry. **Caroll** (1996) is a clear and helpful text on workplace counselling interviews. In addition, Chapter 6 includes several references to the concept of 'emotional intelligence' (EQ), which can be usefully applied to interviewing behaviour.

References

ACAS (2003) *Producing disciplinary and grievance procedures: self-help guide*. Advisory, Conciliation and Arbitration Service, London. (Available at www.acas.org.uk/employment topics (accessed 18th August).)

Burley-Allen, M. (1995) *Listening: the forgotten skill – a self-teaching guide* (2nd edn.). Wiley, London.

Caroll, M. (1996) *Workplace counselling: a systematic approach to employee care*. Sage, London.

Galanki, E. (2002) 'The decision to recruit online: a descriptive study'. *Career Development International*, 7, 4, 243–51.

Hall, E.T. and Hall, M.R. (1990) *Understanding cultural differences*. Intercultural Press, Yarmouth ME.

Healey, M.J. and Rawlinson, M.B. (1994) 'Interviewing techniques in business and management research' in Wass, V.J. and Wells, P.E. (eds.) *op cit.* (123–46).

Hook, C., Rollinson, D., Foot, M. and Handley, J. (1996) 'Supervisor and manager styles in handling discipline and grievance: part one – comparing styles in handling discipline and grievance'. *Personnel Review*, 25, 3, 20–34.

Pearce, C.G. and Tuten, T.L. (2001) 'Internet recruiting in the banking industry'. *Business Communication Quarterly*, 64, 1, 9–18.

Rogers, C.R. and Farson, R.E. (1976) *Active listening*. Industrial Relations Center, University of Chicago, Chicago IL.

Rollinson, D., Hook, C., Foot, M. and Handley, J. (1996) 'Supervisor and manager styles in handling discipline and grievance: part two – approaches to handling discipline and grievance'. *Personnel Review*, 25, 4, 38–55.

Saunders, M.N.K., Lewis, P. and Thornhill, A. (2003) *Research methods for business students* (3rd edn.). FT Prentice Hall, Harlow.

Torrington, D., Hall, L. and Taylor, S. (2002) *Human resources management* (5th edn.). FT Prentice Hall, Harlow.

Ward, A. (2000) 'Online job sites challenge dominance of traditional media'. *Financial Times*, London edition, 25 (15th March).

Wass, V.J. and Wells, P.E. (eds.) (1994) *Principles and practice in business and management research*. Aldershot, Dartmouth.

CHAPTER 12

Presentations and audio-visual technologies

Your brain starts working from the moment you are born and never stops until you stand up to speak in public.
Sir George Jessel, politician and public speaker

Learning outcomes

By the end of this chapter you should be able to:

- identify the distinctive characteristics and requirements of verbal presentations in various organisational settings;
- prepare yourself and your materials in advance of delivering a verbal presentation;
- develop effective techniques for memorising and recalling the content of verbal presentations;
- assess the advantages and disadvantages of audio-visual technologies and associated communication practices;
- deal with the practical challenges relating to the delivery of verbal presentations, including timing, questions, disruptions and facilitating interaction with audiences;
- consider the additional communication issues raised by presentations delivered in culturally-diverse contexts, such as international conferences.

12.1 Introduction

People find themselves on the receiving end of all kinds of presentations. For example, you may have listened to various academic lectures, political speeches and team briefings. They are also widely used by organisational managers and senior executives to brief various stakeholder groups including employees, financial analysts and journalists. In larger international organisations, presentations are often relayed electronically, either as video recordings or as 'live' webcasts, in order to reach staff located around the world (Jones 2003, Turban 2003). Students also find themselves giving presentations as part of coursework exercises; they are also an increasingly common element in organisational recruitment programmes, running alongside more conventional selection techniques, such as interviews (see Chapter 11). However, despite its popularity, the presentation remains a very troublesome communication channel. Everyone has experience of sitting through badly-delivered presentations, while the prospect of actually *delivering* a presentation can often cause an otherwise self-confident person to collapse into a major panic. The dread of addressing an audience is also common amongst experienced managers, and is itself one of the primary causes of poor communication. Nervous presenters commonly resort to reading out pre-prepared scripts, and their audiences are forced to endure a dry and monotonous performance that communicates very little.

This chapter aims to help you improve your own public speaking and presentation skills, and those of others in your organisation. It includes advice on preparing yourself and your materials in advance, using audio-visual equipment and handling an audience successfully. The end-of-chapter case study deals with the additional challenges of presenting to international and culturally-diverse audiences. However, first we begin by considering the distinctive characteristics of this communication channel.

12.2 What makes presentations different?

In the past, the fundamental feature of this communication channel was physical presence; the sender and the receivers were together, in one room. With the expansion of electronically-mediated presentations, this does not necessarily apply to all those participating in the presentation. However, in many cases, these also include a 'live' audience in the room where the presentation is being filmed. When confronted with a sea of faces, whose expressions are generally difficult to interpret, presenters may feel vulnerable and exposed, but giving a presentation can be seen as placing the presenter in a position of considerable power. There are few forms of communication where an audience is so entirely 'captive'. For example, in contrast to people *reading* a report in their office or at home, those on the receiving end of a presentation have virtually no control over the process. More specifically, they cannot easily:

- stop or 'pause' the communication flow;
- return to or reread an earlier part of the message;
- scan through and skip ahead to the end.

Because they are members of an audience, rather than solitary individuals reading a piece of written text, the receiver's power to do these things is constrained by the disruption that it would cause for everyone else listening to the presentation. Consequently, most people, other than a few strong-minded individuals, experience group pressure to allow the presentation to continue. If they want to review or clarify parts of the message, this has to wait until the end of a talk. While this may seem to put the presenter at an advantage, the resulting lack of understanding, and related frustration, can become major barriers to communication. In short, it is not sufficient for presenters to rely on the fact that their audience is captive. Presenters also need to ensure that people are both willing and able to absorb their messages, and in many cases, to use the channel interactively:

- **Willing to receive?** This is a useful point to review the material on persuasive communication (see Chapter 5). Consider the best ways of securing the attention of your audience and holding their interest through the presentation. Though presenters often want to avoid too many questions, particularly during the presentation itself, questions can be a useful way of maintaining interest and involvement.

- **Able to receive?** Since audiences have little or no control over the information flow, it is important to allow pauses between your main points, avoiding information over-load (see section 2.2). It is also important to provide appropriate signposting, equivalent to the headings, sub-headings and contents page of a written report. Presenters can outline the overall framework at the beginning, include frequent reviews as they proceed, and summarise their key arguments at the end.

- **Achieving interaction?** There are a number of ways to stimulate two-way communication in a presentation. For example: the presenter can pose questions or ask for the audience to express its opinion through an informal vote (or 'show of hands'); or the presentation itself can be organised in a way that allows for a period of informal discussion. (In some academic conferences, this process is formalised by appointing a 'discussant', who comments on the preceding presentations, and may attempt to draw out some common themes).

The remaining sections of the chapter consider the practicalities of preparing and delivering a presentation. We begin with the task of preparing the necessary materials to convey the written and spoken messages that will be delivered in the presentation room.

12.3 Preparing the presentation materials

Though it makes use of different media, the supporting materials for a presentation share many of the features of a written report, and both communication channels serve similar purposes (e.g. providing briefings, reporting results, making proposals). As a result, the overall process of preparation is much the same, whether you are communicating through a written report or combining written and spoken words in an oral presentation. For this reason, the following points are essentially a brief summary of the discussion in sections 9.3 to 9.6, which details the main stages in researching and organising source material, and converting it into a suitable format for delivery. The presenter's key tasks can be summarised as follows:

- Answer key questions (audience, objective, context, source).
- Clarify terms of reference/project brief.
- Decide what to include and what to cut out.
- Decide how to organise the material.
- Make the logical structure visible.

If the presentation is to be accompanied by a written report, it is important to ensure that the written version *complements* what is being presented in the oral presentation, rather than simply repeating it. The presenter needs to decide (or confirm) in advance whether the written report is to be circulated before or after the presentation, as this is likely to influence the content and structure of both elements. For example, if the audience has already had a chance to read the written report, the presentation provides an opportunity for discussion and focusing on specific issues of interest. However, if the written report is distributed afterwards, the presentation may work best as a 'broad brush' introduction to the topic, with the written version providing supporting detail. Incidentally, distributing the full written report at the start of an oral presentation is usually fatal; the audience will invariably become distracted, reading the report rather than listening to the speaker.

Sound preparation of the material is, of course, essential to the success of your presentation. However, presenters should put just as much effort into preparing themselves for the occasion. This is especially true if they are relatively inexperienced in this communication channel. Few of us are 'natural' presenters. Fortunately, as the next section discusses, there are some useful 'tricks of the trade' that can help to make the exercise more enjoyable, for presenters and audiences alike.

12.4 The presenter: posture, appearance, voice and memory

Many people, who are happy to spend hours working with a computer software package to perfect their presentation slides and graphics, fail to invest more than five minutes on the most important communication tool of all – themselves. Presenters are rather like athletes, needing a well-organised training schedule to reach competition standard. In this section we work on four of the most common areas where there is a need for improvement: the way people stand in front of an audience; their physical appearance; the way that they speak; and how they manage to remember what to say.

Exploiting non-verbal cues: improving posture

Presenters are sending out messages from the moment the audience first catches sight of them. These initial messages are based on your non-verbal signals (see section 4.7). Many speakers adopt a head down, round-shouldered stance when addressing an audience. This has two powerful and wholly negative effects. First, the voice is projected into the floor, which makes it inaudible, particularly in a larger room or where the presentation is being relayed electronically. Second, presenters adopting this posture are bound to have minimal eye contact with their audiences. Both the posture and the lack of eye contact are often regarded as defensive responses, resulting from nervousness or lack of confidence in the material being presented. Other defensive gestures include:

- leaning on one foot;
- trying to blend in with the background, by standing at the side, or behind items of furniture; and
- folding the arms tightly across the chest, a gesture that symbolically protects the person's 'soft underbelly' from attack.

The audience may perceive these gestures in various ways. For example, they may be interpreted as suggesting that presenters are ill-prepared, hostile or simply uninterested in the topic or the audience. To communicate clear, confident and positive messages, it is essential that presenters use non-verbal cues in ways that reinforce, rather than undermine, their personal credibility. For example (see Figure 12.1), the appropriate posture is likely to be:

- upright and well balanced.
- stable, but not static, allowing for some movement around the room.
- moderately relaxed, but conveying energy rather than apathy.

Figure 12.1 **Giving a presentation**

Achieving this kind of balance and flexibility requires considerable practice, in a number of different situations. It may also be necessary to consider the cross-cultural aspects of these non-verbal cues (see the case study at the end of this chapter). Practical exercises, and careful reflection on the outcome, can be undertaken in seminars, with colleagues, and as part of a 'real world' situation (see the Practical exercises at the end of this chapter). Presenting is much like any sport or performing art, with gradual improvements, some stunning successes and the occasional unexplained disaster. Skills can only be developed and refined after repeated cycles of experience and reflection. However, over time, most 'reflective' presenters begin to feel more confident, positive and alert.

Physical appearance: clothing as a non-verbal signal

A presenter's choice of clothing can help to project the right image, as well as increasing self-confidence. However, there are no fixed rules regarding physical appearance. In the past, some organisations had notoriously strict dress codes, but today there is much greater diversity. As in all areas of communication, presenters may want to consider what messages their clothes are going to communicate to a particular audience. For example, the same expensively tailored suit could impress a group of overseas investors, make little impression on other executives, but completely alienate a group of employees who are being briefed on a major programme of cost-cutting and rationalisation. Clothing is relatively easy to change, so this non-verbal cue is at least worthwhile considering. However, having weighed up the arguments, presenters may simply decide to dress in the way that they feel most comfortable.

Developing the human voice

Though our voices are in regular use every day, they are not always ready for the tougher demands of an extended business presentation. In contrast to informal one-to-one conversations, the presenter has to speak:

- for an extended period;
- in a fairly structured way;
- to many different people simultaneously.

Human voices are rarely *inherently* weak, but in many cases they are seriously under-used in day-to-day activities. Speakers who attempt to address a large audience without practising their vocal delivery are in danger of mistreating their vocal system. If we made a comparison between this system and a sports car, they would be attempting to break the speed limit, without realising that it is necessary to get out of first gear. As Mini-case 12.1 suggests, in order to make more effective use of the human voice, we need a basic understanding of how it functions.

**Mini-case
12.1**

Vocal mechanics: a practical introduction

The human vocal system involves a complex set of interactions, between the brain, which co-ordinates the activity, and various parts of the body, as illustrated below. The lungs are the real powerhouse, responsible for generating the human voice. When people breathe in, they are drawing fresh air into their lungs by tightening the diaphragm, normally an entirely unconscious action. Breathing out is a reversal of this process; the muscles relax and air flows out through the narrow trachea (or 'wind pipe'). The voice is created when air passes up the trachea and over the vocal chords, causing them to vibrate. These vibrations are amplified in the hollow areas of the mouth, the pharynx and the sinuses. They are formed into different words, and paralinguistic sound, as a result of intricate movements made by the jaw, lips, tongue and teeth.

All of this activity is normally undertaken with little conscious attention being paid by the person speaking. Most voices can be improved, for public speaking purposes, by a combination of deeper breathing and a more active use of the mouth. Taking deep breaths ensures a better airflow, which converts into improved tone and greater projection (i.e. the voice 'carries' over a longer distance, so that it can be heard by everyone attending the presentation). Clear and well-projected voices are particularly important if the acoustics are poor, or if members of the audience are unfamiliar with your language (see the case study at the end of this chapter). Voice and singing coaches encourage students to breathe from their stomachs, an action that is much easier when the person is standing upright, with a relatively straight back. Opening and closing the mouth more deliberately helps to ensure that individual words are spoken clearly, as can a greater movement of the tongue. Again, this can be practised, ideally with the assistance of a coach. The primary objective of vocal exercises of this kind is not to alter normal speaking voices, or to remove local accents, but simply to upgrade the voice for the greater demands of public speaking.

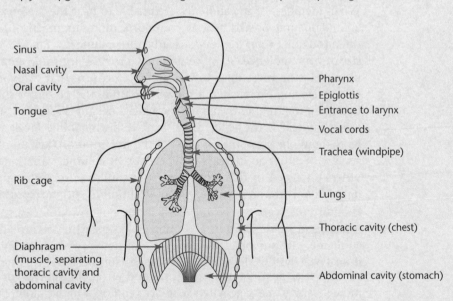

Questions

1 Do the physical aspects of vocalising really make such a difference? Read the following sentence out in your normal voice:

'Speech is an extremely complex cognitive and mechanical process, which appears to be unique to the human species.'

Now repeat the sentence three times, making the following changes:

(a) Do not allow your lips to touch.

(b) Do not move your tongue.

(c) Pinch your nostrils shut.

2 Comment on how these extreme cases might relate to some of the more common weaknesses found in what you would regard as ineffective public speaking voices.

3 It seems likely that vocal delivery styles are shaped by a number of different socio-cultural factors. Try to identify five likely influences on the employees of an international organisation. Would it be appropriate to encourage all employees to develop their voices in the ways outlined in this case?

Having considered how the voice is generated, and how the basic delivery can be improved through physical exercises, presenters can begin to make tangible improvements in their public speaking. The next stage involves working on four main dimensions of vocal delivery – setting the volume, varying the pitch, pacing the delivery and exploiting the pauses.

Setting the volume

When members of the audience are unable to hear the presenter's words, there is a fundamental breakdown of communication. In practice, speakers are more often too quiet than too loud. Clearly, the volume level has to suit the venue and size of your audience. Some venues may provide electronic amplification, but it is ultimately the presenter's responsibility to ensure that everyone is able to hear clearly. Having established a suitable volume, the presenter should try to maintain it; all too frequently, an inexperienced person is asked to 'speak up', but after a few sentences, the voice drops back to an inaudible level. While the volume level should be constant for most of the presentation, key points may be emphasised with either an increase or a decrease in volume. Variations of this kind, and others discussed in this section, serve a similar purpose to upper case letters or italics in a written report; they draw attention to specific words or phrases.

Varying the pitch

A speaker's natural voice may be a shrill *soprano* or deep *bass*, but it is still possible to use variations in tonal range to good effect. In general, presenters convey a more 'positive' message when sentences end on a higher note. Doing the opposite sounds tends to colour the message with a down-beat and depressing quality. Experience suggests that people find it very difficult to judge the way that they use pitch. In addition, some people have a lively and varied pitch in everyday conversation, but revert to either a constant high-pitch, or monotonous drone when they are speaking in public. Consequently, it is essential to obtain the advice of a colleague or friend, who has observed them during several presentations. Variable pitch makes for a much more engaging, and therefore persuasive, presentation. Pitch can also be used, in conjunction with the other variables discussed in this section, to underline particular points. For those with extremely 'monotonous' delivery (i.e. with no perceptible variation in pitch) the answer is to make a special effort, with practical exercises, in order to achieve a greater variety.

Pacing the delivery

Everyone knows that the major fault of nervous and excited presenters is speaking too quickly. However, despite this high level of awareness, many presenters continue to make this mistake. Painfully slow delivery is an equally serious obstacle to good communication, especially when it is accompanied by a monotonous vocal style. To keep an audience interested, the best option is to vary the pace of delivery, avoiding either of these extremes. Almost all presenters, including the author, have made the mistake of including *too much material* in their presentations, and have then compounded the error by attempting to cover all of this material, even though there is clearly insufficient time. The best way to avoid this mistake is to plan ahead, ensuring that the content of the presentation is tailored to the time available. If it turns out that there is still too much to cover (e.g. if the start of the presentation has been delayed by a technical failure, or previous speakers have over-run their allotted times), it is always better to edit out some of the material. Unfortunately, most speakers are insufficiently flexible, and attempt to cover everything at a rapid pace, so losing their audience's attention. Having established a reasonable pace, it is also worth introducing a little variety in order to maintain interest and to highlight key points. Switching from longer to shorter sentences is one simple technique that can help to vary the pace of delivery.

Exploiting the pauses

The so-called 'dramatic' pause can work equally well in the theatre, comedy venue or conference room. Depending on its length, this little piece of silence is the oral equivalent of a comma, semi-colon or full stop. Pauses can be used to separate different ideas and to emphasise a particular argument. Longer pauses are very valuable, yet rarely used; they allow both audience and speaker some much-needed 'thinking time', where ideas can be absorbed or questions can be pondered. It is important to remember that a single pause will seem much longer to the presenter than it does to the audience. Consequently, presenters may need to force themselves to wait, before ending the silence and moving on to the next point. Skilled speakers can exploit (or 'milk') their pauses. Typical techniques include:

- using the pause to build eye contact with the audience;
- appearing to be lost for words, but then returning with a major piece of the argument;
- adding to the dramatic effect by simply walking silently from one part of the room to another.

Each of these elements can be used to introduce more variety into the spoken message. By using them in combination, presentations can be much more powerful, holding the attention of the audience and ensuring that the content is more persuasive and memorable.

Remembering what to say

A stage actor's greatest fear is 'drying', meaning to lose track of the script and forget what to say next. Humans have a great capacity for memorising information, but our capacity to remember can be undermined by the adrenaline rush that often accompanies the start of a presentation. There are four main options for ensuring that the presenter remembers what to say:

- reading a prepared script;
- memorising a prepared script;
- improvising on the day;
- using a prompting system, with key words, cue cards or similar devices.

It is worth reviewing these options and assessing them from a communication perspective. However, only the final option can be recommended for regular use.

Reading a prepared script

Nervous speakers often make the mistake of reading from a prepared script, on the basis that it gives them added reassurance and eliminates the risk of forgetting what to say. However, with rare exceptions, this tactic results in a very ineffective mode of delivery: the presenter's head is usually directed away from the audience, so the volume is inadequate; there is very limited eye contact and minimal use of gestures to reinforce the message; and the vocal style is likely to lack pace and pitch variation. Some politicians and business leaders have perfected the *appearance* of spontaneity using prepared scripts. However, this is usually the result of extensive training. Scripted presentations can also be assisted by display technologies, in which words from an autocue are projected onto glass screens, placed either side of the podium. By glancing from one screen to the other, speakers can retain greater eye contact and give the impression of simply turning to address each side of the hall. However, this technology is not available in most organisations, and reading from a computer laptop is no substitute. With limited exceptions, such as brief introductory speeches, formal declarations and quasi-legal statements, it is best to avoid scripted presentations.

Memorising a prepared script

A few exceptionally gifted speakers can memorise the text of their presentation as though it was the script of a play. However, in an organisational context, a memorised speech can easily sound artificial. It is also a highly inflexible system, and you can be caught out when the presentation is opened up to questions.

While it may be effective for short statements and introductions, unassisted memorising is not a practical option for most people.

Improvising on the day

This is a valuable technique for informal occasions, such as making speeches at the office dinner. Some improvisation is also necessary, and occasionally very impressive, as part of a question and answer (Q&A) session, where the audience has an opportunity to respond to the presentations, and the speakers need to deal with unanticipated issues. In practice, while many contributions give the appearance of being improvised response, they are often based on a great deal of preparatory work. As part of the planning process (see section 12.8), experienced presenters will prepare outline responses to cover all of the most likely questions or counter-arguments that are likely to arise from their presentation.

Using a prompting system

The use of key (or 'trigger') words combines the reassurance provided by a script with the flexibility of an improvised presentation. As a result, it is the most practical option for most presenters. It is still important to prepare the presentation material in a fairly detailed and structured way, particularly where there is an accompanying written report. However, prompting systems work on the assumption that, having become fully immersed in the subject, the presenter can 'trigger' recall of more extensive arguments using a fairly short list of key words or phrases. These are sometimes written on a series of cue cards, usually postcard-sized, which are tied together in case they are inadvertently dropped on the floor. Alternatively, some presenters rely on the key words that they have included as 'bullet points' on the slides that accompany the presentation. Where these are displayed using an overhead projector (OHP), the presenter may simply glance at the transparencies, while slides presented via a data projector are usually displayed on a nearby PC or laptop monitor. In many cases, presenters find that they have very little need of the prompts, because the underlying messages are fresh in their minds. By contrast, if presenters spend too much time checking their prompts, the presentation begins to suffer from similar problems to those associated with reading a prepared script.

12.5 Audio-visual equipment and communication practices

Audio-visual (AV) equipment and materials should be considered as supporting technologies, they can enhance a good presentation, but they cannot cure a bad one. In addition, technical errors, break-downs and crises can often undermine an otherwise satisfactory delivery. It is clearly important to plan and prepare AV materials in advance. However, as we noted previously, this should not be at the expense of preparing the presenters themselves (see sections 12.3 and 12.4). The following headings summarise the main AV technologies in use in organisations today, including their distinctive strengths, weaknesses and peculiarities. It is therefore worth experimenting with these technologies and associated communication practices, in order to become aware of the options available, and to develop the capability to select and employ them effectively.

Projectors (data and OHP)

Traditional overhead projectors (OHPs) are still used to present prepared transparencies containing text, illustrations and photographs. It is also possible to write directly onto a roll of clear film, using a suitable pen. In many organisations, OHPs have been replaced by data projectors, which are used to display images directly from a computer system to a display screen. As technology has advanced, these projectors have become smaller, cheaper and more powerful, with much-improved visual displays. Computer-based projection has many advantages, including:

- the capacity to insert hyperlinks in the presentation text, which allows the presenter to break from the conventional, linear format of the presentation;
- the option of linking to other computer-based sources, including web pages, video clips and spreadsheets, and the related possibility of incorporating presentation materials into a video-conference or webcast;
- the sometimes under-rated luxury of being able to make last-minute changes to a presentation.

However, there are inherent dangers when presenters become over-reliant on the presentation software that is used with this technology (see Mini-case 12.2).
Limitations and user errors include the following:

- standing in front of the display screen;
- talking to the projector or laptop, instead of the audience;
- displaying slides that do not coincide with the spoken delivery;
- using too many software features or too much text; it is important to keep slides simple, ensuring that the text is large enough to be visible from the back of the meeting room, and using colour and graphics in moderation;
- not checking for spelling errors;
- technical failures; it is always advisable to have a contingency plan, spare projector bulbs and a paper copy of the presentations.

Whiteboards

These are a common teaching aid, also useful in organisational discussion and 'brainstorming' sessions, for building up spider diagrams and making rapid changes to the material presented. The presenter can make use of coloured pens to highlight issues (e.g. using alternate colours when listing points). Electronic whiteboards allow the presenter to capture written material, including the contributions of others, directly onto a computer system.
Limitations and user errors include the following:

- presenters turn their backs on the audience while writing on the board, making them difficult to hear; the solution is to practise writing from the side of the board while facing forwards;

- many presenters have illegible handwriting; this also requires practise;
- dried out pens; do not rely on those supplied, have a functioning set available;
- using indelible pens by mistake, a very common error that makes the presenter very unpopular with the next user.

Flip charts

These are a very simple, paper-based system that can be used for pre-prepared sheets or for writing 'live'. (They are useful for group work (e.g. where your audience have an active role, preparing a flip chart sheet in a small group and bringing this back to the front); sheets can also be retained and pinned up around the room for future reference. You can impress an audience by preparing flip chart diagrams, etc. beforehand in pencil, so that you can quickly 'ink them in' during the presentation.

Limitations and user errors: similar to those for the whiteboard, plus the challenge of removing paper and returning to previous flip chart pages; this is simply a matter of practice.

Video players

Short video 'clips' can be very useful to illustrate a point, and may also be presented using a computer and data projector (see above). DVD video has significant advantages over earlier tape-based formats, as it allows for rapid access to specific segments in a longer recording. Extended video playback may have a role in communicating particular messages, but it can be counterproductive if it takes time away from a 'live' presentation; the video element can generally be made available for viewing at other times.

Limitations and user errors include the following:

- technical faults due to incorrect set-up or tampering by other presenters;
- incompatible playback formats;
- inappropriate use during a 'live' presentation.

35mm slide projectors

A traditional choice for highly visual presentations (e.g. in architecture or fine arts), where image quality is a key issue; 35mm projectors now have a very limited application due to improvements in data projectors (see above).

Limitations and user errors include the following:

- inflexibility because slides are in a set order, within a 'carousel' container;
- time required to prepare slides;
- getting slides out of order, upside down or back to front; it is always worth checking them yourself;
- mistakes cannot be altered at short notice;
- projector bulb failures; make sure there is a spare.

Props and 'take aways'

The term 'props' originates in the theatre; in a presentation it refers to additional materials that are used to enhance a presentation and reinforce key messages. Props come in all shapes and sizes, ranging from food samples to scale models of building developments. In some cases, the presenter may also wish to provide the audience with materials to take away after the presentation. This could include:

- an information pack containing supporting details;
- paper or electronic copies of the presentation slides, transcript or a related report; or
- simply a 'goodies bag' of product samples.

    Limitations and user errors include the following:

- handing out material at the beginning of a presentation; the audience look at it instead of focusing on the presentation;
- inappropriate materials, including expensive brochures that the audience is not likely to read.

Mini-case 12.2 reports on a phenomenon that is sometimes termed 'death by *PowerPoint*', referring to the way that many presenters misuse this internationally-known audio-visual aid, and in doing so manage to create some of the world's most tedious and unsuccessful presentations.

Mini-case 12.2	Presentation technologies: 'death by *PowerPoint*'?

This case is based on an article that is highly critical of the world's most popular presentation software package.

A few months ago, Steve McDermott arrived at a breakfast meeting in Harrogate's Majestic Hotel to teach presentation skills to the northern region of the Institute of Directors. He opened his laptop and attempted to launch *PowerPoint*, the ubiquitous presentational software from Microsoft. After two minutes of fumbling, he looked flustered. Members of the audience shuffled uncomfortably, or coughed with embarrassment. A voice from the back called out: 'Bloody hell – I thought you would be better than this.' So he stopped what he was doing and addressed his audience. 'You've probably all experienced death by *PowerPoint*. I don't know which is worse – when it works or when it doesn't.' Then he walked out of the room, returned with a baseball bat and smashed the computer to bits. Mr McDermott, a Leeds-based consultant who styles himself 'Europe's funniest, most insightful motivational speaker', insists that his routine, though contrived – and expensive – serves a useful purpose. It teaches the audience that, contrary to popular opinion, presentations need not always be delivered through the medium of *PowerPoint*.

At a conservative estimate, *PowerPoint* can be found on 250 million computers worldwide. According to Microsoft, 30 million *PowerPoint* presentations take place every day: 1.25 million every hour. A spokesman for Office Angels, one of London's larger recruitment agencies, says *PowerPoint* ranks second only to *MS Word* among the programs with which temporary secretaries are expected to be familiar – just ahead of *Excel*. The program is not restricted to office use: *PowerPoint* has also appeared in churches, at schools and colleges and even for use at family occasions. But business presentations account for the greater part of its commercial success. This is because many executives are expected to use *PowerPoint* as a matter of course, whether they are addressing colleagues or clients. Alastair Grant, another consultant who advises on presentation skills – through his London-based company, GPB Consulting – says managers are sometimes regarded with suspicion if they do not do that: 'They're worried that people might think, "This person hasn't prepared lots of visuals. That's a mark against them."' Brendan Barns, founder of Speakers for Business, believes that many people use the program as some kind of comfort blanket. Watching them, he says, can be like watching classical actors perform Shakespeare with the script in their hands. Rather than preparing audiences for the slide they're about to show, these presenters typically use slides as prompts, reading aloud whatever appears on screen. Since this often consists of bullet points, the process renders speakers unappealingly robotic – and redundant, since members of the audience could just as well read the slides in their absence. The only time it is worth reading slides aloud, says Mr Grant, is when speakers address an audience more familiar with another language: the words on screen help viewers to follow what is being said. Otherwise, he says, 'Senior executives should never be narrators at slide shows. Can you imagine Tony Blair using *PowerPoint* at the Labour party conference? Of course not.'

To be fair, *PowerPoint* does have its uses. It is generally acknowledged – even by Mr McDermott – that speakers, no matter how eloquent, cannot compete with slides that present graphical information. A map is generally easier to grasp than spoken directions and the same applies to financial data in graphs or engineering solutions presented in technical drawings. More generally, graphical effects can be overused. Jim Carroll, London-based deputy chairman of the advertising agency Bartle Bogle Hegarty, says he has endured more than enough from 'clip-art fiends' who pepper their presentations with the 'not-very-amusing cartoons' pre-supplied by Microsoft. Another facility that is often overused combines visual with sound effects: a key word whizzes into place on a slide, halting to the sound of screeching brakes.

PowerPoint was designed so that the originators of content could forgo the services of graphic designers but to prevent excesses, says Mr Carroll, Bartle Bogle Hegarty retains a one-man unit to improve its presentations. ('My job is to tart them up,' says his colleague, Philip Kendrew). Mr McDermott, who previously worked in advertising, remembers that before *PowerPoint* became widely available it was necessary to make real slides. Each slide cost money and that helped to keep the numbers down. 'But with *PowerPoint*,' he says, 'any idiot sitting at a PC can decide, "Oh, I'll have another 50."' He is not the only one who looks back favourably on life before *PowerPoint*. The writer Ian Parker offered the following observation in The *New Yorker* magazine recently: 'Before there were presentations, there were conversations, which were a little like presentations but used fewer bullet points, and no one had to dim the lights.' Mr Parker's thesis was that *PowerPoint* produces a deadening effect on thought itself. Fancy graphics whiz past audiences at speed, in darkness that encourages people to nod off: altogether, the process encourages users to pass off badly constructed arguments and hackneyed ideas. At worst, he says, middle managers can simply add their own company's logo to ready-made presentations, which are provided as part of the software package under the rubric of 'AutoContent'. 'A rare example,' Mr Parker concluded, hardly less fierce than Mr McDermott with his baseball bat, 'of a product named in outright mockery of its target customers.'

▶

12.6 On the day itself – final preparations

This section assumes a 'worst case' scenario: you are giving the most important presentation of your life to a large audience of colleagues, senior managers and international visitors. The venue is an international hotel in a foreign country, neither of which you have visited previously. How can you maximise your chances of success and minimise the risks of a disaster? The scenario may not be typical for all presenters, but the underlying lessons would also apply more generally.

- **Checking the venue:** On arrival at the venue, you have a number of very basic practical questions to ask, including those on the following checklist: In which room is the presentation to be held? Is the room well sign-posted? Are there enough chairs for all of the expected attendees, plus a margin of error? Is there adequate lighting, ventilation, heating? Have the organisers scheduled refreshments, and at what time? If the venue is a large hotel or conference centre, there will probably be specialist staff to help with all of these issues. While liaising with these people can provide useful information and assurance, it is not sufficient. Even in the best-organised venue, you should always check the rooms in person, and at the earliest opportunity.

- **Checking audio-visual equipment and materials:** Again, experienced presenters learn that it is never a good idea to rely entirely on others, however competent and reassuring they may sound. It is good practice to request an early opportunity to check that the AV equipment is working properly, and that your own equipment can be combined with that provided by the venue. In an international setting, the most likely sources of technical problems include: incompatible hardware and software, translation errors and differences in power sockets and voltages (see section 12.5).

- **Checking your personal appearance:** All presenters should try to leave enough time for some last-minute grooming, especially if they have spent the previous hour carrying computers and audio-visual equipment between buildings. The key is to find a suitable mirror and assess whether you are still looking reasonably tidy and relaxed (see section 12.4).

- **Making a good entrance:** This is likely to be the time when you are most nervous, yet your audience's 'first impressions' are likely to have a strong influence on their perceptions of the presentation. Some presenters recommend that you breathe deeply for a short period before taking up position. This simple technique can be remarkably calming and can also help to improve your vocal delivery (see section 12.4). It is tempting to rush into the opening sentence, but experienced speakers take their time to look slowly and calmly around the audience. This helps to establish eye contact with the audience, a positive signal that can be reinforced by taking up a confident stance and giving other non-verbal cues, including a smile. This initial activity may appear superficial, but it does help to create a perception of the presenter as a credible and potentially interesting source of information. It also allows the audience to settle down, and to adjust themselves to the person who is now 'centre stage'. If you are being introduced, the presenter needs to thank the person concerned, focus on the audience and begin your presentation.

The final section of this chapter reviews the four key elements of the presentation:

- creating an 'opener';
- signalling 'transitions' and changing pace;
- closing the presentation;
- dealing with questions, interruptions and dialogue.

However, before moving into the delivery phase, Mini-case 12.3 considers the most common and problematic issue facing presenters on the day itself, dealing with stage-fright.

Mini-case 12.3	**Beating stage fright: 'fight or flight' syndrome**

Why do many people get in such a bad state before a presentation, and during other forms of public speaking (e.g. at a wedding reception)? The explanation can be traced to human physiology; greater awareness of the underlying cause can also help people to isolate and deal with the immediate symptoms. These physical and psychological experiences occur because the body is trying to prepare itself to deal with an imminent crisis. Much of this is driven by the body's release of adrenaline, though cognitive factors also play a part in this process (Schachter and Singer 1962, Parkinson 1987). The experience of 'stage fright', also referred to as 'fight or flight syndrome', occurs when a 'closed circuit' is set up within one branch of the automomic nervous system (Gross 1996: 99–102). Fight or flight syndrome is an essential survival aid that we have inherited from our mammalian ancestors. However, this mechanism is of very limited value in the average presentation room. Its adrenaline-induced symptoms include:

- increased heart rate and higher blood pressure;
- heightened awareness, as the body gives priority to the sensory organs (e.g. dilation of the pupils, to aid vision);

▶

- dryness in the mouth, as the secretion of saliva is suppressed;
- excessive sweating and temporary memory loss, which may be a side-effect of these adaptations.

Perhaps the most inconvenient response is an urgent need to urinate, as the bladder muscles relax; this may also be explained as part of the body's preparation for dealing with the physical demands of defending itself against an attacker, or escaping to a safer location. With practice it is possible to overcome 'fight or flight syndrome', or at least to exert some control over symptoms. Presenters can minimise the fears that help to generate this response by ensuring that presentations are well-rehearsed and that they are familiar with any audio-visual equipment and materials. On the day, a combination of controlled slow breathing and positive thinking can be surprisingly effective.

It is advisable to avoid stimulants like coffee, for obvious reasons, and also to keep away from the bar. Alcohol is a depressant, reducing activity in the central nervous system. In small quantities it may help to relieve anxiety, but drinking also slows the reactions, impairing a person's overall performance. A better option is for presenters to find a quiet corner and spend a few minutes visualising themselves giving an excellent presentation; many professional performers have noted that establishing a positive mind-set can encourage the right kind of physiological response. There are also various training courses in which participants engage in a structured series of exercises, such as reciting poems, to overcome their fear of public speaking (Grenby 2003).

Questions

1 What is your experience of the 'fight or flight' response? Have you found it to be a problem in giving presentations, or in other forms of public speaking?

2 How useful do you think it is for people to be aware of the physiological causes? Can they really be overcome by using the suggestions given in the case?

3 Can you identify any other contributory factors that might explain why some people experience stage fright to a greater extent than others? (Note: It may be interesting to compare your responses to these questions with those of colleagues or friends.)

Source: Schachter and Singer (1962), Parkinson (1987), Gross (1996), Grenby (2003). Case prepared by the author.

12.7 The presentation: four key elements

This section focuses on the delivery of the presentation, though the issues raised here also need to be considered at the planning stage. It suggests that presenters need to pay particular attention to four key elements. Three of these follow the structure of the presentation, from the opening words, to the way that transitions are made between each topic area, and finally to the best technique for drawing the presentation to a close. The fourth element concerns the way that presenters deal with questions, both during and after the presentation. The end-of-chapter case study deals with some additional issues, relating specifically to presentations conducted in an international and culturally diverse setting.

Creating an 'opener'

How do you secure the audience's attention? As with all communication channels, the answer can be found by thinking from the receiver's perspective. In this case, the audience will want to be assured about two aspects of your presentation. First, that your message is *relevant* to them. Second, that you have the necessary *credibility* to deliver it. If either of these aspects is missing, the task of communication will be much harder. Imagine, for example, that your organisation is struggling to meet a 'sustainability' target, set as a result of discussions with external stakeholders. Your task is to talk to a group of office managers about reducing waste paper disposals across the organisation. They are all very busy people, the waste target appears marginal to their main work responsibilities, and they have only attended the meeting reluctantly. What kind of opening statements (or 'openers') might you use in order to get this audience on your side? In reviewing possible solutions, it is important to remain flexible and sensitive to the local context. Many popular guides to delivering a 'winning' presentation claim to have identified the ideal 'recipe' for this kind of communication challenge. In practice, it is always a matter of professional judgement, on the part of the presenter, drawing on the general principles developed in previous chapters.

The following examples illustrate some of the options available to the presenter in our scenario.

- **Pose a question that has relevance for the audience:** 'Let me begin by asking you all a question: how much do you think our organisation spends on waste paper, in one year?'

- **Create a powerful scenario, using visual imagery:** 'Imagine a warehouse about the size of a football pitch, and ten metres high. In six months, we will fill that warehouse with scrap paper'.

- **Quote a statistic that is likely to surprise the audience:** 'Last year, our organisation was spending in excess of €300 per employee on waste paper alone. This year we intend to halve that figure.'

- **Share an informal anecdote or narrative to surprise or entertain:** 'I was chatting to a manager from our Nairobi office last week. They have similar problems to us, trying to meet the sustainability targets. Eventually, we got around to this waste paper issue. "Yes" she said, "we were in a similar position, but now we've got the solution." "So tell me, what's your secret?" I enquired. "Well", she replied, "after considering a number of options ... we bought bigger recycling bins!"'

- **Refer to a relevant and memorable quotation:** 'You probably remember that saying of our founder, Matt Schaebitz, "Saving a few cents in the organisation is better for business than taking the same money from our customers' pockets." So, making more money out of waste inside the organisation, and keeping our external prices competitive, that is exactly what we're here to discuss today.'

Presenters normally follow this their opening statement with a brief explanation of who they are, if this is unclear to the audience, and what they are going to cover during the presentation. While this may seem like background information, it also has an important persuasive role, emphasising what members of the audience will gain by listening (see section 5.2). To recap an earlier point, there must be a perceived benefit for them and, in addition, the presenter must be perceived as having the relevant skills or knowledge to help them secure that benefit. For example, in continuing the waste reduction talk, the presenter might say:

> 'For the last three years, I have been working with each of the organisation's national subsidiaries to introduce our new environmental strategy. Of course there have been some teething problems, but we are now seeing a measurable reduction in waste. This morning I am going to discuss five simple and practical ways that you can reduce your office stationery costs, without affecting staff performance.'

The purpose of this statement, in addition to setting out the structure of the presentation, is to secure the audience's attention. The presenter has calculated that the prospect of relatively painless cost savings should be sufficiently attractive to keep the office managers listening for the next few minutes.

Signalling 'transitions' and changing pace

Presenters can easily lose their audience's attention by moving too quickly from one topic to another. It is essential to remember the inherent limitations of this communication channel and take time to emphasise transitions between each of the main points that you cover (see section 12.2). One of the most useful ways to guide an audience is to give a brief recap of the last topic. Having completed the recap, the presenter pauses for a few seconds before introducing the next topic. The signalling of transitions can be reinforced using non-verbal cues. Presenters can move to another part of the platform, make a symbolic gesture, or introduce an audio-visual prompt, such as a photographic image or an artefact. For example, in the waste paper scenario, we might imagine the presenter introducing the topic 'Practical solutions for reducing waste' by showing a short video extract that demonstrates a new recycling system. Regular transitions and frequent changes in the pace of delivery also help to keep an audience alert and interested.

'Closing' with a flourish

The closing statements are the equivalent to the concluding section of a written report, where the presenter draws the arguments together and attempts to ensure that the audience has absorbed them. It is an opportunity to remind everyone of the initial purpose of the presentation, and to summarise the key points, showing how they combine to achieve that purpose. In a 'live' presentation (i.e. where interaction is either face-to-face or electronically-mediated in 'real time'), the presenter can make use of the distinctive features of this communication channel, discussed in section 12.2, to secure a degree of commitment and action from the audience. In communication terms, this requires a strong persuasive element, where the presenter injects energy and motivation (see Chapter 5). For example, in the waste paper scenario, the presenter might take the opportunity to interact directly with the office managers, challenging them to respond with proposals on how the new recycling system might be implemented in their own departments. In some situations, it may be appropriate to split the audience into groups, as in a traditional university seminar, setting a task and asking each group to report back. This modifies the primarily 'one-way' characteristic of the communication channel, and can allow for genuine dialogue, based on an agenda outlined by the presenter. The final element in the presentation discusses the ways that presenters handle questions from the audience, the most common basis for interaction in this communication channel.

Handling questions, interruption and dialogue

Presentations have a tendency to revert towards a 'one-way' channel, primarily because this is easier for the presenter to handle. Interaction, in the form of questions and other kinds of disruption, is more challenging for the presenter, but these can be essential if the channel is to operate effectively. Questions, whether during or after a presentation, provide presenters and audiences with the chance to engage in a dialogue. In some cases, presenters may decide to initiate the questions, as part of their delivery. For example, the idea of opening the presentation with a single question can be expanded, so that the audience is asked to answer several questions in the form of a 'quiz'. (Note: Each person notes the answers individually, the 'answers' are not given at this stage). The presenter has selected the quiz questions to highlight key points to be made during the presentation. After the quiz, members of the audience are already alert to these themes, and may also be eager to discover whether they have answered the relevant questions correctly.

Presenters need to make clear to the audience whether they are happy to take questions during the main period of delivery. The obvious advantage in deferring questions until the end is that the presenter can side-step unwanted interventions and keep the delivery on track. Unrelated or poorly-worded questions can disturb the presenter's train of thought and distract the audience. However, a few well-handled questions during the presentation can be valuable, confirming that there is a degree of shared understanding between presenter and audience. In a longer presentation, a series of intermediate questions can also be used to signal transitions, as well as bringing much-needed variety.

Sometimes presenters get the uncomfortable feeling that they are 'losing' their audience. This is usually signalled by a number of verbal and non-verbal cues. There may be some talking or whispering, and a distinctive pattern of body language and facial expression (i.e. several people are leaning back in their chairs, eye contact appears to lessen and presenters may detect a phenomenon that was once termed 'EGO', meaning 'eyes glazing over'). It is important not to ignore this kind of disruption, because it is signalling a communication barrier. Experienced presenters display flexibility in order to overcome this barrier, deviating from the 'script' and taking control of the situation. For example, they may decide that the best course of action is to pause at the end of a sentence, look around the room, and ask for questions.

Open questions are generally the most effective in stimulating audience participation and feedback. It is also advisable to allow members of the audience to discuss the question first, rather that asking for an immediate response – and facing an embarrassing silence. Returning to the waste paper scenario, the presenter might say, 'OK, I see a few sceptical expressions out there. What I'd like you to do now is to spend five minutes with the person sitting next to you, discussing the following issue ...'. By altering the pattern of interaction, the presenter is allowing the audience time to recover, in the hope that this restores its interest and brings the presentation back on course. The alternatives to using questions within the presentation are to introduce a short break, or to think seriously about shortening the remaining sections and bringing the delivery to a prompt but dignified close.

Many presenters find it difficult to switch smoothly from 'delivery mode' to engaging in an active dialogue with their audience. In part, this is due to a lack of self-confidence, on the part of the presenter, who feels a need to retain control of the communication channel, by maintaining its 'one-way' emphasis. Presenters can begin to resist the temptation to retain control through careful preparation. This involves trying to predict the kinds of questions that might come up and having a number of prepared answers in mind, and available through techniques such as 'cue cards' (see section 12.4). Handling questions from the floor can be particularly difficult in large audiences, where it may be difficult to provide microphones. One option is to ask questioners to stand up and introduce themselves. This gives the rest of the audience time to adjust to the person's speaking voice. The presenter, should try to retain some control of the interaction, though this involves some difficult judgements. For example, at first sight it may seem reasonable to ask the questioner to stand up, to be brief and to speak clearly. However, the implication is that presenters are seeking to exclude those who lack the self-confidence or the language skills required to meet these requirements. In other words, they are opting for a rather narrow definition of 'effective' communication, prioritising clarity of expression over quality of interaction (see section 2.4). There is no easy solution to achieving an appropriate balance, within the constraints of the organisational setting. However, presenters can make useful interventions, such as attempting to restate the question before giving an answer. This helps to ensure that the presenter has interpreted it correctly, and also gives other members of the audience a second opportunity to hear what has been said.

Question and answer (Q&A) sessions can pose three main problems for presenters. First, they may simply be unable to give an answer. Second, they may know the answer but consider that it is of little interest to other members of the audience. Third, they may know the answer but, for various reasons, be unwilling to give it. In each case, honesty is usually the best policy. In the first case, it may be sufficient for presenters to state that they do not have an answer to hand, but will obtain one if the person can provide contact details after the presentation. Alternatively, the presenter may be able to pass the question on to someone else in the room. In the second case, where the question is either highly specialised or of limited general interest, presenters can make it clear that they do have an answer, and will be pleased to discuss it with the questioner at the end. In the third case, where giving the answer would, for example, be embarrassing to members of the audience, or would breach some kind of confidentiality agreement, the best option is for presenters to state that they are either unable or unwilling to respond to that point at this time, giving whatever justification they consider to be necessary. Giving false information, or being 'economical with the truth' (i.e. using language carefully to encourage a false impression in the audience) in these situations may be unethical and also illegal. Given the free flow of information in most organisational contexts, the tactics of deception or distortion are also likely to be little more than a short-term fix, leading to greater difficulties in the future (Bird 2002, Bowie 2000).

Summary

- Organisations make extensive use of presentations, which range from informal face-to-face briefings to electronically-mediated webcasts.

- The verbal presentation has the potential to be a rich, two-way channel, but presenters need to take account of its distinctive characteristics, including the inability of most audiences to stop, repeat or scan the flow of information.

- The content of presentations can be planned, much like a written report, taking into account factors such as whether the audience will have access to an accompanying report or hand-out, and whether to make use of audio-visual aids to reinforce verbal messages.

- Preparatory tasks include paying attention to physical issues, such as appearance, posture, voice and memorising information. In general, presenters should avoid both prepared scripts and pure improvisation. Cue cards or bullet points on presentation slides can help to trigger recall.

- It is important that the selection and use of audio-visual aids is appropriate to the type of presentation and the needs of the audience. Presenters should become familiar with their technical strengths and weaknesses, including their impact on communication practices.

- Practical arrangements at the venue, including rooms, equipment and refreshments, can have a major effect on the presentation. It is always advisable to check these details in advance.

- There are four key areas to address during the delivery of a presentation: establishing a compelling opening; signalling transitions and changing pace between major themes; concluding the presentation; and handling questions, interruptions and dialogue.

Practical exercises

1 Presentation skills – self-assessment and critique

(a) Think back to the most recent talk or presentation you have *delivered*. Make notes on the following: How did it go? What do you feel were your main strengths and weaknesses? What areas would you most like to improve?

(b) Now think of the most recent talk or presentation you have attended as a member of the audience. Make a second set of notes on the following: How well did the speaker communicate his or her messages? Were you clear about the structure and objectives of the presentation? In what ways could the speaker's performance have been improved?

(c) Compare your two sets of notes. Identify examples where either you might learn something from the other presenter, or *vice versa*.

Seminar option: If you are working in a group, discuss your experiences, as outlined in questions (a) and (b). What are the major presentation strengths and weaknesses within the group? How do these compare to those of the presenters you have listened to recently?

2 Look confident, feel confident

This is a practical exercise, which should ideally be conducted in a small group setting. If possible, make a video recording to demonstrate the 'before and after' effect and to provide a basis for discussion and reflection. Some alternative exercises are included on the companion website and in the tutor's guide.

(a) **The 'before' test:** Walk to the front of a class or meeting room and introduce yourself to your colleagues as though you were beginning a presentation on a topic of your choice. (Note: A 30-second introduction will be sufficient.)

(b) **The practice session:** Make a conscious effort to stand upright, with both feet flat on the floor. Loosen up your head and shoulders; gently 'shake out' any tension in your neck and arms so that you are not standing there like a mannequin! Settle down with your shoulders back, your head centred and your chin up. Breathe slowly and deeply before you begin to speak.

(c) **The 'after' test:** Following the practice session, repeat the exercise adopting the upright stance and taking a few deep breaths before speaking. You should notice the following improvements:

- Your lung capacity is increased, so your voice is more resonant.

- Your voice projects impressively, and is not lost in the floor.

- You have better eye contact with your audience rather than the floor.

- You feel happier and more 'in control' of the situation.

(d) **Consult the audience:** Did they perceive you as more confident and competent, second time around? Check whether you 'over-did' the upright stance. It will *feel* very strange to you at first, but should *look* perfectly normal to them. Continue practising until you reach a happy compromise.

**Case study
L**

'LOGOS 05': diary of an international conference delegate

This case is a fictionalised account of experiences at an international research conference, 'LOGOS 05', which attracts more than 800 researchers, policy-makers and practitioners from around the world. The conference runs over two and a half days, with presentations delivered in a number of 'parallel sessions', running simultaneously in different lecture rooms. It tells the story of Siobhán, a conference delegate from Dublin. It is her first major conference, and she has decided to keep a diary on her electronic organiser, which she e-mails to her partner each evening.

Monday 14th: two nightmare presentations today ...
This is a big conference! It's amazing how many people are interested in 'Learning Organisations, Governance and Strategy'. The opening speaker was a local politician, who spoke mainly about what a really great city this is, and how we should all be considering the attractive foreign direct investment opportunities. 'What, on my salary?!', I thought, as I browsed through the conference handbook. (Note: They have also provided an electronic version on CD-ROM, containing all of the papers, but I haven't managed to load it onto the organiser; so much for compatibility!).

I have sat through two *nightmare* presentations today, plus one that was really rather good. Yes, I quite enjoyed the first talk this morning. The speaker seemed very confident and managed to make a lot of bold statements. He also kept us amused with some humorous anecdotes about his old college professors. He was talking about the rivalry between the major 'Ivy League' universities and something about 'trophy' professor's being traded like soccer stars. For some reason, he didn't have a copy of his paper in the conference proceedings, and there wasn't much information on his presentation slides. I managed to note down a few of the ideas, nothing very original, but it seemed to be in the same area as my own research. Perhaps I will e-mail him later to request a copy of the paper.

At the coffee break I got stuck in a long conversation with a social psychologist from Slovakia. My first attempt at 'networking' went quite well, but it meant that I had to run all the way to the next parallel session. I chose the session on the subject of 'Technology and Learning', mainly because it was being held in the nearest lecture room. This proved to be a big mistake! The first speaker, who I quickly renamed 'The Whisperer', spent the entire 15 minutes of her presentation with her right hand over her mouth. You know, I could have almost believed it was glued there! She also spoke in a very quiet voice, so quiet that I could hardly detect her accent, though I guess from the contact details that she was probably Vietnamese. Fortunately, 'The Whisperer' had produced some fairly clear presentation slides, with plenty of paper copies, so I managed to get to grips with her basic arguments.

My final speaker was probably the worst. Professor Jangler is one of the most famous people in his field, and I was very keen to hear what he had to say about organisational learning and feedback processes. Unfortunately, this man has a nervous habit of playing with the keys and coins in his jacket pocket. It made a *terrible* noise that was picked up by his microphone and amplified very effectively around the room. Occasionally, it seemed as though he was going to stop rattling the keys. For a few precious minutes, everyone in the audience could relax a little and try to concentrate on what the professor was saying. But then there was another loud rattle and we all got distracted again.

Tuesday 15th: the day war broke out!
Well, quite an exciting day, though perhaps for the wrong reasons. I was the second speaker in one of the early afternoon sessions. Fairly nervous, of course, but I was following your advice and trying to keep myself calm and focused. The first speaker in my session

finished his presentation. I noticed that he had been speaking rather quickly, and when I looked up from my notes, all I could see was the back of his head. Of course, I was so busy doing my own last-minute preparations that I had no idea what he had been saying! Anyway, I was just about to get up and check that my presentation was loaded properly on the laptop when someone in the audience stood up and started to make an impromptu speech! I think the man was French, possibly Belgian, and this is roughly what he said:

> 'I am sorry, but I must interrupt. I think we need to remind everyone that this conference is an *international* event. The common language may be English, but for most of us this is a second, third or even *fourth* language. Some of the English-speaking presenters, especially some delegates from North America, Australasia and the UK, seem to have forgotten this essential fact. We are getting *very tired* of you speaking too fast, with not enough clarity, and using your local phrases and humour that nobody else can understand. You know, it is much easier to follow the other 'non-English' speakers; for example, the woman from Latvia, who spoke on Monday. I must say that this is extremely arrogant behaviour on your part; it is a kind of imperialism that you are showing towards us! We demand that you show other nations proper respect and courtesy.'

There was loud applause, then everyone became *extremely* quiet. Of course, I had to break the silence. I decided not to reply directly to 'The Speech', but was extremely careful to speak clearly, and to avoid those idiomatic phrases. I even cut out my little joke about the Irish pub at Moscow airport, just in case somebody was confused or offended. You know, it made me think again about that 'good' speaker I mentioned in yesterday's e-mail. Sure, I enjoyed his talk, with all of the humour and smart remarks. But now I am asking myself whether other people felt the same way, given what the French guy was saying earlier on. It's the conference dinner this evening, so I will try to get some informal impression from some of the other delegates.

Wednesday 16th: the conference dinner
What a dinner! Far too much food, course after course, followed by what seemed to be an endless succession of very formal speeches, each of which had to be translated into English. I ended up on a table full of Brits and New Zealanders, who got very drunk and started passing notes around the table; it seems that someone was trying to form an escape committee. All very entertaining, no doubt, but it would have been good to find out what people really thought about 'The Speech'.

Questions

1 Prepare a list of what you consider to be the five 'worst' presentation practices referred to in the case.

2 Outline the main communication problems that you would associate with each of the practices on your list, and suggest how they might be overcome.

3 People often say that the most important form of communication at international conferences is the informal 'networking' that takes place during coffee breaks, or in the bar. Why do you think this may be the case?

4 Prepare a short (maximum 900 words) guide for LOGOS members, entitled: 'Advice to international conference delegates: the conduct of presentations'. The guide should pay particular attention to the issues raised in 'The Speech'.

Source: Co-written with Tina Fawcett.

Further reading

Most of the literature on presentations comprises 'how to' guides and lists of techniques, such as **Janner** (1989) and **DiResta** (1998). **Jay and Jay** (1996) is an entertaining, yet useful source. There are also many practical manuals on the use of presentation software packages; these have not been listed due to their rapid updating. Research in this area has tended to concentrate on the use of particular technologies in presentations. There is also a great deal of research into the use of lectures in the teaching and learning literature. Beyond this, however, there has been rather limited reflection on the nature of communication in this channel, compared to that for meetings, for example. Additional references are provided in other chapters, relating to particular aspects of the verbal presentation. These include: Chapter 3 (use of spoken and written language in presentations and supporting materials); Chapter 4 (visual aspects of presentation, including graphics used for presentation slides and non-verbal communication related to both the speaker and audience); Chapter 5 (use of persuasive communication in a presentation); Chapter 6 (securing feedback from a presentation audience); Chapter 9 (combining oral presentations with written reports); Chapter 13 (using presentations as part of a meeting).

References

Bird, F.B. (2002) *The muted conscience: moral silence and the practice of ethics in business.* Quorum, Westport CT.

Bowie, N.E. (ed.) (2002) *The Blackwell guide to business ethics.* Blackwell, Oxford.

DiResta, D. (1998) *Knockout presentations: how to deliver your message with power, punch, and pizzazz.* Chandler House Press, Madison, WI.

Flintoff, J-P. (2002) 'A case of visual aids disease'. *Financial Times,* London edition, 13 (9th October).

Grenby, H. (2003) 'Six ways to overcome your fear of public speaking'. *Harvard Management Communication* Letter, 6, 3, 3–5 (March).

Gross, R.D. (1996) *Psychology: the science of mind and behaviour.* Hodder & Stoughton, London.

Janner, G. (1989) *Janner on presentation.* Random House, London.

Jay, A. and Jay, R. (1996) *Effective presentation.* FT Pitman, London.

Jones, J. (2003) 'Using webcasts to inspire staff at the New York Times Company'. *Strategic Communication Management,* 7, 3, 14–17.

Parkinson, B. (1987) 'Emotion: cognitive approaches' in Beloff, H. and Colman, A.M. (eds.) *Psychology survey: no. 6.* British Psychological Society, Leicester.

Schachter, S. and Singer, J.E. (1962) 'Cognitive, social and physiological determinants of emotional state'. *Psychological Review,* 69, 379–99.

Turban, E. (2003) *Electronic commerce 2003: a managerial perspective.* Prentice Hall, Upper Saddle River NJ.

CHAPTER 13

Meetings, teams and negotiations

Talent wins games, but teamwork and intelligence win championships.
Michael Jordan, basketball player

By the end of this chapter you should be able to:

- contrast the different types of business meeting, their purpose and varying degrees of formality;
- identify the characteristics of meetings as a communication channel, assessing their advantages and disadvantages in particular situations;
- apply formal business meeting procedures, including relevant documentation, such as agendas and minutes;
- summarise the tasks involved in chairing a meeting, and identify the communication skills required in a successful chair;
- review the communication process in team meetings and assess the different team roles in communication terms;
- consider the distinctive communication challenges associated with virtual teams;
- assess the effectiveness of 'win–win' negotiation techniques in a inter-cultural context.

13.1 Introduction

People are always complaining about them, yet we all spend much of our working lives in meetings of one kind or another. Meetings have the *potential* to be one of the richest and most creative communication channels (see Figure 13.1). However, they can also pose some of the greatest challenges. This chapter considers why meetings often become so infuriating and unproductive, generating more 'heat' than 'light'. It argues that, with careful preparation and management it is possible to minimise the 'downside' and make the most of these gatherings, be they a top-level committee or an *ad hoc* project team. It begins by reviewing the variety of meeting types and their different purposes, and addresses the general characteristics of this channel. The discussion then turns to the more formal types of meeting, their associated documentation, and the key role of the chair. This is followed by a consideration of communication in the more informal setting of the team meeting, and in the emerging world of 'virtual' team-working. The chapter concludes with a brief review of negotiation meetings, and the skills involved in securing a 'win–win' outcome. The chapter also reflects on the cultural and political factors that have shaped the diversity of meetings encountered in international organisations.

Figure 13.1 **A meeting in progress**

13.2 Meetings: principal types and purposes

Organisations are the venue for many types of meeting, serving a variety of overlapping purposes (Table 8.1). These meetings may also operate with varying degrees of **formality** (i.e. the extent to which they keep written records and follow a set of rules and procedures). One of the most common sources of difficulty results from a mis-match between the meeting format and the nature of the communication being undertaken. For example, a management committee is set up with all the characteristics of an 'executive' (i.e. decision-making) meeting, but its real purpose is to consult or to brief, rather than to decide. A related problem arises when the participants in a meeting have different views on its purpose. For example, imagine the potential for conflict when the sales director thinks she is giving a *briefing*, the regional managers are expecting to be *consulted* and the sales executives are hoping to *participate* in some real executive decisions. As we shall see, it is difficult to separate the technicalities of communication in meetings from the broader political process in organisations.

Table 13.1 Organisational meetings: overlapping types, purposes and styles

Type	Primary purpose	Formal example	Informal example
Briefing	To deliver information	Chief executive presents financial results to investment analysts	Project manager explains the task to a newly-formed team
Investigatory	To gather information	Board of Inquiry interviews witnesses to a serious accident	Architect and structural engineer visit construction site to resolve technical problem
Advisory	To provide information	Panel of experts advise government department on new legislation	Human resources manager consults two colleagues on a disciplinary case
Consultative	Voice opinions	Community leaders speak at public inquiry into new airport runway	Manager asks her staff how they feel about a proposed profit-sharing scheme
Executive	Make decisions	Board of trustees agrees a new strategic plan for hospital trust	Emergency workers at the scene of a fire decide on the best course of action.

13.3 Advantages, disadvantages and channel characteristics

Meetings share the benefits and drawbacks of any face-to-face communication. Benefits derive from instantaneous feedback and intensive flows of verbal and non-verbal communication (Figure 13.2). These have the potential to offer a rapid exchange of ideas and group synergies. In other words, combined efforts of

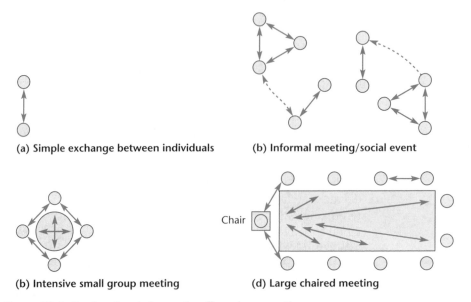

(a) Simple exchange between individuals

(b) Informal meeting/social event

(b) Intensive small group meeting

(d) Large chaired meeting

Figure 13.2 Contrasting information flows in a meeting

a group can often generate better solutions than individuals working alone or communicating through less intensive channels, such as letters or e-mail. Successful meetings can both *inform* and *motivate* those attending. Unfortunately, business meetings rarely succeed in exploiting these opportunities to the full. To understand why, it is necessary to consider the kind of communication that is taking place.

Meetings involve a complex pattern of information flows. Messages criss-cross around the meeting room and are highly vulnerable to noise and incorrect decoding (see Chapter 2). Each attendee arrives with his or her own information, pre-conceived ideas, feelings and prejudices. As the meeting grinds on, the limited attention spans and selective perception of each individual can lead to different interpretations of the material that has been discussed, the arguments presented and any decisions that may have been made. Discussions and arguments can become highly personalised as individuals 'play politics' or begin to identify themselves too closely with particular positions. Meetings often lose direction. In some cases, they may simply drift into unrelated topics, but can also be hijacked by one strong personality or by a faction that wishes to pursue its own agenda. The result is a mis-allocation of time; the meeting spends far too long on relatively minor agenda items, leaving insufficient time for the main business issues. As the hours roll on the most important issues are rushed through by an over-tired chair, who simply wants the meeting to end as quickly as possible.

The role of the chair is crucial, and we will return to it in section 13.4. For example, in a large formal meeting, the chair has the difficult task of co-ordinating information flows, ensuring that individuals are not excluded and closing down 'private' conversations (see Figure 13.2). Poorly-managed meetings generally make bad decisions, which is reason enough to seek to improve this vital communication channel. Equally serious is the demotivating effect of an unsuccessful meeting on everyone concerned.

13.4 The formal meeting

The formal meeting has proved to be a 'necessary evil' in any organisation. During the mid-1990s, the 'dot com' boom generated many new businesses with relatively young and inexperienced senior executives. Anecdotal evidence suggests that this period saw a decline in the formal business meeting, as the new generation of firms sought to operate on a more casual basis. (A colleague recalls how she often arrived at pre-arranged meetings on time to find an empty room; her 25-year-old chief executive and other members of the senior management team would wander in over the following half hour.) Experience suggests that this is not a viable approach – survivors of the subsequent collapse in dot com companies tended to have recruited older and more experienced executives, who insisted on more formalised procedures. Many organisational meetings, notably those with executive powers, require a degree of formalisation if they are to operate effectively. The main features of a formal meeting are:

- established rules and procedures,
- written records of previous meetings,
- usually a specified membership who are able to participate.

Many organisations operate through a system of **committees**, whose members act as representatives for different departments or interest groups. These members may be appointed to their posts or elected by a wider group. The board of directors of a public company, for example, is elected by the shareholders, while charitable organisations are normally governed by a board of trustees. Below the 'main board' (or equivalent) level may also be various sub-committees dealing with more narrowly-defined subject areas, such as finance, social services or directors' remuneration. The decisions and recommendations of **sub-committees** are then reported to their 'parent' committee, representing a formal channel of communication (see Figure 13.3).

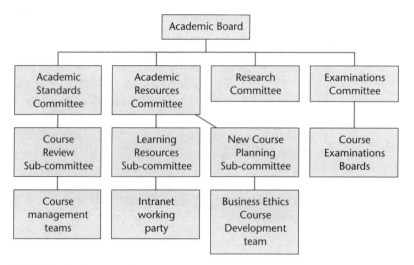

Figure 13.3 **A typical committee structure**

This section describes the main rules governing formal meetings and considers the task of producing two key items of supporting documentation, the agenda and minutes of the meeting. This model is then contrasted with recent research conducted on Chinese meeting practices, indicating the kinds of cultural variation that are encountered in the international organisation.

Rules and order

Most large organisations have a written constitution, or 'standing orders'. For example, in the British legal system, limited companies are governed by their principal legal documents, the Memorandum of Association and the Articles of Association. The company secretary is responsible for seeing that the rules are followed, and that statutory meetings (e.g. the Annual General Meeting) are held, with appropriate notice given. If the board of directors acts outside its rules or powers (i.e. in legal terms, *ultra vires*), the decisions are invalidated, and the individual directors find themselves in a vulnerable position; they have what is termed a 'fiduciary responsibility' to act in the best interests of the company's shareholders. Similarly, under British law, local government councillors can be fined, or 'surcharged', if their spending decisions exceed centrally-imposed limits.

There are a number of specialist terms used in and around formal meetings. As a general rule, it is advisable to become familiar with the procedures and the terminology used in any meetings that you attend (see Table 13.2).

Table 13.2 Specialist terminology associated with formal meetings

Term	Explanation
Adjournment	A break in the meeting before all of the agenda items have been covered. This may because it is inquorate (see below), to obtain information or simply to allow participants to have a break. An adjournment is normally a temporary postponement with an agreed date and time for resumption. However, adjournment *sine die* means that it is for an indefinite period.
Amendment	Motions (see below) can be subject to amendments, which are also proposed, seconded and put to the vote.
AOB	Any other business – committee members should submit items for the agenda in advance if possible; this allows them to be scheduled in a logical order. However, genuinely last-minute items can usually be notified to the chair at the start of the meeting. If time permits, they may be taken as AOB at the end of the meeting.
Ex officio	Ex officio members are individuals appointed to a committee by virtue of the office they hold, rather than by direct appointment or election.
Matters arising	This is a standard agenda item, referring to items from the previous meeting's minutes that require further discussion.
Motion	Motions are part of the voting procedure used in some committee meetings. A motion is normally 'proposed' by one person and seconded (i.e. supported) by another, before being put to the vote.
Point of order	If someone thinks that the meeting is not following its written rules, they can point it out to the chair by calling 'point of order'. Examples include: quorum, *ultra vires*, and speaking on items which are not on the agenda.
Proxy	A proxy is someone acting on behalf of a person who is unable to attend the meeting. Proxies are most commonly used when a vote is called at an Annual General Meeting (AGM).
Quorum	This term refers to the minimum number of members or delegates required for a meeting to proceed. If attendance falls below that number at any time in a formal meeting, it is deemed to be *inquorate* and business must be suspended.
'Through the chair'	It is normal practice for all comments at a formal meeting to be addressed via the chair, rather than in direct exchanges between members. In theory, this rule enables the chair to exert some control over the meeting. It is not always followed!
Ultra vires	This legal term derives from the Latin, meaning 'outside the powers'. It refers to decisions or actions that fall beyond the remit of a particular committee.

Preparing and circulating the agenda

The agenda, listing the topics to be discussed, provides a structure for the meeting. It may be a useful route map, but if poorly-constructed, it can lead everyone astray! A fortnight or so before the meeting, the secretary circulates members, requesting agenda items. The chair and secretary normally plan the 'running order', based on the items submitted. The following factors should be considered when deciding this order:

- **Logical sequence:** If the outcome of one decision is going to affect another, ensure that the 'dependent' topic is further down the agenda.

- **Simple items first:** It is often a good tactic to get straightforward items out of the way, before going on to more complex issues.

- **Consensus items first:** Uncontroversial items at the top of the agenda should be dealt with speedily. However, a seemingly bland item can cause unexpected controversy and time-consuming arguments. It is wise to check, before the agenda is finalised, whether the item really is as innocuous as it sounds.

- **Late arrivals and early departures:** There may be a topic that can only be discussed with a particular individual present. Hence, it may be necessary to defer or advance an item if that person is going to be late, or has to rush off to *another* meeting.

- **Less important/less urgent last?** The chair and secretary may be tempted to place 'minor' items towards the end of the agenda, but this is not good practice. If you have a full agenda, it is best to defer these items to a subsequent meeting or, better still, deal with them via another channel. For example, it is much less time-consuming to circulate a draft report, asking for written comments, rather than to proofread the whole thing, page-by-page, during a meeting.

Having established an appropriate order for the agenda, items of business may simply be numbered in sequence from 01 onwards. Many organisations use a slightly more complex referencing system comprising the current year, followed by number of the agenda item. For example, in 2005, the sequence would begin: '05/01, 05/02 ...'. The sequence of numbers then continues from one meeting to the next (see Figure 13.4). The chair is often provided with an extended version of the agenda. The chair's agenda is annotated, with useful information to assist in running the meeting smoothly. For example, it might include a reminder to provide members of the meeting with a brief update on a rapidly-developing issue, before opening it to discussion. The chair is also likely to note provisional time allocations for each agenda item, to help with time-keeping during the meeting. Once the agenda is drawn up, the secretary sends out copies, normally including details of the date, time and venue. The agenda may be sent as a paper copy, or as an e-mail attachment.

Committees and boards usually have a regular pattern of meetings, which may be planned and notified up to a year in advance. This practice is supposed to increase the chances that members will be able to schedule their attendance around other commitments. However, in practice, 'extraordinary' meetings may also be needed to deal with urgent matters, while others may be re-scheduled or cancelled. It is important to ensure that everyone is included on the circulation list, particularly where the meeting has voting powers.

Greentek plc
FINANCE SUB-COMMITTEE

The next meeting of the Finance Sub-Committee will take place on
Monday 8th January 2006 at 15:00hrs in Room K383, Ryton Tower.

AGENDA

06/01	Apologies for absence	
06/02	Minutes of last meeting	
06/03	Matters arising	
06/04	Response to internal audit report	BJH
06/05	Capital investment proposal: project Alpha	ADR
06/06	Financial information system update	LPN
06/07	Software purchases: 2006/07	LPN
06/08	Any other business	
06/09	Date of next meeting	

Figure 13.4 **Sample agenda and notice of meeting**

Writing up the minutes

It is essential that the minutes provide an accurate and unbiased record of the meeting. The minutes are presented to the following meeting for approval, after which they become the definitive record. If the previous meeting had been contentious, members are likely scrutinise the circulated minutes carefully, and may request corrections. In a formal meeting, the secretary is normally responsible for taking the minutes. Minute taking is something of an art, balancing the requirement of recording proceedings accurately to produce a clear, concise account. There are three main types of minute, ranging from the highly detailed to the briefest summary:

Verbatim minutes

These are 'word-for-word' accounts of the meeting. The records of parliamentary debates and those of some public enquiries are verbatim. For example, *Hansard* is the official record of the British parliament, while the minutes of European Parliament meetings are first recorded in the languages in which members' speeches were given, then translated into the 11 official languages, known as the 'Rainbow' due to their colour coding (i.e. Spanish, Danish, German, Greek, English, French, Italian, Dutch, Portuguese, Finnish and Swedish). Given the resources required for verbatim minute taking, it is not widely used in business organisations.

Narrative minutes

These are a more or less detailed summary of the discussion that takes place around each item, followed by a note of the decision taken. Narrative minutes usually include an 'action' column on the right-hand side of the page, with the name or initial of the person responsible for carrying out any matters agreed by the meeting. Meetings tend to agree things with little thought of how they are to be implemented; the action column counters by specifying a named individual. These actions are then reviewed at the following meeting, exerting some added pressure on the person concerned (see Figure 13.5).

Greentek plc
FINANCE SUB-COMMITTEE

Minutes of the Finance Sub-Committee meeting
held on Monday 8th January 2006
at 15:00hrs in Room K383, Ryton Tower.

Present: Daniel Felton
    Bridget Harris (Chair)
    Jean Lafitte (Secretary)
    Neema Patel
    Lisa Nolan
    Adrian Robertson

		Action
06/01	Apologies Received from Martin Smith and Kerry Jones.	
06/02	Minutes of last meeting The minutes of the meeting held on 20th November 2005, previously circulated, were signed as a true record.	
06/03	Matters arising	
05/13	Computer security: Neema Patel reported that the anti-virus program was updated, effective from 1st December 2005. No further problems had been reported, but a review was to be carried out in June 2006.	NP
06/04	Response to internal audit report A response was submitted on 20th December 2005, covering the substantive points made. Kay Rodgers of internal audit would formally report back to the next meeting.	KR
06/05	Capital investment proposal: project Alpha Following Adrian Robinson's presentation, the sub-committee recommended that project Alpha go forward to the February board meeting.	AR
06/06	Financial information system update A detailed report, accompanying Lisa Nolan's presentation is appended to these minutes. It was agreed that regular updates be given in the development phase.	LN
06/07	Software purchases: 2006/07 The provisional list was agreed, with the addition of the updated virus-checker. Department heads would be asked to provide a list of their requirements by 31st March 2006 at the latest.	LN
06/08	Any other business No other business was notified. The meeting closed at 15:47hrs	
06/09	Date of next meeting The next meeting is scheduled for 8th April 2006 at 15:00hrs in room K383, Ryton Tower.	

Figure 13.5 **Sample narrative minutes**

Resolution minutes

These are the briefest type of minute, stating only what was agreed at the meeting. Resolution minutes are used primarily for statutory meetings (e.g. those required to form or make changes to the legal status of a company). The wording is normally in the form, 'RESOLVED: That Frederick George Wilson be appointed a non-executive director of Greentek plc, with effect from 1st January, 2006.' The alternative form is, 'It was resolved that Frederick George Wilson be appointed a non-executive director of Greentek plc, with effect from 1st January, 2006.'

13.5 On being a successful chair

The task of a chair is to manage the live flow of messages without either stifling useful discussion or showing obvious bias towards one or other viewpoint. This can be a challenging task, particularly when the meeting is affected by 'personality clashes' between members, or where controversial issues are under discussion. The role of chair is common to formal and informal meetings, and is characterised by diplomatic, assertiveness and co-ordinating skills. The chair and secretary have complementary roles, which require close liaison over a number of tasks. These can be summarised under three headings, covering the preparations required before the meeting, activity during the meeting itself, and follow-up action:

Before the meeting – tactical planning

Even where a meeting is scheduled on a regular basis, the chair needs to consider the *purpose* of the forthcoming meeting and establish appropriate tactics for achieving it. Sometimes, there are pragmatic decisions to make. For example, if there is insufficient business, or key personnel are unavailable, it is the chair's role to take the initiative and either cancel or postpone the meeting. Equally, if the proposed agenda is over-full, the chair can make a judgement that some items should be postponed, or dealt with through other channels. These early decisions avoid the depressing prospect of an impossibly long agenda, and the difficult task of rationalising it once the meeting is underway.

There are other practical issues, such as checking that the venue is suitable, with enough seats and reasonable heating, lighting and ventilation. If audio-visual equipment is required, such as flip-charts and overhead projectors, this needs to be in place and functioning before the meeting begins. The chair also needs to read all of the relevant background papers and reports, to be aware of the main issues under discussion.

During the meeting – diplomacy and time management

Above all, the chair needs to keep strict control of the time, ensuring that all business is covered adequately. The chair is also responsible for crowd control.

For example, it may be necessary to stop someone who insists on repeating old arguments, jumping ahead or digressing from the current item. This requires a combination of tact and assertiveness. At the same time, the chair needs to be aware of those signalling a wish to speak, and ensure that everyone has a fair opportunity to contribute. By remaining calm and objective, the chair can help to set the tone for a meeting. Of course, they also have the power to undermine an otherwise successful meeting, by taking the opposite course.

The secretary should be able to assist the chair by having a sound knowledge of the formal rules and procedures; without this understanding, the meeting can become side-tracked by long and unresolved arguments over procedural issues and points of order (see Table 13.2). The chair also needs to ensure that the secretary has had time to record the details of a decision, before moving on to the next item. If a decision has not been expressed clearly, the chair or secretary may ask for it to be re-stated 'for the record'.

From time to time, the chair may also need to get a 'sense' of the meeting. This is often done by summarising the arguments that have been stated, and seeking or proposing a consensus view. In some cases, it is agreed in advance that a meeting will finish by a specified time. In these circumstances, it is even more important for the chair to keep a tight control on timing. Otherwise, the tail-end of the meeting is likely to become disorganised and inquorate, as people drift away for other engagements. The chair should ensure that all the business is either dealt with in the meeting, passed on for action by named individuals, or held over until a specific date. It is important to avoid leaving ambiguities or 'loose ends', especially regarding those responsible for taking agreed actions after the meeting.

After the meeting – prompt follow-up

The Secretary's main and most urgent task at this point is to ensure that the minutes are written up, checked and passed to the Chair for review. They should then be circulated to all of those identified on the circulation list, including those giving 'apologies' at the meeting (Note: This is one of the reasons for recording these names formally in the minutes.) People become irritated if agendas and draft minutes are circulated a few days before the following meeting, as this gives them insufficient time to prepare for the meeting. One of the final tasks is to check the previous 'action' column before the meeting and to seek confirmation as to whether the named individuals have done what was required.

Practical issues

Practical issues, such as seating arrangements and adequate ventilation, may sound trivial. However, as countless good and bad experiences have demonstrated, these simple practical arrangements can have a significant effect on the success of a meeting (Mini-case 13.1).

Mini-case 13.1

Seating your meeting: the role of design

Seating arrangements have a major impact on the way people interact in a meeting. When a meeting is being hosted by another organisation, you may have little influence over the layout of the meeting room. However, there are many good cases of design being used to facilitate improved communication. For example, when the British government's ministers meet in the Cabinet room at 10 Downing Street, London, they sit around a long rectangular table that has a slight curve on either side. The design allows them to see the faces of colleagues on either side.

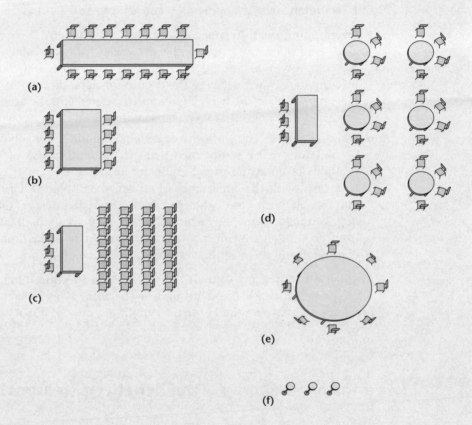

(a)

(b)

(c)

(d)

(e)

(f)

Questions

1 (a) Which of these seating plans have you used or experienced recently?

(b) List the potential advantages and disadvantages of each seating plan.

(c) Based on your assessments, identify the types of meeting where a particular plan would encourage effective communication, and those in which it would be counter-productive.

(d) Are some of the seating plans undesirable whatever the purpose of the meeting might be?

Test your conclusions by experimenting with different seating arrangements during your next meeting or team-based project.

More intractable communication problems in committees

We have seen that formal meetings, and the system of committees and sub-committees, are an important and unavoidable part of organisational life. This section has covered many of the potential pit-falls, showing how they can be avoided with the help of good documentation and well-prepared, competent people in the key roles of chair and secretary. These actions will improve the quality of communication in most formal meetings. However, some weaknesses in committee-based systems can prove more difficult to overcome. Among the most common are overlapping roles and the phenomenon of the 'talking shop':

- **Overlapping roles:** In large and complex organisations, there can be considerable confusion over the respective roles of particular committees or sub-committees. As a result of this, some issues will begin to 'bounce' from one meeting to another, delaying the decision-making process. At the level of the meeting, members are likely to become frustrated and the agenda will be overburdened with items that keep reappearing with no sign of being resolved.

- **'Talking shops':** The authority of certain committees or sub-committees may be undermined by senior management, or in the case of subsidiaries, by decisions taken at the parent company headquarters. Other committees may be formed with the appearance of an executive role, which masks their real purpose. In both cases, those involved find themselves 'rubber stamping' decisions made elsewhere, which can be a very disheartening experience. It is likely to result in members 'voting with their feet'; in other words, attendances fall and the meeting may lose its identity altogether.

In these situations, any solution lies outside the meeting room. The chair and other participants will need to address the underlying structural or political problems that have resulted in these 'symptoms' of poor quality communication (see Section 2.3).

13.6 Informal meetings – the benefits of team-working

Meetings come in all shapes and sizes. People often get together in less formal ways than those described in the previous section. However, the basic reasons for meeting are much the same, however informal it may be. These include tasks such as, tackling a complex problem, planning a future course of action or generating new ideas:

- **The 'quality circle':** At a manufacturing company, a small team of engineers, supervisors and production workers are sitting in a small meeting room, discussing how to redesign a component in order to overcome a technical fault that is affecting factory output.

- **The clinical discussion:** In an orthopaedic ward of a hospital, a clinical consultant, nursing staff and a physiotherapist are meeting to discuss their patient's recent progress following emergency surgery, with the aim of preparing a longer-term treatment programme.

- **The voluntary organisation**: In a local community hall, members of an integrated sports club for disabled and able-bodied people are planning their next fund-raising venture, a stall at the forthcoming town carnival.

Pre-determined agendas and detailed minutes may not be appropriate in these situations, though there is clearly a need for some degree of preparation and note taking. Even in the most informal business meetings, a little time spent on structure and procedures is likely to generate better results. However, the most important requirement is for the individuals concerned to work together as a **team**.

Some writers struggle with the distinction between a team and a group. However, one of the most straightforward ways to clarify the difference is to see a team as a group that combines a joint purpose and a shared sense of responsibility. Hence, there is a qualitative difference between a group of people in a park with a football and the same individuals, once they have formed into two competing teams that are beginning to play. In this section, our primary concern is with the kinds of communication that take place in these 'purposeful' teams.

Team-working as effective communication?

There has been a great deal of management writing concerning the nature and dynamics of organisational teams. While there are differences in presentation and emphasis, the underlying implication is that teams are more likely to achieve better outcomes than several individuals working independently (cf. Adair 1986, Belbin 2000, Hackman *et al.* 2000, Katzenbach and Smith 1998). More specifically, it is argued that an effective team can:

- **Solve complex problems**: Management problems are often wide-ranging and multi-disciplinary, requiring a combination of skills, knowledge and experience. Since these combinations are rarely found in one person, it is often necessary to create problem-solving teams that draw from different parts of the organisation, or spread across a number of related organisations.

- **Stimulate creativity and innovation**: Lively interactions between people can spark off new ideas and provide original perspectives. This often occurs when one person mentions something they have seen recently, prompting someone else to recall a related memory, and a third makes a link between the two. Organisations have sought to foster creativity by encouraging the formation of informal teams.

- **Increase motivation**: Most people have a need to belong, and enjoy mixing with others rather than spending all their time working alone. For example, a field sales force might theoretically spend all of its time on the road, communicating with the office through a laptop computer and mobile phone. Regular face-to-face meetings and social events may be used to build motivation and performance in these dispersed teams.

However, it is equally apparent that a poorly functioning team can cause all kinds of problems for organisations. The symptoms of dysfunction include: expressions of frustration and negativity; unhealthy competition (i.e. 'in-fighting') between team members; lack of involvement or commitment; dishonesty; a climate of revenge (i.e. 'back-stabbing'); and a general lack of strategic direction.

Both the positive and negative aspects of team-working can be investigated in terms of the communication taking place. For example, Tuckman's (1965) widely-cited model of team dynamics can be interpreted as an account of four distinct patterns of communication taking place during the assumed life-cycle of a team (i.e. 'forming', 'storming', 'norming', and 'adjourning'). However, as critics have noted, an 'ideal-typical' stage model of this kind is unlikely to represent the variety of complex situations arising in real organisations. For example, where there are strongly-held norms in the wider organisation, individuals may be capable of making a rapid transition to the 'performing' stage. By contrast, pre-existing conflicts may result in a team being bound into a permanent condition of 'storming'.

Perhaps more interesting for our purposes are the contrasting patterns of intra-team communication taking place over time. Table 13.3 is a tentative re-interpretation of the Tuckman 'stages', highlighting these patterns. Without endorsing the Tuckman model itself, this simple extension indicates the inherent instability and dynamism of team-based communication. At one moment, it may involve intense exchanges between many participants (i.e. multilateral), but at other times it becomes dominated by bilateral exchanges. This phenomenon requires further empirical study, but is strongly supported by anecdotal evidence. Amongst other things, it highlights the challenges faced by a team leader, in managing transitions and handling the contrasting communication flows to balance task, team maintenance and individual development goals (Adair 1986, Hackman *et al.* 2000).

Table 13.3 Indicative communication patterns in the Tuckman model

Stage	Outline of activity	Indicative patterns of communication?
'Forming'	Individuals meet and begin to establish team composition, purpose (task) and process (i.e. ways of working).	Fairly open and multilateral exchange of messages, as team members seek initial indication of capabilities and roles.
'Storming'	Disagreements emerge over task and process issues, potential for internal conflict and hostility.	Strong evidence of bilateral persuasive communication as arguments and counter-arguments are exchanged.
'Norming'	Team establishes agreed standards regarding purpose and process.	Greater attention to bilateral feedback as team leaders confirm consent and establish roles.
'Performing'	Team concentrates on achieving its common purpose, while maintaining process dimension.	Regulated multilateral exchanges between team members engaged in agreed roles.
'Adjourning'	Focus on completion of task and dissolution of the team.	Combination of intensified multilateral exchanges and some unilateral direction as task is pulled together, followed by bilateral leave-takings.

Source: Tuckman (1965 – adapted; indicative communication patterns added).

Communication and the concept of team roles

Another popular approach to the analysis of teams has focused on team roles. This strand of research has been based on the idea that performance can be enhanced by selecting an appropriately balanced team. Belbin's (1981, 1993, 2000) research originated in a series of experiments involving industrial managers who were attending short courses at a management school. The researchers compared the performance of different teams competing against one another in a series of business games. By measuring the behaviour of individuals and then experimenting with teams comprising different mixes of people, they isolated eight distinct team roles (see Table 13.4).

Table 13.4 **The concept of team roles: a communication perspective**

Team role	Primary contribution	Implied communication task
Chair	Organises, co-ordinates and seeks to retain team's focus and involvement.	Monitors and co-ordinates messages between team members.
Team leader	Initiates, provides leadership and drives team towards achieving task.	Generates persuasive bilateral and multilateral messages directed at team members.
Innovator	Creates novel ideas and solutions in support of the task.	Synthesises messages from diverse internal and external information sources.
Monitor-evaluator	Provides objective assessments of performance in relation to stated purpose.	Analyses primarily cognitive task-related messages within the team.
Team Worker	Encourages other members, fosters team morale and reduces negative emotions.	Assesses and generates primarily affective, process-related messages within the team.
Completer	Maintains a check on outcomes in relation to project milestones and deadlines.	Analyses primarily cognitive task-related messages within the team.
Implementer	Carries out much of the practical work required to achieve stated purpose.	Receives bilateral messages (i.e. instructions) and avoids distraction from other internal exchanges.
Resource investigator	Establishes external contacts to secure resources in support of stated purpose.	Engages in bilateral exchanges of persuasive messages beyond the boundaries of the team.

Source: Belbin (1981, 1993 – adapted; communication tasks added).

The higher-performing teams contained balanced combination of these roles, whereas unbalanced teams tended to display signs of dysfunction. Each individual's 'primary' and 'secondary' team roles were identified using a self-perception questionnaire, which was based on an existing personality inventory. In real organisations, the task of constructing the optimum ideal team is complicated by a number of practical constraints. For example, an individual may be required on the basis of technical expertise, irrespective of any preferential team role.

Some work-based teams are simply too small to be 'balanced'. The exercise of team roles may also be constrained by other obstacles, such as formal structures, political, economic and cultural factors. As a consequence, team composition is usually something of a compromise. However, if you accept Belbin's counter-argument, that team members may adopt alternative roles when it becomes necessary, his initial conclusions remain of value. He argues that, 'Teams are a question of balance. What is needed is not well-balanced individuals but individuals who balance well with one another. In that way, human frailties can be underpinned and strengths used to full advantage' (Belbin 1981: 75). Furthermore, team building is an art, which managers can practice and develop (Belbin 1993: 87–95).

The concept of team roles points to some interesting implications for communication within high-performing teams. The notion of a 'balance' between roles, engaged in distinctive types of contribution, suggests that communication tasks are distributed. For example, the chair is concerned primarily with co-ordinating the intense flow of messages between team members, while the innovator synthesises new ideas from a more diverse range of sources, which may extend far beyond the team's boundaries. Similarly, the monitor-evaluator is primarily engaged with cognitive, task-related messages, while the team worker is more concerned with the exchange of affective (i.e. emotional) messages within the team. This interpretation would be consistent with much of the recent research literature in knowledge management, where teams and other forms of human organisation are depicted as purposeful, self-organising systems (see section 6.5).

Creative communication in teams: the case of 'brainstorming'

Brainstorming is a popular and well-established technique for problem-solving and generating novel ideas. However, it is often conducted wrongly, leaving people disappointed with the results. Building on our previous discussion, the activity taking place during a brainstorming session can be usefully analysed from a communication perspective. Consider the general principles for successful brainstorming.

- Appoint a 'facilitator' to write ideas on the board and encourage participation; ensure that this person can write quickly and legibly!
- Everyone else calls out any ideas that come into their heads, keeping them concise (insist on a maximum of two words); encourage everyone to participate.
- Do not reject or criticise any ideas at this stage, no matter how crazy they might appear. Accept, record and acknowledge every contribution.
- Once the initial flow of ideas is exhausted, move to the next stage; begin to link similar words on the board and drawing out common themes, with the person at the board acting as a facilitator, attempting to consolidate the ideas.
- Finally, seek agreement on which of the new ideas is the most promising.

You may have noticed, from direct experience of engaging in brainstorming activities, how difficult it is to follow these guidelines. For example, it is hard to avoid the temptation to engage in a premature questioning of other people's ideas, particularly when the person concerned is less articulate than other members of the team. There is also a fairly common, task-oriented tendency to jump directly from ideas to solutions, without allowing time for the interim stages. From a communication perspective, the brainstorming 'recipe' comprises three stages:

- The first is designed to stimulate the collection of a diverse range of information.
- The second to encourage synthesis, or the creation of 'new combinations' from these sources.
- Third to refine the new information.

Note the similarities between the stages of brainstorming and some of the team roles outlined in Table 13.4. The common feature in both approaches, which is also reflected in the Tuckman model, is that team-based activities depend on people managing complex and dynamic patterns of communication to achieve a stated purpose. The next section takes the idea a little further, by exploring the rise of 'virtual' teams, where a large part of the communication is electronically-mediated.

13.7 The rise of the virtual team

Modern organisations place considerable demands on individuals, who often find themselves needed in several locations at the same time. The symptoms of this trend are the increases in travel distances undertaken for work purposes (NTSU 2001). Transportation technology cannot overcome the basic laws of physics, but innovations in information and communication technologies have enabled cross-functional tasks teams to work together in real time, though team members are dispersed around the globe. Often referred to as 'virtual' teams, they exploit the full range of electronically-mediated communication channels, including text messaging, video conferencing and e-mail. As the reliability of these technologies has improved, the communication issues for virtual teams have become increasingly focused on people. Virtual teams tend to be formed where face-to-face contact is either impossible or not cost-effective. The reasons may be varied, but the underlying factor is the dispersed physical locations of team members. Virtual teams are often formed in high-tech industries, such as software development, where specialist expertise is spread widely. They are also used in alliance-based initiatives involving several organisations, located in different countries or regions. Virtual teams are, by their very nature, disjointed and somewhat artificial. As a consequence, they need particularly sensitive and capable management if they are to function effectively.

In Chapter 7, we reviewed the communication requirements of remote workers (see Section 7.3). This suggested that some tasks, requiring limited bilateral communication, were particularly suitable for remote working. For example, much of the material for this book was prepared in the author's home office. The resulting communication flows (e.g. exchanging e-mails with editors, occasional telephone or face-to-face conversations with other contributors, and specific information searches using libraries and the internet) were mainly bilateral. In other words, they rarely involved more than two people at any one point in time. By contrast, virtual teams engaged in tasks such as developing software programs, economic development strategies or clinical treatments, will be involved in much more complex, multi-lateral interactions. The operating environment may also be more dynamic and uncertain, demanding spontaneous and simultaneous discussions and mutual adjustments. The resulting challenges are intensified where the team is international, and has to address time zone differences, different working practices and similar practical issues (Pauleen and Yoong 2001). Mini-case 13.2 illustrates how one company has made use of virtual teams to provide high levels of customer support to its global clients.

| Mini-case 13.2 | 'Software International': global customer support via virtual teams |

'Software International' (SI) delivers software solutions designed to serve the specialised needs of service industries. Many large and medium-sized organisations in healthcare, retail, professional services, financial services and the public sector rely on SI's systems. Their software helps organisations to automate and integrate key business processes. It also facilitates collaboration among customers, partners, suppliers and employees. SI's software solutions cover functions such as financial management, human resources, product procurement, distribution, and automation systems. SI's customer support is organised through virtual teams, drawing on specialist skills from around the globe. This following account traces the short, but intense life of a typical team.

One of SI's clients, a leading Italian company, headquartered in Rome, has identified an accounting problem at its Berlin office. The issue is both technical and involved, but it requires urgent attention, due to the potentially serious implications for legal compliance. The client's technical staff at the Berlin office place a call to SI's helpdesk in Vancouver, Canada. However, because the client is using a unique product line, with a non-standard hardware platform, the support analyst needs to obtain additional advice. As the problem has been identified as 'business critical', it is immediately escalated to 'second level' status. Within 30 minutes of the initial client call, a new support team is being formed. At this stage, it consists of a second level support analyst, a business analyst with hardware expertise and a software developer. The team assesses the situation, and is in conference with the client in Berlin. After a detailed discussion, it becomes clear that time difference could be an obstacle in resolving the issue quickly. The support analyst decides to bring in another two people. She makes a call to SI's Dublin office, and explains the issue to a client account manager and an analyst from the international team. The Dublin team members are now able to contact the client directly. From conversations, they gain a detailed understanding of the issue and prepare a draft solution document. The document is sent to the client for review. After a further discussion, the client accepts the proposal and is given an assurance that the solution will be available the next day.

That evening, the Dublin office sends the solution document to Vancouver. The team members in Canada now have an opportunity to clarify any issues with their colleagues in Dublin, prior to developing the software 'patch' to deal with the problem. The patch is prepared and sent to the client overnight. The following morning, the analyst in

Dublin is able to assist the customer with the installation, while the support analyst remains on stand-by in Vancouver. Later that afternoon, there is a conference call involving team members in Vancouver and Dublin and specialists from the client firm, based in their Berlin and Rome offices.

The conclusion is that the immediate problem has been resolved, but that further development work is needed to incorporate the patch into the main code for this international product line. The virtual team now disbands, with the members resuming their normal daily activities. The second level support analyst passes the details on to the development team and the patch is incorporated into the next release of the product.

Questions

1 Review the case and prepare a list of the main exchanges of messages, within and beyond the virtual team. In each case, try to identify the communication channel used and the approximate time that exchanges takes place.

2 What do you see as the main communication challenges in operating virtual teams? How would you respond to the challenges that you have identified?

3 Imagine that you were the support analyst co-ordinating this virtual team at Software International. What factors would influence your decisions regarding team composition?

4 What role do you think technology has to play in assisting virtual teams to operate on an international basis?

Source: Co-authored with Richard Foster. 'Software International' is a fictional company.

13.8 Negotiation: applying persuasive communication

The essential nature and purpose of negotiations are much the same, whatever their scale or format. Negotiation is a form of persuasive communication, that may include anything from two parties engaged in bilateral discussion to a large number of participants engaged in many cross-cutting exchanges. The process of negotiation comprises periods of discussion and the presentation of proposals and counter-proposals. After some time, this may lead to an outcome that can be accepted by all sides. The basic 'give and take' interaction that characterises negotiation is first practised in early childhood, when requests in the form, 'Please can I have another biscuit?', are met with counter-proposals containing conditional statements such as, 'Not until you put those toys away.' It is an activity that is found in many aspects of personal and organisational life. For example: when buying a new house or car; agreeing the terms of an employment contract; settling a complaint from a major customer; allocating office space between staff; or securing family agreement on a holiday destination. In this section, we treat the negotiation as a specialised type of meeting, which may take place in either a formal or informal setting.

Two main forms of negotiation: positional and principled

Traditional approaches to negotiation, generally described as 'positional' or 'distributive', have been extensively analysed using game theory and rational choice models (e.g. Raiffa 1982). In essence, each side is engaged in an attempt to maximise the outcome for themselves. The result is a 'zero-sum' game, where the resulting compromise is within the acceptable ranges of each side. In practice, positional negotiations are often undertaken by small teams of negotiators, with tightly defined mandates, giving them limited authority to act on behalf of their respective organisations or departments. The negotiation proceeds as a series of shifts in position, proposals and counter-proposals. If each party's ultimate point of compromise overlaps, an agreement may be reached. However, this form of negotiation often results in deadlock. Another common feature of positional negotiations is that one party may make a 'pre-emptive strike' against the other. For example, a politician can use selective 'leaks' to the media in order to undermine an opponent, or a group of anti-roads protestors may occupy a construction site before a public enquiry. This kind of tactical action, which can also be taken once 'face-to-face' negotiations are underway, is designed to exert additional pressure. In practice, it is usually countered by the other party and can result in a breakdown in negotiations. Responding to the perceived problems of positional negotiation, a group of Harvard Business School researchers developed an alternative approach, known as **principled** negotiation (Fisher *et al.* 1991). This is based on the assumption that the goals of the parties are not necessarily incompatible. Hence, the bargaining process is 'integrative', involving a search for the objective principles underlying each party's position. The aim is to achieve creative and mutually-acceptable outcomes. A key feature of principled negotiation is the attempt to separate the issues and arguments from the personalities of those involved in the negotiations. Above all, it recognises the importance of achieving a 'win–win' solution.

Advantages of 'win–win' negotiation

Since most organisational negotiations are part of an on-going relationship, a short term 'victory' over the other party may not be in your longer-term interests. For example, if you secure a deal that is highly unfavourable to a valued customer or key supplier (i.e. 'win–lose'), they are unlikely to do much business with you in the future. However, it is equally important not to be the victim of the other party (i.e. 'lose–win'). Hence, the best outcome for both parties is referred to as 'win–win' (see Table 13.5).

Table 13.5 **Alternative negotiation outcomes**

	A loses	A wins
B loses	Lose–lose	Win–lose
B wins	Lose–win	Win–win

Negotiation and power

Parties to a true negotiation will have some freedom of manoeuvre. However, this does not necessarily mean that they will come to the negotiating table as equals. In most cases, one party is in a stronger position than the other. For example, the large multiple retailers can exert substantial buying power over their smaller suppliers. However, as skilled negotiators recognise, it is the other party's *perception* of their power that is the key factor. By influencing these perceptions, an apparently 'weaker' party can alter the course of the negotiations in its favour. One approach to dealing with these inequalities is to manage the 'shadow' negotiation, the activity preceding the actual negotiation, but which can have a powerful influence on how the process unfolds (Kolb and Williams 2001).

The negotiation process

The skills required to manage a negotiation are similar to those used in other types of meeting, but the negotiation itself has a distinctive shape. Research on cross-cultural negotiation appears to support the established (i.e. Western) view that there is a common pattern comprising four phases:

● initial relationship building activity;

● the exchange of task-related information;

● persuasion and bidding/counter-bidding;

● concession and agreement (e.g. Mendenhall *et al.* 1995):

Initial relationship-building activity

In all forms of negotiation, there are some ritual activities that serve the purpose of creating an appropriate climate. In the 'principled' negotiation approach, this implies an effort to be cordial, collaborative, brisk and businesslike. However, there are cultural variations, notably in relation to the importance attached to fostering personal relationships. Some negotiators emphasise physical location. For example, that it should be politically neutral and free from interruptions. For example, many recent efforts at securing peace agreements have been hosted in quiet and relatively inaccessible locations. Non-verbal communication can play an important role in these rituals. Hence, skilled international negotiators pay considerable attention to handshakes, appropriate eye contact and non-threatening gestures. This is also a period in which both parties engage in uncontentious 'ice-breaking' conversation. As the memoirs of many political leaders and diplomats have suggested, the formation of good inter-personal relations prior to negotiation can play a crucial role in the outcome.

Exchanging information

Negotiators prepare the ground for bargaining by collecting information, particularly in relation to the other party's situation (e.g. the power relations influencing decision-making in their organisation). In 'win–win' approaches, this phase is associated with efforts to assess your position from the other party's point of view. International negotiators sometimes make use of interpreters to obtain information surreptitiously from the other party, a tactic that is unlikely to generate a climate of trust.

Bargaining and persuasion

The bargaining phase is initiated when the parties begin to make tentative proposals. The 'win–win' emphasis in this phase is on reducing substantive differences between the parties. This is achieved by emphasising areas where there is already consensus, and by ensuring that any remaining disagreements are not personalised. Proposals should always be expressed in **conditional** terms (i.e. 'If you offer us X ...., then we could offer you Y ....'). The principle behind the bargaining exchanges is to identify factors that are most important to the other party, and to value every offer in *their* terms. For example, a busy customer may value 'door-to-door' delivery very highly, even though it costs a supplier very little to add the customer to an existing round. By contrast, the supplier's offer of 'instant credit terms' may be a costly concession, but be of little value to the customer due to the nature of their business (e.g. they may be a cash-rich retailer). It may require a truly creative team of negotiators to put together a proposal that offers a solution satisfying all parties. This kind of creativity requires particular forms of communication, and rarely emerges from a confrontational approach.

Reaching and recording agreement

This phase marks the end of the tentative, conditional exchanges and a move to firm proposals. This transition may be influenced by cultural factors. For example, some may prefer to reach agreement on one issue at a time, while others take a more holistic approach. However, all negotiators emphasise the need to ensure that the terms of any agreement are entirely clear to all parties. This may involve a pause in proceedings to check that everything has been covered. Signifying agreement with a handshake appears to be a generalised ritual of negotiation. There is also a requirement to record the agreement and associated undertakings in writing. Many commercial and diplomatic agreements have broken down because the terms were drafted ambiguously and disputes subsequently arose over the 'small print'. However, international negotiators are also sensitive to differences in approach. It appears that some cultures have tended to place particular emphasis on the formal (i.e. legalistic) aspects, while others may regard such behaviour as indicating a lack of trust.

Negotiation in a cross-cultural perspective: the case of China

Most texts dealing with 'cross-cultural' negotiation continue to emphasise binary oppositions between cultural groups. For example, Deresky (2003), a leading international management text, highlights an earlier study that compared

Japanese, North American and Latin American negotiating styles (Casse 1982). This type of comparison, which is typical of many texts on the subject, has been summarised in Table 13.6. Similar examples of contrasting negotiating styles are reflected in the anecdotal accounts of business travellers, and in empirical studies that have investigated cultural difference (e.g. Buttery and Leung 1998, Graham 1985, Tse *et al.* 1994).

Table 13.6 Cultural difference in negotiation: an outdated approach?

Country/region	Indicative depictions of 'typical' styles
Japanese	Emotional sensitivity is highly valued; interaction involves hiding emotions; face saving is crucial; decision making is step-by-step; decision makers are openly influenced by special interests; the ultimate aim is the good of the group.
North American	Emotional sensitivity not highly valued; interaction is straightforward and impersonal; face saving does not always matter; decision making is methodical; special interests influence decision makers, though this is often considered unethical; the ultimate aim is profit motive or good of the individual.
Latin American	Emotional sensitivity is valued; interaction is emotionally passionate; face saving is crucial; decision making is impulsive and spontaneous; special interests of decision makers are condoned; the ultimate aim of the group equates to that of the individual.

Source: Casse (1982), Deresky (2003: 166).

While it is important for international negotiators to appreciate the cultural backgrounds of others, there is increasing criticism of this kind of approach to cross-cultural management (Holden 2002). To begin with, there is a presentational problem; over-simplified summaries can help to reinforce crude cultural stereotypes, which may themselves present a barrier to communication. However, there is a deeper problem with the way that cultural difference is conceptualised in these frameworks. First, they tend to focus on confrontations between two unitary cultures, whereas much of today's international negotiation involves interactions between individuals and groups from many different cultural backgrounds. In addition, the people who work in today's international organisations often draw on multiple cultural identities. For example, their parents may be from entirely different cultural backgrounds, and they may have work and educational experience in several countries. Indeed, professional negotiators in international organisations tend to be selected on the basis of their multicultural experience and training. The traditional frameworks also take no account of variables other than national culture, such as organisational setting and technical specialism that may have a profound influence on interactions. International business negotiation is itself becoming a professional field, with its own set of cultural norms (Sheer and Chen 2003: 56). In summary, there is a danger in presenting national culture as static and determining, and so underplaying the complex ways in which cultures are actively recreated through human interaction (see section 2.4). Mini-case 13.3 considers this issue in the context of recent research into Chinese negotiators and suggests that it is time for a fresh perspective on this vital communication issue.

Mini-case 13.3

The changing face of Chinese negotiation

Academic researchers from Hong Kong interviewed mainland Chinese and Western business professionals who had several years' experience in intercultural negotiation, ranging from commercial trading to technology transfer, joint ventures, real estate, cultural exchange and joint publishing contracts. A qualitative analysis of the interview transcripts revealed some conventional cases of cultural misunderstanding. For example, a factory director from Shanxi province described how he had 'learned' to maintain eye contact during negotiations with a Canadian investor:

> '[The] interpreter asked me privately whether I was really interested in the joint venture. I was surprised and asked why he asked me such a question. He replied that his boss (the Canadian investor) felt I did not pay attention to him and I always looked away. I learned the lesson. Afterwards, I made an effort to look at the "other side". I am still not very comfortable about this. But it helps negotiations.' (cited in Sheer and Chen 2003: 61)

Both Chinese and Western interviewees identified other differences in communication style, such as a tendency for mainland Chinese negotiators to engage in 'empty rhetoric' (i.e. extended speeches) prior to the main negotiation. However, these factors did not have a decisive impact:

> 'Chinese interviewees conveyed that cultural differences in language, communication, and social etiquette influenced business negotiation in an *insignificant* way. Similarly, Western interviewees saw these as differences in "style", which were obstacles that could be overcome with relatively minor impact on negotiation.' (*Ibid:* 62 – emphasis added)

One-third of the Chinese interviewees believed that the nature of the negotiation (i.e. the supply and demand relationship) and the rituals of international business negotiation were the main driving forces, rather than national culture. The remaining two-thirds identified the *simultaneous* impact of professional and national culture. They gave four reasons for the reduced importance of national culture: the increasing Westernisation of China; increased exposure of Chinese business people to international negotiation practices; closer connection via the internet and related technologies; and the priority attaching to business-related aims. This last point was summarised by a Chinese interviewee, 'Business first, other matters later.' The study concludes that Sino-Western negotiations are being influenced to varying degrees by national and professional cultures. However, it also suggests a rapidly *evolving* picture, as mainland Chinese negotiators engage more actively with the norms and practices of international business negotiation. For example, the Western interviewees made conventional comments on the Chinese concept of *Guanxi* (i.e. the use of personal relationships, often characterised as social networks), in the authors' terms, 'a necessary instrumental strategy to cope with the unstable and inconsistent political environments' (*Ibid:* 63). However, other studies have indicated that Guanxi is itself in a process of transformation, as part of the wider changes occurring in contemporary China (cf. Yeung and Tung 1996, Tsang 1998).

Questions

1 Why do you think both the Chinese and Western interviewees saw differences in language, communication and etiquette as of little importance in their negotiations?

2 How can this view be reconciled with the many popular anecdotes regarding 'culture clash' in international meetings and negotiations?

3 Why do you think the traditional concept of *guanxi* may be changing in the new China?

4 What are the implications of this study for the future of international business negotiation?

Sources: Yeung and Tung 1996, Tsang 1998, Sheer and Chen 2003. Case prepared by the author with acknowledgements to Yan Liu.

Time for a fresh perspective on negotiation?

This chapter has presented one of the most popular Western approaches to negotiation, the 'win–win' model. We have noted how the nature of international negotiation is changing, as cultures interact and new practices and styles are created. The discussion points to the way that negotiation, like any form of organisational communication, is influenced by the context in which it takes place. This view is supported by recent research in large manufacturing organisations, which has shown how negotiation behaviour is influenced simultaneously by individual, relational and organisational factors. In other words, the ways that negotiations are conducted depends on the kinds of people involved, the ways that their parent departments are connected to one another, and the overall strategic goals of the organisation (Nauta and Sanders 2000). However, it would be wrong to conclude that we have no choice regarding the ways in which we negotiate or, more broadly, how we interact in other kinds of meeting and team-based activity. For example, Putnam and Kolb (2000) present a feminist critique of traditional and principled (i.e. 'win–win') negotiation. The authors argue for an alternative model, 'one rooted in feminist values and assumptions about social interaction' (*Ibid:* 80). This approach substitutes conventional assumptions regarding negotiation as a series of exchanges with a process that the authors term, 'co-construction'. The pattern of communication replaces that of reciprocal concessions (i.e. 'if you do this, I will do that'), with a process of mutual inquiry, seeking to make connections and creating mutual understanding. The authors acknowledge that the approach sounds idealistic, but note that it is used in related areas, such as mediation and conflict resolution in the workplace. Like much of the earlier cross-cultural work (see Table 13.6), the authors tend to present their model as a polar opposite of traditional negotiation practice. For example, traditional relationships are, 'Other [party] as distant', 'Instrumental' and 'Rational', whereas relationships in the alternative model are, 'Other [party] as approachable', 'Expressive' and 'Emotional' (*Ibid:* 83 – Table 4.1). This does help to highlight the radical nature of their approach. However, it could be argued that much of its more socially-oriented, collaborative approach is already widely practised in existing forms of negotiation, beyond the dominant 'Western' model.

Summary

- Managers spend a large part of their lives attending meetings. Time invested in these rich but complex communication channels is only productive if they are used appropriately and managed competently.

- Organisations make use of many different types of meeting, which may have a briefing, advisory, consultative or executive role. These differences are also reflected in their procedures and associated communication practices.

- Formal meetings, such as committees, are characterised by rules, agendas, minutes, specific roles and memberships. Procedural aspects include the requirement to plan and circulate agendas in advance and to take accurate minutes.

- The chair of a formal meeting needs to be calm, objective, diplomatic and a good time-manager. The chair provides a structure for the meeting by planning the agenda, and manages the 'flow' of the discussion once the meeting is underway.

- The secretary also has an important role, assisting in the preparation of the agenda, advising on points of order and ensuring that the minutes are clear and unambiguous.

- Organisations also engage in many informal meetings, which are often integral to the work of project teams. Team-working can be a creative and motivating form of communication, given careful management and a sound understanding of team roles and dynamics.

- The rise of the 'virtual' team, connected through information and communication technologies, has extended organisational capabilities, while also creating a need for team members to deal with increased cultural diversity and other practical issues, such as time zones and language differences.

- Negotiations are a specialised type of meeting. Many inter-organisational relationships are long-term, where principled and collaborative approaches are usually most effective. Negotiations in this form require a professional, yet cordial atmosphere, where each party is able to evaluate offers from the other's perspective

- Earlier models of cross-cultural negotiation, based on stereotypical assumptions about 'national' styles, are being challenged by the more collaborative and socially-oriented approaches of some feminist and non-Western writers.

Practical exercises

1 Observing a meeting

Arrange to attend a local meeting that is open to the public (e.g. it may be possible to attend some the meetings at your university or other organisations such as the local council, chamber of commerce, trades union, voluntary bodies or professional organisations). Observe the actions of the chair, secretary and other participants. In particular, look out for the following.

Does the chair:

- Start the meeting at the stated time?

- Ensure that each item received sufficient time for debate?

- Control anyone who strayed from the subject matter of each item?

- Allow those who wanted to speak to do so?

- Get clear and unambiguous decisions?

- Remain calm and diplomatic throughout?

- Close the meeting on time (if stated)?

Does the secretary:

- Distribute copies of all the reports and papers under discussion?

- Advise on any points of order?

- Ask the chair to clarify the wording of any decisions?

- Take any other part in the discussions?

Note: The precise role of the secretary will vary depending on the type of meeting; for example, the secretary of a trades union branch meeting may take more of a leadership role. Much of this work takes place 'behind the scenes' rather than in the meeting itself.

Do the other participants:

- Make positive and well-considered contributions to the discussion?

- Allow others to speak without interrupting?

- Appear to understand the arguments that were being put forward?

- Reach an agreement on items, or resort to a majority vote?

- Become agitated or visibly bored by the proceedings?

- Stay until the end of the meeting?

Take notes on these items at the meeting and discuss the findings with other group members on your return. What are the main lessons to learn from this experience?

2 The negotiation game

This exercise simulates a 'real-world' negotiation, following the approach outlined in the chapter as 'principled' negotiation. It depends upon all parties adopting a predefined role. The negotiation may be based on your own scenarios, or case materials provided by your tutor. For example, the issue for negotiation might be opening hours at the university's computer facilities. One team represents the student union, which is requesting '24/7' access for all students. The other team represents university managers, who want to make a substantial reduction in current opening times. When the scenario has been identified, divide into two teams of four or five and spend 20 minutes preparing a position, using the 'win–win' guidance outlined in this chapter. Appoint one 'negotiator' to represent the rest of the team. The initial period of negotiation should run for about five minutes. During this time, other members of each team should act as observers, noting how the negotiation is progressing, but not making any interruptions. After five minutes, the negotiators may request a short 'time out', giving them an opportunity to consult in private with the rest of their team. Following a second period of five minutes, the negotiation is 'suspended', and the negotiators return to their teams to discuss the outcome. Each team prepares a short presentation structured around the following questions:

(a) What was the outcome? Did you achieve a 'win–win' solution, as described in the chapter? Check whether both parties have the same understanding on what has been agreed.

(b) Comment on the negotiation process. For example, did the discussions get bogged-down at any point? If so, how was the obstruction overcome?

(c) Consider your own negotiation skills. For example, were both parties able to develop creative offers, valuing them in the other party's terms?

(d) Reflect on the wider questions identified in the chapter. For example, how did your experience relate to the closing arguments concerning the influence of cultural and gender on approaches to negotiation?

Case-study M | International meetings: a virtual meeting of minds?

The following article was written by Jagdish Bhagwati, a professor of economics at Columbia University, and senior fellow at the Council on Foreign Relations in the United States. It appeared shortly after the destruction of New York's World Trade Center on 11th September 2001, and following a series of anti-globalisation protests at major international meetings:

We need to think seriously about how international meetings should be handled. The urgency of this task is underlined by what happened to this year's World Bank/International Monetary Fund meetings: first, they were reduced to two from seven days because of threats posed by violent anti-globalisation protests; then they were cancelled as a result of further threats by possible terrorist attacks. We are in a different and ingenious kind of conflict – one in which anti-globalisation protesters target the international agencies and superstructure that were the postwar creation and pride of far-sighted liberals (I mean liberals in the American sense). They strike where you most expect them: at the meetings of these agencies, the Group of Eight leading industrialised nations, and even Davos and the International Chamber of Commerce gatherings.

The world's media gather at these – often dull – events only to be enthralled by the theatrics and the fury unleashed in the streets outside the official meetings. The images of policemen armed with batons and bullets combating unarmed youths quickly undermines support for both the agencies and globalisation. The agencies will never win this battle unless they are prepared to introduce fundamental changes in the way they carry out their business. These changes are essential to assert the values of a dynamic, democratic society and open-world economy that these groups pretend to support but in fact undermine, using our traditions of freedom of speech and protest.

First, these gatherings must be confined to occasions when there is a truly important agenda that requires a large meeting in one place. The cancelled Bank/Fund meetings do not meet that test: nothing of great importance was due to be discussed. In fact, the elimination of such purposeless events would release significant resources – both from these institutions and from the host country, which must provide the security. The funds released could then be used to further the professed aims of the organisations, such as building more schools and hospitals in the poor countries. Second, when an assembly is considered essential, anti-globalisation groups must be allowed to hold alternative meetings but at a reasonable distance – 50 miles, say – from the site of the meeting. At the last Davos meeting, for example, protesters held an anti-Davos meeting simultaneously in Brazil. But the oceans need not divide the two parallel events. The great United Nations Women's Conference in Beijing did precisely this and it advanced the agendas of the more activist women effectively. It would then be up to the media to cover both meetings. Third, street demonstrations must not be ruled out but they have to be regulated so that they do not degenerate into violence. Such groups can democratically select the leaders and rank and file who will be allowed to protest outside the headquarters of the World Bank, for example, if this institution is holding an important meeting. But no one has the right to say that freedom of speech requires that you can get up in a safe theatre and shout 'Fire'. After Genoa, we know where that kind of freedom leads and it cannot be defended. Fourth, when the risk of violence is high and unavoidable and a targeted international agency has a truly important task before it, there is surely a case for shifting an assembly in one place to a 'virtual' meeting.

These principles apply nowhere more importantly than to the forthcoming World Trade Organisation ministerial meeting in Doha, Qatar, scheduled for November 9–13. It is an exceptionally important meeting where we hope finally to launch the new multilateral trade round. Indeed, Pascal Lamy, the European Union's trade commissioner, reminded us this week of the vital nature of the meeting. But do we really need to go to Doha?

Consider the downside. Doha is in the Middle East. It has little security so guests would have to arrange their own – with all the difficulties that would entail. If the US is engaged in retaliation for the recent terrorist attacks, the entire Middle East could suddenly become volatile. The radical anti-globalisation groups are likely to be a further source of insecurity. Add to all of this the limited number of flights out of Doha, and the result is potential disaster. Given the risks, why not have Mike Moore, head of the WTO, launch – with the prior approval of all the various heads of government – the new round via a teleconference link on November 9? A meeting along these lines would put a stop to the increasingly violent protests that we have become accustomed to because there would be no one place in which to protest. That would be a sufficient answer to the anti-globalisers: our business, which will achieve their agendas better than anything they propose, will go on.

Questions

1 Summarise Bhagwati's argument regarding the future of the international meeting, identifying the key factors behind the changes he proposes.

2 To what extent do you think the argument is a product of events at the time of writing? How far do the arguments remain valid today?

▶

3 Consider the implications for communication, if international meetings such as the WTO were run as 'virtual meetings'. For example, how do you think electronically-mediated communication might influence access to the meetings, and the ability of delegates to express their views (i.e. engage in persuasive communication)?

4 Is it possible to negotiate in a 'virtual' meeting? If so, how do you think the process outlined in this chapter might be modified to accommodate the electronic communication channel?

Source: Bhagwati (2001). Copyright Professor Bhagwati. Reproduced with permission.

Further reading

For further advice on the formal meeting, see **Armour** (2002) or **Martin** (2002). (Note: The British professional association, the Institute of Chartered Secretaries and Administrators (ICSA) is a useful source.) **Pan *et al.*** (2002) discuss cultural difference in meetings. **Adair** (1986) develops a useful leadership philosophy, based on the task, team-building and individual development. **Bennis** (2000) is a retrospective collection of writings on leadership and change by an acknowledged commentator. **Aditya *et al.*** (2000) offer a concise summary of the leadership field, including contemporary theories, albeit with a strong US orientation. **Belbin** (2000, 2003) are useful updates and extensions of earlier work on team roles. **Pauleen and Yoong** (2001) is a good example of research into multi-cultural virtual teams. It is also worth reading some practitioner accounts of team-working and leadership, such as **Harvey-Jones** (1994). On negotiation as a form of communication, see **Kolb and Williams** (2000) for a study of 'shadow negotiation', based on research conducted amongst female negotiators, and **Sheer and Chen** (2003) for an insightful empirical study on the complexities of cross-cultural negotiation.

References

Adair, J. (1986) Effective leadership: a modern guide to developing leadership skills. Pan, London.

Aditya, R.N., House, R.J. and Kerr, S. (2000) 'Theory and practice of leadership into the new Millennium' in Cooper, C.L. and Locke, E.A. *op cit.* (130–65).

Armour, D. (2002) *The ICSA company secretary's handbook* (4th edn.). ICSA Publishing, London.

Belbin, R.M. (1981) *Management teams: why they succeed or fail.* Butterworth–Heinemann, Oxford (2nd edn. (2003)).

Belbin, R.M. (1993) *Team roles at work.* Butterworth–Heinemann, Oxford.

Belbin, R.M. (2000) *Beyond the team.* Butterworth–Heinemann, Oxford.

Belbin, R.M. (2003) *Management Teams.* Butterworth–Heinemann, Oxford.

Bennis, W. (2000) *Managing the dream: reflections on leadership and change.* Perseus, Cambridge MA.

Bhagwati, J. (2001) 'A virtual meeting of minds'. *Financial Times*, London edition, 19 (20th September).

Buttery, E.A. and Leung, K.P. (1998) 'The difference between Chinese and Western negotiations'. *European Journal of Marketing*, 32, 132–46.

Casse, P. (1982) *Training for the multicultural manager: a practical and cross-cultural approach to the management of people.* Society for Intercultural Training and Research, Washington DC.

Deresky, H. (2003) *International management.* Prentice Hall, Upper Saddle River, NJ.

Cooper, C.L. and Locke, E.A (2000) *Industrial and organizational psychology: linking theory with practice.* Blackwell, Oxford.

Fisher, R., Ury, W. and Paton, B. (1991) *Getting to yes: the secret to successful negotiation.* Random House, London.

Graham, J.L. (1985) 'The influence of culture on business negotiations: an exploratory study'. *Journal of International Business Studies,* 16, 1, 81–96 (Spring).

Hackman, J.R., Wageman, R., Ruddy, T.M. and Ray, C.L. (2000) 'Team effectiveness in theory and practice'. in Cooper, C.L. and Locke, E.A. *op cit.* (109–29).

Harvey–Jones, J. (1994) *All together now.* Heinemann, London.

Holden, N. (2002) *Cross-cultural management: a knowledge management perspective.* FT Prentice Hall, Harlow.

Katzenbach, J.R. and Smith, D.K. (1998) *The wisdom of teams: creating the high performance organization.* McGraw–Hill, Maidenhead.

Kolb, D.M. and Williams, J. (2000) *The shadow negotiation: how women can master the hidden agendas that determine bargaining success.* Simon and Schuster, New York.

Kolb, D.M. and Williams, J. (2001) 'Breakthrough bargaining'. *Harvard Business Review,* 79, 88–97 (February).

Martin, D. (2002) *One stop company secretary* (3rd edn.). ICSA Publishing, London.

Mendenhall, M., Punnett, B.J. and Ricks, D. (1995) *Global management.* Blackwell, Oxford.

NTSU (2001) *Focus on personal travel: 2001 edition.* Department for the Environment, Transport and the Regions (National Travel Survey Unit), London.

Nauta, A. and Sanders, K. (2000) 'Interdepartmental negotiation behaviour in manufacturing organizations'. *The International Journal of Conflict Management,* 11, 2, 135–61.

Pan, Y., Scollon, S. and Scollon, R. (2002) *Professional communication in international settings.* Blackwell, Oxford.

Pauleen, D.J. and Yoong, P. (2001) 'Relationship building and the use of ICT in boundary–crossing virtual teams: a facilitator's perspective'. *Journal of Information Technology,* 16, 205–20.

Putnam, L.L. and Kolb, D.M. (2000) 'Rethinking negotiation: feminist views of communication and exchange'. in Buzzanell, P.M. (ed.) *Rethinking organizational and managerial communication from feminist perspectives.* Sage, Thousand Oaks CA (76–104).

Raiffa, H. (1982) *The art and science of negotiation.* Harvard University Press, Cambridge MA.

Sheer, V.C. and Chen, L. (2003) 'Successful Sino-Western business negotiation: participants' accounts of national and professional cultures'. *The Journal of Business Communication,* 40, 1, 50–85.

Tsang, E.W.K. (1998) 'Can guanxi be a source of sustained competitive advantage for doing business in China?' *Academy of Management Executive,* 12, 2, 64–73.

Tse, D.K., Francis, J. and Walls, J. (1994) 'Cultural differences in conducting intra- and inter-cultural negotiations: A Sino-Canadian comparison'. *Journal of International Business Studies,* 25, 3, 537–55.

Tuckman, B.W. (1965) 'Developmental sequences in small groups'. *Psychological Bulletin,* 63, 384–99.

Yeung, I.Y.M and Tung, R.L. (1996) 'Achieving business success in Confucian societies: the importance of *guanxi* (connections)'. *Organizational Dynamics,* 25, 2, 54–65 (Autumn).

CHAPTER 14

Communication in perspective

'Torawarenai suao-na kokoro,' which means, 'Mind that does not stick.'
A favourite phrase of Konosuke Matsushita, founder of Matsushita Electric

Learning outcomes

By the end of this chapter you should be able to:

- make connections between communication practices and organisational strategy, drawing on the preceding chapters and other sources, including personal experience;
- recognise the unresolved challenges and paradoxes faced by organisations seeking to communicate 'effectively' in networked, multiple-stakeholder environments;
- develop communication practices, and contribute to the development of communication strategies, that reflect the diversity and dynamism of today's organisations;
- formulate relevant questions and engage in informed argument concerning the wider communication issues raised in this book.

14.1 Introduction

The aim of this short chapter is to draw some useful conclusions, based on our review of organisational communication perspectives, principles and practices. The chapter also points to some continuing questions, regarding the themes that have been addressed in previous chapters. The opening quotation is from the Japanese entrepreneur and business leader, Konosuke Matsushita. These wise words have been cited by several management writers, including the international strategy specialist, Kenichi Ohmae (1989: 132) and the pioneering knowledge management researcher, Dorothy Leonard (1995: 29). They also encapsulate the core message presented in this text, which is that 'effective' communicators need to recognise the importance of remaining both flexible and critical, rather than simply 'sticking' with established patterns and practices. Matsushita's words also echo the opening quotation in Chapter 1, where the architect and designer Walter Gropius celebrated the practical value of working with an 'open' mind.

This chapter is based around five questions, which are designed to encourage further reflection and debate. The themes draw on various parts of the text, but can also be seen as an extension of the discussion that was opened in Chapter 7. This chapter contains just one mini-case (Mini-case 14.1) and the end-of-chapter practical exercises are replaced by additional discussion questions. The final case study, 'Sequencing the human genome', brings together several ideas developed throughout the text. It tells the story of a dramatic communication 'race' involving rival public and private sector scientific teams as they struggled to publish the so-called 'book of life'.

14.2 Five questions for organisational communicators

This section contains questions rather than answers. The questions have been selected on the basis that they pose some of the greatest challenges for those responsible for communicating in today's public, private and voluntary sector organisations. Each question is illustrated by practical examples, with references to previous sections' practices, and is concluded with a topic for further discussion. The list of questions does not provide a comprehensive review of the text, nor is it presented in any particular order. The main criteria for inclusion are that it addresses issues relevant to real organisations, relates to current communication practices and demands the continuing attention of managers. (Note: You may wish to revise some of the questions, or to add others, in order to reflect your own experience).

Question 1: How can we find out what we are communicating?

Throughout this text, we have been concerned with achieving two-way communication in organisations. This has revealed both the importance of interaction, and the practical obstacles to achieving it in practice. We began by considering some of the major barriers to communication, including a mixture of physiological, socio-cultural and political factors (sections 2.3 and 2.4). We also considered how organisations attempt to secure relevant feedback (section 6.2), and assessed the extent to which real dialogue can be achieved with multiple stakeholders (section 7.4) and through various channels. Organisations often carry out communication audits in order to assess the effectiveness of their communication channels and to isolate breakdowns and sources of noise. Various techniques are used to collect the source data. In a typical auditing exercise, managers or consultants circulate questionnaire surveys to employees and, in some cases, to external stakeholders, such as suppliers, customers and members of the local community. Additional audit evidence is collected through other channels, including corporate publications. For example, one of the major US energy companies included a feedback card in its annual *Sustainable Growth Report* (Conoco 2002). It asked stakeholders to evaluate the company on performance criteria (i.e. 'sustainability performance overall', 'environmental performance', 'social performance' and 'economic performance'). It also requested an evaluation of the report itself, based on the following criteria: content; transparency (defined as, 'how openly we have shared information with you'); balance (defined as, 'our willingness to share with you our challenges as well as our successes'); readability; and appearance. The form included a set of tick boxes (e.g. 'environmental advocate', 'government official', 'Conoco retiree', 'interested citizen'), the respondent being asked to check any that apply; there was also space for additional comments and for contact details if a response was required. Organisations may attempt to complement this text-based evidence with richer and more interactive sources, such as focus group discussions or 360 degree appraisals (section 6.3). Focus groups, which are normally facilitated by an independent consultant, are designed to allow an open exchange of ideas. However, discussions are typically based around themes identified by those with a specific responsibility for 'communication' issues, such as human resource and corporate affairs managers.

Topic for discussion: Consider the strengths and limitations of conventional communication audit techniques. Are they likely to be a useful indicator of how an organisation is communicating with its various stakeholders? How might you modify or enhance the audit process, in order to deal with issues raised in previous chapters?

Question 2: How can we make better use of new and emerging technologies?

The text has emphasised the importance of new technologies for the future of organisational communication. Chapters in Part II included several examples of organisations making creative use of new and emerging communication channels, including the creation of new internet-based ventures (Mini-case 7.2), internet-based stakeholder reporting (Mini-case 9.3), text messaging for customer relationship management (Mini-case 10.2), online recruiting (Mini-case 11.3) and virtual team-working (Mini-case 13.2). We also saw how patterns of communication and collaboration are shaped by the established technologies (Yates and Orlikowski 2002), and identified examples where these 'genre systems' are as yet undeveloped (section 8.8). For example, there is still a general lack of agreement over communication practices involving e-mail (Mini-case 8.2) and organisations have faced severe criticism over 'misuse' of text messaging when communicating with employees (Mini-case 8.3). Other on-going challenges include efforts to create more accessible web-based communication channels (Mini-case 2.1), and to avoid the more common abuses of presentation software, a phenomenon popularly known as 'death by *PowerPoint*' (Mini-case 12.2).

Discussion topic: Organisations of all kinds, including multinational corporations and large public and voluntary sector bodies, have had both 'good' and 'bad' experiences of applying new technologies for the purposes of communication. Which recent technological innovations do you think have had the biggest impact on organisational communication? Do you consider this impact to have been positive or negative for organisations and their stakeholders? What lessons might you draw from these experiences?

Question 3: How can we learn to communicate 'with emotion'?

Human emotion is a mysterious and powerful force, which can have a profound effect on the performance of organisations. Indeed, the success or failure of a strategic initiative can be largely determined by the emotional response of key internal and external stakeholders. Consequently, dealing with the emotional aspects of communication is both a demanding and a critically important managerial task. There is a substantial body of research on the role of emotion at work (e.g. Planalp 1999). In this text we have considered the ways that emotion is used in persuasive communication (section 5.3), and the role of 'emotional intelligence' in enhancing feedback (section 6.5); we have also touched on the additional complexities posed by culturally diverse organisational settings, where there may be contrasting approaches to emotional expression (section 2.4) (Kramer and Hess 2002).

Consider, for example, an organisation attempting to implement a new computer system across several sites, perhaps in different countries. Change management initiatives of this kind are bound to generate political tensions, as different factions promote their interests over those of others. People are also exposed to uncertainty, and may feel a lack of control over the process. Research suggests that the success or failure of such initiatives depends to a large extent on how ordinary employees perceive the change process, including the ways that they interact with others, and the socially-constructed meanings that emerge (Zorn 2002).

Discussion topic: What do you think are the main problems to be faced by managers as they attempt to 'handle' emotion across various communication channels? What are the most likely causes of these problems? How would you suggest that an organisation might enhance its capabilities in handling emotional aspects of its communication?

Question 4: How can our communication practices reflect increasing diversity?

The text has referred to many sources of diversity in today's organisations, including varieties of national and organisational culture, as well as differences in gender, and (dis)ability. This has been driven by several factors, including: the internationalisation of businesses, governmental and voluntary sector organisations; organisational responses to stakeholder activism; and the blurring of organisational boundaries (sections 2.4, 7.3 and 7.4). Increasing diversity challenges many traditional communication practices. For example, organisations need to learn how to accommodate cross-cultural team-working, a requirement that is intensified by new technologies that enable virtual teams to engage in real-time working across continents and time zones (section 13.6). While it has always been essential to consider the needs of the 'receiver', this task is complicated when the requirement is for interactive communication that can reflect the diversity of all those involved. For example, report writers need to pay particular attention to the use of language, and may have to make difficult trade-offs between creativity and clarity of expression in order to meet the needs of all stakeholders (section 3.4). Similar issues arise with non-verbal cues, such as the images used to reinforce promotional or campaigning messages, which may be appropriate for some audiences yet ineffective or even offensive to others (sections 5.6 and 10.4). Even human gestures, such as those used in face-to-face interviews or negotiations, may need to be reviewed or modified (sections 11.3 and 13.7).

Discussion topic: Do organisations really need to adjust their communication practices to reflect increasing diversity? How can they engage in a meaningful dialogue with multiple stakeholder groups? What steps would you take to ensure that an organisation was better prepared to meet these challenges?

Question 5: How do communication practices relate to leadership and strategy?

The Irish writer, George Bernard Shaw once noted that, 'For every complex problem, there is a simple solution – that is wrong.' The underlying message in this text has been that organisational communication involves many complex problems, and that contrary to the optimistic words of many popular management books, these problems are rarely open to simple 'recipe book' solutions (section 1.7). For example, we have seen how apparent 'barriers' to communication between members of a committee may be symptoms of deeper structural problems in the organisation, or in its wider environment (section 13.5). The 'solutions' are also likely to reflect pragmatic compromises, which are far from ideal. For example, formal structures and managerial hierarchies are generally the result of trade-offs between competing demands. Furthermore, one set of demands, such as efficient day-to-day operations, is likely to suggest different patterns of communication from other demands, such as stimulating creativity and innovation (section 7.2). Organisations also develop their own distinctive cultures and sub-cultures over time, leading to the potential for misunderstanding and conflict at their boundaries. Given this complexity, organisational communication is often referred to as a key strategic issue, closely connected to the task of leadership. However, as we have seen, organisational leaders often face serious communication problems within their own top management teams (Hambrick 1995) (section 7.2). In addition, there are major tensions between the decentralised approaches to communication indicated in recent stakeholder thinking, and the more unified messages associated with corporate communication (cf. Andriof *et al.* 2002, 2003, Kitchen and Schultz 2001) (sections 7.3 and 10.6).

Discussion topic: What are your views on the argument that organisational communication is a complex phenomenon that should be treated as a key strategic issue? How can the leadership of an organisation seek to influence its communication practices? How would you deal with the tension between maintaining consistent messages and allowing parts of the organisation to engage in real dialogue with stakeholders?

The five questions illustrate something of the challenge of organisational communication. They also suggest that managers need to be willing to reflect on their existing assumptions and practices, in the light of new evidence from a rapidly-changing environment. Mini-case 14.1 tells the story of two senior managers who found themselves reassessing their approaches to organisational communication after taking part in a round-the-world yacht race. The harsh realities of life at sea had a dramatic impact on their long-held views, particularly in relation to the key tasks of leadership and team-working.

Mini-case 14.1	**Leadership, team-working and communication: the 'Global Challenge'**

Going backwards is usually bad for business. Simply staying afloat then becomes the challenge. At sea, the latter is clearly essential. But for skippers who finished the BT Global Challenge round-the-world race this year, backwards was in fact progress. Their east to west race route, known by seamen as the 'wrong way', meant sailing against prevailing winds and the natural flows of the ocean for more than 30,000 miles to reach the contest's seven ports of call. And for at least two skippers, Mark Denton and Manley Hopkinson, the challenge after leaving Southampton in September of last year yielded valuable lessons applicable to business. By their return this summer, some long-held notions of management and communication strategies, and leadership roles, had been discarded and replaced by approaches refined during ten months at sea.

Mr Denton and Mr Hopkinson made it with ten others through a selection process that whittled down 186 applicants to 12 skippers of the Global Challenge boats – 72ft, 42-tonne yachts with 17-strong crews of amateur sailors. Before joining Global Challenge, both skippers had had more than 25,000 miles of sailing experience and had their own theories about how to manage staff.

Mr Hopkinson, who served in the navy and has worked in information technology, most recently for Granada Media managing a team about the size of his boat's crew, believed in the importance of a team leader's mentor role and a simple approach to management challenges based on his time in the services. Modern management theories have their origins in the military, he said last year before setting off on the voyage. Mr Denton agreed with Mr Hopkinson about mentor figures. Before Global Challenge, his management experience was from working in advertising and the music business and running a car valeting service when, he admits, 'I treated my staff as a means to an end.' But back on dry land after completing the Global Challenge, both skippers have changed their approach. Mr Hopkinson stresses the importance of a fluid management structure – and establishing the right culture in which crew/staff could achieve. Mr Denton highlights the need to spend time reflecting on performance, which he rarely did when he ran his own business. In Mr Denton's case, reflection was essential when an error resulted in 12 hours stuck in port while race rivals at sea were free to increase their advantage.

'We were due to leave for Wellington,' recalls Mr Denton. 'But the boat was filled with the wrong fuel. We lost 12 hours and found ourselves 120 miles behind.' Mr Denton's approach to this situation would be how he would now deal with setbacks in business. 'I had to input positive and achievable goals, developing them with the team,' he says. 'It couldn't be that we aimed to win the leg. But in the end we sailed really well. We didn't win, of course, but we felt as though we had. We ended up the

▶

happiest boat in port.' Mr Hopkinson also now firmly believes that team goals must, foremost, be achievable. His main target at sea was to be a 'happy boat', especially as sleep could be scarce and conditions intimidating, not least when heading for the Roaring Forties on the 3,000-mile stretch between Cape Horn, South Africa, and New Zealand. He now holds as very important the early establishment of a culture in which goals are jointly developed and based on what motivates each individual. Targets are then shared and can help bind a strong team together – even when enduring sub-zero wind chill and 100ft swell.

There are techniques of motivation that Mr Hopkinson, having successfully applied them to managing his crew, would now use in business. 'I encouraged people to write down their goals so we could agree them, then no-one could point a finger if we failed and claim "that wasn't my goal". I also established common social rules so that bickering was kept to a minimum. Deal with it, then let it go; support each other; lean on each other.' It was, Mr Hopkinson now admits, different from management styles he had picked up in the navy – he served in the Gulf war – and subsequently applied to team-building in the commercial world. 'In the services, your goal is nominated. On the boat – and so in business – the way was to decide achievable goals.' Mr Hopkinson did not bark out orders every day, with winning the race in mind. 'For me, as the skipper I encouraged the team to grow and its members to develop as individuals. In fact, by striving for these goals we did nearly win one of the legs.'

Both Mr Hopkinson and Mr Denton benefited from establishing a shallow, fluid management structure. In Mr Hopkinson's case that meant an 'almost round table' process of open discussion. 'I also encouraged crew to take decisions,' he says. Mr Denton emphasised in crew meetings how the boat as a whole – 'we' – would handle situations. Finger-pointing was outlawed. Establishing a collective approach also helped when Mr Denton received bad news. 'Leaving Boston for what is known as the 'sunshine leg" to Buenos Aires, I received the weather report which warned that we would run right into a hurricane and 40mph winds. I was able to convey this information quickly and the crew was immediately involved.' Such openness would yield benefits in an office culture, he believes. 'In business, people can work in isolation. Companies operate with everyone in the dark and it is not at all effective.' Both crews also accepted responsibility for mistakes, which were reviewed together, with the emphasis on solutions. Skipper error was also not a taboo subject. But Mr Denton also stresses that he learnt the importance of showing leadership not by banging the table but by 'constantly reiterating goals', having established them early on. 'Time for reflection was important in this,' he believes. 'I hosted debriefing groups and one-on-one talks to see how we could get back on track and achieve what we had set out to achieve. This meant going back to the foundations. That doesn't happen enough in business.'

Mr Hopkinson believes he gained the greatest insight, with future management challenges in mind, from having to incorporate new crew members – 'leggers' – who joined his ship's permanent team for short periods throughout the race. 'In business, staff come and go,' he reflects. 'You have to make people receptive to change. On the final leg of the race back to Britain, fresh leggers joined the boat and the culture was in place to incorporate them. The new people didn't feel estranged, as new staff shouldn't in the commercial world.'

The conclusions drawn by the two skippers is supported by post-race research, carried out by Professors Victor Dulewicz and Malcolm Higgs of Henley Management

College. After each leg, crew members were asked to answer 30 questions on their motivation. According to Prof Dulewicz, the responses highlight that it was crews with shared values and the greatest levels of team work that achieved the best results, and that tangible signs of success were the greatest motivation.

Questions

1 Prepare a sheet of paper, overhead transparency or whiteboard, with two vertical columns. Reread the article and use the left-hand column to list the various 'lessons' identified by the two managers, using key words (e.g. 'fluid structure', 'right culture' ...).

2 Identify and discuss the communication issues raised by each item on your list, referring back to relevant sections in this text where necessary.

3 Which of the 'lessons' outlined in the case do you see as being the most important for your own self-development?

4 How might organisations and managers be encouraged to learn from personal experiences of this kind?

Source: Cameron (23 November, 2001). Copyright Financial Times Limited. Reproduced with permission.

Summary

- Organisational communication is a complex phenomenon, which is not open to simple 'recipe book' solutions. Effective communicators require an open and analytical mind that can draw on multiple perspectives in addition to their own immediate experiences.

- Organisations face important questions regarding their communication practices, including: how to find out what is being communicated; how to make better use of new and emerging technologies; how to communicate 'with emotion'; how to ensure that communication practices reflect increasing diversity; and how to relate communication practices to organisational leadership and strategy.

- Leaders of organisations face their own barriers to communication at the level of senior management teams; they need to be responsive to changing environments and willing to abandon long-established practices in response to experience and informed advice.

- While a great deal can be achieved by drawing on existing knowledge, effective communicators also need to be willing to ask new questions and to experiment with novel approaches.

- Though efforts to improve communication can often be demanding, they are an essential element in achieving personal and organisational goals.

Questions for discussion

Reviewing an organisation's communication practices and performance

Select one organisation for detailed analysis, using the following questions as a guide. Your access to information may be restricted, but could include organisational websites, media reports, direct observation (e.g. as a customer) and interviews with employees or other stakeholders. If you are working with others, it would be useful to compare different organisations. Report your findings verbally, supported with six presentation slides or posters. In the case of presentation slides, you may want to summarise your key points in 'bullet point' format; the posters could be more elaborate, including a combination of text and graphics. For example, you could include examples obtained from the organisation (e.g. sample web pages, promotional materials, letters, reports) to support your arguments.

1 What do you consider to be the main barriers to communication currently experienced by this organisation?

2 What is your assessment of the organisation's use of verbal and non-verbal communication in its efforts to communicate with internal or external stakeholders?

3 How does the organisation make use of persuasive communication to achieve particular objectives? (Try to find evidence that might indicate success or failure in this area.)

4 What mechanisms does the organisation use to secure feedback from various stakeholders? (Try to find evidence that might indicate effectiveness of these mechanisms).

5 How do you see communication practices as being influenced by formal structures and external relationships?

| Case-study N | Sequencing the human genome – the communication 'race' |

Background

Sequencing the human genome has been one of the great scientific achievements of recent times. The human genome has been called 'the book of life' and its three billion 'letters', contained within DNA, form our genetic instruction book. Sequencing the genome means decoding all the letters, in the right order. Researchers can use the genome sequence to understand disease, to gain new knowledge of the body functions and to search for new treatments.

In June 2000, the American President, Bill Clinton, and the British Prime Minister, Tony Blair, announced at a joint press conference that the draft of the human genome had been completed by two rival teams: a public consortium called the Human Genome Project (HGP) and a private company, Celera. In 2001, some months after this announcement, HGP and Celera published separate draft versions of the sequence in different scientific journals (*New Scientist* 2001). By the time HGP had published the final version of the sequence, in April 2003, Celera had abandoned genome sequencing (Couglan 2003). However, just five years earlier Celera's entry into genome sequencing had led to suggestions that the publicly-funded HGP should be closed down. This case describes the 'race' that developed between the public and private sector projects, and examines how communication affected the outcome.

The public sector rivals: the Human Genome Project

The Human Genome Project (HGP) formally began in 1990. It was a loose international collaboration, which still continues today. The single biggest partner was the UK's Sanger Institute in Cambridge, funded largely by the Wellcome Trust, a medical charity. It contributed about 30 per cent of the genome sequence. In the US, four government-funded laboratories contributed about 60 per cent of the sequence between them, while laboratories in France, Germany, Japan and China together provided the remainder. The key aim of the public project was not only that the human genome should be sequenced, but that all the data should made freely-available, without restriction. John Sulston was the director of the Sanger Institute, where he led the British team in their work on the Human Genome Project. Sulston was a scientist with a specialism in the genetics of worms; he was reluctant to become the identifiable figurehead for the HGP. He later wrote: 'I hadn't wanted to take a lead on the PR front for the simple reason that, judging by the usual standards in the scientific community, the human sequence was not my work.' (Sulston and Ferry, 2001:242)

The private sector rivals: Celera Genomics Corporation

Celera Genomics was founded in 1998 by Craig Venter, a long-established genetic scientist, and Perkin-Elmer, a company that manufactured the advanced machines needed for decoding the human genome. Celera was created for the purpose of sequencing the genome. The new company suggested it could complete the task more cheaply and quickly than the public project. Celera's strategy has been described as an 'attempt to privatise the human genome by sequencing it before the publicly funded Human Genome Project.' (*New Scientist* 2002). The company's slogan at this time, 'Speed matters, discovery can't wait' reflected their emphasis on completing the project in advance of their rivals. Craig Venter was the President and Chief Scientific Officer of Celera from its inception until January 2002. He proved to be a very talented communicator, with a gift for putting the Celera case to various audiences, including one highly influential statement that was delivered to the US House of Representatives in 2000 (Venter 2000).

The 'race' begins

By May 1998, HGP had been publicly publishing sections of the genome as they were decoded for several years. It was at this point that Celera announced its intention to sequence the human genome. From then onwards, the quest to sequence the whole human genome was widely perceived as a head-to-head competition between Celera and HGP. As the *New Scientist* reported, 'Like it or not, 1998 was the year in which the genome project turned into a race' (*New Scientist* 1998). During the period 1999–2000, there were tentative negotiations between Celera and HGP to see if they could collaborate. However, these talks broke down over differences in their views about public access to data. From this point, there were reports that the race was becoming increasingly acrimonious.

This was a race that mattered very much to HGP. It feared that, if Celera was able to sequence the genome first, the company could patent the knowledge and prevent it being freely available. HGP did not believe it could guarantee winning the moral argument (i.e. that such knowledge should, by its nature, not be patentable), and decided that it must win the scientific race in order to put this knowledge in the public domain and make it impossible to patent.

▶

HGP's communication challenge

HGP also faced a serious communication challenge. It needed to persuade its key stake-holders, and the world at large, that the public project was successful. HGP had to demonstrate that it was delivering good results and, ideally, that it was out-performing the private sector company. Above all, it was vital to convince the US government agencies, to ensure that they would continue funding the project. Support for the publicly-funded project was far from guaranteed. For example, after Celera announced its entry into genome sequencing, some US politicians began to argue that the public project was redundant and Federal funding should cease (House of Representatives 2000).

From the start, HGP had formidable challenges in conveying its messages. Sulston and others believed that Celera consistently did a better job. As one of the American HGP scientists said, 'The public project was portrayed as labouring with a clumsy, bureaucratic, difficult-to-implement strategy, and these fast-moving folks in the private sector were going to run circles around us...' (quoted in Sulston and Ferry 2001: 184). One of the key problems for HGP was the political sensitivity around any attempts to criticise a private company in the US. For example, within a few days of the private-sector announcement, the UK-based Wellcome Trust announced that it would double the money it gave to the Sanger Centre. An official from the Trust stated, 'To leave this to a private company, which has to make money, seems to me completely and utterly stupid' (House of Representatives 2000). By contrast, the US response was much more conciliatory, with both of the major funding agencies welcoming Celera's initiative, while questioning its ability to deliver data in timely manner (House of Representatives 2000). This difference in approach persists today, as can be seen by the content of the UK and US HGP websites (Your Genome 2003, ORNL 2003).

Science by press release?

In his reflections on the 'race' John Sulston suggests that HGP and Celera were not competing on equal terms. He felt that Celera was not abiding by the scientific ethics that HGP held dear, in particular the convention that results are not announced until the work is completed and accepted for publication in a peer-reviewed journal (Sulston and Ferry 2001:182). Echoing this point, an American HGP researcher accused Venter of engaging in 'science by press release' (House of Representatives 2000).

The genome project was breaking new ground in science, and using technologies understood by very few people. HGP and Celera were using different scientific strategies to try to decipher the genome and Sulston believed that Celera were making over-ambitious claims. For example, in January 2000 the company released a statement that gave the impression it had sequenced nine times as much of the genome as HGP. Sulston believed this was a deceptive comparison of different sorts of data, and in fact the true picture was that HGP had completed more than Celera, and that much of Celera's data came from the publicly available HGP database. However, once Celera had communicated its version of events, Sulston did not think he succeeded in getting his complex scientific rebuttal across, 'I tried hard to explain ... to journalists, but not many got it and most thought it was sour grapes on my part' (Sulston and Ferry 2001:241).

HGP's communication lessons

HGP could be accused of being naïve about what was required to communicate effectively. For example, it took until early 2000 for Sulston to become the generally acknowledged figurehead. Sulston himself was more used to the discipline of science, where the system is geared to finding out the truth, rather than to public relations and journalism, where other factors need to be addressed. As Sulston says, 'I began to realise that presentation matters enormously, that nobody has time or patience to examine the facts for themselves, but rather takes up what is proffered most conveniently' (Sulston and Ferry 2001:242). HGP also suffered from internal communication difficulties arising from its organisational structure, and a lack of specialist resources, 'We were all thrown back on our own resources to present the case as well as we could. We suffered from lack of co-ordination and lack of time' (Sulston and Ferry 2001: 242)

How it ended

The public project succeeded in its goal of ensuring that the genome sequence was put into the public domain and could not be patented. However, it did not feel the media reflected either the importance of its ethical position, or the quality of its science. As Sulston noted, 'The media myth of Celera being ahead of the game became firmly established' (Sulston and Ferry 2001: 241). Sulston's conclusion was that HGP won the scientific challenge, but came a distant second in its efforts to communicate. Furthermore, a combination of HGP's poor communication strategy and Celera's professionalism almost lost them the scientific challenge too. If this had happened, the outcome for the human genome sequence, which is now freely available to the world, could have been very different. When the draft genome was jointly published in 2001, an editorial in the *New Scientist* reflected on what might have been:

> 'Think about what would have happened if the Human Genome Project had been shut down ... Celera would now have absolute power over the human genome. Ask yourself whether the company would now be offering anyone free access to its data.' (New Scientist 2001)

Note: The website http://psci-com.org.uk/ is a guide to quality web-based resources on public engagement with science and technology. It offers free access to a searchable catalogue of websites covering public engagement in science, science communication and the interpretation of science in society.

Questions

1 What do you consider to be the major communication challenges facing:

   (a) the Human Genome Project (HGP)

   (b) Celera Genomics

   (c) both organisations.

2 Use examples from the case to contrast the communication strategies adopted by the two organisations, noting any changes that occurred during the race.

3 How might communication-related factors have contributed to the breakdown in negotiations between HGP and Celera?

4 Draft a set of guidelines (maximum 1,000 words) for scientists/science-based organisations on communicating with the media, politicians and the public.

Source: Co-authored with Tina Fawcett.

Further reading

Chapter 7 contains a number of useful references related to the relationship between organisations, organisational strategies and communication. Full details are given in the Further reading at the end of that chapter. **Huff and Jenkins** (2002) is an edited volume, which exemplifies the links being made between communication-related concepts (in this case, managerial cognition), organisation theory and strategic management. **Sulston and Ferry** (2001) tells the story of the human genome project from the perspective of one of the leading scientists, who headed up the public sector team. **Ridley** (1999) is a fascinating 'popular science' guide to the human genome, which also serves to illustrate how complex scientific information can be communicated effectively to a non-specialist audience. (Note: See also the website reference given at the end of the case study in this chapter).

References

Andriof, J., Waddock, S., Husted, B. and Rahman, S. (eds.) (2002) *Unfolding stakeholder thinking: theory, responsibility and engagement.* Greenleaf, Sheffield.

Andriof, J., Waddock, S., Husted, B. and Rahman, S. (eds.) (2003) *Unfolding stakeholder thinking 2: relationships, communication and performance.* Greenleaf, Sheffield.

Cameron, D. (2001) 'Men at the helm who steered a new course'. *Financial Times*, London edition, 16 (23rd November).

Conoco (2002) *Conoco sustainable growth report.* Conoco Inc, Houston TX.

Couglan, A. (2003) 'First and only edition of the book of life'. *New Scientist*, 178, 2391–19, 19 (April).

Hambrick, D.C. (1995) 'Fragmentation and the other problems CEOs have with their top management teams'. *California Management Review*, 37, 3, 110–27 (Spring).

House of Representatives (2000) *Hearing Charter for Hearing on The Human Genome Project.* Subcommittee on Energy and Environment, US House of Representatives Committee on Science, Washington (6th April). (Available at: www.house.gov/science/ee_charter_040600.htm (accessed 14th August 2003).)

Huff, A. and Jenkins, M. (eds.) (2002) *Mapping strategic knowledge.* Sage, London.

Kitchen, P.J. and Schultz, D.E. (2001) *Raising the corporate umbrella: corporate communications in the 21st century.* Palgrave, Basingstoke.

Kramer, M.W. and Hess, J.A. (2002) 'Communication rules for the display of emotions in organizational settings'. *Management Communication Quarterly*, 14, 1, 50–89.

Leonard, D. (1995) *Wellsprings of knowledge: building and sustaining the sources of innovation.* Harvard Business School Press, Boston MA.

New Scientist (1998) 'The tortoise and the hare'. *New Scientist*, 160, 2165–19, 34 (December).

New Scientist (2001) 'Free for all'. *New Scientist*, 169, 2278–17, 3 (February).

New Scientist (2002) 'Venter quits'. *New Scientist*, 173, 2327–26, 7 (January).

ORNL (2003) *Human genome project and the private sector: a working partnership.* (Available at: www.ornl.gov/techresources/human_genome (accessed 13th August).)

Ohmae, K. (1989) 'Companyism and do more better'. *Harvard Business Review*, 67, 125–32 (January–February).

Planalp, S. (1999) *Communicating emotion: social, moral and cultural processes.* Cambridge University Press, Cambridge.

Ridley, M. (1999) *Genome: the autobiography of a species in 23 chapters.* Fourth Estate, London.

Sulston, J. and Ferry, G. (2001) *The common thread: science, politics, ethics and the human genome*. Corgi, London.

Venter J. C. (2000) 'Prepared statement before the Subcommittee on Energy and Environment, US House of Representatives Committee on Science,' Washington DC (6th April). (Available at: www.house.gov/science (accessed 14th August 2003).)

Yates, J. and Orlikowski, W.J. (2002) 'Genre systems: structuring interaction through communicative norms'. *The Journal of Business Communication*, 39, 13–35.

Your Genome (2003) 'Frequently asked questions'. Wellcome Trust, London. (Available at: www.yourgenome.org/help/faq (accessed 13th August).)

Zorn, T.E. (2002) 'The emotionality of information and communication technology implementation'. *Journal of Communication Management*, 7, 2, 160–71.

Index

Abilene Paradox 36, 37, 129
abstracting *see* summarising
acceptance 266
access issues 26, 32–4, 57
activism *see* campaigning
Adbusters 228
adjournments 305
advertising 106, 117, 223–9
   countering 227–8
   formats/styles 227
   see also promotion
advertorials 67
advice 266, 267
advisory meetings 302
agendas and agenda items 305, 306, 313
alcohol 290
Alderfer, C.P. 109
alertness 27–8, 79
ambiguity 29, 58–9, 93, 200
amendments 305
anecdotes *see* stories
anthropology 13
appearance 75–6, 80, 83, 92, 94–5, 278
   checking 288–9
   see also gestures *and* posture
appraisals *see* performance appraisals
archiving *see* records
argument 106–8, 202
   see also persuasion
Aristotle 107
assembly instructions 78
assessment *see* appraisals *and* feedback
attention 27–8, 303
   demonstrating 255, 257
   and memory 31
   securing 79, 113–14, 275, 291–2
audience 274–5, 293–4
   assessing 109, 198
   encouraging interaction in 294
   securing attention of 113, 291–2
   see also receivers
audio-visual equipment 283–4, 285, 288, 309
   see also visual communication

backings 108
bar charts 85–6
Barnardo's 79

Bartle Bogle Hegarty 287
Belbin, R.M. 315
beliefs 7, 111
Benetton 113–14, 117
bias *see* stereotypes
Bird, F.B. 37, 129
blindness 26, 33–4
body clock 28
body language 64, 75, 77, 92–5, 255, 293
   see also facial expression, gestures *and* posture
BOGOF 225
BP 67, 217–18
BPR (business process re-engineering) 13
brainstorming 316–17
brand awareness 80, 106, 222, 223
breathing 279, 289
briefing 196, 197, 213, 222–3, 302
   see also news releases
British culture 39, 94
BT 98–100, 157–8
bullet points 214, 287
business letters *see under* writing
business plans 219
business process re-engineering 13
business stationery 181–2
businesses, law concerning 58, 182, 304–5
Buy Nothing Day 228

campaigning/activism 130, 157, 227–8, 239–40, 328, 329
   charities and 120–1
CARE 231
Carlson, T. 226
CDP (Communication Display Portfolio) 95–6
Centre for Research in Innovation Management 19
CEO Circle 20
chairing 303, 305, 309–10, 312
change 335
channels 6, 7–8, 234–5
   ethical issues 117
   and feedback 126
   multiple 46, 114
   one-way/interactive 10, 173, 229
   synchronous/asynchronous 173, 184, 186
   see also individual channels
charities, law concerning 120, 182
charts 84–6, 88

chief executives 20
Chinese cultures 40, 93, 323–4
chunking 31
Churchill, Winston 60
CIPFA (Chartered Institute of Public Finance and
    Accountancy) 89–90
circadian rhythms 28
claims 108
clarification 257, 260
clarity 65
    see also Plain English
Clarke, Jane 20
Clarke, Kenneth 61
clichés 61, 83, 180–1
Climate Care 155
clips *see* sound bites
closed questions 259, 260
closeness *see* distance
clothing *see* dress
clustering 19
co-authoring 209–10
coaching 250, 252
coding *see* encoding
colour 91
Comet 91
commitment, perceptions concerning 39
committees 304, 305, 306, 312
communication 4–16
    advertising and 226–7
    channels *see* channels
    dimensions of 9–11
    effects of failure 9, 25
    emotional element 137, 335
    ethics concerning 117–18
    holistic nature 77
    improving 43–6
    linear model 4–8, 115, 229
    one-way/interactive 10, 115, 173, 229
    physiological and neurological factors affecting
        26, 27–34, 289–90
    planning 44, 82
    problems with and factors affecting reception
        26–43, 82–3, 160, 186, 200, 256, 260, 261 (*see
        also* misunderstanding *and* noise)
    records of *see* records
    theories of 4–16
    see also content *and* non-verbal communication
communication audits 333–4
    see also feedback
Communication Display Portfolio 95–6
companies 182, 304–5

complaints 235
complexity 126–7, 160, 336
conferences *see* meetings
conformity 34, 35–7, 129
    see also groupthink
congruence 266
consistency *see* inconsistency
consultative meetings 302
content 6–7
    in letters 177–80
    stories/narratives 66–8, 70–2
    see also message(s) *and* provocativeness
context, meaning and 83
continuous improvement 46
contracts 58
contradiction 46, 75–6, 82
control 46, 71, 153
    physical expression 92, 93
cookies 10
corporate identity *see* organisational identity
correctness *see under* language
counselling 266–7
Crane, A. 158, 159, 232
critical perspectives 13, 14
criticism 45, 46
cross-referencing 210
Crystal Mark 57
cues and cue cards 282, 283, 294
cultural jamming 227–8
culture(s) and cultural issues 14, 26, 38–43, 202,
        255–6, 260, 298
    CDP and 95–6
    definition of culture 38
    multiple identities 41, 255, 323
    and negotiation 321, 322–4
    organisational 70–1, 150–2, 336
    visual communication and 76, 83, 92, 93
    in writing 203, 214
    see also groupthink
cybernetics 8

daily cycles 28
data 6
    electronic exchange of 19–20
    graphical representation of 84–90
    see also facts
data projectors 284
databases and datasets 193, 194
deadlines 185
deafness 26
decision-making 109, 213

decoding 4–5
delayering 148
design 75, 82, 84
    and accessibility 32–4
    forms 134
    letterheads 181
diagramming 44, 45
diagrams 56
    see also visual communication
dialogue, symmetrical/asymmetrical 158–9, 232–3
Digital World Research Centre 173
direct action 114
    see also campaigning
direct marketing 117, 192–4, 222, 230
disability issues 26, 32–4
Disability Rights Commission 34
disciplinary interviews 250, 252–3
discourse analysis 13, 14, 67
dissertations 201, 203–4, 219
distance, personal 77, 83, 92, 93–4
    see also touch
distraction 83, 258, 286
    see also noise
diversity 335–6
    see also culture(s)
double-loop learning 136
drafting 202, 210, 213–14
dress 75, 80, 94–5, 278
    see also appearance
dress codes 94–5, 278

e-mail 19, 20, 58, 171, 173, 183–8
    marketing application 230, 231
    problems concerning 19, 78, 153, 184, 186
    research concerning 19–20, 173–4
ecological issues *see* environmental issues
economic barriers to communication 26
economics 156
Ecover 231
editing 208–9, 210–12, 214
effectiveness 14–16
EGO (eyes glazing over) 293
email *see* e-mail
emotion(s) 7, 93, 335
emotional intelligence 136–8, 140
empathy 266
emphasis 64
employees 11, 130–3, 235, 335
    see also performance appraisals *and* training
Employment Studies, Institute of 18, 19
'empowerment' 13

encoding 4, 5, 8, 46, 114, 117
encouragement, showing 255, 257, 260
English 53, 54–5, 59, 64, 65
    varieties of 60, 65
    see also language *and* Plain English
entrepreneurship 162–5
environmental issues 54, 67–8, 155, 156–7, 231, 243–4
EQ/emotional intelligence 136–8, 140
ethics 34, 37, 116–18, 129–30
    see also religion
ethnography 13
euphemisms 61–2
events *see* performances
executive meetings 302
executive summaries 204, 213
exhibitions 238–9, 240
expectations 9, 254–5
explicit knowledge 136
expression 64, 78, 82, 92–3, 249, 255
eXtensible Business Reporting Language 218–19
external/internal communication 11
ExxonMobil 67–8
eye contact 64, 76, 83, 92, 249, 255, 321
    losing 293
    posture and 276–7
eyebrows, raising 93

face-to-face meetings 18–20, 77, 186
    see also meetings
facial expression 64, 78, 82, 92–3, 249, 255
facts 6, 110–11, 181, 214
    see also information
Fairtrade Mark 80–1
false consciousness 13
families 173–4
fax 8, 173
feedback 8–9, 45, 46, 125–37, 333–4
    distorted 160
    informal 131–2, 152
    internet technology 10
    negative 45, 46, 235
feedback loop 8, 9
feminism 14, 322–3, 325
fight or flight reaction 289–90
figurative language 60–2
financial reporting 55–6, 214, 217–19, 234
first impressions 289
flexibility 332
flip charts 285, 309
flow charts 244–6

focus groups 334
fonts 56, 57, 181, 207
forming/storming/norming/performing/adjourning 314
forms 134
Freeman, R.E. 156, 158
French culture 39
functional structure 146, 147, 161

Gandhi, Mahatma 239
GE (General Electric) 71
gender issues 174, 226
genre systems 189–90
gestures 64, 83, 92, 93, 249, 257, 277
  handshakes 321, 322
glossaries 62
'Golden Bull' awards 57
Goleman, Daniel 137
graffiti 227, 228
grammar 53, 58, 59, 181, 210
grapevines 131–2, 152
graphic communication see visual communication
graphs 86–7, 88
green issues see environmental issues
Greenpeace 239–40
grievance interviews 250, 252–3
Gropius, Walter 1, 332
grounds 108, 110
groups 313
  see also teams
groupthink 26, 35–7, 129
guanxi 324

habituation 28
handshakes 321, 322
hard sales 117
Harvey, J.B. 36
  see also Abilene Paradox
headings
  in e-mails 185
  in letters 177
  in presentations 275
  in reports 56, 57, 204, 207, 210
Healey, Dennis 61
hermeneutics 13
Hewlett, Bill 71
hierarchies 148
histograms 86
Hofstede, Geert 38–9
Hoover 230
Howell, Julie 33–4

humour 79
Huws, Ursula 18, 19
hypothetical questions 261

IBM 80, 150
icons 76, 78
ICT 19–20, 152–4, 213, 286–7
ideas 6–7, 44, 45, 316–17
identity/identities 14, 41, 255, 323
  see also organisational identity
idioms 60–2, 180–1
IKEA 78
illusions, optical 29, 30
image see organisational identity and public relations
images (metaphors) 60–2, 291
images (pictures/diagrams) see visual communication
imagination 29
improvising see spontaneity
incentives 134
  see also motivation
inconsistency 46, 75–6, 82, 92, 210
indexing 206
Indian English 60
influence 107
  see also persuasion
information
  limit for short-term memory 31
  organising 31, 202–3
  overload 213, 275
  see also data and knowledge
information technology see ICT
Innovation Management, Centre for Research in 19
Institute of Employment Studies 18, 19
Institute of Public Relations 232
instructions 200, 223
intelligence 137, 138
interaction 18–20, 275, 294
  see also interpersonal skills
interactivity 10, 115
internal/external communication 11
international cultural differences 38–41, 93, 255–6, 298, 323–4
international meetings/conferences 18, 297–8, 328–9
international teams 318–19
internet technology 10, 227–8, 230
  and financial reports 217–19, 234
  see also world wide web
interpersonal skills 140–1
  see also emotional intelligence, listening and relationships
interpretation 13, 83, 93

see also misunderstanding *and* perception
interpretive research and interpretivist perspectives
  13, 14, 229
interruption 257, 258
interviews 47, 75–6, 106, 249–53, 254–62, 264–5
  counselling 266–7
investigatory meetings 302
isolation 20

jamming, cultural 227–8
Janis, Irving Lester 35, 36
  see also groupthink
Japanese culture 48–50, 323
jargon 62
job applications/interviews *see under* recruitment
job satisfaction surveys 131
junk mail 193, 230

kai-zen 46
kinesics 10, 77, 92
  see also body language *and* facial expression
Klein, Naomi 228
Kluckholm, C. 38
Knight, Peter 20
knock and drop 226
knowledge 202
  individual and organisational 136
  language and 14
  tacit and explicit 136
  see also information
Kolb, D.M. 322–3, 325
Kroeber, A.L. 38

language 10, 54–6, 57–66, 180–1, 335–6
  correctness issues 58–9, 181, 185–6 (*see also*
    grammar *and* punctuation)
  in e-mails 185
  knowledge and 14
  rhetoric and persuasion 106–8
  specialist 62, 180
  see also English
languages 215, 228, 298
  see also English
Latin American culture 323
law *see* legislation
leading questions 261
learning
  from experience 46, 108, 230, 264
  single- and double-loop 136
  stories and 70
  writing and 202

legislation 58, 120, 182, 304–5
Leonardo da Vinci 93
letterheads 181–2
letters 171–82, 195
  direct marketing 193–4
  social aspects 173–4
line graphs 86–7
listening 47, 254–7
  active 257
  in counselling 266
  paralanguage and 64
lists 193
literacy
  visual 82
  see also correctness issues *under* language
Livesey, S. 158, 159, 232
lobbying 106, 235
local authorities 89–90
location *see* physical space(s)
logos 80, 91, 99–100, 158

McClelland, D.C. 109
Maher, Chrissie 57
mail, attitudes concerning 173–4, 193
  see also letters
mailmerge 193
management 109, 145–50, 249, 257, 337–9
maps 88
marginalisation *see* access issues
market research 225, 226, 229
marketing *see* promotion
Maslow, A.H. 109
matrix structures 161
Matsushita, Konosuke 332
Mattelart, A. 4
Mattelart, M. 4
Mayer, J.D. 137
meaning
  context and 83
  stories and 70
media 8, 236–7, 240
  see also channels
meetings 106, 300–17, 321
  continuing need for 18–20, 77, 186, 313
  financial value 19
  formal 305–10
  international 18, 297–8, 328–9
  problems 303
  virtual 329
memory 27, 28, 30–2, 282–3
  paralinguistics and 78

stories and 70
visual images and 80
memos (memoranda) 171, 183, 185
mentoring 250, 252
message(s) 6, 43, 44
    formats 46
    for persuasion 110–13
    reinforcing 46
    see also content
metaphors 60–2
Microsoft 218, 286–7
mind maps see diagramming
minutes of meetings 307–9, 313
misrepresentation 82
misunderstanding 9, 19, 45, 64, 249
mixed metaphors 61
modernism 12, 14
morality see ethics
motions 305
motivation 78, 109
muda-dori 49–50
music 114
myths 70
    see also stories

names 113, 176
    business 182
narratives 66–8, 70–2, 79, 291
Nathan, Max 19
national cultural differences 38–41, 93, 255–6, 298,
        323–4
needs, theories of 109
negotiation 106, 109, 319–25
    see also persuasion
nervousness 45, 273, 274, 289–90
Nestlé 129–30
networking/networks 20, 154, 158, 162–5, 324
neurological and physiological factors affecting
        communication 26, 27–34, 289–90
news 236, 239–40
news releases 236–8
newspapers 236, 237
Nike 228
noise 5–6, 25–6, 160, 229, 303
    see also distraction
Nokia 214–15
non-communication 47
non-verbal communication 10
    see also appearance, body language, paralanguage
        and visual communication
North American culture 323, 324

novelty 28

objectivity/subjectivity 6–7, 9, 12, 14, 41
oculesics 92
    see also eye contact
offices see physical space(s)
one-way communication 10, 115, 173, 229
online recruitment 262–3
open questions 259, 260, 294
open systems 9, 156
openers 291–2
opinions 7
optical illusions 29, 30
organisational culture 70–1, 150–2, 336
organisational identity 76, 80, 91, 98–100, 234, 235
organisations 9, 154, 182, 304–5
    communication in 11, 154, 235, 336
    conditions conducive to groupthink 35
    and individual knowledge 136
    multicultural 41
    networks 154
    as open systems 9, 156
    spokespersons 47
    stakeholders see stakeholders
    structure 145–50, 161, 304–5
Orlikowski, Wanda 189–90
Orwell, George 65
over-optimism/over-simplification 25, 27, 160, 336
overhead projectors 284, 309
Oxfam 120–2

pacing 281–2, 292
packaging 80
paralanguage and paralinguistics 64, 77, 78, 255, 260
paraphrasing 257, 294
Parker, Ian 287
participant observation 13
passivity 36, 37, 129
Pauffley Creative Communication 217
pauses 281–2
Pearl Harbor 36–7
peer pressure see groupthink
perception 27, 28, 29–30, 303
    see also interpretation and misunderstanding
performance appraisals 106, 131, 132–3, 250, 251–2,
        334
performances/events 238–40
    see also presentations
personal distance 77, 83, 92, 93–4
personalisation 45, 46, 303
persuasion 46, 80, 103–4, 105–22

as argument 108–15
  see also negotiation *and* promotion
phasic alertness 28, 79
phone *see* telephone
photography 92
physical appearance *see* appearance
physical contact 77, 83, 92, 93, 94
physical presence 18–20
physical space(s) and location 19, 257–8, 288, 309, 310–11
  personal distance 77, 83, 92, 93–4
physiological and neurological factors affecting communication 26, 27–34, 289–90
pictograms 87–8
pictures 56, 76, 78
  inappropriate 83, 84, 97–8
  see also visual communication
pie charts 56, 84–5
Plain English 54–6, 57–8, 65
Plain English Campaign 57–8, 134
planning/preparation 44, 82
  for advertising campaigns 224–6
  for interviews 257–9, 264–5
  for meetings 306, 309, 310, 313
  for presentations 44, 45, 275, 276–83, 288–9
points of order 305
political barriers to communication 26
political campaigning *see* campaigning
politicians 47, 226
postmodernism 12, 14, 229
posture 92, 93, 249, 255, 260
  improving 276–8
power *see* control
PR (public relations) 106, 230, 231–6
pragmatism 116
prejudice *see* stereotypes
preparation *see* planning
presentation software 286–7
presentations 5, 273–95, 297–8
  combining with reports 276
  interaction in 275
  planning/preparation for 44, 45, 275, 276–83, 288–9
  starting 113, 289, 291–2
  visual/audio-visual aids 283–7
press releases 236–8
printing 181, 208
  see also fonts
probing questions 260
product samples 225–6, 229, 286
product-based structure 146–7, 161

projectors 284, 285, 309
promotion (advancement within organisation) 250, 251
promotion (advertising etc.) 221–40
  see also advertising *and* persuasion
promotional mix 221–2
promotions 225–6, 229–30
proofreading and proof correction 181, 208–9
props 286
protest *see* campaigning
provocativeness 79, 113–14, 117
proxemics/proximity 77, 83, 92, 93–4
proxies 305
psychological factors affecting communication 26
  see also nervousness
public relations 106, 230, 231–6
public speaking 273, 274, 283, 289–90
  see also presentations
punctuation 53, 58, 59, 181
  open 175
  spoken equivalents 10, 281
Putnam, L.L. 322–3, 325
puzzles 113
PwC (PricewaterhouseCoopers) 20, 189

QC (quality control) circles 48–9, 50, 312
qualifiers 108
questionnaires 62–3, 134
questions 47, 259–60, 261–2, 265
  during presentations 275, 293–5
  for securing attention 113, 291, 293
  types 259–60, 261–2
quizzes 293
quorum 305
quotation marks 68
quotations 291

raw data 6
rebuttals 108
recall *see* memory
receivers 4, 5, 43–6, 82
  see also audience
recognition *see* perception
records 173, 184, 193, 307–9, 313
recruitment 250–1, 268–71
  forms 134
  interviews 75–6, 106, 250–1, 258–9, 264–5, 269–71
  online 262–3
referencing 198–9, 205–6
reinforcement 76–7, 78, 80
relationships 321, 324, 325

see also networking
religion 94–5
relocation 19
remembering *see* memory
remote working 153, 317–18
reports 54, 196–212, 214–15, 335–6
    combining with presentations 276
    financial 55–6, 214, 217–19, 234
    multi-authored 209–10, 211
    planning 44, 45, 198–201
    research 12, 13, 14, 201, 253–4
        on attitudes to mail 173–4
        cultural and language issues 40, 62–3
        on effects of visual images 84
        on language and narrative 66–8
        see also market research, reports *and* science
respect, perceptions concerning 92
responses
    to advertising/promotions 230, 231
    deadlines for 185
Reuters 218
rhetoric 106–8
rhetorical analysis 67
RICS 19
RNIB 33–4
Roethlisberger, F.J. 47
roles in teams 315–16, 317
Royal Dutch/Shell Group 67, 91, 159
Royal Institution of Chartered Surveyors 19
Royal National Institute for the Blind 33–4
RSVPi 230
rumours 131–2, 152

sales promotion 225, 229–30
sales techniques 117
Salovey, P. 137
samples 225–6, 229, 286
Sandry, Robert 20
Sapsed, Jonathan 19–20
scare quotes 68
scepticism 82
science 6–7, 12, 13
selection *see* recruitment
self-consciousness *see* nervousness
selling *see* sales
senders 4, 5, 92
Shannon, C.E. 4–5
Shell/Royal Dutch Group 67, 91, 159
signs, visual 76, 78
    see also symbols *and* visual communication
simplicity *see* Plain English; *see also* complexity

single- and double-loop learning 136
situationism 228
slides 285, 287
smell 77, 80, 114
smiling 75, 82, 93, 260
Smith, Adam 156
SMS *see* text messaging
social issues *see* culture(s), interaction *and* relationships
sound bites 47, 236–7
space(s) *see* physical space(s)
speech 10, 64, 278–82, 289
    see also language *and* presentations
speed cameras 104–5
spellcheckers 181, 210
spelling 58, 181, 185–6, 210
spider diagrams 44, 45
spoken communication *see* speech
sponsorship 234
spontaneity 44, 283
stage fright *see* nervousness
stakeholders 128, 156–9, 232–3, 336
    dialogue with, symmetrical/asymmetrical 158–9, 232–3
    see also employees
stationery 181–2
stereotypes 67, 83, 254–5
stimulants 290
stories 66–8, 70–2, 79, 291
stress 160, 186
    see also nervousness
stringers 237
structure *see under* organisations
style 55–63, 65
    advertising 227
    co-authoring and 210
    cultural issues 203, 214
    in e-mails 185
    in letters 178–81
subjectivity/objectivity 6–7, 9, 12, 14, 41
subliminal advertising 117
summarising 196, 204, 205, 213–14, 257, 260
surprise 291
Surrey, University of 173
sustainability *see* environmental issues
symbols 80–1, 91, 94
symmetrical/asymmetrical dialogue 158–9, 232–3
systems theory 8, 9, 12

tacit knowledge 136
taste 114
teams 149–50, 313–17, 337–9

virtual 154, 317–19
technology 27, 82, 288
    blaming 27
    and communication 26, 27, 160, 174, 334
    and office space 19
    see also ICT
telephone 173, 186, 235
    as model of communication 4–5
telephone selling 117
television 10, 92, 226, 227, 234
tension see stress
text messaging 8, 58, 153, 188–9, 230
Thai culture 48–50
theses 201, 203–4, 219
'three-dimensional' images 88
'360-degree' feedback 131, 132–3, 334
time and resource management 49–50
timing 309–10
tonic alertness 28
tools see technology
touch 77, 83, 92, 93, 94
Toulmin, S. 107–8, 110
tourism 243–6
trade fairs see exhibitions
trade marks 80
training 70
translation 10, 62–3
trust, perceptions concerning 39, 71, 92, 322
truth 70
Tuckman, B.W. 314
TV Turnoff Week 228
typesetting 208
    see also printing
typing 185–6

Ugandan English 60
understanding see perception
uniforms 94
see also dress codes
Union Pacific 71
UPS 71
urgency 126, 127, 185
Usnier, J-C. 62–3

vagueness see ambiguity
Venables, Anthony 19
venues see physical space(s)
verbal communication see speech
video 92, 264, 285
video conferencing 78
virtual meetings 329

virtual teams 154, 317–19
visual communication and visual adjuncts to
        communication 54, 56, 75–95
    for presentations 283–7, 288
    problems with 82–4, 336
    puzzles 113
    in reports 199, 207–8
    'three-dimensional' 88
    see also non-verbal communication and pictures
visual generation of ideas 44, 45
visual identity 80–1, 91, 98–100
visual impairment see blindness
visual literacy 82
visualisation 290
vocabulary see language
voice 278–81, 289
    see also speech

W3C/WAI 33–4
warrants 108
Weaver, W.W. 4–5
web see world wide web
web-casting 218
websites 32–4, 215, 217, 262–3
    see also world wide web
whistle-blowers 129
whiteboards 284–5
win–win/win–lose approaches 116, 320, 322, 325
wordprocessing 181, 185–6, 193, 210
Work Foundation 19
working practices and situations 19, 140–1, 153,
        186, 317–18, 335
    cross-cultural issues 48–50
    environmental issues 231
    ICT and 19–20, 152–4
world wide web 154–5, 218
    accessibility issues 32–4
    see also internet technology and websites
writing and written communication 10, 171–90,
        196–214
    business letters 65, 171–82
    co-authoring 210
    emphasis in 64
    formalising agreements 322
    scripts for presentations 282–3
    style see style

XBRL 218–19

Yates, JoAnn 189–90